# Accounting for Aggression

# Accounting for Aggression

## Perspectives on Aggression and Violence

**Gerda Siann**

Boston
**ALLEN & UNWIN**
London            Sydney

**George Allen & Unwin (Publishers) Ltd,**
**40 Museum Street, London WC1A 1LU, UK**

George Allen & Unwin (Publishers) Ltd,
Park Lane, Hemel Hempstead, Herts HP2 4TE, UK

Allen & Unwin, Inc.,
Fifty Cross Street Winchester, Mass. 01890, USA

George Allen & Unwin Australia Pty Ltd,
8 Napier Street, North Sydney, NSW 2060, Australia


First published in 1985.

---

**Library of Congress Cataloging in Publication Data**

Siann, Gerda
  Accounting for aggression
Bibliography: p.
Includes index.
1. Aggressiveness (Psychology)  2. Aggressiveness
(Psychology) – Social aspects.  3. Violence.  I. Title.
BF575.A3S44  1985       302.5′4       84-28319
ISBN 0-04-301187-X (alk. paper)
ISBN 0-04-301188-8 (pbk.: alk. paper)

---

**British Library Cataloguing in Publication Data**

Siann, Gerda
  Accounting for aggression: perspectives on
  aggression and violence.
1. Aggressiveness (Psychology)
I. Title
155.2′32       BF575.A3
ISBN 0-04-301187-X
ISBN 0-04-301188-8 Pbk

---

Set in 10 on 11 point Plantin by Ann Buchan (Typesetters)
Walton-on-Thames, Surrey
and printed in Great Britain by Billing and Sons Ltd,
London and Worcester.

# Contents

*To Julian*

# Thanks and Acknowledgements

I would like to thank the following people very much for their assistance.

For reading and commenting on the whole manuscript – Dr Judy Watson, Robert Irvine and my editor at Allen and Unwin, Gordon Smith.

For reading and commenting on individual chapters:
Chapter 1 – Dr Ian Thomson.
Chapter 2 – Dr John V. Basson, Dr Nigel Leigh, Dr Andre Phanjoo and Professor David Vowles.
Chapter 3 – Professor David Vowles.
Chapters 4 and 5 – Dr Halla Beloff.
Chapter 6 — Dr Bruce Lynch and Dr Alec Sharp.
As I did not adopt every amendment that was offered, I must stress that the views expressed remain my own, and so do remaining errors of omission and commission.

I would also like to thank Annie Davies, Georgina Hunter and Violet Moncrieff very much for their assistance in the preparation of the manuscript.

Every effort has been made to contact the copyright owners or administrators of those works quoted in this book. This has not been possible in every instance. The author and publishers would like to thank the following:

Michael Billig and Academic Press for permission to quote from *Social Psychology and Intergroup Relations*;
Claude Brown and The Macmillan Company, New York, for permission to quote from *Manchild in the Promised Land;*
Jimmy Boyle and Canongate Publishing Ltd. for permission to quote from *A Sense of Freedom*;
*The British Journal of Criminology* and Sweet and Maxwell Ltd., for permission to quote from *The British Journal of Criminology*, Vol. 21, No. 3. 1981;
Anthony Burgess, William Heinemann Ltd. and W. W. Norton & Co. Inc., for permission to quote from *A Clockwork Orange*;
Anne Campbell, Peter Marsh and Basil Blackwell, for permission to quote from *Girl Delinquents* and *Aggression and Violence*;
The Estate of Erich Fromm; Jonathan Cape Ltd. and Holt Rinehart and

Winston Inc., for permission to quote from *The Anatomy of Human Destructiveness*;

William Golding, Faber and Faber Publishers and the Putnam Publishing Group for permission to quote from *Lord of the Flies*;

Graham Greene, William Heinemann Ltd., The Bodley Head Ltd. and Viking Penguin Inc., for permission to quote from *Brighton Rock*;

Konrad Lorenz, Methuen & Co. Ltd., and Harcourt Brace Jovanovich, Inc. for permission to quote from *On Aggression*;

William Marsh, Hughes Massie Ltd. and Harold Ober Associates, Inc. for permission to quote from *The Bad Seed*;

Peter Marsh, E. Rosser and R. Harré and Routledge and Kegan Paul PLC for permission to quote from *The Rules of Disorder*;

I. Page and D. Cairns and Bryan Morrison Music Ltd., for permission to quote from the record sleeve of *Secret Affair*;

Anthony Storr, Penguin Books Ltd. and Atheneum Publishers for permission to quote from *Human Aggression*;

Rollo May for permission to quote from *Power and Innocence* and World Publishing Co. for permission to quote the poem by Bronowski appearing in *Power and Innocence*;

Hans Toch and The Schenkman Publishing Co. Inc. for permission to quote from *Violent Men*.

GERDA SIANN

# Introduction

This book is concerned with different accounts that have been offered for aggression and violence. These include those influenced by biological studies (Chapter 2), by Darwinian theories (Chapter 3), by psychoanalytic approaches (Chapter 4), by experimental psychology (Chapter 5), by social psychology and sociology (Chapters 6 and 7) and by phenomenological approaches to the study of self (Chapter 7).

In presenting these very divergent accounts I will continually be stressing my belief that in adopting a particular viewpoint, a theorist is affected radically, not only by his or her own professional and academic background, but also to a lesser extent by the values and ideologies he or she adheres to. For, as I think will seem apparent throughout the book, all perspectives on aggression and violence have particular implications for social policy. It is not possible, I would argue, to confine the topics of aggression and violence only to academic discussion. Both are too much part of our everyday world.

# 1

# Issues of Definition

We use the terms aggression and violence frequently and easily and so they would appear to hold considerable communicative value. But, in common with other abstract concepts, defining them in an exact manner is not nearly as simple as using them to convey a shared meaning which is what we assume we are doing when we use them in speech or writing. It is precisely this assumption that I would like to look at in this chapter. In doing so, I think two things will become apparent. First, that the terms cover for each of us a complex amalgam of analytical concepts and intuitive understandings, and, secondly, that such meanings may differ considerably. In other words, when we ascribe the descriptions 'aggressive' or 'violent' to ideas, feelings or behaviours, we do so influenced by our own particular value systems. In fact we tend to use the labels 'aggressive' and 'violent' subjectively.

## What do We Mean by Aggression?

Perhaps the first area to focus on in answering this question is whom do I refer to by the term 'we'? Do I mean behavioural scientists like biologists and ethologists (scientists who study the behaviour of animals in their natural settings), clinical workers like psychiatrists and psychoanalysts, social scientists like sociologists, psychologists and anthropologists, or in using the term 'we' do I refer to each of us in our capacity as a member of the general public?

In fact, each group differentiated above does tend to define the terms in rather different fashions. Nevertheless, I think it is worth arriving at a general summational description of the term that would include most of the meanings each of the groups ascribes to it, and so this is what I propose to do in the following sections.

Deriving a general summational description of the way in which the term aggression is used seems to me to be more fruitful than trying to produce a tight and exact definition. This latter approach is one that has been taken by a number of psychologists and has led, I think, to so restrictive an exploration of human aggression that it excludes reference to many aspects of the common everyday usage of the term. To take but one example, most of us use the terms 'aggression' and 'aggressive' in everyday speech, in many instances in a neutral or even a constructive sense. We may, for example, speak approvingly of an aggressive marketing strategy. But many texts in social psychology specifically exclude this usage of the term. Thus, typically, Kushler and Davidson write, 'It should be made clear that what we mean by aggression are those activities that are both undesirable and harmful, as opposed to what some would consider desirable and competitive aggressiveness' (1981, p. 346). It seems to me, however, that if we are to explore aggression in a way that is relevant not only to academic inquiry, but also to the interests of the general public, we will not do so effectively by excluding aspects that both the general public, and indeed clinical workers like psychiatrists and psycho-analysts, see as related. Both these groups use the term in a non-pejorative manner and so I would argue we have to explore both the positive and negative aspects of its usage. Indeed, to return to Kushler and Davidson, if, as they claim, 'Archaeological evidence indicates that the occurrence of excessive aggression is a problem that has plagued mankind from the beginning of civilisation' (ibid), it would surely be helpful to know what it is that they regard as 'non-excessive' aggression and where they would draw the line between the two categories – excessive and non-excessive aggression.

So in the next section I am going to try and build up a summational description of the terms 'aggression' and 'aggressive' using not only different academic sources but also vernacular usage. In order to do this, I am going to list some examples of everyday speech in which the words appeared.

Kids are more *aggressive* these days – no doubt about it. Look at all the mugging – streets aren't safe any more.

Michael just got absolutely furious and he flew at his little brother in an incredibly *aggressive* way.

Susie is a very *aggressive* little girl and there's no way she's going to play with my kids.

No point in arguing with him. You can start off cool as you like but he gets so damn *aggressive* you've soon got a real battle on your hands.

The ministry spokesman said that they had invaded our territory without any provocation and it was a clear case of *aggression*.

I don't know about that marriage. Looks OK on the surface but she's always putting him down with funny little remarks. I reckon there's a lot of hidden *aggression* there.

It's a product that's got to face heavy competition and we're going to need an *aggressive* marketing strategy.

The only resistance came from Hughes who batted fluently and *aggressively*.

Under Jones's *aggressive* captaincy the team soon got into the first league.

Taking these remarks as examples of the way in which the terms are used colloquially and relating this to academic definitions, I would like to pinpoint some conceptual problems underlying their use.

## DOES AGGRESSION ALWAYS INVOLVE PHYSICAL INJURY?

Looking at these examples, the answer must be that it does not. In fact, actual physical injury is probably only on the cards in the cases of the mugging, the angry older brother and the invading army. There is also a suggestion of incipient physical force in some of the other cases, however. For example, perhaps your mental picture of Susie was of a rather tough child not averse to forcibly seizing toys from other children who were engaged in relatively peaceful play. In the case of the football team it is probably not only their frame of mind that is being referred to but it is also likely to be a vigorous style of play involving a great deal of physical contact between members of opposing teams.

Nevertheless, in the other cases, the cricketer, the marketing campaign, the argument and the marriage, the interactions though perceived as aggressive may never lead to the exchange of blows. So we can perhaps conclude, despite the fact that the terms 'aggression' and 'violence' are frequently coupled, that when we use the words 'aggression' and 'aggressive' in conversation we do not automatically allude to situations that even potentially lead to physical injury.

If physical harm or incipient physical harm do not provide a common underlying threat, can we find another? An immediate candidate is obviously the infliction of harm or injury whether that harm be physical or mental[1]. With this base, it would be possible to include the examples of the sarcastic wife, and the belligerent arguer, but could we realistically label the cricketer, the footballers and the manufacturers as actually wishing to inflict injury or harm on their opponents? It seems to me that not only does this change the meaning from that intended by the speakers who were discussing the cricketer, the footballer and the manufacturer, but that using the common thread of the infliction of harm or injury as always underlying the usage of the terms 'aggression' and 'aggressive' would exclude what many see as an important aspect of aggression, and would correspondingly label (as I shall describe in more detail shortly) 'constructive aggression'.

I would therefore suggest that we broaden our description still further, to include not only the infliction of injury, whether it be physical or mental, but to include the concept of emerging dominant. Thus we might regard aggression as occurring when the aggressor is likely to emerge in a relatively stronger position to the other party in the interaction.

So as a first step in a summational description of aggression I suggest the following.

> *Aggression* involves the aggressor emerging superior to or inflicting hurt on others. If hurt is inflicted, such hurt need not be physical. In other words aggression may, but does not necessarily, involve physical violence.

CAN AGGRESSION BE ACCIDENTAL?

Here again I think the straightforward answer is no. In the previous section I argued that the commonality shared by all the exemplars cited was the desire of the 'aggressor' to either harm the other party or at least emerge in a superior position. But sometimes harm occurs accidentally, or without intent, and I would suggest that in such cases applying the term aggression would not be appropriate. Take, for example, Baron's suggestion of the case of an individual who wounds or even kills another by accident while cleaning a gun (Baron, 1977). As Baron says, no one would wish to classify this, in itself, as an instance of aggression. Similarly people sometimes inflict psychological injury without intent. Suppose a physical education teacher says to a 14-year-old girl, 'You're such a big girl now, I'm sure you can jump further than that'. In saying this the teacher's only motive may be to spur the girl on to greater efforts, but if the girl is, as so many young teenagers are, obsessively concerned about her weight, the remark may wound deeply. Here the injury arises out of the girl's vulnerability rather than the teacher's intended desire to humiliate her; I think it would not be likely that an observer would regard the teacher as behaving aggressively.

So it is fair, I think, to conclude that underlying our use of the terms 'aggression' and 'aggressive' is the concept of intentionality – that is, the actor or the person harbouring the emotion has an intention to harm or emerge in a relatively superior position.

As with the vernacular usage, the intent concept in defining aggression is generaly accepted in most reviews of the subject[2], but while the inclusion of this in our description of human aggression may effectively eliminate the misclassification of accidental injury as aggression, it does not delve deeply enough into the area of motivation. And so it is to motives that we now turn.

## MOTIVES UNDERLYING AGGRESSIVE BEHAVIOUR

In looking at different approaches to aggression, it soon becomes apparent that there is a wide divergence in the extent to which these different approaches take into account the subjective feelings and emotions that lie behind behaviour which is labelled aggressive.

Turning, for example, to the case of little Susie referred to in the colloquial examples above, it could be surmised that her motives for seizing other children's toys could be different at different times. Sometimes, for example, she might grab toys because she really wants to play with them herself, and at other times she might do so largely to annoy and upset other children. In yet other cases her motives may be mixed.

This example highlights at a very simple level questions about the extent to which examining the motives underlying aggression are relevant to understanding aggressive behaviour. As I have just indicated, there are wide-ranging approaches to this important issue, an issue to which much attention will be devoted in this book. At this stage I merely want to note that there are important differences between approaches to aggression in the extent to which underlying motives are seen as affecting theoretical explanations of aggression. Consequently I would like to amend the summational description of aggression that I am working to as follows:

> It seems then that *aggression* involves the intent to hurt or emerge superior to others, does not necessarily involve physical injury and may be or may not be regarded as being underpinned by different kinds of motives.

## IS AGGRESSION ALWAYS PERCEIVED NEGATIVELY?

As I noted earlier, it is clear that the terms 'aggression' or 'aggressive' are not always used in a negative or pejorative manner. Indeed, some of the major contemporary writers on aggression argue that it is a drive that has both positive and negative facets. Anthony Storr, for example, writes:

> The aggressive part of human nature is not only a necessary safeguard against predatory attack. It is also the basis of intellectual achievement, of the attainment of independence and even of that proper pride which enables a man to hold his head high among his fellows. (Storr, 1970, p. 11)

Storr sees the major motivation for achievement, at the personal and the professional level, as the positive facet of an aggressive drive. This particular understanding of aggression is one that has been more popular with novelists, psychiatrists and psychoanalysts than it has been with other behavioural and social scientists. It is also a view that is held at a common-sense level by many members of the public, which is why it is so often encountered in day-to-day speech. Thus to quote Storr again, 'we *attack* problems, or *get our teeth into* them. We *master* a subject when we have *struggled with* and *overcome* its difficulties' (ibid, pp. 10–11).

It seems to me then that any summational description must take this implicit sanctioning of aggression into account. Thus, I have widened the meanings ascribed to the terms 'aggression' and 'aggressive' beyond those considered by most experimental psychologists who, as I mentioned earlier, have confined their discussion of aggression and aggressive behaviour to only those aspects of human functioning where injury or harm are intentionally inflicted. For example, Zillman (1979, p. 38) defines aggression as 'any deliberate coercive injurious assault upon another person'; and Baron (1977, p. 12) writes that aggression is 'behaviour which is directed towards the goal of harming or injuring another living being'.

Excluding in this way the non-pejorative connotations of the terms 'aggression' and 'aggressive' has cut such social psychologists off, not only from the colloquial use of the term, but also from the usage of the term made by many psychoanalysts and psychiatrists who, as we shall see in Chapter 4, regard the constructive deployment of aggression as an essential prerequisite of mental health. And it is because I do not wish to exclude two such widespread aspects of the usage of the term that I broaden the summational description as follows:

> *Aggression* involves the intent to inflict hurt or emerge superior to others, does not necessarily involve physical injury, and may or may not be regarded as being underpinned by different kinds of motives. It is not always negatively sanctioned.

THE ISSUE OF CONSENT

In the preceding section I argued that both in everyday speech, and in the definitions of the term presented by some psychologists and psychiatrists, there is an acceptance of the view that aggression is sometimes constructive. They would argue, for example, that if you are interested in marketing a particular product then aggressive marketing is beneficial to you, and that similarly the aggressive captaincy of a football team is laudable if you happen to support that particular team.

Agreeing that there is a constructive aspect to striving for superiority (which is what this view entails) leads those supporting it into complex and ambiguous areas when it come to deciding precisely how the constructive aspects of aggression shade into the negative. Thus while Storr sanctions the aggressive side of male sexuality and the 'aggressive' aspects of human behaviour displayed in sport and the space race, he sanctions it only within certain limits. But how are these limits to be drawn?

One way of drawing such limits, which is not discussed by Storr, who leaves this area relatively unstructured, is to include in the definition of the constructive aspects of aggression the proviso that it is constructive only when the interaction is entered into with the consent of both participants. Thus, for negative aggression to occur one participant, the 'aggressed', has to be an unwilling partner in the exchange. Using this distinction between negative and constructive aspects on the marketing example, it could be argued that any firm entering into the market-place does so with knowledge of the possibility, indeed inevitability, of competition, and thus puts itself willingly into a position where it may fail relative to its rivals; the competition springs thus from the positive aspect rather than the negative aspect of aggression, and this demarcation rests on the willing involvement of all parties.

A similar analysis could presumably be applied to Storr's view of male sexuality. Looking at the relationship between the sexes, Storr argues that 'the proper relation between the sexes' (1970, p. 94) involves an 'important element of aggressiveness' in male sexuality 'which is recognised and responded to by the female who yields and submits' (ibid., pp. 89–90). Such aggression on the part of the male is seen by Storr as wholly desirable, for, according to him, the neurotic male who consults a psychiatrist frequently does so because he has too little aggression; similarly women suffering from too much aggression display equally neurotic tendencies.

Although I find this particular analysis of the relationship between the sexes inappropriate, not to say distasteful, I think it is important to accept that such a perspective is widely held. It is often explicitly stated in fiction. For example, in a recent novel by Ian McEwan, an older man who holds a considerable if ambivalent appeal for a younger couple, one of whom is a self-sufficient, effective and composed woman, says, 'But they [women] love men. Whatever they may say they believe, women love aggression and strength and power in men. It's deep in their minds' (McEwan, 1982, p. 72).

But when does such normal appropriate aggression shade for Storr into negative and inappropriate aggression? This is not an aspect he explores, but perhaps the line can be drawn depending on the extent to which the women acquiesce. Presumably if such normal acceptable aggression moves into rape, this will be negative aggression because in this case the woman has not willingly yielded.

This issue of consent is one which *is* discussed by social psychologists who have tended to include in their definition of aggression a reference to it. Baron, for example, concludes the definition which I have already quoted as follows: 'Aggression will be defined as any form of behaviour directed toward the goal of harming or injuring another living being *who is motivated to avoid such treatment*' (1977, p. 12, my italics).

Recapitulating again we can amend our summational description as follows:

> *Aggression* involves the intention to hurt or emerge superior to others, does not necessarily involve physical injury, may or may not be regarded as being underpinned by different kinds of motives and is not always negatively sanctioned. It is more likely to be negatively sanctioned when one of the participants does not enter willingly into the interaction.

## AGGRESSION, COERCIVE POWER AND THE ISSUE OF LEGITIMACY

In considering this aspect I would like to focus on a particular 'aggressive incident': a mugging. Let us suppose that the incident starts with a younger man simply approaching an older man and asking him to hand over his wallet and any other valuables in his possession; that the older man refused and as a result the younger started to remove them by force. At this stage the older man produced a whistle and, to save himself from being caught by passers-by responding to the whistle blast, the younger man mugged the older before he could actually blow the whistle. It is quite clear that most people would label this mugging as aggressive behaviour by the younger man and, furthermore, such behaviour falls within the summational description of aggression that we have been building up because the young man acted intentionally, and without the other's consent, to injure him.

Suppose further that on an earlier occasion the young man had approached another victim in a threatening manner and the victim in this earlier incident has obediently handed over his valuables without any delay or argument because he feared the younger man's greater power. Should we label the younger man's behaviour on this earlier occasion as aggressive as well? I think the answer is yes, because the intention was to hurt – that is, to remove something the victim would patently prefer to keep. Further, the older person did not willingly enter into the inter-action but it was *imposed* on him.

The younger man was in fact exercising power to force the victim to do what he wanted him to do. Tedeschi has called this 'coercive power' and argued that what is commonly labelled as aggressive behaviour is really only a special instance of the exercise of coercive power – the power to influence another to respond to your wishes rather than follow his own intentions (Tedeschi, 1983).

It seems to me not to matter very much whether we call the young man's behaviour in this instance 'coercive power', as Tedeschi proposes, or 'aggression', but I would like to explore some important points that

Tedeschi and his co-workers make about the subjectivity that is often involved when we ascribe the labels 'aggression' and 'aggressive' to behaviour, thought or feelings.

One of the areas into which subjectivity enters is the following. Somehow, implicit in most people's understanding of the term aggression in its negative sense, is the notion that one who aggresses is one who *initiates* an unpleasant interaction. To return to some of the examples listed in the beginning of the chapter, when the ministry spokesman remarked that the invasion was an act of aggression, he invoked the notion that it was unprovoked. If the ministry spokesman went on to say that his own side had retaliated, he would no doubt have described their action as defensive or reactive. And even if this reaction had involved the loss of lives, the ministry spokesman would not presumably classify this 'intentional inflicting of injury' (to relate it to our summational description of aggression) as aggression, but would class it as defensive behaviour. Similarly, the mother who complains about little Susie's behaviour, is probably not annoyed specifically by what Susie does, but is annoyed by the fact that Susie initiates or provokes play that she disapproves of. For example, if after Susie seizes another child's toy the other child retaliates by taking it back, it will not be the nature of the act (seizing the toy) that is the sole criterion of the mother's disapproval, but the fact that Susie initiates such acts.

This intuitive feeling that injurious behaviour is aggressive only when unprovoked is echoed by dictionary definitions. For example, the Penguin English Dictionary (1979) defines the verb 'aggress' as 'to attack first, to begin a quarrel'. The meaning is clear enough but can we always decide who it is who starts off an interaction in which injury or harm is inflicted? In the case of Susie, it may be comparatively easy, but in the case of the armed invasion perhaps it is not so clear who may be regarded as the aggressor and who the defender. Quite probably a similar type of statement was broadcast on the other side by a counterpart of the ministry spokesman I have quoted, claiming that they had been 'forced to embark on an armed incursion after a series of border incidents'.

There is no doubt that such areas of subjective judgement affect our everyday perception of aggression too. A teacher may argue that a child who answers back is acting aggressively, whereas the child may perceive the retort as defensive action in the face of public humiliation. The teacher has a set of values that preclude a child treating a teacher in the same manner as the teacher treats the child; the child, on the other hand, may have an entirely different set of values which preclude one individual, no matter what their role, humiliating another. Clearly these expectations affect the mutual labelling process.

So we can conclude that whether or not an act is labelled aggressive (in the negative sense) depends not only on the intentional infliction of injury, but on whether or not the labeller perceives this action as, on the one hand, unprovoked and running counter to his or her notions of what

is acceptable (normative) behaviour, when the act may be labelled unambiguously as 'aggressive', or whether, on the other hand, the perceiver
regards the act as reactive and fully within the bounds of acceptable
behaviour, when the act may be labelled as 'defensive' or 'retaliatory'.
Tedeschi's conclusion is, I think inescapable: 'No action can be identified as aggressive or violent without taking into account the value system
of the perceiver' (Tedeschi, Smith and Brown, 1974, p. 557).

We may now amend our summational description of aggression for the
last time:

> *Aggression* involves the intention to hurt or emerge superior to
> others, does not necessarily involve physical injury and may or may
> not be regarded as being underpinned by different kinds of
> motives. It is not always negatively sanctioned but is more likely to
> be negatively sanctioned when one of the participants does not
> enter willingly into the interaction. Applying the label aggressive
> in a pejorative manner to a person or persons is a matter of
> subjective judgement on the part of the labeller. The labeller will
> be affected both by his or her value system and by his or her
> perception of the extent to which the person to whom the label is
> applied is acting provocatively or defensively.

## What Do We Mean by Violence?

Defining the term 'violence' has not been an area of concern for the
numbers of social scientists who have written on the subject. Unlike their
approach to the term 'aggression', which in most cases has involved them
in lengthy, detailed and subtle argument, they have approached the term
'violence' in a manner which suggests that their own use of the term
approximates to its vernacular usage. I have tried to extract the core of
this usage by consulting a number of contemporary dictionary definitions, and the consensual element would appear to be that violence is *the
use of great physical force or intensity*. This meaning does appear to reflect
the use of the term taken for granted by most academics writing about it,[3]
so that I shall start with this as an initial definition and continue by
probing into a number of areas that seem to me worth clarifying.

DISTINGUISHING BETWEEN AGGRESSION AND VIOLENCE

Although the terms 'aggression' and 'violence' are frequently coupled in
psychological reviews and books, an overt distinction between them is
rarely drawn. Thus in their introduction to a recent British book of
readings entitled *Aggression and Violence,* Peter Marsh and Anne
Campbell start off with the assertion that 'Aggression and violence are

aspects of human life that, quite understandably, give rise to considerable alarm and concern' (1982, p. 1), and continue to couple the terms both in their introduction and in their two individual articles without ever attempting to differentiate between their usage.

Nevertheless, I suggest that we should perhaps start to differentiate the terms by relating our summational description of aggression to the preliminary definition I have just given of violence, as follows:

> *Aggression* involves the intention to hurt or emerge superior to others, does not necessarily involve physical injury (violence) and may or may not be regarded as being underpinned by different kinds of motives.

In other words, *violence* may occur as a result of aggressive intent. This leads us on to another question, is violence always a result of aggressive intent?

## IS VIOLENCE ALWAYS A RESULT OF AGGRESSIVE INTENT?

If we continue to define violence as the use of great physical force or intent, is it possible to cite instances where such physical force is used to injure others without aggression being involved? If aggression is seen as the intentional infliction of injury on others, then any violent act must, if intended, be regarded as aggressive, according to the summative description we have derived for aggression.

This issue takes us back to the area which has been briefly touched on before – that of motivation. As I noted at that stage, issues concerning motivation are central to any discussion of violence, and similarly this is an issue that will be dealt with in some depth throughout this book.

At this stage, I only want to suggest that there are some acts of 'violence', that is, acts when physical injury is inflicted, in which the primary intention is not necessarily to emerge dominant, but to engage in the act for the sake of other kinds of gratification. For example, sometimes people engage in controlled interactions which involve physical force but which are enjoyed, and indulged in voluntarily by both participants (or indeed by more than one set of participants). Such acts would include certain martial arts, as well as certain sports like amateur boxing. Yet another related though rather more complex action entered into for no other aim than the intrinsic rewards of the situation would appear to be sadomasochistic relations that are entered into *voluntarily* by both (or all) parties. Neither of these classes of behaviour, though they may include the infliction of injury, could be regarded as being underpinned primarily by the wish to dominate.

It would thus seem that there are instances of violent behaviour that are not easily subsumed as largely aggressive in nature – violent behaviour carried out by individuals in an interaction where all the participants find the behaviour intrinsically rewarding.

So perhaps we can amend our distinction further as follows:

*Aggression* involves the intention to hurt or emerge superior to others, does not necessarily involve physical injury (violence) and may or may not be regarded as being underpinned by different kinds of motives.

*Violence* involves the use of great physical force or intensity and, while it is often impelled by aggressive motivation, may occasionally be used by individuals engaged in a mutual violent interaction which is regarded by both parties as intrinsically rewarding.

## WHEN IS VIOLENCE LEGITIMATE?

When we think of violence or are reminded of it by the media, it is usually within a negative context that suggests that it is 'bad, abnormal, irrational and mindless' (Campbell, 1976, p. 27), but I shall argue in this section that, like aggression, violence is very often legitimized, and that the legitimization or condemnation of a particular violent act will depend on the values, attitudes and ideology of the perceiver or indeed of the participants in the act.

### *'Bad'?*

If violence is defined as the infliction of physical force on others, then war must be the prime exemplar of violence. Yet, it is an example of human behaviour that though seldom justified as 'good' is often rationalized as 'just'. Depending on our ideological predispositions most of us would endorse at least one historical instance of war as just: perhaps on the one hand the war against the Third Reich or an armed struggle against an exploitative imperial power. Or, on the other hand, many would argue that war is justifiable against 'godless' communism or to preserve religious purity against profane infidels, as in a holy *jihad*. Unless we are pacifists, then, it is clear that at some stage we may be prepared to endorse violence, if not as 'good', at least as not unequivocally bad because it is embarked on in the service of what we regard as justice.

In general, it is probably fair to conclude that as in the case of aggression the use of physical force is more likely to be legitimized if it is seen as defensive rather than as a first strike.

As with war, similarly with civil violence. Most of us can imagine a tyranny that is so absolute that assassination is something we might not categorically condemn. As Campbell (1976, p. 28) writes: 'The assassinations of the Kennedys and Martin Luther King . . . were violent acts that outraged us – but the attempts to kill Hitler are not similarly notorious.' Or as Tutt puts it, 'Today's violence may often, through the passage of time, become tomorrow's heroism or martyrdom' (1976, p. 15).

### 'Abnormal'

This term usually implies one of two things – either the behaviour is exceptional or it departs from generally accepted standards. Quite evidently violence is not exceptional. In 1937, surveying the history of eleven nations over twenty-five centuries, Sorokin concluded, 'disturbances occur much oftener than is usually realised . . . On the average from four to seven years as a rule, one considerable social disturbance may be expected', (quoted in Tutt, 1976, p. 28), and more recently Gurr reported serious civil strife in 114 out of the 121 countries he surveyed (Graham and Gurr, 1969).

Does violence depart from generally accepted standards? That depends on one's perspective. While it is common to deplore violence against property if it is perpetrated by ordinary civilians it is less common to deplore violence against those same persons if it is perpetrated by the police. Thus Blumenthal, Kahn and Andrews (1971) found that a representative sample of adult American males, while labelling looting, burning of draft cards and student demonstrations as violent behaviours, did not believe that it was violent if the police shot looters or struck demonstrating college students. As with aggression, it must be concluded that the values of the observer enter into the labelling of an act as violent and further that if violence is classified at the simplest level as using physical force, then this phenomenon (the use of force) is normative and therefore not abnormal, certainly in the USA, though probably less so in the United Kingdom, if exercised by the police.

### 'Irrational' and 'mindless'

A great deal of violence of the kind we deplore appears on the face of it to be completely irrational. One thinks, for example, of child abuse or football violence. There is no doubt that this behaviour is to be deplored but if we are to seek to control it and replace it by more constructive responses, it seems to me it cannot simply be dismissed as being beyond understanding, which is what the phrase 'mindless and irrational' implies.

## Definitions of Aggression and Violence

We can perhaps conclude that while we personally may deplore violence in all but the most exceptional circumstances – for example, we may believe that certain deeply prized ideals are worth defending in a war, or that the custodians of law and order may justifiably use violence in self-defence – the legitimization of violence has been, and continues to be, a commonplace. If we as a species are to learn to control violence we will have to articulate and explore the contradiction between the glib dismissal of violence as 'bad, abnormal, mindless and irrational' and the continued endorsement of what we all see from different perspectives as the legitimate use of physical force.

I would like to conclude this chapter with a summational description of violence and set it alongside the description we have already derived of aggression.

*Aggression*
(a)   Involves the intention to hurt or
(b)   emerge superior to others.
(c)   Does not necessarily involve physical injury (*violence*).
(d)   May be or may not be regarded as being underpinned by different kinds of motives.
(e)   Aggression is not always negatively sanctioned but is more likely to be so when one of the participants does not enter willingly into the interaction.
(f)   Applying the label 'aggressive' in a pejorative manner to a person or persons is a matter of subjective judgement on the part of the labeller.
(g)   The labeller will be affected both by his or her value system and by his or her perception of the extent to which the person or persons to whom the label is applied is acting provocatively or defensively.

*Violence*
(a)   Involves the use of great force or physical intensity.
(b)   While it is often impelled by *aggressive* motivation,
(c)   may occasionally be used by individuals engaged in a mutual inter-action which is regarded by both parties as intrinsically rewarding.
(d)   Though the term 'violence' tends to be negatively sanctioned always, the use of great physical force is often legitimized. How and when the use of great physical force is legitimized or condemned will depend both on the values of the person making the judgement and the extent to which the use of force is seen as provocative (a first strike) or defensive.

These summational descriptions of aggression and violence are not intended to serve as tight, logically consistent definitions. They have been derived for the purpose of aggregating the ways in which the terms are used, both academically and in general conversation. I intend these descriptions to serve as a set of parameters which can be used to check how adequately different theories of aggression and violence cover the overall usage of the terms.

# Notes: Chapter 1

1  For a description of a classification system of aggression based largely on the dichotomy physical–verbal, see Buss, 1961.
2  For a review of this area see Zillman, 1979, pp. 33–7.
3  Although a minority of writers like Norman Tutt use the term to refer to both emotional and physical violence, as for example in the use of the term 'black bastard' to a coloured child, or 'the emotional violence of a strictly observed silence within a home, in which father and mother refuse to talk to one another, the pregnant pause . . . can be a form of violence to the emotions and senses' (1976, p. 17), I would classify both these as instances of aggression, and reserve the use of the term violence for physical force.

# 2

# Biological Approaches to Aggression and Violence

A broad interdisciplinary effort is getting under way to explore the biological nature and origins of violence. Biologists, biochemists, neurophysiologists, geneticists and other natural scientists are probing with increasingly precise tools and techniques in a field where supposition and speculation have long prevailed. Their work is beginning to provide new clues to the complex ways in which the brain shapes violent behaviour. (Bylinsky, 1982, p. 30)

There are wide individual differences in physiology among men. These differences are at times powerful determinants of behaviour. Man has always recognised that behaviour can be changed by altering an individual's environment or his experience. It must now be recognised that behaviour can be changed, sometimes drastically, by altering his internal milieu. That conclusion is now inescapable. The implications of this view of man are profound, and it will change history. (Moyer, 1976, p. 284)

These two quotations represent a view of aggression and violence that is for some inherently attractive and for others repellent in its implications. Stated at its simplest level it assumes that violent behaviour is, in Bylinsky's terms, 'shaped' by the brain and that further (as Moyer implies) such behaviour can be brought under control by physical intervention that changes the physiology of the brain. Such a perspective holds an immediate appeal to many who are frightened and affronted by what they see as a growing contemporary trend to greater violence and the escalation of aggression, for it offers the prospect of an effective and terminal solution. If violence is, in essence, dictated by physiology and, further, if as Moyer suggests some are more predisposed to violence because of their individual physiology, then violence can presumably be eliminated by altering the brain physiology of those individuals who are most predisposed to violence. Few of the natural scientists Bylinsky refers to above would take quite so extreme a perspective, but many would agree that, particularly in the case of those who are habitually violent, there may be biological factors which in conjunction with psychological, social and situational determinants may contribute directly to violent behaviour.

In this chapter I want to examine the evidence for the contribution of biological factors to aggressive and violent behaviour. I would also like to explore in this and the next chapter the reasons which cause other workers in the subject area of human aggression and violence to find the suggestion that some violent behaviour has biological substrates totally unacceptable.

THE SCOPE OF BIOLOGICAL APPROACHES TO AGGRESSION AND VIOLENCE

When investigators with a background in biology or medicine consider the topics of aggression and violence, they do not, in general, pay too much attention to fine discriminations in defining these terms. Three approaches appear characteristic. First, like Mark (1978) they may regard aggression as a characteristic common to all humans and concern themselves only with what they refer to as 'abnormal aggression' and 'unacceptable violence' (ibid., p. 132), leaving unexplored the relationships between the subjective experience of anger and hostility and brain function when such anger or hostility does not reach what they regard as abnormal or unacceptable proportions. Or secondly, like Moyer (1976), they may propose a classification system of aggression that leans heavily on work with non-human species. Or thirdly, like Shah and Roth (1974), they may draw on criminological studies without questioning the relationship between criminal and 'normal' behaviour.

None of these three approaches attempt an exhaustive survey of aggression and violence within a context broad enough to include what, in the first chapter, we labelled as the constructive aspects of aggression, nor do they delve deeply into the influence of ideologies and subjective judgements in the labelling of certain acts as aggressive and the paradox whereby the use of physical force is sometimes legitimized while at other time it is proscribed.

GENERALIZING OF FINDINGS FROM ANIMAL RESEARCH

This book is primarily concerned with human aggression and violence, and little stress will be placed on the study of these topics in other species. One reason for this decision is that if, as is undeniable, aggressive and violent behaviour are intimately intertwined in humans with feelings and higher cortical processes like reasoning and the ability to reconsider and be reflective about one's behaviour, then it is surely inappropriate to draw analogies with other species when we have no insight into their subjective experience. Another reason which has been frequently suggested for confining discussion of human aggression and violence to our own species is that even within animal species and sub-species there is considerable variation in fighting and competitive behaviour, so that generalization from even one species of primates is difficult (Vowles, 1970).

In general, with the exception of this chapter and the next, I will not be concerned with aggression and violence in non-human species. But at this stage, when we are considering biological and physiological factors in human aggression and violence, it seems appropriate to pay some attention to studies in non-human species which take account of our common organic systems. For when it comes to the possible influence of nerve cells and hormones which appear to function similarly in all species, it is at the very least relevant to consider animal studies even if we finally conclude that, in the case of humans, these are far more likely to be brought under cortical control by cultural variables than they are in non-human species.

## 'THE STIGMATA OF DEGENERATION' AND THE THEORY OF THE BAD SEED

We have all felt angry enough at some stage to contemplate inflicting considerable injury on others, if not at the level of physical violence at least at an emotional one; and when we read books, or watch plays or cinema or television in which an aggrieved individual sets out to avenge themselves we often feel a degree of empathy for the protagonist. Similarly, we may occasionally daydream about robbing a bank and even go as far as to imagine using physical force in pursuing such ill-gotten gains. So the experience of angry aggression is one we can sympathize with, and the contemplation of instrumental aggression is something we may allow ourselves. But even in fantasy most of us draw a line – there are some actions that appear so heartless, so enormously sadistic that we shrink from them even in thought. I think few of us could feel empathy with the actions of the 'Moor Murderers' who pursued their own satisfaction regardless of the pathetic pleas of their young victim, and the recent case in which the 'Yorkshire Ripper' was sentenced for the murder of thirteen women filled the British public with disgust, even if that disgust may have been tempered with a measure of prurience. Violence of this intensity which is seemingly unmoderated by any compassion may seem to most of us inexplicably inhumane. And it is tempting to believe that such behaviour is inexplicably inhumane to us precisely because it is in fact 'inhuman' – it is perpetrated by individuals who are totally different from us, who are at a remove from other human beings, not only because of their actions but more basically because they are biologically distinct. The history of criminology reflects this comforting tendency on behalf of the law-abiding majority to come to terms with the criminal, and particularly the violent criminal minority by locating the causes of such iniquities in biological and constitutional factors. This tendency is comforting because such an explanation saves the non-criminal observer not only from examining the law-breakers' environment for any factors or variables which might have caused him or her to behave in so seemingly unintelligible a manner, but also from taking any action to change such an environment.

Cesare Lombroso, while not the first person to suggest that criminals were 'degenerate' at a physiological level, was the first to undertake a systematic effort to study biological factors in criminal behaviour, and in 1876 he suggested that the characteristics of primitive men and inferior animals periodically reappeared in certain individuals who, in fact, revealed the 'stigmata of degeneration' – certain characteristics of the head and skull, lobeless ears, small or receding chins and facial asymmetries. No contemporary criminologist would endorse so simplistic and crude a doctrine; nevertheless, the concept that the criminally violent are, in essence, at least in some respects biologically different from the rest of us continues to exercise an appeal for many members of the public. And a more refined interpretation of Lombroso's nineteenth-century speculations is sometimes echoed in the writing of certain proponents of the biological approach. In this chapter, I shall be looking carefully at the evidence adduced by such investigators to uphold their more sophisticated version of the Lombroso doctrine, which is that there is a class of violent criminals who are marked off from the rest of us by nature of their specific physiological pathology.

I shall be looking in some detail, too, at a specific classification which is concerned with individuals who do not appear to have any moral sense nor any sense of empathy with others. Such people (and I shall return to this classification in greater depth later in this chapter) have been labelled as 'psychopaths'. In addition to showing little if any concern with moral or social codes and to making little or no emotional commitment to others, psychopaths have been regarded as displaying 'callousness and hedonism' (Treves-Brown, 1977). Recently this cluster of personality attributes has been labelled in the USA as 'sociopathic' rather than psychopathic, although the latter term (psychopath) has remained in general use in the United Kingdom – though more often in the media, however, than in technical sources as, for example, in a reference in *The Sunday Times* of 3 April 1977 to 'psychopaths, those flamboyant killers like poisoner Graham Young'.

This image of the cold, calculating and relentless killer has indeed captured the public imagination on a number of occasions. Graham Young exemplifies this stereotype. In June 1972, Young, then aged 24, was sentenced to life imprisonment for murdering two of his workmates and poisoning four others. All his victims had suffered excruciatingly. After sentence was passed, his earlier history became common knowledge. He had ten years earlier been sent to Broadmoor, having poisoned his father, sister and a school-friend; it seems clear that he had, too, fatally poisoned his step-mother. Indeed, even while he was in Broadmoor he tried to poison all the people in his wing with sugar soap.

The fascination of this image of the remorseless, unscrupulous but often ingratiating murderer has been captured by William Marsh in his novel *The Bad Seed* (1973), I would like to describe this novel in some detail, not only because it encapsulates the popular conception of the psychopathic personality, but also because it displays the public's need for an acceptable not too deeply disturbing explanation for such deviance.

### The Bad Seed

The heroine of this thriller is a young mother, Christine Penmark, whose husband is posted in the course of his professional duties to South America. But, instead of accompanying him as he might have preferred, Christine remains behind in a charming small town in the United States so that her 10 year-old daughter, Rhoda, can attend school in the USA.

Rhoda, it soon transpires, though apparently a very well behaved little girl, has already had some sort of unspecified problems of adjustment in her previous school, and at the beginning of the novel the reader is presented with the picture of an exceedingly attractive and sympathetic mother who, although she loves her young daughter, is puzzled by her paradoxical mixture of demureness and resolute independence. Thus, 'when speaking of her daughter, the adjectives that others most often used were "quaint" or "modest" or "old-fashioned" and Christine Penmark, standing in the doorway, smiled in agreement and wondered from what source the child had inherited her repose, her neatness and her cool self-sufficiency' (Marsh, 1973, p. 10).

But despite the mother's apparent reservation about her daughter, Marsh allows us to see that to others she is indeed the epitome of the charming, ingenuous little girl, and throughout the beginning of the novel we glimpse a double image – the cool manipulating Rhoda that her mother loves but deplores, and the child as she appears to most other adults whom she manipulates with very little difficulty, for example, their rich, middle-aged and childless neighbour, Monica Breedlove. In an early episode Rhoda indicates that she would like the locket that Mrs Breedlove is wearing, and she does it in so appealing a manner that not only does Mrs Breedlove give it to her but, in giving it to Rhoda, becomes even more enamoured with the child. Mrs Breedlove, in fact, is very eager to make Rhoda happy:

'But of *course* you may! Why, *certainly*, my dearest!' She seated herself, and went on, 'How wonderful it is to meet such a *natural* little girl . . . '

. . . The child went to her, put her arms around her neck, and kissed her with an intensity that seemed to engage all her consciousness. She laughed softly and rubbed her cheek against the cheek of the entranced woman. 'Aunt Monica', she said in a sweet, shy voice, drawing the name out slowly, as though her mind could not bear to relinquish it . . . 'Oh, Aunt *Monica*.'

Christine turned and went into the dining room. She thought, half-amused, half-concerned, 'What an actress Rhoda is. She knows exactly how to handle people when it's to her advantage to do so.' (ibid., p. 18)

It is not only her mother, however, who has reservations: despite Rhoda's ability to charm outsiders, professionals – like her teachers and her principal at the last school – are more perceptive and their assessment of Rhoda adds to Christine's lonely anxieties (she is reluctant to share with her husband her disquiet because she feels that the problem is too complex and too subtle to be conveyed by letter or telephone). In flashback the reader learns that the problems encountered by Rhoda in her previous school (referred to fleetingly at the beginning of the novel) were concerned with theft and that, unbeknown to Christine, the principal had referred Rhoda to a psychiatrist, not simply because Rhoda had apparently stolen, but because she had done so with such composure and, when challenged, with so little guilt. The psychiatrist had considered that

Rhoda [was] the most precocious child he'd ever seen; her quality of shrewd mature calculation was remarkable indeed; she had none of the guilts and none of the anxieties of childhood; and of course she had no capacity of affection either, being concerned only with herself. But perhaps the thing that was most remarkable about her was her unending acquisitiveness. She was like a charming little animal that can never be trained to fit into the conventional patterns of existence . . . (ibid., p. 46)

Not only has Rhoda stolen to get what she wants, but the reader is allowed to see Christine painstakingly reconstruct another episode from the past to realize that Rhoda had pushed an old lady down the stairs in order to obtain what the old lady had promised she would leave Rhoda in her will, opal crystals in a fluid ball. In the present, the reader accompanies Christine on a bitter path of mixed horror and love as Rhoda cunningly and without discovery by anyone other than the mother, who fearfully is unable to voice her growing convictions, drowns a classmate at a picnic to obtain a medal, and then sets on fire a janitor who is the only person aside from her mother to be suspicious of Rhoda.

Marsh thus presents in *The Bad Seed* the quintessential features of the popular image of the psychopath – a cold amoral but charming killer who, undeterred by guilt, compassion or love, destroys anyone who gets in his or her way. But how did so sympathetic a mother and so loving, if absent, a father as the Penmarks appear to be produce so amoral a child? It is in the resolution of this seeming paradox that Marsh focuses on the second set of stereotypes: such wickedness, such inhumanity can only appear in someone who is inhuman – different from other humans – precisely because they are *born* different; who is, in fact, a 'bad seed'. Marsh now shows us Christine Penmark making a momentous discovery about her own parentage. She discovers that the journalist, who up to now she had always revered and loved as her natural father, had adopted her when she was very young after covering the trial of a woman who was, in fact, her (Christine's) own natural mother. This woman, Bessie Dencker, is shown to have displayed chillingly similar behaviour to Rhoda's, and had in fact been executed for her crimes following the trial which Christine's adoptive father had attended. These crimes had involved the slow annihilation of the whole of her husband's family, to gain control of their property. The only member to survive had been Christine herself, who after escaping the mass slaughter, and after her mother had been caught, apprehended and sentenced, had been adopted by the man and woman who, both now dead, she had regarded as her natural parents. Christine herself had carried, unknowingly, the inheritance of Bessie Dencker and reproduced in her daughter, Rhoda a facsimile of her own psychopathic mother.

Thus Marsh, having built up the horrifying picture of a cold remorseless killer, releases society from any responsibility in the production of so chilling a killer. For the psychopath is not shaped by uncaring parents or deprivation or an unhealthy disadvantaged environment, he or she is an accident of biology – a bad seed. Christine has, unknowingly, been the passive bearer of a malign inheritance.

I have highlighted this particular fictional treatment of psychopathy rather than others in its genre because it focuses on two concepts that have passed from the realms of criminology and psychiatry into myth – the psychopathic personality and the genetic transmission of criminal violence. By implication, of course, it also suggests that violent and deviant behaviour, because it is genetically determined, is physiological in origin. In the rest of this chapter I would like to examine all of these areas – possible biological substrates for aggression, contemporary perspectives of the psychopath and the evidence that the predisposition for violence is inherited.

In doing this I shall cover, in as logical a manner as I can, the numerous suggestions that have been made in the psychobiological, sociobiological, medical and experimental literature about physical conditions that may cause aggressive emotion and/or violent behaviour. These include areas related to neurological function – the limbic system, epilepsy, skin conductance level, head injuries; areas related to biochemistry like neural transmitters, alcohol, drugs and hormones, and areas which have been connected with the genetic transmission of aggression and violence.

## Possible Biological Substrates for Aggression and Violence

THE LIMBIC SYSTEM

Although the entire brain acts as a unit in responding to the world around it, in appraising information about this world and relating it to previous experience, there is some indication that there is a degree of specialization about its parts. For some time now there has been an accumulation of evidence that certain portions of the central nervous system, especially the limbic areas of the brain, have considerable importance in the regulation and control of emotional and sexual behaviour. In vertebrate animals there has been an accumulation of evidence that the limbic system is also involved in the modulation and elaboration of the fight or flight responses which are so important for the preservation of the species when under attack (Mark, 1978). The limbic system, sometimes called the 'old brain', is composed of a series of structures in the upper brain stem and lower cerebrum and includes portions of the thalamus and hypothalamus.[1] I should now like to turn to two sources of evidence linking this system to fighting behaviour in animals and emotions like rage and violent assaults in humans. The first set of evidence emerges from experimental studies and the second from clinical observations and practice.

*Experimental Studies*
Most experimental work in this area has been concerned, as might be expected, with animals rather than humans. In some experiments, particular locations of the animal's brain are stimulated electrically and in other cases locations are actually destroyed. When unanaesthetized animals are stimulated in or near the particular area of the limbic system known as the amygdala[2], defence or flight reactions are produced in many species of mammals. Attacking behaviour is, in the most part, provoked from a much more restricted area of the amygdala.

In many cases electrical stimulation of particular locations in or near this area does not produce an invariant reaction. The type of reaction displayed may depend on the actual experimental situation. For example, when certain species of rats are stimulated in specific points in the hypothalamus, whether or not other animals in the experimental situation are attacked or not may depend on their size – in one study stimulated rats attacked nearby mice and rat pups but not adult rats or guinea pigs. Similarly, cats when stimulated in certain locations attacked only at particularly strong stimulation and only particular targets (Johnson, 1972). Other studies show that the internal condition of the experimental animal (whether, for instance, it is hungry or not) may affect the stimulated animal's responses (DeSisto, 1970, in an experiment with cats).

But certain very rare studies have shown that stimulation of specific areas in particular locations invariably produces attacking behaviour. Such results have been demonstrated mainly in cat studies. For example, Egger and Flynn (1963) claim that electrical stimulation of specific areas in the medial hypothalamus in the cat invariably produces attacking behaviour in which the cat lashes out at any adjacent object. More recent reviews, however (for example, Bandler, 1982) have questioned the validity of these earlier studies, claiming that later studies do not demonstrate that there are any simple organizational schemes in the central nervous system which control specific behaviour.

Studies of the *destruction* of areas associated with fight or flight behaviour in animals do not reveal great consistency. For example, whilst destruction of the amygdala commonly shows a reduction or taming in fight or flight behaviour, in some cases after bilateral amygdaloidal destruction there is an increase in fighting behaviour (for example, in a study with monkeys by Rosvold, Mirsky and Priabam, 1954).

In general animal studies, while showing that areas in the limbic system are associated with fight and flight behaviour, have not shown that there are any identifiable 'aggression centres'; destructive attacks and killing can be elicited from a number of widely separated portions of the limbic system. Further, the elicitation of such behaviour is in most cases dependent on the experimental situation, for example, the animals or objects present, the strength of the electrical stimulation and the condition of the experimental animal. However, isolated studies, notably on cats, do suggest that certain specific locations can invariably produce stereotyped attacking behaviour. Indeed, Moyer (1976) has extended this kind of approach to suggest that there are organized neural systems in the brain for various kinds of aggression and has proposed systems for predatory, inter-male, fear-induced, maternal, irritable and sex-related aggression; thus, for example, he proposes that stimulation of the lateral portion of the basal nucleus of the amygdala of the cat stimulates fear-induced aggression but inhibits predatory and irritable aggression.

In support for his claim for these specific neural substrates (which all involve the limbic system) for particular kinds of aggression, Moyer relies almost exclusively on animal studies, and in the main on those of non-primates like rats and cats. In primates it is clear, however, that there is no area of the limbic system that functions autonomously or directs all other brain areas (Shah and Roth, 1974) and, in primates, unlike the lower animals on which Moyer bases his conclusions, the limbic system is massively inter-connected with the brain's thinking and reasoning centres in the cortical mantle surrounding the limbic structures.

Turning from the animal studies, there are some reports of direct stimulation of the limbic areas in humans, but the conclusions that can be drawn from them are far from clear. For example, stimulation of the same area in the brain in certain patients can produce both fear and anger (Heath, 1962). And when the amygdaloidal area of forty-six epileptic patients was stimulated in a study by Jasper and Rasmusson (1958), only two patients responded with fear while the rest reported confusion or did not respond. On the other hand, a handful of individual cases have been reported (see Moyer, 1976, for example) in which stimulation of the amygdala in a patient produced aggressive emotion and/or a tendency towards violence.

Rather more direct evidence of the involvement of the limbic area in aggressive emotions or violent behaviour in humans comes from clinical studies of structural brain disease in the limbic system, and it is to these that we now turn. It is important to bear in mind that, while it is not entirely appropriate to extrapolate from studies of pathological conditions in which patients behave in an aggressive or violent manner to aggressive emotion and violent behaviour in physically healthy individuals, such studies may lead us to consider whether aggressive and violent behaviour in certain ill people may, at least in part, be provoked or stimulated by physical pathology.

## Clinical Studies
Malfunction of the nervous system, of which the limbic system forms a part, is generally expressed in two ways, which often interact. First, there may be a delay or slowness of function (negative or hypofunction) and, secondly, there may be a facilitation of function (or hyperfunction), but usually these interact so that there is a net result of the disturbance of balance in functions. It is therefore not surprising that there are a number of reports of atrophy or tumours or other lesions of the limbic system leading to abnormal. and sometimes extremely irritable, even explosive behaviour in humans (Shah and Roth, 1974).

An extreme example is provided by the case of Charles Whitman. Whitman, a student at the University of Texas, had tried to speak to psychiatrists about his periodic violent impulses, but had not been given any detailed examination. In fact, on the evening of 31 July 1966, he wrote a farewell letter which indicated that he considered that his extreme emotions were due to physical causes and that he wished to have a post-mortem conducted on his corpse.

Later that night he killed his wife and mother and the following morning he barricaded himelf on the top of the observation deck of the university tower with a high-powered hunting rifle, and in ninety minutes shot thirty-eight people, killing fourteen. On post-mortem it was discovered that he had a malignant tumour in the area of the medial part of one temporal lobe.[3] It is, of course, open to conjecture whether a similar tumour in another individual, leading as it must have to considerable pain and experience of what Whitman himself called 'mental turmoil', would have led to so violent an explosion. Not all tumours or lesions in the limbic system lead inevitably to assaultive behaviour, although there is a source of evidence from individual studies and clinical surveys to suggest that limbic tumours have been associated with abnormally aggressive behaviour (Mark, 1978).

Some further evidence for the importance of the limbic structures in modulating and influencing aggressive emotion and assaultive behaviour is also provided by the results of some neurosurgical procedures performed over the last decade or so. These surgical interventions usually involve destruction of small and specific areas of the limbic system. In some but by no means all cases, it is reported that these procedures are followed by a reduction in rage and anger without accompanying disturbance of intellectual or social functioning (see, for example, the paper by Sano *et al.* 1970), but in others the procedures have not led to a decrease in rage attacks and violent behaviour, and in yet other cases the accompanying social and emotional changes have been very disturbing.

One of the largest studies was reported by Balasubramaniam *et al* (1972). They treated 128 patients with bilateral amygdalotomy. In nine, destructive rage behaviour was eliminated, and forty-five showed some improvement, but the surgery apparently had no effect on the disturbed behaviour of the remaining seventy-five.

Whether such extreme and irreversible procedures are ever ethically acceptable is of course an important issue, but here I simply want to point out that, in the cases where the surgical procedures have led to a diminution of aggressive emotion and violent behaviour, there is some support for the contention of some biologically oriented researchers that, in the cases of some abnormally aggressive and violent individuals, their behaviour may result from specific brain pathologies. However, it should always be remembered that such neurological procedures, which have been carried out because surgeons suspected that violent behaviour was linked to pathologies in the limbic system, do not necessarily suggest that the limbic system in healthy individuals controls or directs emotion. Indeed, detailed recent study of the mechanism of nervous transmission in healthy humans indicates that in the case of the amygdala, in particular, specific structures in the limbic system are linked in complex and multiple ways with the cerebral cortex, thus ensuring that motivated behaviour is always influenced by memory and other cognitive (thinking) processes.

Turning again to neurosurgical procedures, numbers of these in the past were performed on epileptic patients with at least a partial objective of modifying what has been regarded as anti-social behaviour. But in general current opinion seems to be that the performance of such neurosurgical procedures on epileptic patients largely to modify behaviour is not justified and, when we turn to the connection between epilepsy and aggression and violence as we do in the next section, we shall see that this more recent cautionary approach is warranted by the sketchy nature of the connection between epilepsy and a tendency to aggressive emotion and violent behaviour.

EPILEPSY-RELATED DISORDERS, AGGRESSION AND VIOLENCE

Epilepsy is a disorder involving spontaneous activations of various neural systems in the brain. It cannot really be regarded as a specific disease entity and is better thought of as a dysfunction of the nervous system. Although many people associate epileptic seizures with convulsions in which the patient falls to the floor, loses consciousness and has no subsequent memory of the fit, such paroxysmal seizures are characteristic of only one of the classifications that are commonly made of epileptic seizures, the *grand mal* attack. In the second type, *petit mal*, the patient shows lapses of consciousness without significant motor activity or falling. It is the third type, *psychomotor (or temporal lobe)*[4] epilepsy which is most common in adults. This involves, as well as some paroxysmal motor disorders which may include fumbling, lip smacking and postural changes, a variety of subjective experiences such as compulsive thinking, anxiety, dream states and depression; sometimes there is some memory of the seizure but at other times there may be complete amnesia.

Some confusion has arisen in the reporting of epilepsy because, in some cases, the diagnosis has focused on the electroencephalograph (EEG) record (which traces electrical activity in the brain) and sometimes the diagnosis has rested on the clinical picture presented.[5] And perhaps because of the comparative bluntness of the EEG records, these two methods do not always lead to a consistent diagnosis. For example, about twenty per cent of those who have *grand mal* seizures have apparently normal EEG records (Jones, 1965). Such inconsistencies in diagnoses permeate the studies that have been made linking epilepsy with disturbances in psychological functioning, and in particular, with behaviour that is relevant to this book – disruptive and violent outbursts. It is nevertheless possible to systematize such studies by looking at the association of disruptive and/or violent behaviour with three different levels of epilepsy–related disorders – ictal disturbances (actual seizures, inter-ictal disorders (periods between seizures for patients who suffer from seizures) and EEG abnormalities in people who do not suffer from seizures.

There is very little association between classical epileptic seizures or ictal disturbances and directed[6] violent behaviour, and it is currently thought that where aggressive reactions are encountered in a classical seizure, they are related to the patient's confused attempts to fight off restraint. In addition, when Gunn and Fenton (1971) reviewed the history of 158 epileptic prisoners and 29 hospitalized epileptics, they concluded that automatic behaviour in a seizure was a rare explanation for crimes committed by epileptic prisoners.

When attention is focused on the behaviour *between seizures* of patients suffering from epilepsy, particularly on the behaviour of those who have been classified as suffering from temporal lobe epilepsy, there are a large number of studies reporting that some such patients are likely to show hostility and aggressive outbursts between seizures. Indeed, some reviews tend to give the impression that the great majority of temporal lobe epileptics are likely to show extremely disturbed and violent behaviour between seizures. Yet detailed studies indicate that the association between such behaviour and temporal lobe epilepsy is by no means consistent; for example, Rodin (1973) reviewed the history of over 700 patients with temporal lobe epilepsy and identified only five per cent who had committed aggressive acts. Indeed, some neurologists are sceptical of any strong relationship between temporal lobe epilepsy and violent behaviour.

Further, when temporal lobe epileptics do show such behaviour, they are likely to be younger rather than older (Serafetinides, 1970) and to show brain damage in addition to the clinical picture of epilepsy (Ounsted, 1969). It would seem that, in general, there is little to support the contention that temporal lobe epileptics typically tend to show aggressive emotion and violent behaviour between seizures, an impression that is easily gained by reading the works of some biologically oriented researchers into aggression and violence. Instead, it seems that such behaviour is characteristic of a minority of such patients.

Turning away from patients who actually suffer epileptic seizures, the third strand of evidence connecting epilepsy-related disorders with aggressive emotions and/or violent behaviour comes from studies of *electroencephalographic investigations* of certain target groups. For example, some studies have suggested that certain violent children show a maturational lag in cerebral development. Thus Surwillo (1980) reported that when six boys, who had been classified as aggressive because of fighting, bullying, being physically abusive and cruel, were asked to do a simple reaction task when attending a child guidance clinic, they showed EEG tracings that were typical of the tracings of subjects younger than the boys' respective chronological ages. Other investigators have suggested other specific EEG features for subgroups of violent individuals. For example, Lorimer (1972) reported that he had identified two subgroups in a study of violent individuals; one group was characterized by excess slow cerebral activity and the other by excess fast cerebral activity.

However, despite the association of EEG abnormalities with disturbed behaviour in studies such as these, the general consensus seems to be that the overall results of such studies are not very clear and there have been some contradictory findings (Shah and Roth, 1974), and even Moyer is

forced to conclude that 'However, at best the EEG has very little prog-
nostic value in regard to aggressive behaviour' (1976, p. 41). More
recently Whitman *et al.* (1982) have concluded after a study of eighty-
three epileptic children that in understanding the behavioural problems
shown by epileptic children a consideration of 'situation centred
variables' is more important than trying to relate such disorders to
biological variables, for example, type of seizure.

Finally, it must always be borne in mind that epilepsy is far more likely
to occur in disadvantaged social groups than in more advantaged groups,
and that even when a connection is shown between disturbed behaviour
and epilepsy-related disorders, how the association is interpreted may
'often be a matter of the investigator's background and disciplinary bias'
(Shah and Roth, 1974, pp. 121–2). In other words, if a study does
indicate, say, that violent offenders are more likely than non-offenders to
show EEG abnormalities, whether this is interpreted as showing support
for the physiological base of violence or whether it is interpreted as
showing that socially disadvantaged people are likely to be both un-
healthier and more disposed to anti-social behaviour than their more
advantaged peers may depend on whether the investigator is disposed to
look for a physical or a sociological interpretation.

## HEAD INJURIES

A number of studies have shown that violent criminals are likely to have
suffered head injuries at some stage. For example, approximately
seventy-five per cent of 400 violent adult prisoners studied by Mark and
Ervin (1970) had histories that included loss of consciousness from head
injuries.

However, this association between head injuries in general and violent
behaviour does not necessarily lead to the conclusion that brain injuries
*cause* violent behaviour. As I shall show in Chapter 6 people who are
habitually violent are more likely than other individuals to have suffered
a history of social and emotional deprivation during which, both in
childhood and adulthood, they may have suffered violent assaults. Their
own violent behaviour may be as much a response to their social and
psychological history as it is to their experience of head injury.

## PSYCHOPATHY AND THE AUTONOMIC NERVOUS SYSTEM

As I mentioned earlier in this chapter, the term psychopath, as used by
laymen, tends to refer to individuals who behave in anti-social, sometimes even cruel ways, without experiencing any remorse for the effect
their actions may have on others. But the use of the terms by psychologists, psychiatrists and sociologists has been so diverse that any effort
to define the nature of psychopathy 'remains elusive', as Treves-Brown

notes in his review, 'Who is the psychopath?' (1977).

The first contribution to the concept of psychopathy is usually attributed to Pinel, who wrote in 1835 about *manie sans delire* that:

> The moral and active principles of the mind are strongly perverted or depraved, the power of self-government is lost or greatly impaired, and the individual is found to be incapable not of talking or reasoning upon any subject proposed to him, for this he will often do with great shrewdness and volubility, but of conducting himself with decency and propriety in the business of life. (Quoted by Treves-Brown, 1977, p. 56)

This description, that is, of an individual who appears to be aware of a generally accepted moral code, but who neither acts in accordance with it, nor experiences remorse nor anxiety because he or she does not act in accordance with it, remains at the core of most descriptions of what has been variously labelled the psychopathic, sociopathic or anti-social personality. Related to this inability to feel remorse or compassion is the concept that an essential feature of the psychopath is an inability to form relations with others, or indeed to feel any trust in other human beings. A final component that seems to run through most descriptions of the psychopath is that he or she is 'impulse-ridden'. But while there seems to be a measure of agreement that psychopathy involves a lack of remorse, an inability to make emotional relationships and a tendency to impulsive action, there is agreement about little else. For example, many psychiatrists see as the central tendency in psychopathy an inability to profit from experience (Gray and Hutchinson, 1964), while others such as McCord and McCord (1956) do not consider this a central attribute. While some recent workers see psychopaths as manipulative, others see them as 'lacking judgement or foresight' (Henderson and Gillespie, 1969). Again, while most workers consider it necessary to differentiate between types of psychopaths, there is no acceptance of a common typology.

There is also no agreement about whether or not psychopaths are predisposed to aggression or violence. Taking the former term first, while the McCords see aggression as central to the definition of a psychopath, classifying a psychopath as an 'antisocial, aggressive, highly impulsive person', Curran and Partridge (1969) classify psychopaths into two types, the 'predominantly aggressive' and the 'predominantly inadequate'. Turning to violence, the literature shows a similar lack of consistency with disagreement as to whether psychopaths are predisposed to violence (Heilbrun, 1979).

Despite this lack of consensus about the concept of psychopathy, a number of attempts have been made to link psychopathy with specific physiological abnormalities. It has been suggested by some workers, for example, that psychopaths show EEG abnormalities particularly when activating procedures are used. (For instance, subjects are exposed to flashing lights, given certain drugs or told to breathe deeply.) There is, however, no general acceptance that psychopaths do show specific EEG abnormalities. Similarly, while some recent studies have suggested that psychopaths show neurological abnormalities associated with the functioning of the right and left cerebral hemispheres, such studies have not been reliably replicated (Reid, 1981).

But the most heavily researched area in the physiology of psychopaths has been related to their skin conductance level. This is measured by monitoring the sweating in the palms of subjects' hands. Psychopaths tend to show a lower skin conductance level than non-psychopaths under normal conditions (though this difference is not always statistically significant). They also tend to show a lower skin conductance level when exposed to stresses like sudden exceptionally loud noises and, if warned that a blast of noise is going to occur, they tend to show anticipatory skin conductance response later than non-psychopaths and at a lower level (Mednick *et al.*, 1982). This difference in anticipatory response has led to speculation about fear levels in psychopaths. It has been suggested that because psychopaths tend to show lower anticipation, they feel less fear when faced with the prospect of an unpleasant stimulus. And it is further speculated that such lowered levels of anticipatory fear lead to lowered levels of sensitivity to the threat of punishment.

Mednick *et al.* (1982) conclude that it is these physiological differences in skin conductance levels and responses between non-psychopaths and psychopaths which make the psychopath more prone to anti-social behaviour. The reasoning goes like this. Psychopaths show low anticipation of punishment (as evidenced by the finding that they show lower anticipatory skin conductance levels) and are in genernal less anxious than non-psychopaths (as evidenced by their lower skin conductance level under normal conditions). They therefore not only fail to anticipate punishment but also fear it less (because of lower base anxiety levels).

Implicit in this explanation is the assumption that most of us do not behave like psychopaths because we fear punishment if we do. This explanation for psychopathy rests on another assumption, which is that we acquire moral values by learning them without examining them, much as children learn their multiplication tables by rote, whereas most contemporary psychologists would argue that moral values are acquired primarily through social interaction and through active thinking about moral issues rather than by simply internalizing, without reflection, a social code.

But to return to the subject matter of this chapter, does this physiological difference in skin conductance level shown in many (but by no means all) studies of psychopaths provide a specific physiological basis or substrate for aggressive emotion and violent behaviour in human beings in general? The answer is clearly no – psychopaths are in fact regarded as less emotional than non-psychopaths, their 'emotional flatness' is often remarked on (Shah and Roth, 1974), and with respect to violence many of us know that the reason we do not commit violence is not primarily because we fear punishment if we do, but because of a whole complex of inhibiting factors like compassion, empathy, and an active and dynamic moral code. Finally, it is important to remember that by no means all individuals classified as psychopaths have behaved in a violent manner.

BIOCHEMISTRY, AGGRESSION AND VIOLENCE

In this chapter I am concerned with all those biological variables that have been associated in the socio/psychobiological literature with aggressive emotion and violent behaviour. So far we have looked at the limbic system, at relevant research on epilepsy-related disorders, at head injuries and finally at skin conductance level, and I now want to turn to biochemical and endocrinal factors. I shall look in turn at chemical messengers, sex-hormones and factors associated with what Mark has called 'brain poisoning'.

*Chemical Messengers*
This is a term I shall use to cover those substances which are thought to carry messages associated with motivated behaviour either in the bloodstream or in the nervous system. The substances which have most often been associated with the neural transmission of messages about motivated behaviour in the nervous system are the neurotransmitters noradrenalin, dopamin and serotonin. All three have been found in high concentration in the limbic system and it might thus be anticipated that they would be involved in fighting behaviour in animals. This has indeed been demonstrated: for example, if fighting behaviour is produced in cats by stimulation of the amygdala, there is a subsequent change in the biochemical background (Vowles, 1970), and according to Moyer (1976) there is good evidence that the brain chemistry of isolated and aggressive rats is different from that of normal animals with respect to turnover rates of serotonin, noradrenalin and dopamin. Nevertheless, there is no clear evidence that particular neural transmitters are associated with aggressive emotions and violent behaviours in humans. For example, while some studies implicate serotonin in the manifestation of violent behaviour, other studies do not (Bioulac *et al.*, 1980). Further, recent research by Bradley has shown that brain cells are affected in different ways by the same neurotransmitter depending on the state of the cell, the amount of neurotransmitter and how often the chemical is administered (Bylinsky, 1982).

Aside from the action of the neurotransmitters in conveying messages between individual cells, messages associated with motivated behaviour are also carried in the bloodstream by adrenalin and noradrenalin (which also acts, as I have noted above, as a neurotransmitter). It has been known for some time that these two substances are secreted into the bloodstream in stressful or emotional states and it has been proposed in the past that high aggressiveness is associated with noradrenalin and high anxiety with adrenalin. But this rather neat set of relationships has been increasingly questioned. Turning first to the relationship between anxiety and adrenalin, evidence has been accumulating that the effect of a rise in adrenalin in humans produces (aside from physiological changes such as an elevation in heart rate) psychological changes in mood but that the nature of the mood change is related to the particular situation the individuals concerned find themselves in. For example, when students were administered with synthetic adrenalin and compared to a group who had been administered a placebo, not only did the students with the adrenalin rate themselves as feeling more emotional than the students who had received the placebo, but how they rated their mood depended on the experimental conditions. In one experiment in Germany, for example, after students had been injected with adrenalin, those who had been needlessly denigrated reported that they felt angry and those who had been praised reported that they felt happy (Erdmann and Janke, 1978)

Rather more support has been shown for the noradrenalin–aggressive-ness relationship. The support derives from the proposition that amphe-tamines increase the propensity for violent behaviour and that amphe-tamines are thought to act on the nervous systems, in part at least, by releasing noradrenalin (Shah and Roth, 1974).[7] But while this does provide a rationale for the aggressive–noradrenalin connection, the finding that the administration of amphetamines reliably causes an in-crease in the propensity to violent behaviour has itself been questioned. As we shall see shortly when we turn to 'brain poisoning', the action of amphetamines has been found to vary with specific environmental con-ditions, the individual's personal characteristics and the extent to which the individual is taking other drugs (Moyer, 1976).

In general, it seems that while adrenalin, noradrenalin, dopamin and serotonin are implicated in motivated behaviour, in the case of humans there is no simple one-to-one correspondence between any one of these and aggressive emotion or violent behaviour. But rather more directly implicated in these areas have been a particular set of biochemical agents – the sex hormones. It is to a discussion of these and their effects on aggressive emotion and violent behaviour that I now turn.

## Sex Hormones, Aggression and Violence

A large body of literature is concerned with sex differences in aggression and violence, and I shall be returning to this area repeatedly in the course of this book. That men appear to show a greater propensity than women for violent behaviour has been extremely well documented. Though women are now more likely than they were in the past to be involved in violent crime, so are men, and recent research appears to indicate that, in the USA and the UK, men continue to show a far greater propensity to be indicted for crimes of violence (Steffensmeier, Steffensmeier and Rosenthal, 1979; Box and Hale, 1983).

Measuring differences in aggression between the sexes is, of course, a far more complex conceptual problem. Naturally, it will depend to some extent on how aggression is defined by the evaluator and on the setting, whether natural or in the laboratory. In Chapter 3 I will look in some detail at reports of sex differences in aggression in natural settings, in Chapter 4 at psychoanalytic views of sex difference in aggression, in Chapter 5 at laboratory studies of sex differences in aggression and in Chapters 6 and 7 at social influences on sex differences in aggressive and violent behaviour. At this stage I will take for granted that there appears to be a consensus that there are well-established differences in this area.

In this chapter, I want to consider only one aspect of sex differences and that is to what extent such sex differences, when they are shown, can be ascribed to a particular biological causation – the influence of sex hormones. The particular type of hormone which has been chiefly associated with aggression are the androgens. In the male (in the absence of any genetic abnormality) these are secreted early in foetal development and they appear to be the main agent in the organization of sexual dimorphism, that is, in causing changes in the foetus which result in the production of a child with masculine, rather than feminine, physiological characteristics. Androgens, and in particular testosterone and andro-stenedione, also show a sudden and dramatic increase in males with the onset of sexual maturity, though they are present, as I have mentioned, in smaller quantities before puberty as well. Although androgens are the main agent of sexual dimorphism, they are found in minute quantities in the foetal stage in females as well, and it is now thought that, in terms of hormones, the difference between males and females is quantitative rather than qualitative. This means that, throughout life, males have relatively high levels of androgens and relatively low levels of estrogens (the chief female hormone) and females have relatively high levels of estrogens and relatively low levels of androgens.

It has been suggested that sex differences in aggression are the result of the impact of androgens on the *prenatal* organization of those areas in the brain that 'mediate aggression' (Tieger, 1980), and secondly it has been hypothesized that *at puberty* hormones in males lower the threshold for angry, aggressive behaviour (Moyer, 1976). As I indicated earlier in this chapter, no specific areas in the brain or nervous system have been pinpointed as controlling aggression, and with the exception of certain stereotyped behaviour in rats and cats no areas have been shown to be specifically concerned with aggression, so it is not surprising to find that the studies which cite the role of hormones in aggression do not rest on precise physiological details. Speculation about the connection between hormones and aggression is based rather on the following types of evidence. First, that abnormal prenatal levels of sex hormones affect later levels of aggression; secondly, that castrated males show changes in particular types of behaviour which are relevant to aggression; and thirdly, that levels of testosterone in males correlate with levels of aggressive behaviour.

I shall now consider these three strands in turn but, in so doing, I shall confine the discussion to studies concerning primates, and humans in particular. Studies concerned with the action of sex hormones before birth fall into two categories. First, there are studies of children who, before birth, were exposed because of pathological conditions to naturally occurring abnormal sex-hormone levels and, secondly, there are studies of children whose mothers were given hormone treatment when they were pregnant because their pregnancies were high risk.

If females are exposed, before birth, to higher levels of androgens, then, if there is a reliable link between androgen level and the tendency to aggression, we might expect such girls to show higher levels of aggression than the control group. There are three studies containing information on levels of aggression in early androgenized girls. Money and Erhardt (1972) compared fifteen such girls with controls and found no significant difference in childhood fighting, and Money and Schwartz (1976) studied another sample of such girls in some detail and concluded that there was no evidence that these girls showed any tendency to manifestations of overt aggression during childhood or adolescence. Erhardt and Baker (1974) compared seventeen such girls with their sisters and mothers and showed no statistically significant differences in fighting, though there was a tendency for the androgenized girls to initiate more fights than their mothers or sisters (as reported in interviews). Finally, Money and Schwartz, reviewing evidence on males who were exposed to abnormally high levels of androgens before birth, conclude that such males

> have proved not to be noteworthy in dominance assertion or in their readiness to fight and attack. Despite a physique that would enable them to win in combat with agemates, they have avoided disputes. In fact, they have frequently shown themselves to be unusually gentle people. (1976, p. 28)

The evidence does not seem to support the contention that abnormally high levels of androgens at the foetal stage contribute to higher levels of aggression in humans.

In some cases, in order to avoid further complications of pregnancy, mothers with high-risk pregnancies are given female hormones such as progestogens and estrogens, and a number of studies have investigated whether the children resulting from such pregnancies are lower in levels of aggression. If androgens are implicated in aggression, it might be surmised that the administration of higher levels of female hormones would suppress the sexual dimorphism that it has been proposed leads males to develop a tendency to higher aggression than females. But, when mothers are given hormones prenatally, these are often a complex mixture of androgen and progesterone-related synthetic hormones (e.g. Reinisch, 1981), so that it is difficult to draw clear conclusions.

Interpretation is further complicated because the children of such pregnancies might be expected to show differences in activity-related comparisons with other children of normal pregnancies simply because of the pathologies suffered by their mothers during pregnancy. This is the conclusion reached by Meyer-Bahlberg and Erhardt in a recent review of such studies (1982). In any event, comparisons between such children and matched controls rarely reveal strong differences. For example, Meyer-Bahlberg and Erhardt themselves compared twenty-eight children whose mothers had been given medroxyprogesterone in pregnancy with twenty-eight children born of normal pregnancies who had been matched by sex, race, birth date and socio-economic status. The children and their mothers were interviewed when the children were between 9 and 14 years of age. Differences in 'aggression' were found in only eight out of thirty three comparisons and only one of these was statistically significant: the child's report of 'indirect aggression against the father'. It must be concluded, I think (and see also Mazur, 1983), that such studies show little evidence that children exposed to 'feminine' hormones when their mothers were pregnant are subsequently less aggressive, and that in any event the results of such studies are difficult to interpret because, as Meyer-Bahlberg and Erhardt note, 'the influence of pregnancy pathology cannot be excluded' (1982, p. 39).

The second line of evidence linking aggression with hormones is concerned with studies of the effects of castration. Studies have been made of the hundreds of men (Mazur, 1983) who have been castrated in America and Europe in this century in an attempt to curb those aspects of their behaviour that were regarded as anti-social by law enforcing agencies. As might be expected, the majority of these studies have been concerned with the effect of castration on sex drive, and in particular on the propensity to commit sexual offences (Moyer, 1976). Results from studies that are concerned with the effect on aggressive behaviour, other than sexual attacking behaviour, are not consistent. For example, Bremer (1959) reports that castration of mental cases had no definite pacifying effect while Hawke (1950) described some cases where generally aggressive men, after castration, became less liable to create disturbances. These studies, whatever one may think of the ethics of castration, do not present any conclusive evidence that aggressive behaviour is linked to the male hormone because castration in human males is generally accompanied by such profound changes in the subjective evaluation of self that behavioural changes are very difficult to interpret. In addition, it is worth noting that castration of other primates does not produce any change in dominance relationships (Kedenburg, 1979).

The final thread of evidence linking male hormones to aggression comes from those studies which have linked the level of plasma testosterone and either self-reports of aggressive behaviour or observations of aggressive behaviour. Once again the results are inconsistent.[8] Kreuz and Rose (1972) tested a prison population of young offenders who were in prison for crimes like murder, rape and assault. They found that there were very large individual differences in plasma testosterone levels but these differences were not related to aggressive behaviour in any consistent manner. For example, while plasma testosterone levels were related to the degree of violence shown in crimes the men had committed before sentencing, the testosterone levels were not related to fighting behaviour in prison, neither were any overall differences found between the testosterone levels of prisoners compared to guards. Similarly inconsistent findings were recently reported by Olweus *et al.* (1980) who measured plasma testosterone levels in fifty-eight normal 16-year-old Swedish boys. They correlated these levels with the boys' responses to questionnaires dealing with self-reports of aggressive feelings and behaviour. On one aggression inventory there was evidence of an association, but on another there was none. Comparing across studies, the same pattern of inconsistent results appears. For example, while Kreuz and Rose (1972) showed an association between plasma testosterone levels and violent crime in a sample of offenders, Mattsson *et al.* (1980) found no such association in a study of juvenile offenders.

Thus we can conclude that these three strands of evidence do not show any clear and unambiguous relationship between male hormones and the propensity to display violent behaviour or feel aggressive emotion. Indeed, the likelihood of such a simple unidirectional relationship has been thrown into doubt by two additional lines of investigation. The first shows that the secretion of male hormones is itself directly affected by environmental and social variables, and the second is concerned with the speculation that female hormones may also be implicated in violent behaviour and aggressive emotion.

The circularity of the relationship between emotional and aroused behaviour and hormones is currently under increasing investigation. It has been shown in a number of studies that if primates are placed into situations where they suffer defeat they show a reduction in testosterone levels. For example, Rose, Bernstein and Gordon (1975) introduced four adult males into a large, well-established breeding group of rhesus monkeys with the result that the four were seriously attacked and defeated by the resident males. After this the introduced animals showed a significant reduction in testosterone levels, and the dominant males showed an elevation in testosterone levels (Meller, 1982). Similarly in humans testosterone level has been shown to be responsive to levels of stress in the environment. For example, one study showed that shortly after young men entered the Officer Candidate School in the United States Navy, they showed a marked suppression of circulating testosterone (Kedenburg, 1979). Recovery or subsequent elevation of this testosterone level was ascribed to the reduction of stress as they became accustomed to their new environment. This study and other similar findings have been interpreted as lending support to the hypothesis that the level of testosterone is itself affected by situational variables.

The relation between female hormones and aggressive and dominant behaviour has also been investigated and early primate studies suggested that estrogen injected into female chimpanzees whose ovaries had been removed increased dominant behaviour. But recent research has showed a more complex relationship between estrogen and aggression or dominant behaviour. As in the studies linking testosterone in primates to male aggression and dominance, the relationship has been shown to be circular and not one-directional. That is, the social rank of the primate concerned is a major determinant of the effect of the hormone, and dominant and submissive females react differently to the administration of estrogen (Meller, 1982).

The influence of female hormones on human emotional behaviour has been studied intensively, mostly in connection with what has been termed the 'premenstrual' syndrome. This term refers to the fact that some, but by no means all, women report various symptoms premenstrually. These may include a variety of physical changes ranging from headaches to oedema (swelling of tissues because of increased fluid content) and weight gain. Simultaneously many women report a subjective feeling of increased emotionality. The emotions experienced are nearly always unpleasant, ranging from depression and anxiety to hostility and irritation (Parlee, 1976). Whether or not this syndrome is directly associated with hormonal changes has not been established. Some researchers ascribe the syndrome directly to the action of hormones, claiming that progesterone (which shows a relative fall in level premenstrually) has an irritability-reducing effect on the brain. Other researchers claim a more indirect role for hormones, hypothesizing that hormones affect the level of sodium and water retention, and that it is this retention which results in general feelings of discomfort. Yet other researchers into the premenstrual syndrome ascribe it to cultural and societal factors, arguing that when menstruation is called 'the curse' and that when other women report feelings of physical and psychological discomfort premenstrually, the developing girl learns to interpret the physiological changes she experiences before menstruation in a negative manner.

But even if we accept the hypothesis that links the premenstrual syndrome most directly to hormones, there is still no absolute link between a particular hormonal state and a particular emotional one. For as we have seen some women report that they are tense and irritable premenstrually, while others report that they are depressed and anxious (Moos, 1977). And while some studies show that women are more likely to commit violent crime premenstrually, other studies show that suicide attempts also increase (Moyer, 1976).

What then can we conclude about the influence of hormones on aggressive emotion and violent behaviour? I think it is probably only reasonable to draw three conclusions. First, there is no evidence for a direct one-directional association between any particular hormone or class of hormones and aggression and violence. Secondly, while it is possible that hormonal change may result in subjective mood change (for example in the case of the premenstrual part of the menstrual cycle, or just after the birth of a baby for women), the change in mood experienced varies from individual to individual. Thirdly, while hormones may affect emotions and behaviour, so may social interaction and other environmental factors influence the secretion of hormones.

*Brain Poisoning, Aggression and Violence*
I should like to turn now to the third biochemical factor, those substances Mark refers to as 'brain poisons'. But before doing so I want to refer briefly to the effect of certain pathological conditions on emotional behaviour. Certain pathological conditions do affect mood. For example, when diabetics are in a state of hypoglycaemia (that is, their blood sugar levels are extremely low, perhaps because of the administration of too large a dose of insulin), they may experience emotional imbalance as well as showing physical symptoms. In such cases the patient may become very disruptive, and so some psychobiologists and sociobiologists claim that this condition is an example of a well-established link between a particular physiological state and aggressive emotion or violent behaviour. In fact, not all hypoglycaemic patients *do* show such emotions, but many become instead sullen and withdrawn (Moyer, 1976). Once again there is no direct, invariable link between any specific state of blood chemistry and a particular emotion.

The link between alcohol and violent behaviour is well established. For example, Wolfgang (1958) examined Philadelphia records of homicides and found that fifty-four per cent of the offenders and fifty-three per cent of the victims had been drinking shortly before, or at the time of, the killing. But for the purposes of this chapter we are really only concerned with one aspect of the link: to what extent does alcohol *directly cause* aggressive emotion and violent behaviour? Alcohol clearly has a number of indirect effects on such emotions and behaviour. For example, under the influence of alcohol thought processes become distorted and so it is probable that inhibitions, whether moral or social, will be lowered, making people far more likely to act out negative emotions and behave in an anti-social manner. Further, when people drink excessively they often do so in circumstnaces where violent behaviour is, relatively speaking, reasonably common. Finally, a number of studies suggest that when people drink alcohol, they expect to feel more emotional than normal.

In particular, some studies have shown that people expect to react aggressively after they have consumed alcohol. For example, in a study reported by Powers and Kutash, Lang and his co-workers gave subjects a beverage to drink, telling one group that it was alcohol and the other group that it was tonic water. Actually half of each group were given alcohol and half tonic. Then in half of these four groups, a confederate of the experimenters tried to provoke aggressive responses, while in the other half a confederate simply maintained a social interaction. The results showed that, comparing the subjects who had actually been given tonic water, those who thought it was alcohol behaved more aggressively than those who thought they had been given tonic (Powers and Kutash, 1978).

Alcohol then is associated with aggressive emotion and violent behaviour for a number of indirect reasons – it lowers inhibitions by clouding thought, it is often drunk in an atmosphere which is suggestive of aggressive or violent interactions (for example, in certain pubs with established reputations), it is regarded as conducive to comparatively aggressive and anti-social behaviour, particularly when it is consumed in excess, and finally, those who drink in excess are often (but by no means invariably) those who have a record of violent interactions. For example, Mayfield (1976) investigated the drinking habits of 307 people who had been convicted of serious assaults and found that problem drinkers had more often committed assaults than those without a drinking problem.

But does alcohol have a direct action on the brain or nervous system that leads unambiguously and invariably to aggressive emotion and violent behaviour? It would appear not. The relationship between alcohol and emotional behaviour is, as Powers and Kutash put it, both very complex and paradoxical:

> Aggressive individuals can become more aggressive; yet passive individuals can also become aggressive; and, additionally, aggressive individuals at times may become more passive. In the last instance, when the aggressive individual becomes more passive with alcohol use, the relaxing and euphoric effects of the drug may help the person to overlook frustrations and negative feelings, such as rejection and inadequacy. Some of our own clients with problems of high aggressiveness have told us that alcohol helps them control hostile or violent feelings – for instance, when they are extremely angry at another person or at some frustrating occurrence. (1978, p. 322)

In conclusion, although the consumption of alcohol, particularly in excess is associated with aggression and violence, the link, as Taylor and Leonard (1983) conclude, is complex and there is no simple, invariant relationship between the action of alcohol on the brain or nervous system and a specific emotion or particular class of behaviour.[9] In fact, as many of us know from experience, alcohol can lead to a wide range of emotions ranging from euphoria to depression, depending on our existing mood and the setting we find ourselves in.

Next to alcohol the substance most often linked to violent behaviour has been amphetamine. In the past even moderate doses of amphetamines have been associated with a predisposition to disruptive behaviour, but currently there is general agreement that moderate dosages of amphetamines do not have such an effect. There is, however, some evidence that if amphetamines are taken intravenously, in excess, and over a long period, individuals may start to feel increasingly paranoid and, as a result, they may become destructive and assaultive. However, because such individuals habitually take other drugs and because they often are involved in a subculture which is heavily involved in violence, it is by no means easy to establish the precise role of amphetamines on the violent behaviour (Moyer, 1976).

Reviewing the evidence on the three categories of biochemical agents we have considered – chemical messengers, hormones and brain poisons – it should be clear that we have identified no particular biochemical agent that acts directly and invariably in such a way that all individuals will, under its influence, feel more aggressive or act more violently. Nor should we expect to find such an agent. Human beings after all are exceedingly complex. Their values and attitudes and past experience are so varied that we should surely not expect to predict in any unambiguous manner an individual's reaction to the action of any particular neural transmitter or any specific change in blood chemistry.[10]

GENES, AGGRESSION AND VIOLENCE

The failure, as summarized in the preceding sections, to identify any specific physiological substrates for aggression destroys the most powerful claim of the psycho- and sociobiological view of aggression and violence – that is, that in Moyer's words we can change an individual's behaviour in a predictable direction by 'altering his internal milieu' (1976, p. 284). It could, however, be argued by biologically oriented researchers that the failure to identify specific substrates is not because attitudes, values, expectations and social settings are the ultimate determinants of emotion and behaviour, but because neurological and endocrinological techniques remain as yet too blunt and unsophisticated to pinpoint the biological substrates. As further support for the essentially physiological determinance of aggression and emotion they could point to the studies that are concerned with genetic factors in aggression and violence.

The evidence that links aggression and violence in humans[11] to genetic factors comes from four areas: first, laboratory and experimental studies; secondly, studies of levels of criminality; thirdly, studies of the genetic transmission of psychopathy; and finally, studies of chromosomal abnormalities. In the following sections I shall consider each of these in turn.

*Laboratory and experimental studies of the genetic transmission of aggression*
A number of studies have attempted to investigate the hereditary transmission of aggression in children and adults by using 'twin studies' in the experimental situation. The 'twin study' technique involves comparing the 'concordance rate' for identical twins with the 'concordance rate' for fraternal twins by obtaining two sets of twin pairs, identical and non-identical and estimating how similar members of the twin pairs are on the attribute being studied. If the members of identical twin pairs are more similar on that attribute than the members of non-identical twin pairs are, this is interpreted as indicating that there is a degree of genetic transmission in the attribute being investigated because identical twins have identical genetic make-up whereas non-identical twins do not.

Using this technique, Plomin, Foch and Rowe (1981) studied two samples of twin pairs – fifty four identical twin pairs and thirty-three non-identical twin pairs – whose average age was 7½ years. They compared the level of similarity between the pairs of identical twins to the level of similarity between the pairs of non-identical twins on 'Bobo clown aggression'. (This is one of the most commonly used measures of aggression in experimental studies of aggression in children, and involves measuring how often children hit a 5 foot inflated clown-like doll, after they have been exposed to an adult model repeatedly hitting the doll.) Identical twins, in Plomin's study, were no more similar to each other on this measure of aggression than were non-identical twins, leading the authors to conclude that there was no evidence of an hereditary influence on this measure.

Their finding was similar to the findings of other twin study investigations of aggression in the laboratory situation which have not shown significant differences between the levels of similarity on measures of aggression for identical twins as compared to non-identical twins (e.g. Loehlin and Nicols, 1976; a review of these studies can be found in Plomin, Foch and Rowe, 1981).

*The genetic transmission of criminality*
A number of investigations have used the 'twin study' technique just described to explore the evidence for the hereditary transmission of

criminality by comparing the concordance rate for criminal convictions among identical twin pairs with the concordance rate for non-identical twin pairs.

In a review of these investigations, Mednick *et al.* (1982) conclude that such studies do show a higher concordance rate for identical twins than for non-identical twins on criminality, but they point out that such studies are methodologically weak because it is very difficult to separate out hereditary and environmental factors in such studies. They further conclude that while there is a higher rate of concordance for criminality for identical twins, no such higher rate has been observed for the sub-category of violence. (Of course such studies of criminality cannot be used to estimate concordance for aggression, however it is defined, because court records do not contain such a category.)

A similar technique to the 'twin study' technique focuses on adoption. In 'adoption studies', concordance rates are also compared, but this time it is the concordance between adopted people with on the one hand their natural parents and on the other hand their adopted parents. If the concordance rate between adopted people and their natural parents is higher than the concordance rate between adopted people and their adopted parents, it is interpreted as offering evidence for a genetic transmission of the attribute being studied.

Results for adoption studies on the heritability of criminality are very similar to the results obtained on the twin studies of the heritability of criminality. Once again, there does appear to be a hereditary transmission in level of criminality[12] but when attention is focused on violent crimes there is no evidence for a genetic factor. This was shown for example in a large study of 14,427 Danish adoptees that separated out crimes of violence (Mednick *et al.*, 1982).

I think it must be concluded at this stage that concordance studies, whether of twins or adoptees, do not show any evidence for the genetic transmission of aggression or violence.

## The hereditary transmission of psychopathy

As I have noted earlier, the definition of psychopathy is by no means clear cut. Nevertheless, many reviews of criminality discuss the role of genetic factors in psychopathy (e.g. Shah and Roth, 1974; Reid, 1981), basing their discussion on the study done by Fini Schulsinger (1974) in Denmark. Schulsinger used an adoption study and compared the concordance rate between adoptees and their natural parents to the concordance rate between the adoptees and their adopted parents for fifty-seven Danish adoptees who had been diagnosed as psychopaths. He found that none of the mothers (natural or adopted) could be diagnosed as psychopaths, but the diagnosis of psychopathy occurred more than five times as frequently among the natural fathers of the fifty-seven diagnosed psychopaths than it did for their adopted parents, leading, he argued, to the conclusion that there is a genetic factor in psychopathology.

However, Schulsinger's criteria for psychopathy do not bear much similarity to the core components for psychopathy that most other studies include (see discussion above). For example, his criteria make no mention of personal coldness in relationships or disregard for moral values. Furthermore, while his criteria were strictly applied to the adoptees, the application of the criteria to the parents proved far more difficult, as he himself acknowledges, because of the quality of the parents' case record material. From the point of interest of this book, his study does not provide any evidence for the genetic transmission of a predisposition to aggressive feelings or violent behaviour, because neither of these attributes (aggressive or violent) are mentioned in his criteria. Indeed, he appears to have included in his diagnosis of psychopathy some individuals who were 'mainly passive-asthenic' (depressed) (ibid., p. 184).

## The genetic transmission of aggression and violence in chromosomal abnormalities

When a sperm unites with an ovum to produce a female baby, the mother contributes one sex hormone, an 'X', and the father another, also an 'X'. In the case of a male baby however, while the mother contributes an 'X' sex chromosome again, the father contributes a 'Y' chromosome. One particular abnormality of the sex chromosomes has been cited as being implicated in violent behaviour and this is the XYY configuration, where a male baby receives not one but two Y chromosomes from the father.

The first study to isolate this abnormality was reported in 1961 and shortly after that, to quote Mednick _et al._ (1982), some surveys began to suggest that 'XYY men are disproportionately represented in maximum security hospitals. The descriptions presented of the crimes perpetrated by these XYY men would supply material for a series of horror films. A media image quickly developed of the huge, dangerous hulk of a ."supermale" with superaggressiveness spurred on by his extra male chromosome' (1982, pp. 22–3).

More recent evidence, however, based on a number of studies has shown no association between the XYY chromosome and the predisposition to violence (for example, Witkin _et al._, 1976), and it is now clear that while some, but not all studies, show that XYY men are more likely to be criminal than other men of their height, intelligence and social class, there are considerable variations and no consistent behavioural syndrome (or pattern) can be described for XYY men. Indeed, Shah and Roth (1974) estimate that there must be 'literally thousands' of men with the XYY sex chromosome configuration in the general public who are, in all but their chromosomal abnormality, indistinguishable from their fellows.

On page 42 I noted that any evidence for the genetic transmission of the predisposition to violent behaviour or aggressive emotion would support the claim that there is a specific physiological substrate for aggression and violence. I then went on to review studies in this area, and I think it is fair to conclude that, at this stage, no such evidence for the genetic transmission of aggression or violence is available.

## Overview of the Biological Approach

I would now like to draw together the threads of this chapter by looking at the following six issues:

(1) Who are the biologically oriented researchers into aggression and violence?
(2) Are these researchers consistent in their use of the terms 'aggression' and 'violence'?
(3) Have they provided convincing evidence for the physiological determination of aggression and violence?
(4) What are the social implications of their claims that there are physiological substrates for aggression and violence?
(5) How may their research be evaluated?
(6) Does their use of the terms aggression and violence cover all the parameters discussed in the summational description of aggression and violence derived in Chapter 1?

WHO ARE THE BIOLOGICALLY ORIENTED RESEARCHERS?

In this and the next chapter of this book I discuss theories and approaches which have been labelled in some cases as psychobiological (for example, by Moyer, 1976) and in other cases sociobiological (Mark, 1978). What distinguishes these approaches from the approaches in the remainder of this book is that socio– and psychobiologists believe that aggression and violence are intimately related to physiological processes and man's genetic endowment. In general, they tend to regard physiological processes or genetic predispositions as extremely powerful influences on human behaviour. Though they accept that such controlling influences are modified by social situations and psychological factors, they tend to underplay the effect of the psychological and social environment. In particular, they place very little emphasis on the influence of cognition and emotion on behaviour.

I think that it is possible to trace two seminal traditions in the work of socio- and psychobiologists. The first, the one we have been concerned with in this chapter, is largely biological, and the second, which we will look at in the next chapter, is ethological, drawing heavily on the Darwinian model of evolution.

In this chapter I have drawn on the work of neurosurgeons, for example Mark, and physiologically oriented psychologists such as Moyer as well as the work of the group of scientists gathered at the Psykologisk Institut of Copenhagen, who include Mednick and Schulsinger.

## HOW CONSISTENTLY DO RESEARCHERS WORKING WITH A BIOLOGICAL ORIENTATION USE THE TERMS 'AGGRESSION' AND 'VIOLENCE'?

At the beginning of this chapter, I noted that people using the biological approach seldom feel it necessary to define terms such as 'aggression' and 'violence'. They tend to use the words interchangeably but if any pattern can be discerned it would seem to be as follows.

There are biological substrates that control aggression. By aggression they seldom if ever mean 'aggressive emotions or feelings'. They appear rather to use the term 'aggression' always in the context of behaviour. For example, they are not interested in aggressive dreams or fantasies. In general, though it is never explicitly stated, they appear to regard violence as very intense aggression. Thus a patient will be 'aggressive' – shout, for example, or act 'disruptively'. When his aggression becomes severe, he may behave 'violently' – physically attacking people and property.

## ARE THERE SPECIFIC SUBSTRATES FOR AGGRESSION AND VIOLENCE?

In this chapter I have tried to evaluate as impartially as possible the many investigations that have been made into specific biological processes and functions that could control aggression and violence. These may be summarized as follows. [13]

### The limbic system
Although there is some evidence that particular individuals have displayed violence because of pathologies in this system, the weight of evidence does not support the concept of an 'aggression centre or centres' in this system.

### Epilepsy related disorders
Evidence linking temporal lobe epilepsy to violent behaviour is weak and controversial. No specific abnormalities in EEG have been convincingly linked to violent behaviour (though there is some suggestion that cerebral maturational lag and violence may be linked). However, even

were an association between EEG abnormalities and violent behaviour consistently shown, this association could not necessarily be taken to indicate that the EEG abnormality causes violent behaviour because social and environmental factors may be implicated (see page 29).

### Head injuries
The fact that some studies indicate that violent individuals have a history of head injuries cannot be taken to indicate that head injuries *cause* violence.

### The autonomic nervous system and skin conductance level
Although there is some indication that individuals diagnosed as psychopaths show abnormalities in skin conductance level, the reasoning linking this finding to violent behaviour is tenuous and based on speculation about psychological rather than physiological processes.

### Biochemistry
No particular chemical messenger, neural transmitter, hormone or substance (such as alcohol or drugs) has shown to have an invariant, specific effect on the predisposition to aggressive emotion or violent behaviour.

### Genetics
There is little firm evidence for the genetic transmission of the predisposition to aggressive emotion or violent behaviour.

It must, however, be stressed that while this biological approach does not seem to offer a general theory for violence and aggression, it cannot be disputed that in individual cases, physical pathologies, for intance PMT or hypoglycaemia, or limbic lesions, *may* lead to the individual concerned feeling aggressive or behaving violently. To a limited extent, then, individual cases of aggression and violence can be 'caused' by physiological processes and this conclusion will be borne in mind in the final chapter. But the conclusion will be examined in the light of evidence that suggests that mood, values and situational dynamics will always play an intermediary and modifying role on the subjective experience of mood and on behaviour.

## SOCIAL IMPLICATIONS

In this section I want to discuss some of the potential implications of the belief that aggression and violence are largely mediated and/or controlled by physiological processes or genetic endowment. I stress that these implications are potential because not all people who accept this belief would necessarily accept the implications I am going to explore.

At the beginning of the chapter I quoted a passage which referred to the possibility of changing man's behaviour by 'altering his internal milieu'. This phrase can cover a variety of procedures from the administration of drugs (with or without the consent of the individual whose internal milieu is considered to be in need of changing) to irreversible psychosurgery.

Physical interventions of this nature are not necessarily to be condemned out of hand. For example, some drugs undoubtedly act to alleviate depression. Further, compassionate psychiatrists like Anthony Clare (1980) concede that psychosurgery may have its place in cases of chronic, distressing, and intractable psychological suffering when neither psychotherapy nor drugs have been able to alleviate crippling anxiety and depression.

But the use of medical interventions in altering behaviour has not always been so benign. For example, in the belief that the amygdala was implicated, two Japanese surgeons have reported on a follow-up of twenty-seven children, ranging in age from 5 to 13, who had amygdalotomies performed on them because they were characterized by unsteadiness, hyperactive behaviour disorders and poor concentration (Narabayashi and Uno, 1966). This example of active psychosurgery is by no means unique (see, for example, the studies quoted by Clare, 1980).

Some biologically oriented researchers extend their belief that aggression and violence are 'shaped by the brain' (Bylinsky, 1982, p. 30) even further than the individual case. They argue that social unrest is linked to undiagnosed brain pathology. Thus Mark, Sweet and Ervin, concerned about the urban riots that swept through the United States in the 1960s, suggest not the amelioration of social disadvantage, but clinical studies of people who were involved in the rioting, arguing that 'the goal of such studies would be to pinpoint, diagnose and treat those people with low violence thresholds before they contribute to further tragedies' (1967, quoted by Clare, 1980, pp. 321-2).

EVALUATING THE PHYSIOLOGICALLY ORIENTED APPROACH TO AGGRESSION AND VIOLENCE

In evaluating the different approaches to aggression and violence that are to be considered in this book, it seems to me that two sets of criteria can be used. The first set relates to those approaches that rest on what might be termed scientific methodology and are concerned with the extent to which such approaches meet the criteria that are usually applied to scientific studies – for example, experimental design, replicability of results, sample size and so on. The second set of criteria concern the assumptions the approach under discussion makes about human nature and the extent to which such assumptions are made with consistency and rigour and the extent to which they aid the evaluator to extend his or her understanding of aggression and violence.

Looking at the first set of criteria it seems to me that there is considerable variation in the degree to which the studies reviewed in this chapter successfully meet the criteria usually applied to scientific studies. Some (for example, the later studies on epilepsy) meet such standards reasonably well while others, such as the Schulsinger (1974) study on the genetic transmission of psychopathy described above, seem to be radically flawed.

Turning to the reviews of physiological studies, the same divergence is apparent. If we look, for instance, at hormonal influences on aggression and violence, it seems to me that while some reviews seem to go beyond the findings on which they are supposedly basing their conclusions (for example, Maccoby and Jacklin, 1980), other reviews, notably Mazur's (1983), are eminently balanced and cautious.

While I do not personally believe that there is any substantial evidence for unique physiological substrates that underpin aggressive and violent behaviour in such a way that there is an invariant and causal relationship between stimulation of such substrates and aggressive or violent behaviour, in general I would suggest that a number of the studies that investigate this relationship are carefully and rigorously carried out.

Looking at the second set of criteria – those concerned with the assumptions about human nature on which the approach rests – it seems to me that although an assumption about human nature does underpin the physiological approach to aggression and violence, it is rarely spelt out, and in many cases it seems that the researchers concerned are not even aware that they make any such assumption.

The assumption on which the physiological approach to aggression and violence rests is, I believe, essentially reductionist. By the use of this term I refer to the proposition that biological organisms are essentially reducable to physical systems (Bullock and Stallybrass, 1977, p. 530). The theorists whose work has been discussed in this chapter appear to believe that aggressive and violent behaviour, whether individual or social, can be accounted for by pathologies and can be modified by physical intervention. While their adherence to this belief is consistent, it seems to me (as I have indicated in this chapter and will continue to argue in the rest of the book) essentially limited, in that it fails to take into account either the subjective experience of individuals or the social circumstances in which they live.

HOW EXTENSIVE IS THEIR USE OF THE TERMS 'AGGRESSION' AND 'VIOLENCE'?

In Chapter 1 I derived a summational description of the ways in which the terms 'aggression' and 'violence' were used in order to check how adequately different theoretical approaches covered this usage. Referring back to page 14 it can be seen that researchers working with biological orientations use the terms in the following way.

*Aggression*
(a)  Intention is seldom discussed (Moyer being the exception here).
(b)  Only 'hurt' is considered; aggression is never discussed in the context of achieving superiority as in 'aggressive marketing' or 'aggressive sport'.
(c)  Aggression does not necessarily involve violence.
(d)  Motives are never discussed.
(e)  Aggression always appears to be negatively sanctioned.
(f)  The issue of subjectivity in applying the term aggression is never considered.
(g)  The values of the person using the term and the issue of provocation are never taken into account.

I think it is fair to conclude that the term aggression is taken for granted. With the exception of Moyer, who differentiates its use in a manner that is not relevant to human aggression (see page 24), substantive attention is not paid to defining the term.

*Violence*
(a)  Biological researchers would agree that violence involves the use of great force or physical intensity.
(b)  They are not interested in the motivation for violence.
(c)  They do not consider physical force when it is used in a mutually rewarding interaction (for example, in martial sports or sado-masochism).
(d)  With the exception of Mark, who differentiates between 'acceptable' and 'unacceptable' violence,[14] they do not consider issues concerned with the legitimization of violence.

As with aggression, the term 'violence' tends to be taken for granted.

## Notes: Chapter 2

1  The limbic system includes portions of the thalamus and the hypothalamus, upper parts of the brain stem, and the other structures lying in a C-shaped arrangement outlining or bordering (the Latin word *limbus* means border) the inner surfaces of the cerebral hemispheres, the cingulum, hippocampus and hippocampal gyrus. Also included are nuclear masses within the temporal lobe (the amygdala), and portions of the frontal lobes as well as other portions of the temporal cortex.
2  A nugget-like mass of grey matter in the anterior portion of the temporal lobe.
3  Because of the extensive damage to the brain from gunshot wounds when he was

eventually shot by a police marksman, it was not possible to establish the precise position of the tumour.

4 Recently these have tended to be termed 'partial seizures and temporal lobe fits' or 'complex partial seizures'.

5 Though in clinical practice (as distinct from research reports) the diagnosis of epilepsy is always a clinical one, supported in most (but not all cases) by EEG evidence of paroxysmal activity.

6 By 'directed' I mean behaviour that appears to be specifically directed towards a particular target or targets.

7 A recent poorly documented and sensational linkage between violent behaviour and adrenalin and/or noradrenalin levels has been proposed by Erin Pizzey and Jeff Shapiro (1982). They suggest that exposure to violence in early childhood may cause certain individuals to fuse pain-and pleasure subjectively and may also cause a permanent imbalance in the level of noradrenalin and adrenalin. This imbalance leads them in later life to seek similar experiences in order to restore some equilibrium to these chemical levels. Aside from being riddled with logical inconsistencies these speculations are not backed up by any supportive physiological data.

8 Blood levels of testosterone are often extremely difficult, if not impossible, to monitor reliably, because testosterone is secreted in spurts, giving transiently high blood levels. And further difficulties in relating serum levels to human behaviour arise because there are complex interactions between cells, hormones and cellular DNA which affect responsiveness to hormone levels.

9 Further difficulties in looking at the link between alcohol and violent behaviour lie in the fact that most studies have taken place amongst prisoners who are more likely than other people to have a record of violence.

10 However, it must be noted that biologically oriented researchers continue to seek for causal links between levels of particular chemicals and aggressive behaviour. See, for example, Virkkunen's work on enhanced insulin secretion in young offenders (1983), and see also Anderson (1982).

11 Because most of the genetic studies in animals that are concerned with aggression and violence have been done in non-primate species, like cats, dogs and rats, I have not included these in my review of genetic factors.

12 Precisely how 'criminality' can be conveyed genetically is not discussed in these studies. Criminality is taken to mean having been indicted for a criminal offence but, according to Mednick *et al.*, 'minor offenses are omitted' (1982, p. 28).

13 In making this summary I draw on my own conclusions about the data that have been discussed in this chapter. Recent reviews that are perhaps rather more sympathetic to the physiologically oriented view on aggression and violence can be found in Mazur, 1983 and Wolfgang and Weiner, 1982. However, it must be stressed that neither of these reviews concludes that there is a stronger case for physiological substrates for aggressive and violent behaviour than that there is a *general* relationship between physiological factors and aggression and violence.

14 Mark defines 'acceptable violence' as 'the controlled minimum action necessary to prevent personal physical injury or wanton destruction of property' (1978, p. 132). He has, however, taken into account the criticisms levelled at his earlier work in his recent definition of 'unacceptable violence', and he writes: 'Obviously, any definition of unacceptable violence, however carefully articulated, will be construed according to the judgement of the people participating in or observing a given violent action' (ibid., p. 132). Nevertheless, despite this acceptance of the subjectivity involved in his labelling of acts as 'unacceptably violent', he does not discuss the subjectivity involved in deciding when aggression shades into the term he commonly uses, 'abnormal aggression'.

# 3

# Ethological and Sociobiological Approaches to Aggression

. . . human behaviour, and particularly human social behaviour, far from being determined by reason and cultural tradition alone, is still subject to all the laws prevailing in all phylogenetically [deriving from the evolution of the species] adapted instinctive behaviour. (Lorenz, 1966, p. 204)

The biologist who is concerned with questions of physiology and evolutionary history, realises that *self-knowledge is constrained and shaped by the emotional control centres in the hypothalamus and limbic system of the brain.* These centres flood our consciousness with all the emotions – hate, love, guilt, fear and others . . . (Wilson, 1975, p. 3, my italics)

Without aggression as an inborn force, survival throughout all the natural world would be impossible. (Ardrey, 1982, p. 8)

But it is not our very nature that is the problem, for that is totally unproblematical. It is not violence that is the problem, for this is part of the unproblematical nature. It is not aggressiveness or killing that is the problem, for these are as natural as copulation and eating. (Fox, 1982, p. 13)

In Chapter 2, I considered the work of biologically oriented researchers who believe that aggressive emotions and violent behaviour have identifiable physiological substrates. In the main, they are concerned with pathologies in these substrates that lead to 'abnormal' levels of aggression and violence, and their approach has been influenced by a medical perspective which tends to equate social and emotional abnormalities in behaviour, not with environmental stresses, but with physiological pathology.

Another major strand in biological approaches to aggression and violence derives from a rather different tradition, the evolutionary theory of Charles Darwin. Although the implications of Darwin's theory were strongly resisted by the general public in the nineteenth century, who found the idea that humans and primates were linked because they had common ancestors not only revolutionary but also repugnant, Darwinian theory is currently very much part of the general consciousness. Most people nowadays believe that characteristics found in many species must have evolved genetically because they were in the interests of the species.

Of course, the fact that a characteristic is commonly found in a species is no indication that it is innately determined. For example, most pet dogs will wait at the gate or front door at the time their owner is usually expected to return, but it is hardly likely that a gene exists governing such behaviour. And currently there is considerable discussion and controversy about precisely what is to be understood by 'in the interests of the species'. Nevertheless, the idea that if a particular mode of behaviour is observed frequently and over time in humans, it must be 'part of human nature' and be controlled by our genes, is fairly widespread among the general public and it has allowed a particular perspective on aggression and violence to gain general acceptance, particularly in the mass media.

This perspective is exemplified by the work of Lorenz, Ardrey and Fox who, as the quotes at the beginning of this chapter suggest, see aggression and violence as 'instinctive behaviour' (Lorenz), 'an inborn force' (Ardrey), and 'as natural as copulation and eating' (Fox). In this chapter we will be considering their views, the evidence cited in favour of them and the criticisms that have been levelled against them. Following this we will look at a further development of Darwinian theory, the work of sociobiologists such as Wilson and de Vore whose understanding of the genetic basis of human aggression is rather more complex than the simple determinism of Lorenz and Ardrey.

## Aggression and Genetic Determinism

This section is concerned with the approaches of Lorenz and Ardrey. Their writing has had, and continues to have, a considerable impact on the public imagination. In particular their contention that it is natural for man to behave aggressively and violently finds an echo in the history of Western thought, for as Ashley Montagu puts it,

For Man-as-Killer is no more than the present-day secular version of an idea that has had a fierce grip on the Western imagination for many centuries: the doctrine of original sin.

When Lorenz and Ardrey state flatly that there is in every man the instinct to kill other men, and that it is locked into his genes in the same way that the color of his hair is locked in, they are telling us again, in different words, the age-old religious story that men are conceived in sin, born in sin, live all their days and finally die in sin. (Montagu, 1978, p. 33)

Because the work of Lorenz and Ardrey is so readily assimilated into the consciousness of the general public, it is not surprising to find that their theories are echoed as well in the arts, notably in film, drama and fiction. For example, the influence of their perspectives is very clear in the work of film directors like Sam Peckinpah and Michael Winner, whose films are characterized by multiple killings and underpinned by plots that indicate that rationality and reason can never solve emotional and social problems. Their plots seem to support the alternative proposition that such problems are best dealt with by an open acceptance that even contemporary society rests on an abyss of violent, irrational instinct. Peckinpah indeed acknowledged his debt to Ardrey when he said, as he handed out copies of Ardrey's books,

The myth of the noble savage is bull. People are born to survive. They have instincts that go back millions of years. Unfortunately some of these instincts are based on violence in every human being. (Quoted by Montagu, 1978, p. 30)

But perhaps the most elegant and extended reflection in the arts of this perspective is to be found in the novel *Lord of the Flies* by William Golding, in which Golding shows that man is a 'fallen being'. 'He is gripped by original sin, his nature is sinful and his state is perilous' (Golding, quoted by Tiger, 1974, p. 45).

'LORD OF THE FLIES'

I would like to make a point about the writing of *Flies* and its position in the world of scholarship.

I said to Ann [Mrs Golding] in about 1953, 'Wouldn't it be a good idea to write a book about real boys on an island, showing what a mess they'd make?' She said, 'That *is* a good idea!' So I sat down and wrote it. You see, neither I nor she nor anyone else could dream of the sheer critical firepower that was going to be levelled at this mass of words scribbled in a school notebook. (Unpublished letter by Golding, 1970, quoted in Tiger, 1974, p. 38)

Since its publication in 1954, *Lord of the Flies* has been subjected to a barrage of interpretation ranging, according to the particular interests of the commentators, from the political to the religious. But perhaps the most sustained thread of interpretation has been social and psychological. The book, according to Tiger, 'tugged at one's private hunch that males – even small boys – enjoyed aggression, group hierarchies and the savour of blood' (1974, p. 39). As Moody puts it, the novel 'does depict a fairly frightening, indeed pessimistic sense of human nature' (1966, p. 33). So despite the rather disingenuous disclaimer by Golding in the letter quoted above, a large number of critics and commentators seem to have been convinced that a more valid interpretation of Golding's aims in this novel, whether unconscious or conscious can be found in Golding's answer in reply to a literary magazine's questionnaire, which raised the question of a writer's 'engagement', that 'I am very serious. I believe that man suffers from an appalling ignorance of his own nature. I produce my own view, in the belief that it may be something like the truth' (quoted by Hynes, 1968, p. 3). Indeed Golding does seem to be the sort of writer who forces the reader to draw conclusions; and in the main these conclusions are about mankind's ignorance of its own nature.

> All at once, Robert was screaming and struggling with the strength of frenzy. Jack had him by the hair and was brandishing his knife. Behind him was Roger, fighting to get close. The chant rose ritually, as at the last moment of a dance or a hunt.
> *"Kill the pig! Cut his throat! Kill the pig! Bash him in!"*
> Ralph too was fighting to get near, to get a handful of that brown, vulnerable flesh. The desire to squeeze and hurt was over-mastering. (Golding in *Lord of the Flies*, 1958, p. 126)

The story of *Lord of the Flies* will undoubtedly be familiar to most readers. A group of English schoolboys, most of them with a public school background, are stranded on an island in the Pacific or Indian Ocean, where they are faced with the task of survival. To this task, they first bring the certainty that they will be able to cope rationally and sensibly with all the needs and pressures of an existence where they are totally unprotected by adult society. For, as Jack puts it, 'After all we're not savages. We're English; and the English are best at everything.'

But despite an attempt to model their microcosm of society on what 'grown ups' would do, by establishing government and laws, providing for food and water and lighting a signal fire, their rational society soon begins to break down under two pressures – fear, and what Hynes (1968) has called 'blood lust', or as Tiger (1974) puts it, 'superstition' and 'aggression'. At night when they can sense but not see the dark unknown, they endow the uncertainty with a terrifying identity, 'the darkness was full of claws, full of the awful unknown and menace' (1958

p. 108); they become convinced of the existence of a beast, which moves in the trees at night and is 'big and horrid'. They try to propitiate this beast with the totem of a pig's head on a stick, and hunting becomes killing as some of the boys break away and form a society of their own with gods, rituals and territory. When two of the boys from the remaining group invade their territory, aggression and violence take over. Two boys are killed, one in ritual as a symbol of the beast:

> '*Kill the beast! Cut his throat! Spill his blood! Do him in!*'
> The sticks fell and the mouth of the new circle crunched and screamed. The beast [a boy called Simon] was on its knees in the centre, its arms folded over its face. It was crying out against the abominable noise something about a body on the hill . . . The beast struggled forward, broke the ring and fell over the steep edge of the rock to the sand by the water. At once the crowd surged after it, poured down the rock, leapt on to the beast, screamed, struck, bit, tore. There were no words, and no movements but the tearing of teeth and claws. (ibid., p. 168)

A second boy is killed, not in the same spirit of 'blood-lust' but because he reminds the others of the lost world of adult restraints and social inhibitions when he challenges them with the words: 'Which is better – to have rules and agree – or to hunt and kill?' (ibid., p. 199). His plea for restraint is met with a 'solid mass of menace' as the boys, chanting 'an incantation of hatred', advance on their victim and stone him. Finally, only one member of the original group is left. He too is pursued, in a mounting orgy of violence, but is saved by the intervention of the adult world in the shape of a naval officer who has come to rescue them. And the book ends with the haunting image of this last victim, saved at the very moment of sacrifice, filthy, with matted hair, weeping for 'the end of innocence, the darkness of man's heart'.

The novel or fable tells us a great deal about what Golding considers to be the root of violence and evil – it is in the nature of the human being and is kept at bay, precariously, by rules, laws and restraints. We must, I think, assume that Golding believes that ultimately darkness must triumph in the human condition, because while 'the novel tells us a good deal about evil; . . . about salvation it is silent' (Hynes, 1968, p. 16). We have an instinct for violence but none for compassion.

Before looking at academic sources that provide a backing for this view of man as destroyer, I would like to turn to an account of a true episode in which children were shipwrecked, which is reported in Ashley Montagu's book *The Nature of Human Aggression* (1978).

A Melanesian group, possibly an extended family, had embarked on a routine voyage between some islands off the coast of South-East Asia. At one point they left some six or seven children aged between 2 and 12 on an atoll planning to pick them up later, but a storm ensued, and the children were isolated for some months. When the children were rescued, it seemed that they had coped very well indeed. They dug for water and they lived on fish, and 'in general they flourished, without any fighting or falling out or issues of leadership' (ibid., p. 28). This anecdote suggests that, while one can imagine English schoolboys who are accustomed to discipline being imposed on them relapsing into immature and destructive ways of behaving in such circumstances, we could equally well imagine that children from a culture close to the island situation could adapt with ease and equanimity to an adultless existence on a deserted island.

The writers whose work we are now going to look at echo Golding's message – most of human behaviour, and aggression and violence in particular, is pre-determined, and arises because it is innately pre-programmed. They contend that although modern man may deny this simple truth, we do so at our peril, because if we do not accept this predisposition, we cannot cater to it in a controlled manner. And if we do not allow it to manifest itself in such a controlled manner then, to use a phrase that Ardrey is very fond of, we shall all descend into a 'behavioral sink'.

This viewpoint has profound implications for social policy and I shall explore these throughout this chapter. But here I would like to note two implications. The first is that this view leads to an acceptance of the *inevitability* of violent conflict. If Lorenz and Ardrey are right, attention must be shifted away from *avoiding* such conflict and towards *containing* it. Inevitably, too, attention must shift away from ameliorating the social ills that some suppose at least to contribute to social conflict. Instead, according to these writers, we must move towards the acceptance that since violence is man's destiny, social policies designed to make people less reliant on violence as a solution to conflict are misguided and illusionary.

Secondly, this viewpoint leads to the conclusion that attempting to understand the psychological causes of anti-social and aggressive behaviour in children is bound to fail. Research into such areas will provide only a diversion for at the root of such behaviour is not fear, frustration or the desire to avoid humiliation, rather it is the heart of human darkness, the inborn need to aggress.

## KONRAD LORENZ AND THE INSTINCT FOR AGGRESSION

Konrad Lorenz, who was director of the Department of Behaviour Physiology at the Max Planck Institute in Bavaria and who shared a Nobel Prize with Niko Tinbergen, Professor of Animal Behaviour at Oxford University, is an ethologist.[1] Before we can consider his theory of human aggression, we must look at the nature of this discipline, which

emerged around the middle of the twentieth century from a background
of biology and zoology.

Ethology developed as a separate discipline because certain biologists
and zoologists, working primarily in Germany, became dissatisfied with
the then current emphasis in studying animal behaviour, on laboratory
work and observing animals in captivity. Drawing partly on the work of
the nineteenth- and early-twentieth-century naturalists, they claimed
that far more could be learned about animal behaviour by studying
animals in their natural habitat. In particular they felt that observation of
animals in their natural settings would aid our understanding of the ways
in which the behaviour of any species is influenced by the processes of
natural selection, outlined in the last century by Charles Darwin. So they
argued that zoologists and biologists should concentrate on methodical
and detailed observation of animals in their own habitat and, in doing
this, attempt to understand how their observations related to the natural
evolution of the species being investigated. Thus ethology was born: 'a
branch of behavioral biology concerned with the evolution and function
of species-specific behavior' (Schuster, 1978, p. 75).

When ethologists consider any class of behaviour, whether a very
specific action or set of actions like the mating movemens of the duck, or
whether a general series of related actions like birds nurturing their
young, they are concerned with four issues (Hinde, 1982): what immediately causes the behaviour, how such behaviour has developed over the
animal's life cycle, what the useful consequences of such behaviour are
and how the behaviour has evolved within the species. Consideration of
these issues, ethologists claim, enables them to draw conclusions about
the ultimate nature of such behaviour. For example, if two stags are
observed fighting, an ethologist might ask what set of events has led to
the fighting, how much fighting have the stags been involved in before,
what are the consequences of the fight and how does fighting contribute
to the survival of the species.

Briefly, then the ethological approach to fighting behaviour would be
concerned both with why fighting occurs in a particular instance and how
such fighting behaviour affects both the individual concerned and the
survival value of the species.

While many ethologists are concerned with fighting behaviour in
particular species, not all such ethologists would classify fighting behaviour as 'aggressive'. But a certain influential group of ethologists has
become well known to the general public because their observations of
fighting and conflict behaviour in various animal species have led them to
generalize from such observations on animals to conclusions about
human behaviour. Prominent amongst these have been Lorenz and
Eibl-Eibesfeldt. Their branch of ethology has been further publicized by
popular writers like Ardrey and Desmond Morris and some anthropologists like Robin Fox.

At this stage, it should be pointed out that while ethologists like Lorenz and Eibl-Eibesfeldt have achieved considerable prominence, their work is not really part of the mainstream of ethology, and while writers like Ardrey, Morris and Fox draw on ethological sources, they themselves have never studied ethology in any formal sense. (An excellent introduction to ethology which highlights the differences between the rather popular nature of the work of Lorenz and his associates and the more academic researches of other ethologists can be found in Hinde, 1982.)

The work of Lorenz, Ardrey, and Fox rests on the premise that it is legitimate to draw conclusions by analogy from one species to another. And, in the particular case of Lorenz's approach, the analogies have been drawn in the main from non-primates, indeed in many cases from non-mammals, like fish and insects. Lorenz defends such extrapolation not directly, but indirectly. Instead of substantiating reasons for making the extension, he attacks those who ask for the substantiation, claiming that such people refuse to face the implications of the extension because it is too emotionally charged for them to do so.

Lorenz operates on the assumption that drawing analogies between species is logically and scientifically acceptable and is only questioned by those who are emotionally affected by the comparison of human behaviour with animal behaviour.

But leaving aside for the time being the question of human–animal analogy, let us consider Lorenz's theory of aggression which appeared in its most extended form in the publication of *Das Sogenannte Böse; Zur Naturgeschichte der Aggression* in Vienna in 1963, subsequently translated and published in English as *On Aggression* in 1966.

### 'On Aggression'

In order to do justice to Lorenz's argument, which is not presented in a linear manner in *On Aggression,* it seems to me preferable to first summarize his own development of his thesis, and later to extract his major premises.

Lorenz starts off with a very simple and straightforward definition of aggression; it is 'the fighting instinct in beast and man which is directed *against* members of the same species' (1966, p. ix, Lorenz's italics). Two points of interest emerge from this pithy definition. First, Lorenz is not overly concerned with fine distinctions of meaning – as between say physical and verbal aggression, or between aggression and violence. As the definition indicates, any conflict, whether the infliction of force in animals or humans engaged in combat or verbal argument between two people, is subsumed under fighting behaviour. Secondly, aggression is not seen as emerging from experience or the environment or from imitation or modelling; instead it is an inborn predisposition – an 'instinct'.[2]

The first three chapters of *On Aggression* are concerned with 'the description of simple observations of typical forms of aggressive behaviour' (ibid., p. xii). The most extended descriptions are of fighting behaviour in birds, rodents, dogs, cats, and insects. Of these observations, Lorenz asks two of the four questions suggested by Hinde (see above); what is the immediate cause of the fighting behaviour, and how does such behaviour contribute to the survival of the species? The first question elicits some vivid descriptions of, for example, the fights of sticklebacks; in this case the cause is disputed territory. The second question he answers not only for specific animals and insects but for all the species he has discussed, and he concludes that intraspecific aggression (that is, aggression between members of the same species) 'is good for' three purposes: (i) the even distribution of the animals of a particular species over an inhabitable area, (ii) the selection of the most powerful individuals for breeding, and (iii) selection of the most powerful animals for defending the young.

At this stage he points out that while aggression may serve all these purposes in the preservation of a particular species, in some species, for example those with no territorial behaviour, aggression may serve only some of these purposes. In addition, he notes that

> It would be wrong to believe that the three functions of aggressive behaviour dealt with in the last three chapters – namely balanced distribution of animals in the same species over the available environment, selection of the strongest by rival fights and defence of the young – are its only important functions in the preservation of the species. We shall see later what an indispensable part of the great complex of drives is played by aggression. It is one of those driving powers which students of behaviour call 'motivation'; it lies behind behaviour patterns that outwardly have nothing to do with aggression, and even appear to be its very opposite. (ibid., pp. 34–5)

This last observation prepares the ground for one of Lorenz's central contentions – that 'aggression, far from being the diabolical, destructive principle . . . is really an essential part of the life-preserving organisation of instincts' (ibid., p. 39). Lorenz believes that in animals this instinct is always constructive at root, but in humans, though basically constructive, it can become distorted. And it is towards understanding this distortion of aggression in humans that Lorenz devotes the rest of his book.

But before we can attempt to understand how and why Lorenz sees this distortion of a basically constructive instinct occurring, we have to follow the development of his argument along his next three propositions: that aggression is a spontaneous drive, that in the case of animals, but not men, this drive is under control by behavioural rituals, and that it is the nature of the social organization of the human species that makes man a very aggressive species.

**The spontaneity of aggression**:    Lorenz's view of motivation is based on an energy model. He believes that all innate predispositions are fuelled by reservoirs of innate energy. This applies both to the predisposition to perform certain stereotyped behavioural acts, like nest building in birds, or licking the young after birth in female mammals, and to the four drives (or instincts) that Lorenz considers fundamental and which he calls the ' "big four" – hunger, sexuality, flight and aggression' (ibid., p. 89). Each innate predisposition has its own specific energy, which *must* be discharged. Thus aggression does not occur in reaction to the environment, but it occurs because the energy specific to it must be dissipated. Aggression is therefore described by Lorenz as spontaneous and rhythmic. The energy for it builds up, discharges, and then builds up again. The evidence he adduces for this is very slight; a description of a cichlid male fish attacking its mate and the following example of spontaneity in humans:

> Analagous behaviour [to the male cichlid fish] can be observed in human beings. In the good old days when there was still a Hapsburg monarchy and there were still domestic servants, I used to observe the following, regularly predictable behaviour in my widowed aunt. She never kept a maid longer than eight to ten months. She was always delighted with a new servant, praised her to the skies, and swore that she had at last found the right one. In the course of the next few months her judgement cooled, she found small faults, then bigger ones, and towards the end of the stated period she discovered hateful qualities in the poor girl who was finally discharged without a reference, after a violent quarrel. After this explosion the old lady was once more prepared to find a perfect angel in her next employee. (ibid., p. 45)

For Lorenz then, aggression is *not* reactive – it is spontaneous and inevitable.

**Behavioural rituals in animals**    Lorenz considers, as I have just noted, that aggressive behaviour is innately predetermined because it has a reservoir of specific energy associated with it, which must be discharged. Now, in animals, Lorenz sees this discharge as following a fixed pattern that has been shaped by a special evolutionary process known as ritualization. Ritualization preserves the adaptiveness of aggression by producing a victor in any contest without too much harm occurring to either the victor or the loser.

Thus, if two deer engage in a fight, the contest proceeds in such a way that while 'fighting behaviour' is engaged in, neither animal gets hurt, because the fight is ritualized, rather than 'real'. The animals swing their crowns into collision, lock together, then goose-step beside each other, wrestling with their locked antlers; the victor is the deer who holds out the longest.

Sometimes, however, animals approach each other aggressively, but do not actually engage, because one animal will display another set of rituals, 'appeasement rituals', which succeed in deflecting the other from actual conflict. For example, Lorenz cites the case of a species of jackdaws who live in very close quarters and therefore, according to Lorenz, need 'a specially effective appeasement gesture' to avoid internecine strife. These birds have a nape section at the bottom of the head, which is very clearly marked off from the rest of the body by its plumage and colouring. When a jackdaw turns its head away, offering the nape, from another jackdaw, 'the aggressor never attacks, even if on the verge of doing so, when the weaker bird assumes a submissive attitude' (ibid., p. 115).

Similarly, according to Lorenz, in many species of animals a male never seriously attacks a female, because the female displays the appropriate appeasement rituals when the male shows aggressive tendencies.

So it can be seen, concludes Lorenz, that the aggressive drive or instinct in animals has evolved in such a way that while it remains adaptive for each species, it is sufficiently under the control of ritual and appeasement gestures to avoid distortion into destructive behaviour. In man, however, while aggression remains adaptive, it has ceased to be under the control of appeasement gestures, which in man are, according to Lorenz, smiling, laughing, making submissive gestures and showing appeasing attitudes. This is because the use of weapons has moved combat from the eye-to-eye situation to a distance that precludes the use of such appeasement rituals. Incidentally, the only extended reference to such appeasement behaviour in man occurs in a passage in which Lorenz visualizes the scene when 'two enemy American Indians became friends by smoking a 'peace pipe' together.

**Social organizations:**   Lorenz suggests that all species fall into one of four categories of social organization. In the first three of these, herds or flocks (for example, starlings), colonies (for example, night herons) and large families (for example, rats), individuals do not know or recognize other individuals and because of this inability they do not form love or friendship bonds. In the fourth type of social organization, such as greylag geese (Lorenz's particular field of study), cichlid fish and man, individuals *do* recognize each other and are therefore capable of forming friendship and love bonds. These species are the most aggressive because friendship and love, according to Lorenz, have evolved in order to appease aggression, and therefore aggression *must* be present in this fourth category *because* species in this category show such strong evidence of love (pair formation) and friendship.

Lorenz's theory of aggression is now nearly complete but before I go on to complete it and present his conclusions and inferences, I would like to summarize the thread of his argument so far:

(1) A theory of human aggression can be based on analogies drawn from observing the social behaviour of any, and all, animal species.

(2) Aggression has developed adaptively and is an instinct that is found in all species. Intraspecific aggression (aggression against the members of one's own species) is particularly prevalent and deep-seated in species like man that show friendship and love bonds.

(3) Aggression in such species is spontaneous and must be dissipated periodically.

(4) Animals who are aggressive contain and control intraspecific aggression by the use of rituals and appeasement gestures. Thus aggression in animals is primarily constructive.

(5) Man, because he has developed weapons, indulges in combat in situations that are not eye-to-eye, and thus appeasement gestures are not effective and man is unable to control this aggressive instinct.

Lorenz makes two final points in support of his theory that man is by nature aggressive. These points, though they perhaps belong logically to the development of his argument, are buried in his penultimate chapter among his conclusions and recommendations. They offer, he considers, proof that his theory is correct, because they show that spontaneous aggression is natural to humans. They can perhaps be summarized as a sixth and seventh thread of his argument.

(6) All human societies are characterized by aggression which is spontaneous and not reactive in nature because it has developed, in the evolutionary sense, from a necessary adaptation to the conditions in which early man lived. Lorenz argues that 'warrior man' emerged because when man had mastered the physical environment by means of clothing, fire and tools, a state of affairs must have prevailed in which the counter-pressures of the hostile neighbouring hordes had become the chief selecting factor determining the next steps of human evolution. 'Small wonder indeed if it produced a dangerous excess of what has been termed the "warrior virtues" of man' (ibid., p. 209).

(7) Some societies, because they needed to use aggression, and because they are in addition inbred, show an extremely high level of aggression – what he calls a hypertrophy of aggression. Such a society, and he cites only one, is the Ute, a 'Prairie Indian' tribe. According to

Lorenz, who draws on the work of a psychoanalyst, Sydney Margolin, in the past the Ute led a 'wild life consisting almost entirely of war and raids' (ibid., p. 210). During this time, 'there must have been an extreme selection pressure at work, breeding extreme aggressiveness'. Present-day Ute, according to Lorenz, show evidence of this hypertrophy of aggression in three ways – a high crime rate, neuroses (due, Lorenz argues, to the repression of their aggression) and a high degree of accident-proneness (and 'it has been proved the accident-proneness may result from repressed aggression', ibid., p. 211).

## Lorenz's conclusions and inferences

Lorenz's chief conclusion should be abundantly clear: man is by nature aggressive and needs to give vent to this instinct or drive. It then follows, he argues, that we must not only acknowledge this drive and its demands but learn to control it.

So according to Lorenz, as distasteful as we may find it to acknowledge that we are similar to some species of animals, we must nevertheless accept this conclusion in the spirit of what he calls 'scientific humility', and pursue research into the areas he has started investigating in *On Aggression*: 'we must deepen our insight into the causal concatenations governing our own behaviour'.

Observation of animals shows, according to Lorenz, that one way of discharging aggression is by displacing it on to substitute objects. Thus we reach Lorenz's solution to the problem of human aggression. We cannot obliterate aggression, it is in our nature, so we have to redirect it and the focus he suggests is sport – which not only provides a simple outlet but also educates man to a conscious and responsible control of his own fighting behaviour. The Olympic Games, for example,

are virtually the only occasion when the anthem of one nation can be played without arousing any hostility against another. This is so because the sportsman's dedication to the international social norms of his sport, to the ideas of chivalry and fair play, are equal to any national enthusiasm. The team spirit inherent in all international sport gives scope to a number of truly valuable patterns of social behaviour which are essentially motivated by aggression and which, in all probability, have evolved under the selection pressure of tribal warfare at the very dawn of culture. (ibid., p. 242)

Indeed, any hardy and dangerous pursuit which can be pursued by people from different nations and ideologies should be cultivated. This would include mountain climbing, polar expeditions and the exploration of space.

In sum, Lorenz's recommendations are that we accept the aggressive side of human nature, learn more about it by studying aggression in animals, and displace it from military and violent interactions to sport, expeditions and explorations.

### Criticisms of Lorenz's On Aggression

After the publication of *On Aggression* and in the wake of a series of books that draw on it, like Robert Ardrey's *Territorial Imperative*, Desmond Morris's *The Naked Ape*[3] and Anthony Storr's *Human Aggression*,[4] a distinguished group of ethologists, zoologists, anthropologists and psychologists hastened to challenge the conclusions drawn by Lorenz, Ardrey, Morris and Storr. It could be argued that such a response was fuelled by two main causes. First, despite Lorenz's beguiling style and wealth of knowledge of animal behaviour, these scientists claimed that he not only argued from illogical bases on many occasions but that he actually misrepresented some of the ethological findings and nearly all of the anthropological findings that he presented. Secondly, some but not all of his critics argued that his theory with its stark message that humankind is by nature aggressive, and its simple conclusion that this aggression cannot be contained but must be diverted, is not based on scientific data and his own observations, but in fact preceded his collection of the data and his summary of his observations. Such critics argue that Lorenz's particular ideological position leads him to hold the view that man is by nature aggressive and that he has, consciously or unconsciously, bent his presentation of his own and other people's scientific data to fit in with his own belief system.

In dealing with the criticisms I will look first at those that focus on the content of his argument and leave the speculations about how his values have affected his scientific objectivity until later. In looking at the criticisms that have been made of the content of his theory of aggression I will draw on the seven threads I extracted from his writings.

**On drawing analogies:** Nearly every critic of Lorenz has pointed out that he is very free-wheeling in his use of analogies. He frequently attempts to explain various human actions by drawing analogies between these behviours and supposedly similar patterns in animals. Then he attaches the same label to these human and animal behaviours and maintains that he has explained the human actions (Berkowitz, 1982a). For example, consider his discussion of the mating behaviour of greylag geese. After describing the behaviour of geese he had observed, who tended to form stable pair relationships which were not easily disrupted, he notes that

> If, in the greylag goose and in man, highly complex norms of behaviour, such as falling in love, strife for ranking order, jealousy,

grieving etc., are not only similar but down to the most absurd
detail the same, we can be sure that every one of these instincts has
a very special survival value, in each case almost or quite the same
in the greylag and in man. (1966, p. 187)

This example illustrates Lorenz's propensity to note a similarity (for
example, a goose's disrupted behaviour patterns when a mate disappears
and a human being's emotion when a loved one dies), to label them
identically (in this case as grief), and to assume that in both cases the
'grief' occurs as a result of an innate instinct for bond formation.

It should, however, be noted that not all of Lorenz's critics disapprove
of using animal studies to try and understand human behaviour. A
number (e.g. Schneirla, 1973) insist explicitly that this is not the point at
issue. What is at issue, they insist, is the *manner* in which Lorenz makes
the comparisons between man and other species.

Barnett (1973), for example, complains that many of the key terms
Lorenz uses in making his analogies are undefined. And Eisenberg
(1973)[5] notes that in drawing his analogies, Lorenz often has no detailed
knowledge of the conditions which evoke the behaviour.

**Aggression as an instinct:**   A major issue seized on by most of Lorenz's
critics, particularly by those who are themselves biologists, is his understanding and use of the term 'instinct'. Lorenz does not actually define
the term in *On Aggression* and he has since admitted this lack of precision
(Berkowitz, 1982a). But he appears to be using it in the following sense:
an instinct is a drive, that is already in existence within the nervous
system when an animal is born. When the appropriate conditions are
present, whether these conditions are internal, such as the presence of
certain secretions in the organisms, or external, such as the presence of a
certain stimulus, the instinct will cause the animal to behave in a certain
stereotyped way. For example, certain gastric secretions cause an animal
to set off to find food, and the presence of a receptive female can cause a
male animal to initiate mating behaviour.

None of his critics deny that certain propensities are innately determined – for example, the tendency to seek food. But all claim that in
emphasizing the innately determined nature of much of animal behaviour, Lorenz ignores the extremely powerful role of learning and
other environmental factors.[6]

Particularly in the case of higher animals such as primates, almost all
behaviour involves a mixture of the learned and the innate. Thus all
baboons of one species will grow up making the same range of sounds,
but the sounds may have different meanings from troop to troop. And,
while in one area male baboons may defend the troop, male baboons of
the same species living in a different environment may run away from
danger (Pilbeam, 1973).

In sum, contemporary biologists and most contemporary ethologists believe that it is extremely difficult to regard any aspect of animal behaviour as purely 'instinctive'. Behaviour is always affected by the developmental experience of the animal in question as well as the environment in which his particular group lives. Lorenz, on the other hand, his critics claim, places far more emphasis on the innate determinants of behaviour, which he frequently ascribes to 'instincts'.

If Lorenz's critics cannot agree with him on his use of the term 'instinct' it is not surprising to find that they are in even greater disagreement with his conception of an 'instinct for aggression', arguing that what Lorenz classifies as innately determined aggression is very often fighting behaviour, which may occur not because there is an innately determined need to be aggressive, but because no other response is possible. As Edward Wilson puts it, 'aggression evolves not as a continuous biological process, as the beat of the heart, but as a contingency plan. It is a set of complex responses of the animal's endocrine and nervous system, programmed to be summoned up in times of stress' (1975, p. 248).

Finally, in considering Lorenz's view of the instinct for aggression in man, and its relationship to the social organization of the human species, Lorenz's critics cite a number of inaccuracies in his fourfold categorization of animal societies (see page 62). For example, Lorenz's contention that animals that flock do not display fighting behaviour is noted to be inaccurate by Barnett (1973).

**Aggression is spontaneous:**   Criticisms of Lorenz's contention that there is an accumulation of energy, specifically directed towards aggressive behaviour, that leads to the likelihood that aggression is spontaneous and not reactive, have been made on two grounds. First, physiologists have argued that if this were so it should be possible to show specific changes in some physiological levels, before and after aggression. It has not been possible to demonstrate this (Swanson, 1976). Secondly, they have claimed that Lorenz himself only documents two cases of spontaneous aggression. The first is the case of a cichlid fish who attacked his mate, and the second is the anecdote (reported above) about his aunt and her problems with maids. As far as the first instance is concerned, his critics have argued that because of the conditions in which the fish were kept it was impossible to claim that the fish was spontaneously aggressing; with respect to the second instance, it is generally felt that this anecdote reveals more about Lorenz's social attitudes than it does about the spontaneity of aggression.

Richard Schuster has recently examined Lorenz's claims in the light of his own field experience with a species of African antelope. In discussing the evidence for the spontaneity of aggression, he notes that according to Lorenz:

Social isolation should lead to increased aggressiveness, just as starvation causes increased hunger. But the effects of isolation are unpredictable . . . Long deprivation [of the chances of aggressing against others] ought to produce rhythmic, spontaneous aggression *in vacuo* or against inappropriate targets, but this is almost never reported. Fighting should lead immediately to a period of reduced aggressiveness but often has the opposite effect for a short time . . . An appetite for aggression is rarely seen. (1978, pp. 93–4)

In brief, there is very little empirical support for Lorenz's belief that in animals, aggressive acts are caused mainly by the build-up of aggressive motivation, making, as Schuster puts it, 'aggression both spontaneous and inevitable, even in the absence of any eliciting situation' (ibid.). Instead, contemporary biologists and ethologists tend to believe that aggression in animals is reactive, and that it is modifiable by a variety of internal and external conditions (Hinde, 1974).

**Rituals and appeasement gestures in animals:**    A detailed discussion of the role of ritualization in animal behaviour is perhaps not really very central to a book primarily concerned with the field of aggression and violence. Looking at ritualization, from the viewpoint of a critique of Lorenz's theory on aggression, it is worth noting that in general there is little disagreement with Lorenz's argument that fighting between animals of the same species is typically ritualized in such a way that, by signalling, a beaten combatant can indicate when it is ready to leave the field to the victor (Wilson, 1975). However, some of Lorenz's critics, for example Schuster, point out that Lorenz's treatment of rituals in fighting behaviour does not take into account the way in which the goals of behaviour affect the degree of ritualization. For example, when antelopes fight they are far more likely to use rituals in fighting over territory than they are in fighting to displace a sexual rival. Nevertheless, there is a general acceptance that Lorenz is justified in his contention that many animals have a specialized set of rituals that they use in the course of fighting behaviour, and which serve to minimize the chances of the combatants being critically wounded.

**Human appeasement rituals:**    While agreeing with Lorenz that many animal species use rituals as appeasement gestures, in the manner described above, there is very little agreement with Lorenz's extrapolation of appeasement gestures in animals to the use of such appeasement gestures in man. First, it is argued that neither early man nor his closely related primates showed or shows much aggressive behaviour. Detailed studies of primates, for example, Schaller's with gorillas and the Reynoldses' with chimpanzees show that the behaviour within troops and between troops is predominantly peaceful (Helmuth, 1973).

Further, it is argued that Lorenz's depiction of early man as 'warrior' man is misleading, and his critics contrast his picture of early man facing 'hostile neighbouring hordes' with a picture of small clans of individuals living peaceably together, who were seldom likely to encounter members of other similar clans. For evidence to support their view of early man, they turn to present-day populations of hunter-gatherers like the Eskimo, various Malayan groups, the Punan of Borneo, the Pygmies of the Ituri forest, the Hadza of Tanzania, the Birhor of Southern India, the Bushmen of the Kalahari and the few remaining Australian aboriginal populations. All of these live in small clans who seldom if ever encounter other people. And most of these people are notable for their peaceful and co-operative life-style. Secondly, Lorenz's critics argue that man's behaviour, in common with the behaviour of most primates, is shaped far less by genetic programming than it is by social development. Primate behaviour is, they argue, characterized by its responsiveness to environmental conditions like terrain, weather, the food available and so on. Primates adapt and respond to the world around them; their behaviour is not stereotyped and predictable. Man, moreover, is not only as adaptable as other primates but possesses a unique ability to pass on the experience of each generation to succeeding generations by the use of language and customs. As Barnett puts it:

> Man is the one species whose social behaviour (except in infancy) does *not* depend on a uniform set of social signals: all our customs, including language, depend on the training we receive in our own family or community. Hence arises the immense diversity of *mores* within the single species, *Homo sapiens*. (1973, p. 81, his italics)

So, Lorenz's critics argue, the belief that in man destructive aggression occurs because appeasement gestures have lost their evolutionary significance is invalidated by three sets of evidence. First, primates in general did not need to evolve such appeasement gestures because fighting behaviour in such species is relatively uncommon secondly, early man in particular did not need to evolve such gestures because his society was not characterized by intraspecific violence; and thirdly, the behaviour of man is a complex response to the demands of the particular environment, such a response being powerfully influenced by custom, language and culture.

**Spontaneous and not reactive aggression is characteristic of all human societies because aggression has been inbred in man as a result of its early adaptive value to the species:** While few anthropologists would claim that there are a significant number of societies where aggression and violence are rare, there is a large measure of agreement that there are well-substantiated cases of isolated groups of people who have developed societies characterized by interpersonal harmony and a relative rarity of aggression and violence. For example, the two Canadian Eskimo groups described by the anthropologist Jean Briggs in her book *Never in Anger* condemned any open display of anger or animosity. Disputes were solved without violence by the traditional method of song contests in which combatants competed in 'assaulting' each with reproachful songs. There are, in fact, a number of well-documented descriptions of the way in which Eskimo societies, before their contact with other non-Eskimo groups, lived a life that was characterized by an impressive degree of interpersonal co-operation and a relative absence of conflict (e.g. Birket-Smith, 1959). A similar picture of a co-operative, harmonious and non-violent life-style emerges from anthropological studies of other societies such as the Tasaday of the Philippines, the !Kung of the Kalahari, some of the aboriginal societies of Australia and the Zuni indians of North America.[7] While aggressive instances were recorded in all such societies they were extremely rare and were reactive rather than spontaneous. So that while Lorenz's critics concede that aggression and violence are invariably observed, they point out that there is such a wide range of diversity in these areas across cultures to suggest that there is no stereotyped innate programming of aggression. Such diversity suggests instead, his critics argue, that aggression and violence are reactions to external circumstances rather than the product of internal motivation. And clearly, substantiation for their viewpoint is offered by the common observation that where such peaceable societies encounter differing external pressures, when for example they come into contact with other cultures, their behaviour alters considerably.

**The hypertrophy of aggression:** Lorenz's contention that certain societies have inbred and extremely high levels of aggression rests on a single example – the Ute of North America. His description of this people, their history and their social behaviour has been challenged by anthropologists such as Omer Stewart (1973) of the University of Colorado, who worked amongst these people for forty years. Stewart disputes Lorenz's classification of the Ute as Prairie Indians, arguing that they are more commonly classified as Mountain and Great Basin Indians, disputes that their history showed them to be uniquely violent, questions the evidence that the Ute are more prone than other neighbouring peoples to accidents, neuroses and crimes and claims that their dominant religion, peyotism,[8] specifically promotes love, charity, forgivingness and transcendental practices. The picture of the Ute that emerges is at considerable variance with the Lorenz–Margolin picture presented in *On Aggression*.

In sum, Lorenz's critics question not only the substantive content of his approach to human aggression but also the detailed representation of a number of the ethological studies and all of the anthropological data he reviews. I think it is fair to conclude that such criticisms are, in the main, justified and that *On Aggression* is someimes inaccurate and sometimes circular in argument. (See, for example, the argument summarized on page 63 above that we can expect a species to be aggressive if it shows social bonding, and that because the human species shows a very strong tendency to make social bonds this proves that the human species is by nature extremely aggressive.) It is also very often anthropomorphic; that is, it ascribes to animals human motivation and emotions.

However, as I mentioned above, yet another set of criticisms have been levelled at Lorenz. Sometimes these are quite explicitly stated, as in Eisenberg's 1973 article, and sometimes they are implicit, as for example in Montague (1978). Such criticisms suggest that Lorenz started off with an ideological position which was heavily biased towards believing that human behaviour is largely shaped by inborn pressures and that this belief led him consciously or unconsciously to *bend* his observations and scientific reports to correspond with his beliefs.

Eisenberg puts it like this: 'What I do inveigh against is the formulation of pseudo-scientific support for a priori social ideologies that are projected onto, not "found" in nature' (1973, p. 58). Is there any support for this rather extreme accusation?

It is a central thesis of this book that scientists and social scientists will be led by their own training, experience and indeed social position to select those approaches and interpretations that are congruent with such training, experience and social variables. For example, a physician trained in orthdox medicine will probably find it easier, in trying to understand human behaviour, to refer to physiological rather than social causations. And, as we shall see in Chapter 5, those psychologists who have worked within a formal laboratory paradigm tend to ignore aspects of aggression and violence that cannot be explored in the laboratory. So that it is surely not particularly reprehensible nor even remarkable for Lorenz, working within a discipline, ethology, which is centrally concerned with the evolution of behaviour, to focus on its innate aspects. Perhaps it is a matter of degree, and of the extent to which Lorenz is prepared to consider his own motivations. For example, a number of studies (to which I shall return at the end of this chapter) have suggested that in most animal species the male tends to be more aggressive than the female. But when Lorenz describes such studies, he seems to carry his description a step further than most scientists and social scientists would, and it is difficult, from his discussion, to accept that he has not *started off* with a belief that only 'abnormal' men are ever submissive:

> The social precedent of the female among bullfinches and canines is thus only an apparent one, and it is elicited by the 'chivalrous' inhibition of the males against biting females. Western civilization

offers a cultural analogy between human customs and animal ritualization, of exactly similar form. Even in America, the land of boundless respect for woman, a really submissive man is not appreciated. It is expected of the ideal male that, in spite of mental and physical superiority, he should submit according to ritually laid-down laws to the smallest whim of his wife; but there is an expression, taken from animal behaviour, for the contemptible really submissive man: he is called henpecked , a metaphor that well illustrates the *abnormality* of male submissiveness, for a real cock does not let himself be pecked by any hen, not even his favourite. (1966, pp. 109–10, my italics)

Some of his critics however go further. They argue that not only does Lorenz allow his general values to permeate his presentation of scientific material, but they claim that his early years in Germany, during the period of the German Reich, influenced him to such an extent that his work has always retained an eugenicist bias. These contentions are explored in some detail in Eisenberg (1973). It seems to me that in reading Lorenz it is difficult to escape the belief that Lorenz's views are on the right of the political spectrum, but it hardly seems reasonable for critics writing in the 1970s and 1980s to hold against Lorenz's writings of the 1960s statements he made more than twenty years earlier.

In summary, it seems fair to conclude that although the suggestion of a political bias sometimes appears to colour Lorenz's work, this is almost unavoidable when the subject matter is that of aggression and violence. And the major impact of Lorenz's *On Aggression* is that it is based on a systematic exploration of a great deal of academic material. The same observation cannot always be made of the next writer I shall consider.

ROBERT ARDREY AND 'THE VIOLENT WAY'

Robert Ardrey's genesis as a writer on human nature has been long and complex. He brings to this endeavour enormous skills as a popularizer of the work of anthropologists, ethologists and biologists. As Geoffrey Gorer puts it, 'He is a skilled writer with a lively command of English prose, a pretty turn of wit, and a dramatist's skill in exposition; he is also a good reporter, with the reporter's eye for the significant detail, the striking visual impression' (1973, p. 159). He also brings to this endeavour a series of succeeding beliefs, often presented in an obsessive manner, which relate to man's inborn propensity for violence.

Ardrey graduated from the University of Chicago during the Great Depression of the 1930s, having attended some courses on 'the sciences of man' (Ardrey, 1976, biographical notes). After some time spent lecturing on anthropology at the World Fair, he had no further contact with the social sciences for a period of about twenty years during which time he became a reasonably successful playwright, journalist and writer of film scripts. But in 1955 he met the South African paleo-anthropologist Raymond Dart and became convinced that the orientation of his life should change – his mission was no longer to amuse, but to educate the general public about the effect of man's evolutionary progress on contemporary social and political life.

Raymond Dart, whom Ardrey has always continued to hold in enormous esteem, himself had at this stage some very pronounced beliefs about the nature of man. He had written that man was, at heart, violent, cruel and a killer, and that these attributes were inbred as a result of mankind's evolutionary history as a carnivorous cannibal. For, 'The loathsome cruelty of mankind to man forms one of his inescapable, characteristic and differentiative features; and it is explicable only in terms of his carnivorous and cannibalistic origin' (Dart, 1953, p. 207).

After this initial contact with Dart, Ardrey began to develop a series of beliefs about human nature. Most of these beliefs were related to man's predisposition to violence and conflict. The first of these concerned man's use of weapons. This happened, according to Ardrey, as man moved from a vegetarian to a flesh diet. This move was accompanied by the use of weapons, the change to a two-legged posture, the increasing use of the thumb and the enlargment of the brain. All of these led carnivorous man to overcome his earlier progenitors. And so

> with his big brain and his stone handaxes, man annihilated a predecessor who fought only with bones. And if all human history from that date has turned on the development of superior weapons, then it is for very sound reason. It is for genetic necessity. We design and compete with our weapons as birds build distinctive nests. (Ardrey, quoted by Gorer, 1973, p. 162)

So, according to Ardrey, man is predisposed to violence because his genetic predisposition is to develop ever more efficient weapons. This is one of the messages of the *African Genesis* (1961), and has remained a continuing theme in Ardrey's writings on human nature.

But, according to Ardrey, it is not only man's history as a weapon user that predisposes man to violence. Further 'genetic compulsions' were to emerge in Ardrey's later writings. The first of these (see *The Territorial Imperative*, 1970 and *The Hunting Hypothesis*, 1976) is that man is a territorial species and that it is part of his nature to defend his territory, and the second of these (see '*The Violent Way*', 1982) is that man has an innate tendency to xenophobia, or the rejection of those that he considers outsiders.

I have included some reference to Robert Ardrey's work in this book not because I believe it to be in any way comparable in analytic rigour or

scientific methodology to Lorenz's, but because it has had an unques-
tionable impact on popular thought. But even the most cursory reading
of any of his work will reveal that, despite his extensive (if obscure)
references, Ardrey's writing is extravagant and speculative rather than
reasoned and logical. It would seem, therefore, that because of Ardrey's
tendency to make sweeping and often unsubstantiated generalizations,
his proclivity for basing his arguments largely on analogies, and his
biased and often inaccurate reviews of anthropological literature, it is
inappropriate to grant Ardrey's theories about human nature much
validity. His books may be dramatically and skilfully written, but on the
whole they have not been treated seriously by social and natural scientists. And so it is not surprising to discover that in his massive survey of
the field of sociobiology, *Sociobiology: The New Synthesis* (1975), the
eminent American authority, E. O. Wilson, makes only two references
to Ardrey; one in passing and one that is critical.

Before we turn to the work of Wilson himself, however, I should like
to refer briefly to the writing on aggression and violence by the American
anthropologist Robin Fox, whose views reflect and amplify the writings
of Lorenz and Ardrey.

ROBIN FOX AND 'THE VIOLENT IMAGINATION'

In his article, 'The Violent Way', Robert Ardrey claimed, as I have noted
above, that human beings are fascinated by violence. Robin Fox (1982)
has expanded on this theme at some length, claiming that it is very rare
indeed to find an individual who is not drawn to violence. Man has both
violent drives and violent needs and those who deny this, according to
Fox, show by their very vehemence that they are violent. (Though it is
difficult to grasp from the quotation below quite how Fox knows that
pacifists are, in private life, violent people.)

> To use the modern slang expression that is extremely expressive,
> we can say that the human animal is very easily 'turned on' to sex
> and violence. And while not every human animal is exactly the
> same in this respect, it would be very rare human beings indeed
> who had *no* propensity to violence and *no* attraction to sexual
> activity. Critics to this point of view are very fond of pointing out
> that the wickedness of its proponents is subtly visited upon the
> whole species: because, for example, my friends and I are easily
> turned on by violence, we assume the rest of the world is the same.
> I have a great many friends who are not all that easily turned on by
> violence, but none who are not turned on at all, although such
> people must exist; I have some friends who are·extremely timid
> about sex, but none who would maintain that they are not turned
> on somewhat by the appropriate erotic stimuli. But then, no one

suggests that sex drives and sex needs do not exist, as a great many people wish to do with violent drives and violent needs. (I am always very curious about the lives of these loquacious pacifists who, certainly in print and very often in their personal behaviour, are most extraordinarily violent people.) (1982, pp. 21–2)

How does Fox substantiate these claims that man is 'turned on' by violence?

Fox's first contention is that because man has evolved as a 'hunting omnivorous species', it follows that man will destroy any animals, plants and members of his own species who get in his way. This is a natural and comprehensible state of affairs, according to Fox, and only leads to difficulties because we have imbued killing with meaning. While we accept that other innate drives like eating and copulation are natural and we do not condemn such behaviour in man, Fox argues, we refuse to accept that killing is natural, and we ascribe to killing a condemnation that is not justified,

> If one considers that the desire to kill is in itself a problem, it is a little like saying that the desire to eat or copulate is a problem. In what sense is it a problem? . . . Only if one wishfully decides that there should be no killing does the very existence of the desire to kill become a problem . . . It makes as much sense to say that killing *per se* is a problem as it does to say that the herbivore's desire to eat grass is a problem because it destroys the grass: it is a problem not for the herbivore, but only for those who can imbue behaviour with meaning. The herbivore and the carnivore do not do this: omnivorous man does. And the problem exists because he is the animal that creates problems, not because he is the animal that kills, or eats, or copulates. (ibid., p. 7)

Fox argues that man within a hunting society could absorb into his way of life the innate urges for food, sex and violence. But he goes beyond saying that these urges were a natural part of day-to-day living because he argues that all these urges were also comprehended and come to terms with, in the evolving systems of ritual, religion and art. Early man 'did not use magic and religion to question the very nature of violence, or to ask whether it was necessary, but merely to supplement and help it, and also to comprehend it' (ibid., p. 9).

Contemporary man, on the other hand, suffers, according to Fox, from two problems in coming to terms with this innate urge to violence. First, like Lorenz and Ardrey, Fox claims that weapon development and military technology have outstripped our capacity to deal with violence at a personal level; we are cut off from the roots of violence. We no longer need to kill to eat, and therefore have no way of satisfying this urge for violence. We have problems because 'the upper palaeolithic hunters that we are continue to behave as though huge armies are skirmishing bands, as though atom bombs are stone arrowheads, and as though the destruction of three-quarters of mankind is a raiding expedition against the next tribe' (ibid., pp. 12–13). So far, Fox goes no further than Lorenz or Ardrey. But he also claims that contemporary man has another problem with the innate urge to violence, and this is that the human imagination cannot control its fascination with violence. Where early man could, in a sense domesticate this fascination in appropriate, small-scale religious customs, rituals and art forms, contemporary man can use his violent imagination to create immeasurable havoc. 'The problem lies with the capacity of the human imagination to create its encompassing, consummatory systems with violence as their focus and purpose. We call these systems battles, wars, pogroms, feuds, conquests, revolutions or whatever' (ibid., p. 14). The general who is fascinated with violence can play out his creative urge to violence with maps, communiqués and troops. Our technology allows the violent imagination devastating scope.

The crux of Fox's argument is that we should not regard our violent nature as a problem but that we should see that the problem lies in our violent imagination which enables us to use our innate urges to violence to such devastating effect.

Humans need not only to be violent but to transmute this violence through imagination, into elaborate cult activities. Early man could ritualize this fascination with violence comparatively harmlessly when he went on the warpath, but contemporary man, living as he does in the 'supposedly orderly framework of a modern city', can only achieve satisfaction for his violent imagination in the ritualistic violence of gang street battles. For violence is an appetite like hunger and sex:

> both sexual desire and the lust for combat, as it were, have to lie somewhere near the surface . . . they cannot be eradicated . . . With sufficient punishment, or with sufficient bribery, one can suppress them, but one can do so in the long run only with great damage to the integration and stability of the organism's behaviour . . . the human animal is very easily 'turned on' to sex and violence. (ibid., p. 21)

It is in this way that Fox then substantiates man's fascination with violence – violence is a natural attribute and so is the violent imagination. Is there any hope that man can control these two innate dispositions? According to Fox there is. 'In much the same way as violence itself is a natural attribute, so the regulation of violence is an equally natural attribute' (ibid., p. 23). As man is turned on by sex, food and the joy of combat, so, according to Fox, is he turned on too by 'rules and regulations'. 'Left to his own devices, in other words, man would regulate his sex and his violence with as much relish as he copulates and fights' (ibid., p. 23).

Why then, he continues, do we find such regulation of violence so difficult to achieve in modern society? Apparently it is because we do not cater to the actual needs of our violent imagination. We need the opportunity to explore the benefits of violence – 'all the excitement, the danger, the exploration, the comradeship, the compassion, the daring, the beauty and the glory . . . and the reality of death'. The last is most important; it is the reason that, 'whatever its popularity, football can never have the religious fascination of bullfighting' (ibid., p. 25).

According to Fox, we need to encourage ritualized small-scale violent interchanges, like duels and single combats. We also need to try and understand how we can use war, in a limited manner, so as to obtain a balance between regulation and restriction, and finally we need to accept that we will always live as a species, in a balance of violence and the regulation of violence and endeavour as far as possible to move the cockpit of violence away from large-scale issues where 'real interests (territory, population, women) are involved', and towards the small-scale ritualization of our violent needs and our violent imagination.

I have included a section in this chapter on Robin Fox for two reasons. The first is that I find it surprising that so sensationalized and personalized an account of violence can be found in a set of recent academic readings on the subject. Although Fox starts off with a base in science (in this case evolutionary theory), he soon moves through reasonably informed speculation to extremely tendentious and confident statements about human nature. He cites only one reference, and that to a previous book of his own. And despite his disclaimer (see page 74 above), he does seem to be extending his own personal fascination with violence to a conviction that all human beings, at all times, are 'turned on' by violence. In essence, his account is subjective, but is presented as an objective representation of the universal human interaction with the issue of violence, whether that violence be real or imagined.

The second reason for including a section on Fox concerns the observation that violence does undoubtedly exercise a fascination for many people. Were this not so there would not have been the proliferation of films in the early 1980s like *Cruising*, which is an extremely sensationalized and graphic account of homosexual assaults, killings and rape. But not everybody wants to watch films like *Cruising*, and while videos and films like this continue to be profitable, so too do films like *E.T.* It is obviously important in a book dealing with violence to grapple with the fascination violence exercises for many, and it would be naive and hypocritical in the extreme not to consider why sadomasochistic and violent subjects continue to be explored in fiction, films, dramas and personal fantasies. But this fascination with sensationalized and ritualized violence is not universal to all cultures, neither is it felt by all members of any particular culture, nor is it felt by those individuals who do find violence attractive equally strongly at all times. In sum, it is perfectly valid for Fox to try and understand and interpret what he calls 'the violent imagination', but it is too easy and too simple to assume that the violent imagination is universal and innate, and that everyone regards violence as embracing 'comradeship, compassion, beauty and glory'.

Fox, like Ardrey and Lorenz, is convinced that two principles hold. The first is that certain traits or attributes are built into human beings because such attributes have contributed to the survival of the human species. The second is that predominant amongst these attributes is aggression and violence. These two principles are not currently acceptable in contemporary ethology (see for example, Hinde, 1982), the discipline on which Lorenz's work originally rested, but they have been taken up by the adherents of what E. O. Wilson has called sociobiology – and it is to this new field that I would like to turn now.

## Sociobiology and the New Synthesis

As Peter Smith (1983) has noted, the 1970s and 1980s have seen a renewed attempt (following the ethological studies of the earlier part of the century) to apply evolutionary theory to human behaviour. Aiming to provide a systematic account of the evolution of behaviour, and particularly of social behaviour, it seeks to relate these to the concepts of genetic advantage and biological fitness. The most influential propagator of this approach has been Edward O. Wilson, a professor of zoology at Harvard University who proposed that sociobiology could provide a core for a 'new synthesis' for social behaviour (Wilson, 1975). In the broadest sense he defined sociobiology as the 'systematic study of the biological basis of all human behaviour'. Behaviour, he argued, is always in the service of three evolutionary mechanisms – the personal survival of the individual, the reproduction of the group to which the individual belongs, and altruism. By altruism he refers to the tendency to help and co-operate with others in the group, even if this help and co-operation involve personal cost.

Under behaviour he included not only observable and overt conduct, but also the experience of emotions and the understanding of self (or 'self-knowledge'). He argued that subjective experience such as emotions and self-knowledge, like observable behaviour such as mating and fighting, are also constrained by genetic predispositions which have evolved to enhance reproduction, personal survival and altruism. In other words, when individuals face a stressful situation, their reactions, both behavioural and emotional, will largely be determined by genetic mechanisms. In the case of their emotions, these will be under the control of the 'hypothalamic-limbic complex'; this hypothalamic-limbic complex in man 'knows or more precisely it has been programmed to perform as if it knows' (ibid., p. 5) that the genetic survival of the individual and the group will be favoured if it 'orchestrates' a set of responses that favour individual and group survival.

In other words, Wilson argues that when human beings are under stress, their behaviour will be affected by emotions that are themselves determined by genetic predispositions. We may feel hate and aggression in order to aid personal survival, love in order to aid reproduction and guilt in order to aid altruism. All these emotions are adaptive and are in the service of the three evolutionary mechanisms of personal survival, reproduction and altruism.

Wilson considers that sociobiology, the 'systematic study of the biological bases of social conduct', should focus on the population structure, castes and communication systems and social structure of animal societies and early human societies, because an understanding of the way in which these have adapted will lay the basis for illuminating how genetic transmission shapes contemporary man's predispositions not only to behave in particular ways, but to feel particular emotions and mixes of emotions.

But even though Wilson emphasizes the need to study the genetic bases of behaviour, he does not deny the role of learning and culture in individual behaviour. He acknowledges that the individual is of course affected by the circumstances and experience of his own particular environment and the norms and demands of his own particular culture. Wilson argues, however, that the values and social structures of any society are themselves shaped by evolutionary forces. For example, magic, totemism and religion emerged in turn as adaptations to the environment, and can be regarded as kinds of 'environmental tracking devices'. For example, as a plant contends with irregularities in humidity on a daily basis, and a plant species adapts over time to changes in the rainfall pattern, using sensitivity to humidity as an 'environmental tracking device', so individuals turn to ritual and magic to deal with an environment that they cannot predict or understand, and communities evolve a steadily changing set of sects or religions in such a way as to enhance the interests of the group.

> A form of group selection also operates in the competition between sects. Those that gain adherents survive; those that cannot, fail. Consequently religions, like other human institutions, evolve so as to further the welfare of their practitioners. (ibid., p. 561)

Individuals too, according to Wilson, are affected by their genetically inherited traits. (Here it should be pointed out, that Wilson accepts without any question that individuals can be characterized as possessing

measurable amounts of operationally definable traits – a viewpoint which
many contemporary psychologists would dispute.) Wilson notes that in
primates males are more likely to carry the trait of 'aggressive dominance' (ibid., p. 551),[9] but he does not explore this observation in any
further detail.

Wilson's *Sociobiology*, then, argues for the causal influence on our
behaviour of our evolutionary history, at both the social and at the
individual level. And the influence is shown both in overt behaviour and
in subjective experiences like emotions and the internalization of social
norms, ethics and value.

In Wilson's formulation of human nature, altruism is much more
salient than aggression. In fact, altruism is, as I have noted above, one of
the three central determining evolutionary mechanisms, the other two
being individual survival and reproduction. So before I consider how
aggression features in Wilson's sociobiology, I would like to describe his
understanding of altruism.

Wilson defines altruism as occurring when an individual increases the
fitness of another at the expense of his own fitness. That such behaviour
occurs in a number of species was first noticed by Charles Darwin
himself, who observed that in insect societies worker castes evolved that
were sterile. In some families, individual members were reproduced who
were incapable of furthering their own interests (because they were
sterile) but were important to the welfare of their fertile relatives.

The modern genetic theory of altruism was launched in order not only
to account for this type of phenomenon, but also to account for other
'altruistic behaviour', for example, the way in which turkey male siblings
co-operatively attract the attention of females and allow only the most
dominant male to mate, the others yielding voluntarily to him. Wilson
accounts for this altruism in evolutionary terms by postulating the
concept of group selection (based on the work of William D. Hamilton),
which suggests that if individuals are closely related to each other, then
altruistic self-sacrifice can be advantageous to the group to which both
individuals belong. The closer the relationship, the more likely the
individual will be to behave in an altruistic manner. But such kinship
selection cannot explain why it is that numerous examples of co-
operative behaviour are observed even in non-related animals; for
example, the behaviour of male baboons who place themselves in dangerous and exposed conditions while the rest of their troop forage for
food. Trivers (1971) presented some solution to this problem for natural
selection theory with his concept of reciprocal altruism. This occurs
when an individual performs a favour to another at a relatively slight
personal cost because he can expect that in future the other individual
will reciprocate. This principle of reciprocal selection will favour the
evolution of strong emotions not only of liking and gratitude, but also of
hatred and indignation when aid is not reciprocated (Vine, 1983). Thus

Wilson and other sociobiologists now provide a basis for their contention that *emotions themselves will be genetically predetermined in man*. As Vine puts it,

> Because of the inherent vulnerability of systems of reciprocal altruism, a species like our own, whose members are highly reliant on temporally extended reciprocity, must also require highly elaborated cognitive-affective capacities and dispositions for the moral regulation of social relationships and interactions. (1983, p. 4)

If altruism provides the motive force for emotions, can one of the emotions necessarily emerging be aggression? Wilson would accept this because, according to him, the theory of group selection and altruism predicts

> ambivalence as a way of life in social creatures . . . the individual is forced to make imperfect choices based on irreconcilable loyalties – between the 'rights' and 'duties' of self and those of family, tribe, and other units of selection . . . (1975, p. 129)

Or, as Wilson puts it in a later book,

> our brains appear to be programmed to the following extent: we are inclined to partition other people into friends and aliens . . . [therefore] We tend to fear the actions of strangers and to solve conflict by aggression. (1978, p. 119)

Aside from the predisposition to aggression as an emotion, Wilson also considers that aggressive behaviour, which he defines as 'an abridgement of the rights of another, forcing him to surrender something he wins or might otherwise have attained either by physical act or by the threat of action' (1975, p. 242), is also adaptive in man. He puts it this way:

> Is aggression adaptive? From the biologists' point of view it certainly seems to be. It is hard to believe that any characteristic so widespread and easily invoked in a species as aggressive behaviour is in man could be neutral or negative in its effect on individual survival and reproduction. (ibid., p. 254)

But, in accepting that aggression is adaptive, he points out that 'overt aggressiveness is *not* a trait in all or even a majority of cultures' (ibid., p. 254). The predisposition exists for it to be evoked under certain conditions, but this predisposition does not necessarily ever have to be shown in behaviour. In addition, Wilson points out that it is possible that aggression may be affected by learning;

> It also does not matter whether aggression is wholly innate or is acquired part or wholly by learning. We are sophisticated enough to know that the capacity to learn certain behaviours is itself a genetically controlled and evolved trait. (ibid., p. 255)

In *Sociobiology* Wilson explicitly distances himself from the view of Dart and his followers whom he claims espouse 'very dubious anthropology, ethology and genetics'. But he also makes it very clear that he himself believes that all human behaviour, aggression included, owes a great deal to genetic programming. According to him, the potentiality for aggression to be shown will always be present in man because under certain circumstances it is adaptive.

More recently in *On Human Nature*, Wilson has explored the topic of aggression at a more popular level, continuing his argument that 'human beings have a marked hereditary predisposition to aggressive behaviour' (1978, p. 100). In this work he claims that the plasticity of human behaviour points, not as might first be supposed to the determining influence of the environment, but to the importance of innate predispositions. Thus when he presents evidence that the Semai of Malay, who until 1950 'seemed to be innocent of even the concept of violent aggression' (ibid., p. 100), became with the advent of the British campaign against the Communist guerilas, hardened soldiers, he concludes that the change occurred not because of different environmental pressures that exposed them to conflict, but because the conflict awakened in them the hereditary predisposition to aggress. He also pursues further his interest in territoriality, arguing that the 'biological formula of territorialism translated easily into the rituals of modern property ownership' (ibid., p. 109). And he claims that the rituals with which different cultures surround access to their personal space owes less to cultural norms that it does to 'the products of neural chemistry'.

Wilson's position on aggression[10] offers a considerable challenge to social scientists because it tends to minimize the effect of social factors on behaviour, but before I consider the implications of the sociobiological stance in any detail I would like to turn briefly to the issue of sex differences in aggression, focusing on non-human studies because such studies are often quoted by sociobiologists and some biologists in support of their claim that aggression is innately determined.

## Sex Differences in Aggression in Non-Human species

I have mentioned before that there are well-documented sex differences in violent behaviour. In Chapter 2 I looked at the effect on such differences of the different hormonal secretions of the sexes and concluded that such hormonal differences do not account for the observed sex differences in violent behaviour. In Chapter 4 I will look at psychoanalytic views of such sex differences and in the remaining chapters I will look at the effect that learning and gender stereotypes have on sex differences in the areas of aggression and violence. But, at this stage, before we leave the field of ethology and biology, I would like to look very briefly at sex differences in aggression and violence in animals.

In many species, for example mice, fighting fish, bears, elephants and pheasants, there are striking sex differences in the tendency to show combative and violent behaviour, with males being more combative. However, there are a number of exceptions to the general rule that the male of the species is more likely to show aggressive behaviour. For example, in bees it is the female who possesses stings and fights predators, and while male mice tend to be bigger and more aggressive than female mice the same rule does not hold for hamsters, where the female is more aggressive (Johnson, 1972). Similarly, among the black eagles of South Africa, the females are more aggressive than the males (Cowden, 1969).

When we turn to primate species, a number of studies indicate that amongst non-human primates more aggression is displayed by males than females (Moyer, 1976). But, once again, there are exceptions to this general rule. Some primate species show no sex differences (Tieger, 1980), and in some primate species, for example tamarins and plata monkeys, the females are said to be more aggressive than the males (Maccoby and Jacklin, 1980).

But where sex differences are observed such that males are more aggressive that females in primate species, a number of intriguing findings are relevant. These findings suggest that it is the social patterning of the environment rather than an innate disposition to be aggressive that makes male primates show more aggressive and fighting behaviour than females.

For example, rhesus mothers punish young male infants more often and earlier than female infants, and these punishments may promote male assertiveness because the offspring of brutal mothers tend, in general, to be more aggressive than other monkeys, thus suggesting an association between such socialization and later aggressiveness (Mitchell, 1969).

Further, amongst such primate species, male infants interact mostly with male peers and are avoided by the closely knit group of females which includes their mothers and sisters (Poirer, 1974).

In sum, comparative data suggest that males are generally more aggressive than females in most species, but in all species and especially in primate species this rule is not invariant. Further, in primate species, while such sex differences are obviously ultimately determined by sexual dimorphism, because mothers treat males differently to females, and males associate more with each other than they do with females, the tendency to behave aggressively may be largely influenced by socialization habits (Boice, 1976).

It seems that an examination of sex differences in aggression in non-human species, because the differences are not universal and because they are often modified by environmental factors, does not offer support for the innate origin of aggressive behaviour.

## Overview of the Ethological and Sociobiological Approaches

In the concluding section of this chapter I would like to look at the following issues:
(1)   Can there be a reconciliation between the views of most social scientists and the sociobiologists?
(2)   What criteria can be used in evaluating the work of the socio-biologists and those ethologists whose work has been discussed in this chapter?
(3)   Does the use these researchers make of the terms 'aggression' and 'violence' cover all the parameters discussed in the summational descriptions of aggression and violence derived in Chapter 1?

### SOCIOBIOLOGY AND THE SOCIAL SCIENCES – RIVALRY OR RECONCILIATION

Lorenz, Ardrey and Fox have in turn provoked considerable hostility from a large number of social scientists. Some of the reasons for this hostility have been made clear in this chapter – social scientists have claimed their work is characterized by excessive over-generalizations and is often explicitly prejudiced, and their lines of argument are frequently illogical. In addition, as I have noted, their critics have asserted that Lorenz, Ardrey and Fox are often scientifically, and occasionally polit-ically, reactionary.

But, while I think it is fair to accept much of the criticism that has been made of the work of writers like Lorenz, Ardrey and Fox, such criticisms cannot be made with as much justification of the more recent approaches to sociobiology of scientists like E. O. Wilson, whose arguments in *Sociobiology* are more scholarly and more careful. Nevertheless, any sociobiological approach, no matter how cautious, tends to be attacked with considerable vehemence by social scientists who have seen such approaches as 'an irrelevance or a menace to an emancipated social psychology' (Vine, 1983, p. 2). In this section I should like to ask why this should be so and whether it is possible to reconcile sociobiology with the social sciences.

It could be argued that sociobiology robs the social sciences of their traditional remit and that is why such opposition to sociobiology has been generated within the ranks of social scientists. For if human behaviour is essentially predetermined by genetic programming, then exploring the mechanisms of evolutionary adaptation to the ecology is the chief key to understanding human behaviour. Wilson, in fact, argues precisely this:

> Taxonomy [study of the classification of organisms according to their resemblances and differences] and ecology, however, have been reshaped entirely during the past forty years by integration into neo-Darwinist evolutionary theory – the 'modern Synthesis', as it is often called – in which each phenomenon is weighed for its adaptive significance and then related to the basic principles of population genetics. It may not be too much to say that sociology and the other social sciences, as well as the humanities, are the last branches of biology waiting to be included in the modern synthesis. One of the functions of sociobiology, then, is to reformulate the foundations of the social sciences in a way that draws these subjects into the Modern Synthesis. (Wilson, 1975, p. 4)

If sociobiologists believe that the social sciences can be 'truly biologicized in this fashion' (ibid., p.4), it is not surprising that sociobiology provokes so heated a response from social scientists, a response, for instance, that leads Simon (1982) to call it the 'Aesop's Fables of Science'. To some extent, then, it could be claimed by sociobiologists that social scientists reject their approach not on rational grounds but on the grounds of what Vine has termed 'rivalry'. And it is open to argument that the rejection of sociobiology by some social scientists owes at least something to such motivation.

Is it possible for social scientists and sociobiologists to reconcile their approaches? This is a question that I, in common with many other social scientists, believe must be answered in the negative. For, as Stephen Gould has put it, this is

> not just a quantitative debate about the extent of ranges. It will not be settled amicably at some golden midpoint, with critics [of sociobiology] admitting more constraint, sociobiologists more slop. Advocates of narrow [sociobiologists] and broad [most social scientists] ranges do not simply occupy different positions on a smooth continuum; they hold two qualitatively different theories about the biological nature of human behavior. (1984 p. 329)

Like Stephen Gould, I myself see a number of obstacles to a reconciliation between sociobiologists and most social scientists. But before looking at these obstacles it might be appropriate to look first at some common ground.

Both sociobiologists and social scientists would agree that human behaviour rests on an *interaction* of environmental and genetic variables (see Slater, 1980). This is a truism which few of either persuasion would deny: we are all interactionists these days. But beyond this measure of agreement, there appear to me to be two major theoretical areas of disagreement. The first of these concerns the nature of the interaction between the environment and genetic variables, and the second concerns what predisposes specific individuals to experience specific emotions.

With respect to the interaction between the environment and genetic variables, there would not seem to be any dispute between sociobiologists and social scientists when attention is focused *on the individual*. For example, in the case of physical strength, even with an optimal environment, there will be some tasks such as lifting really heavy weights that individuals born with a small frame may never be able to perform. Similarly, a child born with Down's syndrome (a mongol), even given the most enriched environment possible, will not reach high levels of academic achievement. In both cases behaviour will be limited and affected by the environment and the individual genotype.

At the level of the species, dispute enters. For while the sociobiologists argue that the human species is ultimately limited by its genes, many social scientists argue for almost limitless plasticity. Not perhaps at the level of physical capacities and endurance, because, for example, there *are* certain weights that humans will never be able to pick up on their own, no matter how rich their environment, and no human group can survive indefinitely without food or water. To that extent both would agree that the human species is limited by its genetic make-up. When, however, we turn to other than purely physical capacities, the schism between sociobiologists and many social scientists opens. Sociobiologists argue that where universals of human behaviour are seen (for example, jealousy, aggression, selfishness, altruism), because such emotions are due to innate traits, any human society, no matter what its values and culture, will ultimately be limited by these parameters of human nature. Human nature is not 'perfectable'. Many (but not of course all) social scientists would disagree with this claim, arguing that what is most distinctive in humans is 'their adaptability, their capacity to learn what in other animals is already programmed into the genes' (Simon, 1982, p. 55).

Thus where sociobiologists would appear to believe that the intrusion of others into a group's territory will inevitably be met with innately determined predispositions to react aggressively and violently, many social scientists would argue that a non-aggressive culture and a set of non-violent norms would enable a society to react to such incursions with learned strategies of social interaction like diplomacy and bargaining.

There seems, then, to be a major area of disagreement in the *extent*, to which sociobiologists and social scientists believe that human social and emotional behaviour is affected, at the species level, by 'human nature'. For while sociologists and other social scientists tend to believe that there are social processes and structures that have developed within societies which ultimately guide our behaviour, sociobiologists hold that human behaviour is ultimately guided by powerful evolutionary forces over which we have no control. As de Vore puts it, 'we will survive only if we have the courage to discover our own, human nature' (1982, p. 53).

The second major theoretical divide between sociobiologists and most social scientists concerns the subjective experience of emotions. As I have already indicated, sociobiologists believe that where emotions like jealousy, aggression and altruism are shown across all, or most, cultures and societies, such universality, or near-universality, indicates that these emotions are programmed into the human genotype. But they go further than this belief, for they argue that when an individual shows a specific emotion at any time, such an emotion is not dictated by the individual concerned integrating and interpreting his values and experiences in complex response to a set of social dynamics, but is guided instead by a 'trait' which is genetically controlled, and which is believed by certain sociobiologists like Dawkin to be carried in some cases on a single gene.

Two examples can illustrate this. The first example concerns an individual who does a favour for another, and does not receive a favour in return when he or she asks for this reciprocation. In many cases the first individual will feel angry and resentful. According to the sociobiologists, these emotions emerge because reciprocal selection will 'tend also to favour the evolution of strong emotions, not only of liking and gratitude, but also of hatred and indignation when aid is not reciprocated as expected' (Vine, 1983, p. 4). In other words, the resentment and anger that are experienced are predetermined and, in a sense, involuntary; emerging not from the violation of socially learned norms and expectations, but from the individual's possession of a particular innately determined trait.

A second example concerns the treatment of step-children. If, for example, a step-parent experiences ambivalence over their relationships with a step-child, sociobiologists believe this is due largely to an innate tendency to favour those we are related to by blood ties, and a step-child does not fall into this category. Thus in a conversation with Scot Morris, the sociobiologist Irven de Vore concurs with Morris's proposition that he, de Vore, believes that 'the legend of the wicked step-mother may have some basis in our DNA' (de Vore, 1982, p. 48).

Both these examples illustrate the sociobiologists' belief that

It is simply that millennia of evolution have equipped [humans] with a whole complex of motivations, inclinations, propensities, emotions – what we call proximate mechanisms – that guide [human] behaviour appropriately . . . in most instances, the sources of these emotions are beyond the limits of ordinary awareness. What counts is that we are left with emotions – love, friendship, gratitude – that are expressive of our deepest biological nature, *entirely natural* and adaptive. (ibid., p. 49, my italics)

In sum, sociobiologists underplay learning, culture, values and traditions, arguing instead that any ' "cultural value" can be predicted from the genetic consequences alone. It doesn't require assumptions about the socialization of the child, cultural experiences, or other intervening variables' (ibid., p. 49). I think it is clear that such a reliance on the guiding mechanisms of evolutionary adaptation represents a viewpoint of human behaviour that is difficult to reconcile with the stance of most social scientists. Therefore the relationship between sociobiology and the social sciences seems likely to continue to be characterized by rivalry rather than reconciliation.

EVALUATING THE WORK ON AGGRESSION OF ETHOLOGISTS AND SOCIOBIOLOGISTS

In evaluating particular approaches to aggression and violence[11] I intend to use the twofold set of criteria suggested in the last chapter, that is, first, looking at how all the approaches meet the accepted criteria that are used in evaluating scientific studies, and secondly, looking at rather more subjective issues which are concerned with the rigour and consistency of the approach and the extent to which it enhances the evaluator's understanding of aggression and violence.

When considering the extent to which the approaches discussed in this chapter meet the criteria that are usually applied to scientific studies, I think that in the discussion of Lorenz's work it was made clear that his approach to aggression suffers from severe limitations when it comes to the presentation and interpretation of the empirical studies he bases his theory on. The same is true of Ardrey.

Wilson's work with non-human species is justly acclaimed for its careful presentation and meticulous scientific methodology. But when it comes to his extension of some of the models he has derived from non-human species to humans it can, I think, be argued with justice that, in Crook's phrase, Wilson is guilty of 'excessive biological reductionism' (1980, p. 152). For Wilson's extension relies largely on analogy as the empirical data on human behaviour comes either from a very narrow and selective range of anthropological studies or is anecdotal.

Turning to the second set of criteria, as I have already indicated the work of Lorenz and Ardrey is flawed in a number of important ways. Aside from the examples of misreporting and misrepresentation referred to earlier in this chapter, both Lorenz and Ardrey are prone to make unjustified analogies between discrete bits of animal and human behaviour, and use these analogies as the basis for very broad and confident statements about the similarity of human and animal motivation. Finally, they often generalize about human nature from a very ethnocentric point of view, drawing on observations and data observed in Western twentieth-century man.

With respect to the work of later sociobiologists like de Vore, and particularly Wilson, it seems to me that no one who is seriously interested in the areas of aggression and violence can fail to pay attention to their work and their theories. However, while I, like most social scientists, would accept that the predisposition to experience emotions such as altruism and aggression must ultimately be related in some way to genetic variables, I do not accept that their claims that there are innately determined 'traits' for emotions like selfishness, altruism and aggression are justifiable. It is of course possible that this reluctance to accept biological arguments may spring, at least in part, from my training as a social scientist, a point I mentioned in the introduction to this book. Nevertheless, it seems to me in common with many social scientists that, as Gould puts it, 'the classical arguments of biological determinism fail because the features they invoke to make distinctions between groups are usually the product of cultural evolution' (1984, p. 325).

At this stage I would like to emphasize an interesting divergence that has emerged in this chapter between the views of Lorenz, Ardrey and Fox on the one hand, and Wilson and de Vore on the other. This is that the first three regard aggression and violence as pre-eminent in man's genetic programming, whereas Wilson and de Vore believe that aggression is but one of the genetic emotional tendencies that is programmed in. So that while Lorenz refers to aggression as one of the four big drives, Wilson and de Vore both see the tendency to altruistic behaviour as more salient in the human condition than the drive to aggression.

Finally in this chapter I want to look at the use that has been made by sociobiologists of the terms 'aggression' and 'violence' relating this to the parameters discussed in Chapter 1 and my summational description of aggression and violence.

## HOW EXTENSIVE IS THE USE MADE BY ETHOLOGISTS AND SOCIOBIOLOGISTS OF THE TERMS 'AGGRESSION' AND 'VIOLENCE'?

### Aggression

(a)   In the definition of the term, neither Lorenz nor Wilson (pages 59 and 81) refer to intention. Ardrey does (by implication) when he refers in his 1982 paper to aggression as the 'determined pursuits of one's interests'. (I take determined to imply intention.)

(b)　　Lorenz, Wilson and Ardrey all use the term 'aggression' in contexts that are related to achieving dominance or superiority. In fact their overall treatment of aggression is as a generalized determination to succeed or overcome obstacles.

(c)　　For these writers, aggression does not necessarily involve violence.

(d)　　The treatment of motives by Lorenz, Ardrey and Wilson rests on an implicit assumption that what individuals perceive as a conscious motive to aggress is often underpinned by a biological and almost involuntary predisposition to experience the emotion of aggression. But they tend not to draw a distinction between different classes of motives.

(e)　　Aggression is often positively sanctioned.

(f)　　All of the writers whose work is discussed in this chapter pay some attention to the fact that not everyone would always label the same act as aggressive. But such references are made in passing and very little attention is paid to the overall issue of subjectivity.

(g)　　None of the writers considered in this chapter explicitly discuss the intersection of values and the act of labelling an emotion or action as aggressive. In general, sociobiologists do not deal with the other variable I outlined as affecting the labelling of an act as aggression – the issue of provocation. In most instances of aggression they focus on combative behaviour between individuals without distinguishing between the individuals concerned in terms of who initiated the behaviour.

In general I think it is fair to conclude that the term 'aggression' is used by the writers under consideration here very broadly and in such a way as to embrace all the types of usages I discussed in Chapter 1. But little attention is paid by them to issues of motivation or to the issue of subjectivity.

*Violence*

(a)　　Lorenz, Ardrey and Wilson tend to regard violence as an outcome of aggression in which physical force is used. As Ardrey puts it, 'Aggressiveness, by definition, is the determined pursuit of one's own interests. Violence is the pursuit of such interests through force, or the threat of force' (1982, p. 8). Fox, in his article on violence, never explicitly defines aggression or differentiates between aggression and violence, although he sometimes uses the term 'violence' to refer to behaviour that does not involve the use of physical force, as for instance when he refers to pacifists who are violent in print (see page 75 above).

(b)　　The motivation for violence is seen as emerging from the drive for aggression (Lorenz and Ardrey), the trait for aggression (Wilson and de Vore) and the innate drive for violence (Fox).

(c) When it comes to the issue of violent behaviour that is mutually satisfying to all parties, all the writers considered here, except Wilson, do discuss this, particularly in the area of dominance in male and female relations, and sometimes in the area of fighting between males (for example, gang fights). All seem to imply that such behaviour can be enjoyable for all parties (provided not too much harm is inflicted) and that females prefer to be dominated by males in this way. [12]

(d) In general ethologists and sociobiologists do not discuss issues concerned with the legitimization of violence. To the extent that they all regard violence as 'natural', some legitimization is granted to it.

In sum, as with aggression, their treatment is wide, but they are not in general concerned with issues of subjectivity that may involve consideration of values and cultural, religious or ethical mores.

# Notes: Chapter 3

1  Although some contemporary ethologists may be inclined to regard his work as representative of a rather over-simplified approch to the discipline, there is no doubt that Lorenz with Niko Tinbergen laid the foundations of contemporary ethology (see Hinde, 1982, pp. 13–15).

2  Defining the term 'instinct' is an extremely difficult task because its use has changed over time. At this stage I use it colloquially as 'an inborn tendency to behave in a stereotyped manner' and I will return to its discussion later in this chapter.

3  Morris has written a number of very popular books in which he draws a series of analogies between the behaviour of animals and the behaviour of people, in order to illustrate how closely human behaviour is related to animal behaviour. Morris's books are not particularly well received by social scientists.

4  Anthony Storr's book is discussed in some detail in the next chapter.

5  Thus, according to Eisenberg, Lorenz ignores the very different conditions that may evoke attack behaviour in various species. For example, in insects attack behaviour may be triggered by trace chemicals; in birds by territorial defence, but only during the breeding season; in carnivores by prey, but only if the appropriate internal state of arousal is present; in apes by the appearance of a predator, but only under specific conditions; and in man by a verbal insult. Eisenberg notes that 'the mere observation in divergent species of similar behavioral outcomes that fit the generic label "attack" justifies no conclusion about an underlying aggressive instinct, without detailed study of the conditions evoking, and the mechanism governing, the behavior of each' (Eisenberg, 1973, pp. 58–9)

6  In order to illustrate the kind of interplay between innate and environmental factors that Lorenz's critics accuse him of ignoring, let us consider the case of bird vocalization. For a long time biologists and ethologists considered that a bird produced its particular song because it was innately determined. And research shows that this is true in the case of song sparrows, because if these are isolated from their own kind and foster reared by canaries, they still produce their own song patterns. But meadowlarks similarly isolated as fledglings, acquire the song of their particular foster-species. And the white-crowned sparrow must hear the adult model of its song during a 'sensitive

period' of development in order to acquire it (Eisenberg, 1973). In other words, even in as lowly a species as birds, learning and environmental factors can affect behaviour that early ethologists tended to regard as 'instinctive'.

7 A detailed description of some of these studies can be found in Montagu, 1978.

8 Peyotism is a religious cult which incorporates ancient Indian as well as Christian elements, in which the Christian teachings about love, charity and forgiveness have been merged with Indian ritual and visionary states.

9 Wilson also speculates whether there are genetically transmitted traits like homo-sexuality, which may be governed by 'homosexual genes' (1975, p. 555), and whether traits like being a 'doer' rather than a 'verbalist' might also be genetically conveyed (ibid., p. 555).

10 Following Wilson's pioneering work on sociobiological aspects of aggression, certain sociobiologists (for example Durham, 1976, and Dyson-Hudson and Smith, 1978) have continued to explore the nature of territoriality, proposing that a model may be set up to account for inter-tribal conflict which regards territoriality as an optimum strategy that may be resorted to when there are problems with the distribution and scarcity of resources.

11 In this evaluation, and in the succeeding section, when using the term 'ethologists' I refer only to Lorenz and the extension of his work that has been made by Ardrey and Fox. There are a number of recent studies of aggression in non-human species by contemporary ethologists which have not been used as a basis for discussing human aggression (see Hinde, 1982).

12 Wilson too takes a fairly stereotyped view of male–female relations, though not in the particular area of sex, when he writes:

The building block of nearly all human societies is the nuclear family . . . The populace of an American industrial city, no less than a band of hunter-gatherers in the Australian desert, is organized around this unit. In both cases the family moves between regional communities, maintaining complex ties with primary kin by means of visits (or telephone calls or letters). During the day the women and children remain in the residential area while the men forage for game or its symbolic equivalent in the form of barter and money. The males cooperate in bands to hunt or deal with neighbouring groups. If not actually blood relations, they tend at least to act as 'bands of brothers' (1975, p. 553).

# 4

# Psychoanalytic Approaches to Aggression and Violence

Nevertheless I should like to linger for a moment over our destructive instinct . . . As a result of a little speculation, we have come to suppose that this instinct is at work within every living creature and is striving to bring it to ruin and to reduce life to its original condition of inanimate matter. Thus it quite seriously deserves to be called a death instinct while the erotic instincts represent the effort to live. The death instinct turns into a destructive instinct when with the help of special organs, it is directed outwards, on to objects. The organism preserves its own life, so to say, by destroying an extraneous one. (Freud, 1932)

Malignant aggression . . . is specifically human and not derived from animal instinct. It does not serve the physiological survival of man, yet it is an important part of his mental functioning. It is one of the passions that are dominant and powerful in some individuals and cultures, although not in others . . . its generation results . . . from *the interaction of various social conditions with man's existential needs*. (Fromm, 1977, p. 294)

Aggression is a drive as innate, as natural and as powerful as sex. (Storr, 1970, p. 148)

In this chapter I should like to look at psychoanalytic approaches to aggression and violence. Perhaps at the beginning I should make clear that it is rather difficult to define precisely what a psychoanalytic approach is, because popular conceptions of psychoanalysis do not necessarily take account of the complicated schisms and controversies that have characterized the work of psychoanalysts since Alfred Adler and Carl Gustav Jung broke ranks with the founder of psychoanalysis, Sigmund Freud, in the second decade of this century.[1]

In this chapter, I have included the work of those people who would themselves regard their approach to aggression and violence as psycho-analytic,[2], and who share the belief that Kristal has recently identified as the 'basic assumption' of psychoanalysis that 'much human functioning is to be explained by the operation of forces buried in our unconscious selves' (1982, p. 190). Thus I shall look in some detail at the approaches of Sigmund Freud, Erich Fromm and Anthony Storr. I also intend to look at the implications of a particular view that many psychoanalysts hold which is that male sexuality 'does contain an important element of aggressiveness' (Storr, 1970, p. 89).

## Freud and the Death Instinct

Sigmund Freud (1856–1939) has had a unique impact on Western under-standing of the human mind. He was born to a middle-class Jewish family in Moravia in 1856 and migrated with his family to Vienna in 1860, where he was educated, eventually qualifying as a doctor in 1881 after some years spent studying physiology. It was not until he was 30 that he first turned to psychology, and this interest led to his distin-guished career as a psychiatrist and as the founder of the particular approach to psychology and psychiatry which he termed psychoanalysis. His domestic life was marked by stability and predictability – his marri-age was reputedly extremely happy and he was a devoted father to a family of three sons and three daughters; indeed for the greater part of his life, from 1891 to 1938, he lived in the same house and used the same consulting rooms, leaving Vienna for London in 1938 only with the advent of the Nazi regime. But his creative and professional life was markedly more stormy, being characterized not only by the public controversies that surrounded the evolution of his ideas but also by a series of bitter disputes with those who, initially his devoted followers, later publicly took issue with him over the development of the theories and practice of psychoanalysis.

Before looking in some detail at Freud's changing views on aggression and violence,[3] I would like briefly to examine what Freud meant by the term 'psychoanalysis' and to look at the relevant aspects of his psycho-analytic approach.[4]

The term 'psychoanalysis' is usually used to describe a particular method of psychotherapy which was originally outlined by Freud, in which the psychoanalyst uses the three techniques of *free association*, *interpretation* and *transference* to help the client (or patient as psycho-analysts continue to refer to them) resolve his or her psychological difficulties. All three of these techniques rest on the psychoanalytic belief that such difficulties arise from unresolved conflicts in the unconscious mind.

*Free association* allows the psychoanalyst to glimpse what the 'patient' may unconsciously be attempting to hide, and essentially it is a technique in which the psychoanalyst encourages the patient to report all his or her thoughts, fantasies and dreams freely and without reservation. The psychoanalyst then interprets the latent meanings that underlie the material that the patient has produced in free association, thus using *interpretation* to demonstrate to the patient the operation of those powerful and normally hidden impulses and conflicts that lie in his or her unconscious and shape his or her functioning. The forces operating in the unconscious are believed to have arisen largely as a result of the patient's early experience with other people who are important to him or her (notably, for Freudian psychoanalysts, the parents), and using *transference* the psychoanalyst attempts to displace on to his or herself any unresolved feelings towards these people that the patient may still be harbouring and which may be directing the patient's behaviour. So that in classical psychoanalysis, the patient attends the analyst's consulting rooms and is encouraged to talk freely and unreservedly while the analyst, preserving an impersonal distance, uses this material to uncover the client's unconscious conflicts by, for example, explaining the hidden content of the dreams that the patient describes. During this process (and typically in classical psychoanalysis, psychoanalytic sessions will take place two or three times weekly for a period of years), the analyst interprets the material for the patient and the patient (through the process of transference) undergoes an intense and changing set of emotions, focusing on the analyst.

These three techniques of psychoanalysis rest on the belief that, because it is assumed that human functioning is largely directed by unconscious processes, psychological dysfunction rests on unresolved unconscious processes. While, as I noted earlier, this assumption of the primacy of unconscious processes underlies all psychoanalytic approaches, other assumptions about human functioning are not necessarily shared by all schools of psychoanalysis, though all make use of the three techniques I have just listed. Freud's own approach altered over time, and in no aspect more than in the area of aggression. For this reason I would like to present first the central assumptions which Freud held throughout his life and the implications of these assumptions for his early views on aggression. Then I would like to focus on the major change he made in his approach and consider how this change affected his understanding of aggression.

## FREUD'S CENTRAL ASSUMPTIONS

As I mentioned earlier, Freud's first area of study was physiology, and throughout his life, in his attempts to understand the nature of human psychological functioning, he was influenced by his early training as a scientist. Although his approach rested in the main on his clinical material, his thinking undoubtedly was affected by a desire to integrate these clinical insights with what he had initially learned when, as a young man, he studied neurology and physiology (Breger, 1981). Perhaps because of this influence, Freud placed a great deal of reliance on the concept of instincts, which he saw (rather in the way Lorenz was to) as sources of energy which directed human functioning and which human beings were motivated to discharge or consummate. Pre-eminant amongst these instincts for Freud were the two instincts of sex (repro-duction) and self-preservation.[5] It was the first of these instincts that assumed a central importance in Freud's approach for he saw this sex drive or instinct, energized by what he termed *libido* (sexual energy), as motivating human functioning, even in infancy.

According to Freud, human beings are impelled to discharge this energy, and the way in which this is done depends on the individual's developmental stage. Thus Freud described stages or phases that all human beings passed through in the discharge of this libidinal or erotic energy.

The first phase, occurring in the first year of life, is the *oral* phase, in which the mouth is the main source of pleasure and the centre of experience. The oral stage is followed by the *anal* phase in which the anus replaces the mouth as the main focus, and after that by the *phallic* phase in which stimulation centres around the genitals. These three phases are all regarded as pre-oedipal because, taking place in the first two or three years of life, they pre-date the most influential developmental phase – the *oedipal* phase. In this phase the focus of the libido is the parent of the opposite sex, and it is only after considerable emotional conflict that the child learns that it cannot, as it wishes to at the beginning of the phase, really take possession of the loved object – the parent of the opposite sex.[6]

After passing through the emotional maelstrom of the oedipal stage there is a phase of *latency* in which, as Rycroft puts it, 'the psychosexual maturation marks time' (1972, p. 82), and consequently there is a period of emotional quiescence until puberty, when the young person enters the last phase, the *genital* phase in which mature heterosexual relationships start to take place.

A central tenet of Freud's thought about these phases, which as we shall see Fromm was to draw heavily on, was that *fixation* could occur at any phase. If a person fixates at any stage, that is if he or she fails to progress through it appropriately, he will throughout his life tend to return to that phase and its focus. So that, for example, fixation at the anal stage can cause an individual to have an anal personality which, according to Freud, is characterized by the need to be compulsive about being orderly and parsimonious (symbolically wanting to hoard their faeces) or, in another kind of reaction to fixation at this phase, to be compulsive about being untidy and generous (symbolically wanting to expel their faeces). And, as we shall see, Fromm considers that fixation at this stage may lead to a predominance of anal sadistic characteristics which may, later in life, result in a tendency to behave in a cruel and sadistic manner.

During all these phases, the child's interactions with his or her parents are most important, according to Freud. This is, of course, particularly true during the oedipal stage. And it is these early relationships with the parents, in conjunction with his or her course of psychosexual development, that provide the richest source of material for the child's unconscious.

The unconscious, as I have noted before, played an extremely important part in Freud's understanding of human motivation. He used the term to refer to mental processes of which people are not consciously aware but which direct their thoughts, feelings, dreams and behaviour. The unconscious was for him 'an entity influencing the self, unbeknownst to itself' (Rycroft, 1972, p. 173). The forces in the unconscious were thought by Freud to be so powerful that they intruded into all aspects of the individual's life. So that almost anything an individual does, or consciously feels or thinks, or indeed dreams of, can be traced back to unconscious processes.[7] Thus the conflicts and preoccupations of the unconscious may spill over into behaviour. For example, if a child suffers from frequent accidents a psychoanalytic investigator might regard this predisposition as springing primarily from the child's need to punish itself, and such an investigator would then be likely to explore the child's thoughts and feelings about itself, rather than focus on other forces like the quality of the child's supervision, the child's physical constitution or hazards in the child's environment.

The final area of the Freudian approach that I want to outline is Freud's delineation of the human mind into the *id, ego* and *super-ego*. The *id* represents the seat of the instincts. It is, according to Freud, 'the dark, inaccessible part of our personality', and it operates according to what Freud termed the 'pleasure principle', which leads it to avoid pain by always seeking to release instinctive energy. Thus the id leads people to gratify their instinctive needs, and for most of Freud's life the primary instinct he saw the id as seeking to gratify was the sex drive. The id is of course rooted in the unconscious rather than the conscious mind. The *ego*, on the other hand, is largely conscious, and mediates between the instinctive striving of the id and the demands of everyday life; the ego brings the id under control of reality and operates according to the 'reality principle'. For the ego 'has been modified by the direct influence of the external world . . . The ego represents what may be called reason and common sense, in contrast to the id which contains the passions' (Freud, quoted in Rycroft, 1972.) Finally, Freud suggested a third component of the mind, the *super-ego*, which represents the part of the mind in which self-observation, self-criticism and other reflective properties of the mind take place. Freud believed that the content of the super-ego derived mainly from introjecting (or taking for the individual's own) the values and precepts of the parents in the oedipal stage.

Freud thus outlined an approach to psychology in which much of human emotion was seen as springing from sexual motivation. And it is not surprising that, writing as he did in the aftermath of the puritanical Victorian era, his views were treated with astonishment, disapproval and in many cases derision. Despite this a number of distinguished physicians, including Jung and Adler, were attracted to his viewpoint and in 1907 the Vienna Psychoanalytical Society was established. But, although psychoanalysis as a movement was to become an extremely influential focus of Western thought in the twentieth century, dissension soon emerged within the ranks of this group, and within five years Jung broke with Freud, rejecting the idea that libido is primarily sexual, and Adler broke away from Freud, believing that aggression rather than sex provided man's primary motivation. As we shall see, this belief of Adler's was to have an influence on the development of Freud's view of aggression, but before considering this I would like to turn towards a consideration of Freud's earlier viewpoint on aggression, which was based on the psychoanalytic approach just outlined.

## FREUD'S EARLY VIEWS ON AGGRESSION

As Fromm has noted, perhaps the most surprising aspect of Freud's study of aggression is the comparative lack of attention he paid to it until after the First World War. Although his case histories frequently contain references to anger, competitiveness and hatred, these emotions are seldom discussed, except in as much as they are related to erotic feelings. Freud himself was to note this when he wrote in 1930: 'But I can no longer understand how we have overlooked the ubiquity of non-erotic aggressivity and destructiveness and can have failed to give it its due place in our interpretation of life' (Freud, quoted in Fromm, 1977, p. 581).

A number of reasons have been offered for this. Fromm himself ascribes it to the mood of the European middle classes at the turn of the century. There had been no major war since 1871, and from the vantage point of Vienna it appeared to its affluent citizens that not only was their civilization, with its emphasis on material well-being, in ascendency but that its progress was unlikely to be interrupted. Those psychological problems that Freud was uncovering within the ranks of his particular patient population were more concerned with the effects of a repressive and puritanical moral code than with overt conflict. So, according to Fromm, 'he simply failed to attach much importance to the problems of aggressiveness, until it could not be overlooked any longer due to the First World War' (1977, p. 582).

Paul Stepansky adds two other reasons to this: first, Freud's inability to come to terms himself with his own hostility and rivalry to members of his family and to his colleagues; and, secondly, the emergence of the topic of aggression as the focus for one of the most salient of the battles of loyalty which were to characterize Freud's relationships with his followers – the controversy which resulted in Alfred Adler splitting from Freud. Aggression was thus, according to Stepansky, an area 'whose rich personal, social and institutional connotations, substantially undermined Freud's conscious efforts to deal with it' (1977, p. 188).

Nevertheless, despite the absence of any extended discussion of aggression at this earlier period, Freud often made references to both aggression and associated emotions like envy, hatred and competitiveness in his case histories. For example, in his final discussion of the case of Little Hans (a five-year old boy who displayed a phobic fear of horses),[8] after he has described the roots of Hans's conflicts as lying in Hans's latent sexual feelings, Freud notes that, in addition, there were 'tendencies in Hans which had already been suppressed and which, so far as we can tell, had never been able to find uninhibited expression: hostile and jealous feelings towards his father, and sadistic impulses (premonitions, as it were, of copulation) towards his mother' (Freud, 1909, p. 295).

This passage was typical of Freud's earlier references to aggression and it illustrates how he regarded the emotion. He saw it as a derivative of the conflicts that arose when erotic urges (in this case Hans's love for his mother) were impeded. Similarly, Freud suggested that the frustration of the young infant's oral satisfaction could lead to rage and anger (a view that was to be developed by one of Freud's British followers, Melanie Klein).

Thus rage, anger and hostility are emotions that, according to Freud, may spring from the frustration or repression of the erotic urge.[9] But these negative emotions, although mentioned in passing, were for Freud far less important than an emotion commonly thought to relate to aggression which he discussed at great length – sadism.

Sadism, the enjoyment of the infliction of pain on another, was for Freud a very important component of the child's early emotional life. For example, in the oral stage early oral eroticism is followed, as the child develops teeth, by an 'oral sadistic stage' when the child enjoys biting, and similarly certain situations in the anal and later stage were also inferred to lead to feelings of satisfaction at the pain of another. But at all phases, in this stage of Freud's thought, sadism was related to, and derivative of, the erotic impulses. Cathexis provided the link beween the comparatively benign nature of oral and anal sadism and its later pathological manifestations. Cathexis, according to Freud, occurred when libidinal energy becomes vested in an idea, an object or a person. So that if at any phase fixation occurs, sadistic impulses may become cathected to the focus of that phase. Thus parental mishandling or excessive frustration at the oral stage may lead to a strong 'oral sadistic component' in the individual's later life, showing itself in a well-established tendency to express negative emotions through oral or verbal means. It may lead, as Kutash puts it, to a predisposition to indulge in 'verbal biting criticism' (1978, p. 9). Similarly, in the 'anal sadistic stage', fixation may lead to an individual characteristically giving vent in later life to hostile outbursts of anger. In this way, according to Freud, individual manifestations of aggression, such as sarcasm, oubursts of temper or sadistic sexual practices, can be traced back to fixations at respectively the oral, anal or phallic stage (a view developed, as we shall see, by Erich Fromm).

Fixation at the oedipal phase can lead to 'inverse or negative oedipal wishes; that is, fantasies of incest with the parent of the same sex and murderous wishes toward the parent of the opposite sex' (Brenner, 1973, pp. 115–16). Thus an unresolved oedipal phase can lead to strongly hostile emotions towards the parent of the same sex which continues throughout life.

Throughout Freud's life he was concerned with sadism and its converse, masochism (where the individual enjoys having pain inflicted on him). But when he discussed sadism, and particularly during the period we are presently concerned with, he seldom differentiated it from other negative feelings like rage, hate and destructiveness.

In general then, in his early writing, Freud specifically denied any belief in aggression as a separate motivator. 'I cannot bring myself', he noted in 1909, 'to assume the existence of a special aggressive instinct alongside of the familiar instincts of self-preservation and of sex, and on equal footing with them' (quoted in Fromm, 1977, p. 582).

But Freud was to change his view radically. The change, however, was slow and cumulative as he gradually became aware that not all destructive or aggressive behaviour was primarily motivated by an erotic enjoyment of the suffering of others. Although his case studies and writing slowly began to reflect this realization, he only began to comment in any extended manner on the evolution of his thinking about aggression after he had come to terms with the defection from his circle of Alfred Adler.

Alfred Adler, who became a member of Freud's inner circle of psychoanalysts after he left medical school in Vienna in 1895, himself went through a number of phases in his own views on aggression.[10] But throughout all phases he retained a belief that the prime motivational force in development was not 'libido' but the child's feeling of helplessness. According to Adler, this feeling of impotence led to an 'inferiority complex' which in turn propelled the child to compensating struggles such as striving for superiority and power. Aggression was seen by Adler as an attitude that an individual could take in his or her desire to achieve superiority and power; an attitude that, in most people, was ever-present and very powerful. In this formulation of aggression Adler prefigures the general approach towards understanding individual power needs that both May (1976) and Toch (1972) were to deal with almost half a century later, and to which I will return in Chapters 6 and 7.

At the time that he was first starting to develop his views on the importance of aggression in human motivation, Alfred Adler was still very much part of Freud's inner circle. And there is no doubt that Adler's increasing emphasis on aggression as a major motive force for human nature presented an important challenge for orthodox Freudian psycho-analysis. Adler thus became one of the first of a series of Freud's followers who were to part from the master, in an atmosphere of rancour on the part of the followers and 'analytical condescension' (as Stepansky, 1977, puts it) on the part of Freud. The issue of aggression became then not only an area of academic controversy within the inner circle of psychoanalysts, but a symbol of Adler's divergence from Freud's views. This may well, at least in part, 'account for Freud's resistance to accept-ing the concept [of aggression] as an independent urge in human life' (May, 1976, p. 154).

## FREUD'S LATER VIEWS ON AGGRESSION

Because Freud was basically an instinctivist theorist his views on aggres-sion are intimately linked to the evolution of his ideas on instincts. Bibring (1941) has suggested that his views on instincts went through four phases. The first two phases underpinned his earlier work on aggression which I have just reviewed. They were that there were two separate instincts, those for sex and life-preservation (the *first phase*), and that although there were two instincts it was not possible to differentiate between the energy linked to these two instincts (*second phase*). So far aggression as part of an instinct does not enter directly into the picture. It is only in the third and fourth phase, which I would now like to discuss, that agression is seen first as a trend, then as a drive, and finally as an instinct.

As I noted earlier, it was only some time after he split with Adler that Freud began independently to consider such an approach to aggression. In moving in this direction he was partly propelled by the desire to put the libidinal impulses he had labelled as 'sadistic' on a sounder theoretical basis, and partly propelled by a re-examination he made of the development of instincts in *Instincts and Their Vicissitudes* (1915).

In this work, which represents the *third* phase of the evolution of his views on instincts, Freud attempted to integrate into his overall theore-tical approach an examination of the predisposition to 'hate' that he had noted in his case studies. In discussing this predisposition, he considered it for the first time as separate from the impulse to obtain sadistic enjoyment.

But as Freud began to trace the natural history of this predisposition, he still remained reluctant to see it as an instinct or drive on its own. Indeed, at this stage in the evolution of his thoughts on aggression, he noted that the predisposition was not present at birth. For, according to Freud at the time when he wrote the *Instincts and Their Vicissitudes*, at birth, and shortly afterwards, the infant is in the stage of 'primal narcissism' in which the ego's instincts are directed wholly to itself. The ego can in fact be simply 'loving', or it can be indifferent, but it is concerned only with its own satisfactions and the outside world is not hated, but simply ignored. But, as the child grows older, and as the ego continues its search for satisfaction, it encounters pain-inducing objects in its environment and pain-inducing internal stimuli. At this stage, according to Freud, a change occurs in the polarity of the ego, from love and indifference to love and hate.

In this way, and for the first time, Freud started to ascribe to 'aggressive inclinations' an existence not only separate from sadistic impulses, but also not directly related to the sexual instinct. As he himself noted, 'love and hate' did not 'arise from the cleavage of any originally common entity, but sprang from different sources' (1915, p. 138).

The ego's aggression is no longer simply a by-product of the development of erotic impulses but it is now ascribed a large dose of positive survival value. Here, for the first time in the evolution of Freud's thoughts on aggression, we encounter the tentative equation of aggression with positive aspects of development, in that hatred of a hostile environment may lead to survival. Further, Freud now also began to suggest that it was part of the human development to come to terms with a basic ambivalence in the need to reconcile the dual forces of love and hate.

In this way Freud reached the *fourth* and final phase of the evolution of his approach to instincts. Once again, external circumstances played a part. In this case, Freud was influenced by the bloody course of the First World War, which filled him with a profound depression. Thus in 1916 he told his colleague Abraham, 'It is a desolate world. There is no prospect of a pleasing, peaceful end, and there are all sorts of dark threats to the necessary victory' (Freud, quoted in Sepansky, 1977, p. 155). It was the impact of wartime aggression that provided the impetus for a slowly gestating but total reworking of Freud's understanding of human aggression. In 1920 in *Beyond the Pleasure Principle* and later in *The Ego and the Id* (1923a) he postulated a new dichotomy of instincts – not the dichotomy of his first three phases, the sexual and the self-preservation instincts, but instead two sets of instincts which were polar opposites: the life instinct(s) and the death instinct(s).[11] The mechanism he suggested for these instincts changed over time. To begin with he proposed that the energy for the instincts arose from chemically produced tension, but later he suggested a biological mechanism in which each living cell is endowed with the two basic qualities of living matter, the life force and sexual drive (*Eros*) and the striving for death (sometimes referred to as *Thanatos*).

Freud's assumption of the death instinct allowed him to propose a new root for aggression. The death instinct requires man to strive for his own personal obliteration, but in doing so it runs counter to the life instincts; thus 'the libido has the task of making the destroying instinct innocuous, and it fulfils the task by diverting that instinct to a great extent outwards – soon with the help of a special organic system, the muscular apparatus – towards objects in the external world. The instinct is then called the destructive instinct' (Freud, 1930, quoted by Fromm, 1977, p. 587). This then was Freud's final position on aggression: aggression occurs as a result of the death instinct – it could be turned inwards in impulses of self-destruction or, more commonly, by displacement, it could be turned outwards in hostility towards others. [12]

Aggressive conflict thus became for Freud inevitable:

> It really seems as though it is necessary for us to destroy some other thing or person in order not to destroy ourselves, in order to guard against the impulse to self-destruction. A sad disclosure indeed for the moralist. (Freud, 1933, quoted in Fromm, 1977, p. 588)

In this final phase, Freud also reviewed his understanding of both sadism and masochism. Previously, as I have noted, sadism and its converse masochism had been regarded as stemming from erotic impulses alone. In this final phase, Freud now regarded such emotions and behaviour as arising from a combination of the death instinct with erotic impulses.

THE IMPLICATIONS OF FREUD'S APPROACH TO AGGRESSION

In this section I should like to look first at the lessons Freud drew for himself from his proposition of a death instinct, and then very briefly at the overall impact of his views on aggression.

As I mentioned in the preceding section, Freud's later view of aggression included the belief that it is part of development. Indeed, he noted in 1938 that 'Holding back aggressiveness is in general unhealthy and leads to illness' (quoted in Fromm, 1977, p. 613). How then did Freud resolve the dilemma occasioned by the need to express the aggressive instinct and its effects on the organism itself (if turned inwards) or the world at large (if turned outwards)? If we are not all to be destroyed by our own death instinct, was war and conflict inevitable for Freud? Fromm (1977) has summarized Freud's own attempts to solve this dilemma by suggesting that Freud's writings in this area converge towards three possible (and not mutually exclusive) positions.

In the first instance, he suggested that the aggressiveness is redirected from the id, through the intermediary of the ego, into the super-ego; here, in what we commonly call the conscience, aggressive feelings are turned into guilt; destructiveness becomes introjected and internalized into a need for punishment. 'Civilisation, therefore, obtains mastery over the individual's dangerous desire for aggression by weakening and disarming it and by setting up an agency within him to watch over it, like a garrison in a conquered city' (Freud, 1930, quoted in Fromm, 1977, p. 613). In some ways, of course, this represents a full circle; the death instinct is turned outwards towards others in order for the individual to avoid self-destruction, but the ensuing hostility to others is itself censored by the conscience and turned inwards again.

The second set of suggestions made by Freud centre around the concept of 'sublimation', where the aim of the instinct is redirected. In this case, Freud suggests that the energy of the death instinct is redirected into activities other than destruction, such as domination over nature, over objects and over the environment in general. Finally Freud suggested that the life instinct, its antagonist, should be brought into play against the ravages of the death instinct. Thus anything that contributes to emotional ties between people should be encouraged.

But the final vision was bleak; the suggested ameliorations for the death instinct were offered unconvincingly and tentatively. Ultimately, Freud appeared to believe that the death instinct was an inevitable assumption on both biological and psychological grounds and that pessimism seemed a conclusion that could not be avoided, because in life there was a continual struggle between *Eros* and *Thanatos*.

Freud's overall approach had of course an unprecedented effect on public thinking about psychology in general and the interior world of emotions, dreams and fantasies in particular. His ideas swept through areas as diverse as anthropology and sociology on the one hand and art, theatre and aesthetics in general on the other. Despite their controversial nature (Farrell, 1981; Breger, 1981) and the hostility and criticism they encountered on many occasions (for example, Eysenck, 1952), his views have had an indelible effect on Western culture. But in the area of aggression, his ideas made little impression on the general public until Anthony Storr united them with Lorenz's ethological approach in *Human Aggression* in 1968 and Fromm produced his massive tome *The Anatomy of Human Destructiveness* in 1973.

At the more specialized level Freud's views on aggression were taken up largely within the clinical setting, particularly by Hartmann, Kris and Lowenstein in America and Klein in Great Britain.[13] They had, however, little general effect on the burgeoning field of experimental and laboratory approaches to aggression, with two exceptions: first, as we shall see in the next chapter, Dollard and his associates followed up Freud's early suggestion that aggression emerges a result of frustration, and secondly in the experimental work on 'catharsis' which I shall also explore in the next chapter. (Catharsis is the term used to describe the amelioration of emotion supposedly experienced after an individual has given vent to his or her feelings in an active and intense manner.)

Freud's views on aggression thus had, until recently, a comparatively limited impact, affecting only the clinical practice of psychoanalysts. I shall touch on this effect very briefly, before moving on to the rather more general approaches to aggression and violence developed by the contemporary psychoanalysts Anthony Storr and Erich Fromm.

## NEO-FREUDIANS AND AGGRESSION IN THE CLINICAL SETTING

Freud's concept of a death instinct was not readily taken up in the clinical situation by his followers but they were, on the whole, very receptive to his somewhat earlier view that mankind has somehow to reconcile the opposing forces of sexual and aggressive impulses. Hartmann, Kris and Lowenstein (1964) in particular developed the view that the two mainsprings for behaviour in man are the sexual and aggressive drives which are very similar in nature. Both drives are instinctive,[14] both give rise to tension whose reduction is pleasurable and both can be converted into other behaviour. So that in the same way as Freud had argued that the sexual drive could be sublimated in creative activities, Hartmann, Kris and Lowenstein (ibid.) suggested that the aggressive drive could be 'neutralized' to provide the motor power for activities like mastering the environment.

But sometimes, according to neo-Freudians like Hartmann, Kris and Lowenstein (ibid.) and more recently Kutash (1978), the aggressive drive is internalized but not effectively 'neutralized'. When this happens the results may lead to very negative consequences for, as Kutash puts it, 'Internalized aggressive energy without neutralization can lead to self-destructive impulses' (1978, p. 20). In such circumstances, in extreme cases, the internalized aggression focuses on 'homicidal fantasies, suicidal preoccupations, sadistic ideas, and a variety of tabooed or forbidden antisocial thoughts' which lead the individual concerned to become 'indecisive and beset with self-doubts and uncertainties'. If faced with threats from the environment, the individual concerned will tend to deny them, but if the threat becomes overwhelming he or she may resort to 'homicide, suicide or irrationally violent behaviour' (ibid., p. 24).

This claim that pathological behaviour, and violence in particular, is largely due to the inadequate neutralization of aggressive impulses underpins the work of Hartmann, Kris and Lowenstein and Kutash. It is one of two salient themes in their work in the area of aggression and violence. The other theme that emerges is that aggression is fundamentally positive. So that unless the individual concerned suffers from a 'weak ego', aggressive impulses are 'positive and benign'. Whether or not an individual suffers from a 'weak ego' depends, of course, as far as psychoanalysts are concerned, on that individual's early interpersonal experiences. And so it is perhaps reasonable to conclude that Freud's legacy in the area of aggression and violence emerges in three interlocking assumptions. The first of these is that aggressive behaviour derives from innate sources; the second is that the manner in which an individual displays aggression in later life is dependent on his early emotional history, and the third is that if this history was traumatic or if the experience of personal relationships, particularly with the parents, was negative rather than positive, aggression, basically benign in nature, can become 'malignant or pathological' (Kutash, 1978, p. 29).

But before I move on to the work of the two contemporary psychoanalysts, Anthony Storr and Erich Fromm, who have expanded these assumptions in the most extended form, I should note in passing that reading the work of the neo-Freudians like Kutash and Hartmann (who are often referred to as 'ego psychologists') can be fairly demanding for the non-specialist, because their writing tends to be studded with phrases like 'an over-cathected, too rigid ego–id boundary' (ibid., p. 23), and it is easy to sympathize with Farrell's complaint that 'Ego-Psychology seems to be primarily a way of talking or mode of description, from which it is difficult to extract confirmable generalisations' (1981, p. 171).

## Anthony Storr and the Aggressive Drive as 'an Inherited Constant'

Anthony Storr's book, *Human Aggression*, is dedicated to Konrad Lorenz; it was first published at the time that Lorenz's own book on aggression was making its initial impact. It is not therefore surprising to find that Storr's book is often grouped with the work of Lorenz and Ardrey, particularly in the series of articles collected in Ashley Montagu's book *Man and Aggression* (1973)

Like Lorenz and the other sociobiologists discussed in the previous chapter, Storr is in no doubt that aggressive behaviour is based on 'an endogenous, instinctive impulse that seeks discharge' (1970, p. 35). Indeed, three chapters of his own book are devoted to substantiating this claim, the substantiation being based almost entirely on Lorenz's work. So that by the time he is ready to launch into the more psychological and more original sections of the book, Storr has reviewed the evidence cited by Lorenz and concluded that aggression is an instinct,[15] that aggression plays a positive role in animal life because it contributes to optimum spacing, sexual selection, defence of the young and the creation of social order, and that aggression in man has played a positive role in his evolution because it has contributed to the maintenance of social order. Storr sums up this section with a remark attributed to Professor Washburn: 'Throughout most of human history, society has depended on young, adult males to hunt, to fight, and to maintain the social order with violence' (ibid., p. 58).

Storr is, as I have mentioned earlier, a practising psychotherapist, and in *Human Aggression* he is concerned to fuse the understanding of human aggression that he has gained from Lorenz with his own background in psychoanalysis. But, in doing so, he is very careful to distinguish his own viewpoint from those psychoanalysts like Melanie Klein, whom he claims have regarded man's aggressiveness as 'a deplorable impulse which ought to be eliminated'. Rather, Storr argues, psychoanalysts have to come to terms with the fact that aggression is 'a necessary part of our biological inheritance with which we have to learn to co-exist, and which has served and serves to preserve us' (ibid., p. 17).

How then does Storr characterize this 'necessary part of our biological inheritance'? For him, aggression subsumes an exceedingly large part of human behaviour; indeed he quotes approvingly the words of another psychoanalyst, Winnicot, that 'aggressiveness is almost synonymous with activity'. For Storr, it seems, aggression includes all human activities that cannot be linked to interpersonal dependency. Aggression is 'the basis of intellectual achievement, the attainment of independence, and even of the proper pride which enables a man to hold his head high among his fellows' (ibid., p. 11); it is a drive to 'explore and master the environment, to act independently' (ibid., p. 67) and it includes the needs for 'disagreement, controversy and even competitive striving' (ibid., p. 83).

Storr, then, accepts the first of the three assumptions which I suggested above underpin psychoanalytic views on aggression, because he claims that aggressive behaviour derives primarily from an innate drive. I would like to consider the extent to which Storr can be regarded as accepting the other two assumptions: that the manner in which an individual handles this drive is dependent on his or her early emotional history, and that pathological aggression may derive from negative experiences in the handling of this aggressive drive.

## INTERPERSONAL EXPERIENCES AND THE AGGRESSIVE INSTINCT

Storr's views on childhood development, as outlined in *Human Aggression*, paint, for me at any rate, a rather one-sided picture of child–parent relationships. The child is seen as requiring not guidance but opposition. For it is only by opposing the child's urge to independence that the parent allows the child to come to terms with his 'innate urge to independence':

The normal disposal of aggression requires opposition. The parent who is too yielding gives the child nothing to come up against, no authority against which to rebel, no justification for the innate urge towards independence . . . If there is no one to oppose, the child's aggression tends to become turned inwards against the self so that he pulls his own hair, bites his own nails, or becomes depressed and self-reproachful'. (1970, p. 69)

Thus Storr does not see the child as learning to accommodate the wishes and needs of others, by for example acquiring moral values and by emphazing with the feelings of others; rather, according to Storr, the essence of interpersonal interaction is the pitting of one individual's set of desires against another's. Thus, for Storr, optimum development occurs when the urge for self-expression, autonomy and achievement, springing as it does from instinctive sources, is met with sufficient opposition to allow for independent behaviour, but not too much to turn the journey to independence into a retreat into depressed self-involvement.

But it is not only in relationships with the parents that the child expresses the oppositional aspects of the aggressive drive. For Storr, peer relationships too are permeated with the need to attain power. 'Most of the games children play have an obvious aggressive content. Cops and robbers, cowboys and Indians are examples of struggles in which the child, identifying itself with one or other side, is attempting to prove that it has some power in the world' (ibid., p. 70).

Similarly, Storr sees the child's fantasy life as dominated by the need to resolve his or her aggressive drive. According to Storr, it is thus no wonder that myths and fairy tales are pervaded by 'all kinds of horror from castration to boiling oil' (ibid., p. 72).

Childhood provides a time in which each individual learns to resolve and cater for the aggressive drive; balancing against the need for dependency on the parents is the opposing need to move away towards independence and autonomy, for Storr sees childhood as dominated by this dichotomy – and the need to resolve it. According to Storr, however, the dichotomy does not cease in childhood but persists in adult life in a modified manner, as the adult strives to resolve his need for the company and support of others with the need for maintaining a separate identity. For Storr, identity arises in opposition, and thus the striving for identity is a derivative of the aggressive instinct, while the need for the support and company of others is a derivative of the child's dependency urges.

It is quite clear in reading Storr that for him the shaping of identity is always an oppositional process. Identity is maintained by differentiation, and differentiation for Storr inevitably requires competition. Human beings are seen as necessarily and desirably competitive, for:

Utopias in which men did not compete or struggle would be

unimaginably tedious: mass associations of indistinguishable non-entities. Man can only be safe from strife when in the womb or in the grave: both fine and private places which we may long for or regret. But in the one the dynamic of life has hardly begun, while in the other it has disappeared for ever. (ibid., pp. 83–4)

Thus for Storr, human development is characterized, both during childhood and adulthood, by the individual's attempts to reconcile two opposing and innate tendencies: an affiliative need for dependency and support, and an oppositional need, deriving from the aggressive instinct, to strive against and compete with others. This second drive is 'Janus faced' – that is, it may manifest itself both as a positive, constructive force or as a negative and malign one. Which face is presented will depend on emotional experiences, particularly early ones. So it can be seen that Storr accepts the second of the two assumptions that I suggested underpin psychoanalytic views on aggression: that the manner in which an individual displays aggression in later life is dependent on early emotional experiences. I now want to turn to the third assumption and consider the extent to which Storr endorses the idea that a basically benign force can be transformed into a malignant and destructive one.

## AGGRESSION AND PSYCHOPATHOLOGY

As I noted above, Storr considers that the aggressive drive plays a basically positive part in the life of the individual both as he or she is growing up and as an adult. In addition, as I shall consider later in this chapter, for Storr the satisfactory resolution of the aggressive drive is an integral part of healthy sexual relationships. But in *Human Aggression* he is also concerned with 'psychopathological' aspects of aggression – that is, with

individuals who have developed in such a way that they have been unable to come to terms with their own aggressive drive. In such individuals, aggression is either repressed and turned inwards towards the self; or else disowned and attributed to others; or else expressed in explosive and childish forms. In other words, these individuals have been unable to integrate their aggression in a positive way, and can therefore be regarded as mentally ill or maladjusted. (1970, p. 101)

The four forms of psychopathology which Storr considers to be largely attributable to the inadequate resolution of the aggressive drive are depression, schizoid behaviour, paranoia and psychopathy.

Depression is, for Storr, the mildest instance of this lack of resolution, and it is likely to occur[16] when an individual's experience in infancy, with his or her mother, has been such that he or she does not acquire any conviction of his or her mother's essential goodness, and as a result 'He will find it impossible to achieve any conviction of his own essential "goodness" or lovability' (ibid., p. 109), and this sense of inadequacy will lead him or her to be unable to tolerate any rejection from others. So that when he or she becomes angry with others, fear of the consequences of expressing such anger, will lead to a suppression of the outward expression of the aggressive drive. The drive will turn inwards, and the person concerned will become apathetic and depressed. Such an individual does, according to Storr, at least openly express emotion (for example, dependency and depression), whereas the schizoid personality, according to Storr, is unable to express any emotion, and endeavours to detach itself completely from any emotional involvement with others. Such a predisposition arises because the schizoid's early experiences have been so distorting that the individual in infancy feared to express either dependency or aggression. Like depressives, the schizoid then contains within himself hostile feelings but, unlike the depressive, who turns his hostility inwards, the schizoid, who has withdrawn completely from any resolution of his or her emotions, and who fears any emotional contact at all, turns his or her energies into maintaining an 'icy coldness or detachment' (ibid., p. 118).

In this way Storr accounts for at least two types of what he calls 'psychopathology' in terms of an inadequate resolution of instinctive needs in early life. He is, however, not only concerned with explaining depression and emotional withdrawal, he is also concerned to account for 'man's unique capacity for cruelty'. This Storr sees as arising largely as a result of two more severe types of psychopathology, 'paranoid hostility and psychopathic hostility'.

In discussing cruelty, Storr suggests that it is necessary to differentiate between aggression and hatred. For while aggression is largely positive in nature, hatred represents the negative aspect of aggression: 'Aggression turns to hatred when it comes to contain an admixture of revenge; and the tendency to persecute those who are already defeated, or who are obviously weaker than the aggressor' (ibid., p. 126). Hatred is to be explained, according to Storr, in terms of the 'aggressor's' need to revenge himself for past humiliations.

Once again, the seeds for this corruption of the aggressive drive are sown in early childhood. In the case of those who Storr labels as 'paranoid',[17] the hatred is due to the paranoid's projection on to others of the intense negative emotions acquired in a childhood that has been characterized by a total denial of the need for self-assertion and by subjection to humiliation and disregard. This treatment leads to 'impulses of hate and revenge, which have a vindictive quality that is absent from "normal" aggression' (ibid., p. 129). These deeply felt impulses lead such people in later life not only to deny their own 'normal' aggression but to project their hatred and vindictiveness on to others. Thus they become subject to paranoia, in that they are led 'to descry hostility when none exists' and to attribute to others motives of malignant antagonism when the antagonism is really not felt by the other but by the paranoid himself.

For Storr, however, paranoia embraces not only the projection on to others of malignant and vindictive hostility, but also the enjoyment by the paranoid person of the suffering of others. For, according to Storr, when the paranoid individual (who, Storr claims, is far more likely to be male than female) was a child the experience of total helplessness that he suffered enabled him to identify with victims and to 'enter imaginatively into his enemy's agony'. This combination of the desire for revenge and the understanding of the role of the persecuted fuels a need to make those whom he considers his inferiors suffer even more. In this way the condition of paranoia embraces not only the projection of negative feelings on to others, but also the potentiality for the bullying and humiliating of those whom the paranoid has identified as objects of hate or contempt.

The paranoid personality, however, according to Storr does not necessarily vent this malignant potentiality in violent behaviour. But, he claims, there are a certain group of paranoid people whose extreme feelings do spill over into violent behaviour and these are the people whom he calls *paranoid psychopaths*:

> a group of persons who combine certain paranoid characteristics with an habitual lack of ability to control their immediate impulses . . . They are, however, much more dangerous than depressives, schizoid personalities, or paranoid schizophrenics,[18] since they have a strong propensity to 'act out' their hostility, and are therefore responsible for much violent crime. (ibid., p. 137)

Storr accounts for this capacity, on the part of some paranoid personalities, to indulge in violence in two ways. To begin with, he argues (using some of the data discussed on pages 31–2 above) that some psychopaths may be organically different to normal people, but he also believes that nurture as well as nature may account for psychopathy, in that 'psychopathic conduct can be explained, at any rate in part, by a failure to develop any affectional ties' because 'there is no doubt that a high proportion of psychopaths come from homes where affection is lacking' (ibid., p. 143).

The paranoid psychopath is, for Storr, an individual who goes beyond the paranoid's destructive combination of projection and vengefulness, because combined with the paranoid's malignant cocktail of suppressed emotion, he has never acquired the capacity to care for or indeed consider the feelings of anyone except himself, and 'thus psychopaths are capable of treating other people as most of us might treat a wasp'.

In sum, Storr uses his theory of an innate drive for aggression, which may be distorted from a fundamentally positive orientation to a destructive and malign orientation, to account for a wide spectrum of individual behaviour ranging from chronic depression to crimes of violence. But his exploration of the power of the aggressive drive is not confined only to instances of what he refers to as individual pathology – it covers as well the influence of the aggressive impulse on social behaviour, for he claims that man's propensity to behave cruelly to his fellows is rooted in the 'normal' course of childhood development. The paranoid and psychopath, for Storr, lie at the one end of a continuum of paranoid characteristics; ranging along the rest of the continuum are the rest of us: 'Although most obvious in the insane, the capacity for paranoid projection is, regrettably, not confined to them. Indeed we must assume that the whole of mankind possesses some underlying potential' (ibid., p. 131). And it is this paranoid potential that explains, according to Storr, 'man's unique capacity for cruelty'.

The key to this capacity, for Storr, lies in the universal experience of childhood, where all individuals experiencing the position of being totally helpless acquire some of the characteristics of paranoia. Because we have all been at the mercy of adults who at some stage have disregarded our needs and desires, we not only store up the need to avenge this humiliation but also understand what it feels like to be a victim. This combination of hostility and identification fuels a desire to avenge ourselves when others suffer, and so when we come across others who are suffering we not only wish to see them continue to suffer but we also wish to intensify their suffering. 'Upon this basis also rests man's capacity for cruelty. His wish to torture and humiliate someone over whom he has already proved his superiority is clearly related to his ability to enter imaginatively into his enemy's agony' (ibid., pp. 133–4). It is this scenario from early childhood that accounts for man's potential for torture and scapegoating.

## SOME CONCLUSIONS ABOUT STORR'S APPROACH TO HUMAN AGGRESSION

Storr's debt to both Lorenz's brand of ethology and psychoanalysis are clear. To Lorenz and to Freud he owes his belief that aggression is instinctive. Going somewhat further than Freud, and concurring with Lorenz, he argues that aggression, in addition to being instinctive and therefore unavoidable, is also potentially positive. But he also unites Lorenz's psychobiological position with a psychoanalytic stance from which he sees adult behaviour as shaped not only by instinctive forces but also by unconscious motivations which emerge out of the early inter-section of the instinctive impulse to aggress with the child-rearing ex-perience.

His recommendations for reducing hostility also show this dual lineage for, like both Lorenz and Freud, he argues that we have to come to terms with our aggressive instincts rather than strive to eliminate them. In addition to this general recommendation, however, he proposes four specific strategies for reducing hostility. It seems to me that two of these derive from the influence of Lorenz and two from the influence of psychoanalysis.

First, like Lorenz and for the same reason, he urges that we increase competition both at the international and the individual level, thus directing our aggressive impulses into constructive channels. Secondly, basing his argument on Lorenz's claim that man has territorial impulses, Storr suggests that we strive to reduce the world's population by birth control, for 'to reduce world population, or at least to stem the flood of its increase, is the most important single step which can be taken by mankind to reduce hostile tension' (ibid., p. 162).

His next two proposals are closer to psychoanalysis in that they are based on his belief that hostility emerges from deep-seated emotions as well as from the direct operation of the aggressive drive. Thus his third proposal is that we attempt to circumvent some of the projections of hostility that we have developed. Nations, he argues, often project hostile feelings onto other nations. If we increase communication and co-operation between nations, then we would be less likely to rely on these paranoid projections.

Storr's fourth proposal also emerges from his belief that hostility is fuelled by emotions as well as by instinct. This proposal is that we attempt to reduce the scale of human institutions so that each individual has a sense of dignity and power and is not simply an unimportant cog in a vast bureaucratic machine. For, Storr argues, the feeling of resentment engendered by impotence is likely to convert smouldering discontent into active hostility and hatred.

Although Storr does not specifically deal with modes of ameliorating individual psychopathology, presumably he would believe that, in addition to the four proposals he explicitly lists for reducing conflict in group situations, individual acts of violence would be less likely to occur if there were a concerted shift to the kinds of child-rearing practices he recommends.

*Human Aggression* is a very ambitious book. Within its 164 pages, Storr aims not only to diagnose the roots of individual psychopathology but also to diagnose the source of group conflict. Furthermore he moves beyond diagnosis to prescription. Trying to accomplish so much within such a restricted frame must inevitably lead to oversimplifications, parti-cularly when so much of the actual material is polemical. It is not surprising therefore, to find that Storr's work is often grouped with Lorenz's and Ardrey's, not only because of Storr's acknowledged debt to Lorenz but because all three are seen as presenting a 'highly simplified conception of the causes and possible remedies of aggression' (Berkowitz, 1982a, reviewing the work of Storr, Ardrey, Morris and Lorenz, p. 14).

Berkowitz's criticism is difficult to refute. For example, consider Storr's confident assertion that in all families 'there are bound to be perpetual struggles for dominance' (Storr, 1970, p. 127), or his claim that 'the child feels insecure with parents who never show any aggression' (ibid., pp. 68–9) or that 'man is a competitive, aggressive, territorial animal' (ibid., pp. 154–5). All these statements may be true for most individuals or families in Western societies, but an acquaintanceship with the body of anthropological data would, I suggest, lead to less certainty.

Although Erich Fromm, the next writer I intend to discuss, shares with Storr the three basic assumptions which I suggested on page 106 underpin psychoanalytic approaches to aggression, his work is characterized by considerably more complexity and caution. His book on aggression is, as a result, far longer and far more carefully and fully referenced than Storr's, and it may be that the aims of the books differ as well. It is possible to see Storr's book as primarily polemical in its impassioned plea that we discard the 'futile optimism' of the belief that aggression is primarily reactive rather than innate, and that we 'face the fact that, in man, as in other animals, the aggressive drive is an inherited constant, of which we cannot rid ourselves, and which is absolutely necessary for survival' (ibid., p. 148), while the primary aim of Fromm's book is not to persuade the reader to adopt a particular orientation to aggression, but to examine at great length the support for a rather less unidirectional approach. For while, as we shall see, Fromm does use the psychoanalytic approach to understand pathological instances of aggression, he is also concerned to point out that not all destructive behaviour owes its existence to any one drive.

## Erich Fromm and *The Anatomy of Human Destructiveness*

In *The Anatomy of Human Destructiveness*, the German-born American psychoanalyst Erich Fromm produced the most comprehensive theory of aggression to emerge from within the ranks of psychoanalysts. In this book he not only presented his own over-view of the whole field of aggression, but also surveyed much of the earlier work on aggression in the areas of physiology, ethology and psychology.

Using the term 'aggression' to cover emotions and behaviour which are motivated to enable the 'aggressor' to preserve or enhance his or her own position, Fromm centres his approach around four premises, each of which I would like to explore in some detail. These are, first, that man, like most other animal species, has a 'built in' potential for defensive aggression and that such aggression is fundamentally benign. Secondly, the pathological aspects of aggression that man displays, such as cruelty and destructiveness, are not due to this inbuilt potential but to aggression-producing conditions in the environment. Thirdly, cruelty and destructiveness can be woven into the character structure of individuals by their early emotional social experiences. Finally, intensive explorations of the early experience of historical figures like Stalin, Himmler and Hitler can be used to substantiate his claim that early experiences condition character structures which are basically cruel, sadistic and exploitative.

## 'BENIGN' AGGRESSION

It seems to me that the only possible way to differentiate the varied emotions and behaviours that Fromm characterizes as 'benign' is by exclusion. This is because the major thrust of his book concerns 'malignant aggression' where behaviour is motivated by the desire to inflict, and enjoy inflicting, cruelty and destruction on others. 'Benign' aggression is *the term Fromm uses to distinguish emotion and behaviour which, while causing suffering to others, is motivated by causes other than the desire to inflict cruelty and destruction.*

Under the term 'benign aggression' Fromm groups three different categories. First, defensive behaviour; secondly, what he calls pseudo-aggression; and finally behaviour which, while it involves fighting or harming others, is not primarily directed by motivations concerned with the desire to harm others.

In discussing the category he calls 'defensive aggression' Fromm argues that it is in the interests of all species to have a 'phylogenetically programmed' set of possible responses to threats (1977, p. 139). Basically he considers such responses fall into two categories: rage and attack, and fear and flight.

Drawing on some of the earlier studies of hypothalmic stimulation and on the work of Mark and Moyer (see Chapter 2 above), he claims that there is a great deal of evidence to support the hypothesis that specific areas of the brain are mobilized when an animal or person is threatened. Such mobilization prepares the individual for a set of flight responses or a set of fight responses. Both sets of responses are biologically adaptive and both are essentially reactive. Unlike Storr, Fromm does not believe that there is an innate drive for aggression. Rather he argues that there is a potentiality for fight or flight which is aroused only in the face of threat. When this happens, whether in man or animal, the individual concerned, if moved to fighting, is not motivated to destroy for the sake of destruction, but is primarily motivated to defend him or herself. Thus 'defensive aggressiveness' [19] is "built in" in the animal and human brain and serves the function of defence against threats to vital interests' (ibid., p. 251).

Fromm thus believes that there are 'benign' aspects of aggression in both man and animals which stem from the need for defence. Man is, however, far more likely to be aroused to such defensive aggression than animals for three reasons, all of which are linked to man's greater cognitive and emotional range. First, man, unlike other species who perceive only 'clear and present danger', is endowed with foresight and therefore may foresee dangers; secondly, man sometimes reacts to imagined rather than real threats, as for example occurs when people react to propaganda; and thirdly, man has a far wider range of vital interests than other species, extending from the need for food and physical shelter to the need to defend values and ideals.

Thus under 'benign aggression' Fromm subsumes, as may be expected, behaviour that is primarily defensive, such as fighting in the service of deeply held beliefs and ideals, fighting for human rights, as when colonized peoples revolt, and verbal aggression when people's deep-seated psychological defences are attacked, as for example when a client in psychoanalysis is confronted by the analyst with motivations he or she finds it painful to think about.

In addition to defensive behaviour and emotions, however, as I have noted above Fromm includes under the heading of 'benign aggression' emotions and behaviour which, while not defensive, are not primarily in Fromm's eyes malignant or destructive, although their eventual consequence may involve harming others. For example, he lists a number of categories of what he calls 'pseudo-aggression' – 'those aggressive acts that may cause harm, but are not intended to do so'. These acts include accidentally hurting others, hurting others in sport or play and 'self-assertive aggression'. This last term refers to being aggressive in the sense of 'moving towards a goal without undue hesitation, doubt or fear' (ibid., p. 256).

Self-assertive aggression, for Fromm, is more characteristic of the male than the female. For 'since the male capacity to function sexually is a basic requirement for the survival of the species, one might expect that nature has endowed the male with some special aggressive potential' (ibid., p. 257). This hypothesis leads Fromm to speculate whether men are not intrinsically better suited to being 'generals, surgeons or hunters' and women to being 'physicians and teachers'. But he concludes that even if this is so, 'many men lack self-assertive aggressiveness, and many women perform excellently those tasks that may require it' (ibid., p. 262). In any event, for Fromm, there is a category of behaviour, self-assertion, intimately tied to the need to achieve, that may be more characteristic of males than females and that, while it may involve the discomfiture of others, is primarily concerned with promotion of the 'aggressor's' need for success.

The third category of what Fromm calls 'benign aggression' covers a wide variety of behaviour, a great deal of which most of us would hesitate to call 'benign'. It includes *conformist* aggression – when, for example, a soldier fights only because he is directed to and he considers it is his duty to obey orders; *instrumental* aggression (this term is also used by experimental psychologists, as we shall see in the next chapter), where the aim is to obtain something desirable rather than to destroy or harm another; and, finally, the aggression that occurs *in war*.

Although conformist aggression, instrumental aggression and war all harm others, for Fromm they are saved from 'malignancy' because they are directed not by any destructive urges, but by a whole complex of motivations springing from the wide range of human behaviour and emotion. Thus Fromm, castigating those whom he sees as offering a simple-minded and superficial explanation of war, writes:

> It has become fashionable to consider war as caused by the power of man's destructive instinct . . . [But] The thesis that war is caused by innate human destructiveness is plainly absurd for anyone who has even the slightest knowledge of history . . . [For example] the First World War was motivated by the economic interests and political ambitions of the political, military, and industrial leaders on both sides, and not by a need of the various nations to give vent to their damned-up aggression. (ibid., pp. 283–6)

War, according to Fromm, is not only a strategy for obtaining economic or political ends, but may also provide for the combatants 'more subtle emotional motivations . . . that have nothing to do within aggression'. It may supply an excitement and stimulation that is absent from the 'boring routine of everyday life' (ibid., p. 289). In short, for Fromm, war answers needs that have little to do with innate drives for aggression and much to do with the pressures, limitations and constraints of the societies that enter into them.

Fromm extends this line of reasoning to argue that all aspects of 'benign aggression' in man could be controlled by changing social conditions. For if people are not threatened, if their needs both for the essentials of life and human dignity and freedom are met, and if the 'misery, monotony, dullness and powerlessness' that exist in large sectors of the population are eliminated, then the factors which cause benign aggression would be removed.

## MALIGNANT AGGRESSION

While Fromm's delineation of benign aggression is relatively straightforward, his conception of malignant aggression rests on a complex infrastructure of premises about human nature. Briefly, he believes that man, unlike other species, is rooted in biological contradictions. These contradictions arise out of an evolutionary development which have allowed man to emerge as the species with the minimum of innate programming and the maximum of cerebral development. As a result, man is the only species to be self-aware. This self-awareness, according to Fromm, enables man to appreciate the true nature of his condition; his relative powerlessness in the face of natural forces and his inevitable individual oblivion in death. Lost, powerless and separate from nature, man is driven to 'find new ways of relating himself to the world to enable him to feel at home' (ibid., p. 304). He is driven, in short, to satisfy what Fromm calls his 'existential needs'.

Fromm lists these existential needs as the need for an abiding system of values and belief in order to give life focus and meaning; the need for reciprocal personal relationships; the need for an inner sense of personal unity or identity; the need to feel effective; and the need for stimulation and excitement. How an individual meets these existential needs depends, according to Fromm, on two sets of conditions. The first of these concern his or her own personal emotional experience (and here Fromm emphasizes what I have suggested is one of the lynch-pins of the psychoanalytic approaches to aggression), while the second concerns the particular culture in which the individual lives.

These twin sets of circumstances dictate whether the strategies the individual chooses are basically constructive or basically destructive. Malignant aggression is potentiated when the only strategies available are destructive.

For Fromm, then, malignant aggression is always a possibility. Though not innate, it is nevertheless 'a human potential rooted in the very conditions of human existence' (ibid., p. 305). When people are not able to satisfy their existential needs with positive strategies such as 'love, tenderness, striving for justice, independence [and] truth', they will turn to the use of negative strategies, such as 'hate, sadism, masochism, destructiveness [and] narcissism' (ibid., p. 305). Thus, for Fromm, the central question in the quest to control malignant aggression is to identify which circumstances predispose the use of such negative strategies. Or, as he himself puts it, *'the problem is to examine in what manner and to what degree the specific conditions of human existence are responsible for the quality and intensity of man's lust for killing and torturing'* (ibid., p. 253, Fromm's italics).

In the *Anatomy of Human Destructiveness*, Fromm strives for a solution to this problem by outlining two categories of malevolent aggression, and suggesting how they are potentiated. The first category concerns 'spontaneous' forms of aggression and the second, the category to which he devoted the major part of the book, malignant aggression which is 'bound in the character structure'.

Turning very briefly to 'spontaneous' forms of malignant aggression, it seems that Fromm considers this is likely to occur when individuals or groups are subjected to a particular extreme and traumatic set of experiences, and that it can take the form of either 'vengefulness' or 'ecstasy'. Vengefulness occurs when the individual or group has been subjected to intense and unjustified suffering, and becomes driven by the need to avenge their own pain. It is exemplified in the notion of blood revenge, when 'revenge is a sacred duty that falls upon the member of a family, clan or tribe who has to kill a member of the corresponding unit if one of his people has been killed' (ibid., p. 363). Ecstatic destruction on the other hand, though also a response to a particular set of circumstances, occurs in ritualized orgies or states of trance that certain societies use in order to give vent to extreme rage. Both forms of spontaneous destructiveness, however, are relatively harmless, according to Fromm, in that they do not characterize an individual lifespan but are specific responses to particular sets of circumstances. On the other hand, when aggression is 'bound in the character structure' it is particularly destructive, for it will characterize the whole of the individual's way of life.

## CRUELTY AND DESTRUCTIVENESS WOVEN INTO THE CHARACTER STRUCTURE

For Fromm a central premise of human psychology is the belief that each individual has his or her own particular 'character'. This term refers to *'the relatively permanent system of all non-instinctual strivings through which man relates himself to the human and natural world'* (ibid., p. 305, Fromm's italics). According to Fromm, differences in character are rooted in differences in social experiences, both personal and cultural, although 'genetically given' dispositions may also play a part. Some individuals, according to Fromm, experience so destructive an early environment, both personal and social, that predispositions to behave in particularly destructive and cruel ways become bound into the character structure.

Consider, for example, Fromm's view of what he calls the 'sadistic character'. 'For the sadistic character everything living is to be controllable; living beings become things. Or still more accurately, living things are transformed into living, quivering, pulsating objects of control. Their responses are forced by the one who controls them' (ibid., p. 388).

Such a character, according to Fromm, is shaped by the interaction between a variety of forces. At the level of individual experience, a child who is severely and arbitrarily punished and who is made to feel impotent and unworthy may satisfy his or her denied existential need by compensation, and may endeavour to control the environment in much the same way as he or she has been controlled by dominant adults. He or she would, according to Fromm, be likely to develop the syndrome of character traits Freud referred to as 'anal': stubborness, orderliness, parsimoniousness, extreme punctuality and extreme cleanliness.

But while developing anal traits might lead to a life of sterility and rigidity, the possession of an 'anal character' would not necessarily lead to the display of sadistic behaviour. For this to happen, the social as well as the individual environment would have to be propitious. For 'a person whose character is sadistic will be essentially harmless in an anti-sadistic society' (ibid., pp. 307–8). It is only in a society which, by being exploitative in itself, is conducive to sadistic behaviour at the general level, that the potential sadist is able to extend his or her potential for malignant aggression.

Malignant aggression is manifested not only in sadistic behaviour, where the prime impulse is to control and dominate, but also, according to Fromm, in the behaviour that results from the impulse to destroy. This impulse dominates the character type Fromm labels 'necrophiliac'. For necrophilia is *'the passionate attraction to all that is dead, decayed, putrid, sickly; it is the passion to transform that which is alive into something unalive; to destroy for the sake of destruction; the exclusive interest in all that is purely mechanical. It is the passion to tear apart living structures'* (ibid., p. 441, Fromm's italics).

Necrophilia, for Fromm, like sadism, is rooted both in individual and social conditions. At the individual level it rests on the distortion of the relationship with the mother at the oedipal stage,[20] when the child, instead of developing 'benign incestuous bonds' with the mother, develops bonds that are pathological in that the mother is not related to as a real, affectionate, warm love-object but is related to as a phantom who is at times attractive and desirable and at other times cold and repelling. This distortion of the early bond with the mother leads to a predisposition to relate to other people in a shallow manner, for example by sadistic control or by 'narcissism'. Narcissism occurs when the potential necrophiliac demands boundless admiration. Once again, individual experiences do not by themselves lead to destructive behaviour. For that to occur, as with sadistic behaviour, the social environment must also offer an appropriate climate. Such a climate is provided by social conditions in which technology, organization and alienation dominate; when the emphasis is on technique rather than feeling, and when lifeless machines assume dominance over warm human relationships.

Fromm acknowledges that his own understanding of malignant aggression emerges from his experience as a psychoanalyst, so that it is not suprising to find that he validates his categorization of such aggression by reference to the early life of particular individuals. But his choice of case histories to provide such validation illuminates not only his psychoanalytic roots but also his belief that individual development rests as much on the socio-political environment as it does on interpersonal relationships. It is for this reason that he illustrates his approach to aggression by reference to individuals whose social and political background is at least as accessible as their early life.

## HIMMLER – A CLINICAL CASE OF ANAL-HOARDING SADISM

For Fromm, the case study of Heinrich Himmler, Hitler's deputy, provides an excellent example of the 'connection beween sadism and the extreme forms of the anal-hoarding bureaucrat, authoritarian character' (ibid., p. 398). Drawing on biographical studies of Himmler and Himmler's own diaries, Fromm sets out to show how Himmler's early family life predisposed him towards sadism and how contemporary German society allowed him to vent this predisposition on others.

Himmler's early life, Fromm argues, was dominated by a controlling father who imposed submission to himself and to his values on the growing boy. This imposition of submission led Himmler, Fromm claims, to himself seek to impose his will on others, for it was only by controlling others that Himmler could compensate for his own inner feelings of impotence, shyness and unease. Paradoxically, while Himmler sought to control those others he saw as his inferiors, his early relationship with his father also predisposed him to offer to those whom he accepted as his superiors a submission and fanaticism. He was, in effect, predisposed to be a disciple to someone who, stronger than himself, reflected similar values. Thus, according to Fromm, the psycho-dynamics of Himmler's early life produced in Himmler the typical attributes of the authoritarian character – the propensity to play the dual role of fanatical follower and ruthless overseer.

There were, however, according to Fromm, other aspects of Himmler's early life that also prepared him for the place he was to occupy in history. These aspects concerned the development in Himmler of what Freud had labelled as the 'anal-hoarding' syndrome, where the individual concerned is regarded by psychoanalysts as being excessively orderly, rigid and stubborn. Such attributes, according to Fromm, stood Himmler in good stead as he carried out his ghastly duties with 'inhuman bureaucratic conscientiousness and methodicalness' (ibid., p. 399).

For Fromm, Himmler exemplifies the way in which if the child's early existential needs are not met, he or she can become, as Fromm considered Himmler did, 'an example of the typical anal-hoarding, sadistic authoritarian character' who, themselves weak, can only develop security in orderliness and pedantry, and whose inner uncertainties and sense of impotence leads to the 'malicious wish to humiliate and destroy' others.

But, as I noted above, Fromm moves beyond the position of classical psychoanalysis, with its emphasis on psychodynamic forces, to consider the interaction of such forces with the social and cultural environment. And so Fromm poses the question: 'What would have become of Himmler had he not lived when he did?' (ibid., p. 429), and answers it in this way:

The answer is not too difficult to find. Since he was of average intelligence and very orderly, he would probably have found a place in a bureaucratic system say as a school teacher, postal clerk, or employee in a large business enterprise. Since he ruthlessly sought advantage, by cleverly flattering his superiors and intriguing against his colleagues he might have risen to quite a high position . . . He would have been thoroughly disliked by his colleagues and perhaps would have been the favourite of a powerful superior . . . (ibid., pp. 429–30)

In short, Himmler in unexceptional times might have remained unexceptional.

Instead, according to Fromm, the time he lived in transformed his potential for enjoying controlling and humiliating others into the reality of a career devoted to the extermination of those he regarded as his inferiors.

The case history of Himmler exemplifies Fromm's approach to what he defines as malignant aggression. Such aggression arises not out of innate predispositions to hurt or humiliate or control others, but out of the joint operation of a social and emotional climate that directs individuals to seek to meet their existential needs for meaning, personal relationships, identity, achievement and excitement, not by the strategies of love, tenderness and seeking justice, but by hate, sadism and destruction.

Because, for Fromm, those aspects of aggression that he labels as malignant are not innate, his prescription for avoiding the excesses of 'malignant' aggression and violence are more optimistic than those of Lorenz, Freud or the sociobiologists. Thus, in his view, the malignant aspects of aggression can be substantially reduced when the socioeconomic conditions are replaced by conditions that are favourable to the full development of man's genuine needs and capacities, to the development of 'human self-activity and man's creative power as its own end . . . [for] all factors that make man into a psychic cripple turn him also into a sadist or a destroyer' (ibid., p. 576).

## SOME CONCLUSIONS ABOUT FROMM'S APPROACH TO AGGRESSION

Reading Fromm, it is not possible to remain unimpressed by his immense erudition. It is also not possible to remain unimpressed by the manner in which he acknowledges how his own approach to aggression deals with only limited aspects of mankind's turbulent history of conflict and violence. Unlike all the approaches we have looked at up to now, Fromm does not aim for a macro-theory which extends to cover the whole range of behaviours and emotions that are labelled aggressive and violent.

As I indicated at the beginning of this section, the approach Fromm adopts rests on four premises. First, there are aspects of aggression that are innately 'built in' but such aspects are basically benign; secondly, malignant aggression, while not innately built in, is rooted in the human condition; thirdly, the predisposition to malignant aggression can be woven into the character structure; and, finally, the second and third premises can be substantiated by reference to case histories. Essentially he accepts the three assumptions that I suggested underpin psycho-analytic approaches to aggression – that it derives (in Fromm's case only partially) from innate sources, that the manner in which an individual displays aggression in later life is dependent on early emotional experiences, and that these experiences can cause pathological and malignant aggression.

But, as I have already noted, Fromm broadens his approach beyond psychoanalysis. In particular he is far more sophisticated than the ego-psychologists like Hartmann and his associates, Kutash and Storr, in his understanding of social and political factors and their impact on individual psychology.

In evaluating Fromm's approach to aggression and violence, I think it is important to remember that his work, while drawing to some extent on physiological and ethological studies, is essentially based on a subjective conceptualization of human nature that is not open to substantiation or refutation, and this is an issue I would like to return to at the end of this chapter. But before doing so I will turn briefly to the issue of the psychoanalytic approach to the role of aggression in sexual relationships.

## 'Women in Love'

That males are more aggressive than females is a recurrent theme in different approaches to aggression and violence. In Chapter 3 we looked at the ethological studies bearing on this theme, we will look in Chapter 5 at documented studies of sex differences in human aggression, and in Chapters 6 and 7 at social aspects of these differences, but in this chapter I want to move away from the rather 'scientific' approach of these other sections on sex differences in aggression and violence and concentrate on the rather more intuitive approach to this theme that is offered by psychoanalysis.

Freud himself, though he always admitted the bisexual nature of much of human behaviour, believed that there were major differences in the psychology of men and women. (For example, he argued that compared to men, women were more likely to be plagued by envy, jealousy and shame, and that women, relative to men, had on the whole 'little sense of justice'.)[21] Nowhere, according to Freud, was this difference more apparent than in the approach to heterosexual relations, where 'Maleness combines [the factors of] subject, activity and possession of the penis; femaleness takes over [those of] object and passivity' (1923b, p. 312, editor's brackets).

Although Freud traced this passivity on the part of women to the psycho-dynamics of early childhood, he also appeared to believe that men are innately more aggressive than women, for 'the accomplishment of the aim of biology has been entrusted to the aggressiveness of men', and that consequently women are more passive because their active involvement is not necessary for the procreation of children (1933, quoted by Rohrbaugh, 1980, p. 92).

The polarity between the active male and the passive female that Freud posed was not, and indeed is not, unique to Freud, and the duality he wrote about has permeated literary works from Samuel Richardson through to Norman Mailer. But at the time of publication, Freud's thinking in this area found its most immediate literary reflection in the writing of the contemporary novelist D. H. Lawrence. For, even though he explicitly rejected many of the assumptions of psychoanalysis in *Psychoanalysis and the Unconscious* and *Fantasia of the Unconscious*, Lawrence was nevertheless heavily influenced by Freud, as he himself acknowledged when he wrote 'We are thankful that Freud pulled us somewhat to earth, out of all our clouds of superfineness. What Freud says is always partly true. And half a loaf is better than no bread' (1971a, p. 17).

It seems to me that Lawrence's debt to Freud is most apparent in those novels like *Sons and Lovers*, *The Rainbow* and *Women in Love* when he shows most clearly his belief in the centrality to the psyche of the sexual drive. I would like to focus briefly on the last of these to demonstrate how Lawrence illustrates Freud's identification of masculinity with aggressive activity and femininity with passive receptivity. But before I do this I want to consider what Lawrence actually said about the nature of male–female differences in *Fantasia of the Unconscious*.

Focusing first on the masculine ideal, Lawrence wrote: 'Now, in what we call the "natural" mode, man has his positivity in the volitional centres, and women in the sympathetic' (1971b, p. 97). So that for men, action is prescribed: 'Man in the daytime must follow his own soul's greatest impulse, and give himself to life-work and risk himself to death' (ibid., p. 100). Consequently, according to Lawrence, boys should be treated like this: 'First and foremost establish a rule over them, a proud, harsh, manly rule. Make them *know* that every moment they are in the shade of a proud, strong, adult authority. Let them be soldiers' (ibid., p. 99). Whereas the programme for women is rather different: 'Let her learn the domestic arts in their perfection. Let us even artificially set her to spin and weave' (ibid., p. 87), and 'Make her yield to her own real unconscious self, and absolutely stamp on the self she's got in her head' (ibid., p. 191) so that 'Ah, how good it is to come home to your wife when she *believes* in you and submits to your purpose that is beyond her. Then how wonderful this nightfall is! How rich you feel, tired, with all the burden of day in your veins, turning home' (ibid., p. 193, Lawrence's italics).

These views of Lawrence find their closest literary expression in the novel *Women in Love*. This is a complex and subtle book concerned not only with the centrality of sexual tensions but also with the disintegration and dissolution of traditional English life, so that focusing as I am on one aspect of the novel necessarily detracts from its overall structure and unity. Its central theme is nevertheless clear – it continues the search, begun in *The Rainbow*, for a lasting relationship between the two sexes (Daleski, 1965). This relationship is portrayed by following its course in the pairing of two contrasting couples, Ursula and Birkin and Gudrun and Gerald. Ursula and Gudrun are sisters and at the beginning of the novel both teachers, but there their resemblance ends. While Ursula is the protagonist of an essential femininity, Gudrun, sexually aggressive and dominant, symbolizes a category of women that Lawrence was to be repelled by throughout his life, those whom Spilka (1978) has called 'wilful women'. As Lawrence poses the women in contrast, so too does he contrast their relationships. Ursula and Birkin, comparatively similar in background, meet in a number of unexceptional, almost domestic settings, where they 'work their way painfully towards fulfilment in life', whereas Gudrun and Gerald move through a number of highly charged dramatic encounters as 'they follow their road to spiritual death' (Pinion, 1978).

Shaping the benign relationships of Ursula and Birkin is Ursula's essentially passive responsivity to Birkin. As Birkin strives to define the relationships between men and women, she moves to an acceptance of the feminine role that Lawrence outlined so passionately in the excerpts from the *Fantasia of the Unconscious* quoted above.

This role is highlighted in a scene where Ursula and Birkin are shown discussing another male–female relationship, one that they are watching – a meeting between Birkin's cat, Mino, a lordly 'slender young gentleman', and a young female stray, 'a fluffy, soft outcast . . . with wild eyes that were green and lovely as great jewels'. As the stray alternatively draws Mino to her and repels him, Birkin says of Mino, 'He is only insisting to the poor stray that she shall acknowledge him as a sort of fate, her own fate: because you can see she is fluffy and promiscuous as the wind. I am with him'; and later, 'with the Mino, it is the desire to bring this female cat into a pure stable equilibrium, a transcendent and abiding *rapport* with the single male. Whereas without him, as you see, she is a mere stray, a sporadic fluffy bit of chaos' (1960, pp. 165–7).

At first Ursula finds this conception of masculinity and femininity difficult to accept but ultimately, despite quarrels and misunderstandings, her relationship with Birkin grows and develops as she learns

that for Birkin's sake she must learn to reflect his moods and accept his
more prepotent will.

But while Birkin and Ursula's relationship flows into a harmony and
companionship, Gudrun's relationship with Gerald moves jerkily and
destructively towards a violent climax as Gerald, maddened and be-
wildered by Gudrun's superior power and wilfulness, destroys himself in
a skiing accident in the arctic snows of the Alps. For, unlike Ursula,
Gudrun does not accept her feminine destiny. Unlike Ursula, Gudrun
does not wish to complement but to compete and indeed dominate:
'They were of the same kind she and he [Gudrun and Gerald] a sort of
diabolic freemasonry subsisted between them. Henceforward, she knew,
she had her power over him. Whenever they met, they would be secretly
associated. And he would be helpless in the association with her. Her
soul exulted' (ibid., p. 135).

For Lawrence, as for Freud, there is a dynamic polarity that characterizes mature sexual relationships: the active controlling male and the
passive complementing female. Storr, writing long after Lawrence,
emphasizes even more than either Lawrence or Freud the destructive
results that follow when the polarity is ignored or reversed. For, as I
noted before, Storr argues that satisfactory sexual relationships involve
an important element of aggressiveness in male sexuality and of yielding
and submission in females. For 'in the relation between the sexes, the
spermatozoon swims actively, while the ovum passively awaits its pene-
tration' and thus 'the anatomy of the sexual organs itself attests the
differentiation of the sexual role' (Storr, 1972, p. 89). From this description of the early progenitors of sexual relationships Storr goes on to
develop the theme that for satisfactory sexual relationships, and happy
emotional ones, male dominance is essential:

> However emancipated a woman may be, she will still, at one level,
> want her husband to be the dominant partner; whilst the hen-
> pecked husband with his more formidable spouse will continue to
> excite our ridicule, however full of civilised compassion we may
> think ourselves to be. (ibid., p. 92)

As at the emotional level, so also at the sexual level. According to
Storr, mature sexual relationships must include an element of sexual
aggression on the part of the male. The evidence, according to Storr, for
this claim comes both from the consulting room and from looking at
sexual fantasies. Even fantasies reflect this polarity between male aggression and female submission:

> It is significant that there is a difference between the sexes in the
> type of phantasy which will appeal to each. The idea of being seized
> and borne off by a ruthless male who will wreak his sexual will

upon his helpless victim has a *universal appeal to the female sex*. It is the existance of this phantasy which accounts for the wide popularity of such figures as *The Sheikh*, Rhett Butler, or even King Kong. (ibid., p. 91, my italics)

While women fantasize about being dominated, men, according to Storr, fantasize not only about dominating women but also about inflicting suffering on them: 'In contrast to women, men very frequently have sexual phantasies in which they behave sadistically' (ibid., p. 91).

For Storr, then, sadism within the sexual act is a derivative, at least in part, on a kind of innate predisposition on behalf of men to dominate women, and of women to enjoy that domination. Fromm also comments on this, though his remarks are more cautious and less generalized than Storr's:

It would seem that sexual sadism is more frequent among men, than among women, at least in our culture; whether masochism is more frequent among women is difficult to ascertain because of lack of reliable data on the subject. (Fromm, 1977, p. 375)

Of course, it is not only psychoanalysts who suggest that women are attracted by aggressive, powerful males, for as Roth puts it,

the belief that aggressiveness and power are inseparably intertwined with sexual desirability and success in the male has been handed down through the ages in many, but not all, cultures, and is fostered and reinforced from many sources. (1982, p. 13)

Recently, particularly in the West, the theme has become insistent and male domination and machismo are salient messages in sources as diverse as romantic novels and hard core pornography. As Smith concluded after an analysis of paperback novels on sale at American news stands between 1968 and 1976, the attitude that is conveyed is often, 'No matter how much she says no, go ahead and do it anyway, because she'll be grateful to you afterwards' (Smith, 1976, quoted by Nelson, 1982, p. viii).

The ubiquity of the message, within Western culture, can of course be ascribed to a complex of interlocking variables ranging from inequalities in power, influence and prestige of the two sexes to the increasing amount of capital invested in pornography from sex shops to video-tapes. Its roots are diverse, interlocking and deeply embedded in our culture. In particular, as I shall describe in Chapters 6 and 7, it is vitally important to examine just how much this message has been amplified recently by pornography such as 'video nasties'; but for psychoanalysts the major root is clear, it is that the coupling of male sexuality and male aggression are deeply embedded in human nature.

## Overview of Psychoanalytic Approaches

In the last section of this chapter I would like to look at two issues:

(1) The evaluation of the psychoanalytic approach to aggression and violence.
(2) Whether the use psychoanalysts make of the terms aggression and violence covers all the parameters discussed in the summative descriptions of aggression and violence in Chapter 1.

EVALUATING THE PSYCHOANALYTIC APPROACH TO AGGRESSION

In the concluding sections of the last two chapters I suggested that there are two possible evaluative perspectives that can be taken in looking at different approaches to aggression and violence. Applying the first perspective, experimental and clinical results are evaluated using criteria like experimental design, replicability of results, sample size and so on, thus basing the evaluation on what might be termed a 'scientific' model. Applying the second perspective, the evaluator looks at assumptions that are made about human nature, using criteria that are essentially more subjective, like judgements about rigour and consistency and whether or not the approach helps the evaluator extend his or her own understanding.

Because so much of the content of psychoanalytic writing is concerned with assumptions about human nature and development rather than with empirical findings, it seems to me that any evaluation of psychoanalysis must be slanted in the direction of the second rather than the first perspective. But before I look at this perspective I would like to point out that all three of the psychoanalysts whom I have discussed in detail in this chapter base their initial premise – that aggression is innate – on 'scientific' data; in Freud's case on physiological data that is now essentially out of date, in Storr's case on Lorenz's ethological data, and in Fromm's case on the studies of hypothalamic function and electrical stimulation of the brain that were reviewed and evaluated in Chapter 2.

Turning now to the second perspective, I want to look first at the work of Freud. It seems to me that Freud's major contribution to an understanding of human aggression and violence lies not in his writing that is specifically about the subject area, but in his illumination of the nature of psychodynamic processes. Freud's description of unconscious processes leads to the hypotheses that some people may, in general, behave more aggressively than others, not for physiological reasons, nor because they have learned to be more aggressive than others, nor because of socio-political factors, but because at some deep-seated and non-rational level they feel more resentful and hostile, and that these deep-seated feelings may derive, at least in part, from emotional experience. To me an acceptance of these hypotheses, which derive from Freud's seminal work on the unconscious, is an essential prerequisite to an understanding of aggression and violence, and I shall return to this in the final chapter.

While accepting the importance of Freud's illumination of psycho-dynamic processes in human feelings and behaviour, I, like most other social scientists, have difficulty in accepting his specific assumptions about aggression and violence; in particular his final position that aggression derives from a death instinct. For, as Berkowitz (1962) argues, rather than seeking quiescence in death, most organisms seem to desire an optimum level of stimulation.[22]

When it comes to evaluating the work of Storr, I think it cannot be disputed that he tends to take up a fairly polemical stance. Furthermore, it seems to me that, in his attempt to produce a comprehensive theory of aggression, Storr underplays the kind of complex social, economic and political variables that are undoubtedly involved in human conflict. His more interesting contribution, to my mind, lies in his discussion of the ways in which the experiences of early childhood may lead to deeply laid feelings of impotence, rejection or hostility, which may fuel aggressive emotion and behaviour in later life.

Like Storr, Fromm develops Freud's assumption that early emotional experiences predispose to later emotional predispositions. I personally do not find Fromm's typology of malignant aggression into 'spontaneous' and 'character bound' particularly illuminating; nor do I find that his further classification of malignant aggression into 'sadistic' or 'necrophilic' varieties aids my understanding of aggressive individuals. It seems to me that such tight classificatory systems of individual 'character' types are not necessary to account for the fact that, under pressure, different individuals will respond in particular ways.

But, while I would dispute the value of Fromm's detailed typology of malignant aggression, I would argue that he has developed and extended the psychoanalytic approach to aggression and violence in a significant and valuable manner. He has done this, to my mind, in his deepening of the level of complexity of the psychoanalytic approach. Unlike earlier psychoanalysts, he argues that we have to look *beyond* the bounds of the individual psyche to wider social, economic and political conditions to understand the *full range* of aggressive emotion and violent behaviour in human beings. Furthermore, he is the first of the theorists I have considered so far to discuss in any depth the different classes of motives that may underpin aggressive and violent behaviour. That is, he argues that there is a difference in motivation between, say, a man who kills his wife's lover and a robber who, in fleeing, kills a bank guard, in that the former is likely to feel more *personally hostile* to his victim than the latter.

In conclusion, I believe that psychoanalytic approaches can deepen our understanding both of the aggressive feelings and violent behaviour of individuals and of certain group processes like scapegoating (a point I shall return to in Chapter 7). But that is not to suggest that all the aggressive emotions and violent behaviour of individuals are explicable in terms of such psycho-dynamic mechanisms; nor is it to suggest that complex social processes like scapegoating are wholly explicable in terms of such mechanisms. For it seems to me that it is impossible to attempt to understand aggression and violence without also referring to factors like social learning, and the influence on emotions and behaviour of variables like values, cultural traditions, ideology and socio-economic conditions. It is with these factors that the next chapters are concerned.

## HOW EXTENSIVE IS THE USE PSYCHOANALYSTS MAKE OF THE TERMS 'AGGRESSION' AND 'VIOLENCE'?

In Chapter 1 I derived a summational description of the ways in which the terms 'aggression' and 'violence' were used in order to check how adequately different theoretical approaches covered this usage. Referring back to page 14, it can be seen that psychoanalysts use the terms in the following ways.

*Aggression*
(a)  Psychoanalysts discuss intention in aggression to the extent that all consider the nature of sadism as well as the innate drive (or in Freud's and Storr's case, instinct) to aggress.
(b)  Psychoanalysts use aggression both in the sense of 'hurting', and in the sense of achieving dominance.
(c)  Psychoanalysts would agree that aggression does not necessarily involve physical injury.
(d)  Fromm is the only psychoanalyst to explicitly differentiate between the different kinds of motives that may underpin aggressive and violent behaviour.
(e)  Aggression is seen by psychoanalysts as having both a positive and a negative aspect and both aspects are dealt with in depth.
(f)  Perhaps because aggression is so often seen as positive rather than negative, the issue of subjectivity in applying the label aggressive to emotions or behaviour is not discussed by psychoanalysts.
(g)  Although Fromm does discuss how value systems influence aggressive behaviour, he does not explore how values affect the labelling of behaviour as aggressive. With respect to provocation, Fromm differs from other theorists in his labelling of retaliatory behaviour as 'aggression', referring to such behaviour as 'defensive aggres-

sion'. Other psychoanalysts do not deal with the issues of values or of provocation.

*Violence*
(a)  Psychoanalysts would agree that violence involves the use of great physical force or intensity.
(b)  For psychoanalysts other than Fromm, violence is seen as being motivated solely by an aggressive drive. By Fromm, violence is seen as having many possible causes of which 'malignant' aggression is only one.
(c)  All psychoanalysts discuss physical force when it is used in mutually rewarding interactions – particularly in the sexual context.
(d)  When it comes to the issue of the legitimization of violence, Fromm is the only psychoanalyst to deal with the topic, and he argues that violence in the defence of 'existential needs' can be regarded as an extension of 'benign aggression', as for instance when a colonial people fight for their freedom.

In general then, psychoanalysts explore the wider aspects of aggression and violence. But with the exception of Fromm, they seldom consider aspects like the subjectivity that may be involved in labelling an act aggressive, or in the legitimization of violence.

## Notes: Chapter 4

1   In a *Critical Dictionary of Psychoanalysis*, Charles Rycroft summarizes some of the ways in which subsequent schools of psychoanalysis have parted company with Freud's original formulations of central psychoanalytic terms and concepts.
2   The exception to this general rule is the work of Rollo May. May regards himself primarily as a psychoanalyst but I have decided to discuss his work in Chapter 7 rather than here because his underlying perspective seems closer to a phenomenological than to a strictly psychoanalytic approach.
3   In the course of this chapter I have not cited detailed references to Freud, but his most important specific references to aggression can be found in Freud, 1905, 1915, 1920, 1923a, 1930 and 1932, while Freud, 1933 and 1940 provide a good general introduction to his psychoanalytic approach. An excellent discussion of Freud's views on aggression can be found in Fromm (1977) and a shorter introduction in Kutash (1978).
4   Most commentators on the status of psychoanalysis (for example, Farrell, 1981, and Breger, 1981) do not regard psychoanalysis as a 'theory' but rather as a set of formulations about the processes underlying human behaviour, and for this reason I have decided to use the term 'psychoanalytic approach' rather than 'psychoanalytic theory'.
5   As we shall see, later in life Freud re-formulated his description of human instincts.
6   The oedipal phase is named after the mythical Greek hero who killed his father and married his mother. The oedipal phase, according to Freud, occurs around 4 or 5 years of age in chidren of both sexes, though the details of the phase differ considerably for the sexes. In general, however, the process is similar, in that during this phase attention moves from the phallic focus of the preceding phase to the person of the

opposite sex parent; and the young child is filled with desire to possess this parent and simultaneously get rid of his or her rival – the parent of the same sex. But the child soon realizes that both these aims are unrealistic, and begins to fear and at the same time to want to propitiate his or her rival – and so the child resolves the emotional conflict of fear and desire by 'identification'. This means that the child takes on the identity of the same sex parent; in this way little boys learn to behave like their fathers in a 'masculine' way and little girls begin to behave like their mothers in a 'feminine' way.

7   'Mistakes', for example, according to Freud are seldom if ever random. Thus verbal errors can usually be traced back to unconscious needs or preoccupations; and the person who says to a colleague, 'I've been trying to avoid you all week' when she intended to say 'I've been trying to contact you all week' would be regarded as having made a 'Freudian' slip dictated by unconscious feelings of fear, resentment or rivalry towards her colleague.

8   The case of Little Hans provided much of the material on which Freud based his thinking about the oedipal phase.

9   Repression was seen by Freud as the process by which an unacceptable impulse or idea is made unconscious. For example, in the case of Little Hans, according to Freud, the little boy was not conscious of his deep hostility to his father because he had repressed this hostility.

10.   Adler's changing views on aggression can be traced in Adler (1927, 1931a and 1931b).

11   In further works Freud tended to speak of *a* life instinct and *a* death instinct.

12   Freud also sometimes suggested that the death instinct contained components concerned with the drives for mastery and power. But he did not develop these suggestions to any great extent, concentrating far more on the destructive aspects of the death instinct.

13   Although I have mentioned Hartmann and his associates and Kutash in particular, Freud's work also affected the approaches of others like Klein, Fenichel, Horney and Stone. References to these can be found in Kutash, 1978, or Zillman, 1979.

14   Hartmann, Kris and Lowenstein were never very clear about what they meant by 'instinctive' beyond claiming that the instinct could be hypothesized because people need to fight and this need cannot be traced to any physiological or behavioural source other than an innate predisposition.

15   Storr, while acknowledging the controversial concept of the term 'instinct', defines his use of the term as follows:

> in man, as in other animals, there exists a physiological mechanism which, when stimulated, gives rise both to subjective feelings of anger and also to physical changes which prepare the body for fighting. This mechanism is easily set off, and, like other emotional responses, it is stereotyped and, in this sense, instinctive. (1972, p. 27)

16   Storr does however acknowledge that depression may be caused partly by other factors like 'loss or failure of a personal kind . . . by changes in the body chemistry which accompany the menopause, infections like influenza, or social factors such as depression' (1972, p. 103).

17   Storr uses the term 'paranoid' in its generally accepted sense of a mental disorder where the individual concerned has persistent delusions of persecution and/or power.

18   Storr (1972) considers that paranoia 'in its clear-cut form is best seen in the mental illness known as paranoid schizophrenia'. A balanced account of contemporary perspectives on schizophrenia can be found in Clare, 1980.

19   In his differentiation of a category 'defensive aggression', Fromm moves away from more general conceptions of aggression (see page 9 above), which tends to associate aggression with provocation rather than defence.

20   This description of necrophilia is only developed for boys.

21  A good discussion of feminist issues and psychoanalysis can be found in both Miller, 1973 and Mitchell, 1974.

22  Many experimental studies, both with animals and humans, have shown that the absence of sensory stimulation is a very aversive condition. For example, the experiments performed by Bexton and his associates at McGill University showed that sensory deprivation caused disturbances in perception, irritability, restlessness and emotional distress.

# 5

# Laboratory and Experimental Approaches to Aggression and Violence

This study takes as its point of departure the assumption that *aggression is always a consequence of frustration*. More specifically the proposition is that the occurrence of aggressive behaviour always presupposes the existence of frustration and, contrariwise, the existence of frustration always leads to some form of aggression. (Dollard *et al.*, 1939, pp. 23–4)

A complete theory of aggression, whatever its orientation must explain how aggressive patterns of behaviour are developed, what provokes people to behave aggressively, and what maintains their aggressive actions. (Bandura, 1973, p. 43)

. . . it seems that an enormous educational accomplishment would already be achieved if hostility and aggression were no longer construed as an undeniable part of human nature. Great strides would be made if it were not believed that the inhibition of supposedly built-in or reactive destructive urges is ultimately pathogenic and if it were recognized that the destructive treatment of adversaries, suitable substitutes, or the self is not necessarily a 'healthy' means of coping. (Zillman, 1979, p. 376)

Perhaps the most exhaustive treatment of aggression and violence in the twentieth century has emerged from the studies of academic researchers working within the disciplines of psychology, sociology and criminology, and this chapter and the next are concerned with the approaches of these social scientists.

The volume of work produced by social scientists in the topic area is daunting, ranging as it does from massive tomes presenting individual approaches, through collected sets of readings and published records of symposia, to innumerable articles in academic journals. (For example, Stonner records that between 1970 and 1976, when he wrote his review, over 1,200 articles were listed under the topic of aggression in *Psychological Abstracts*.)

In trying to summarize this enormous body of work, I have decided to divide my presentation into two chapters, drawing for this division on recent analyses of the historical development of the academic disciplines of psychology and sociology (for example, Harrè and Secord, 1972; Billig, 1982). But this division is bound to be idiosyncratic to some extent, and the summary of so much work in such a relatively short account is necessarily condensed and selective. With this last point in mind, a short bibliography is given in the first note of this chapter and of Chapter 6.

This chapter reviews the work of some experimental psychologists whose major influence has been what Armistead has called the field of 'general psychology'. By this term he refers to the mainstream of psychology which has tended to take what could be termed a positivist approach to understanding human nature.[2] Armistead defines positivism in social science rather neatly by stating that positivist accounts 'make the assumption that social facts, like other facts, are out there in the world and it's just a question of measuring them somehow' (1974, p. 18). Thus psychologists working within this tradition tend to focus on those aspects of human (or animal) functioning that are observable and preferably measurable; they have their roots, in fact, in what Stonner has called 'psychology as science'.[3] Not surprisingly, their data is culled mainly from experimental studies, though they also regard as valid data collected from field situations and surveys.

In this chapter I will refer to psychologists who work from this standpoint as 'experimental psychologists'. Armistead has suggested that experimental psychologists all tend to share three interlocking beliefs. The first of these is that psychologists should not seek their material in the verbal or written accounts people may give of their thoughts, feelings, dreams or fantasies, but should concentrate instead on the *observation of behaviour*. Secondly, they believe that not only should behaviour be observed, but it should be *quantified*, in much the same way as physicists measure temperature in degrees. This emphasis on measurement has led to a reliance on data observed under conditions that allow for reliable quantification, that is to a reliance (as noted above) on data obtained within the confines of the experimental situation. Finally, it is contended that the *use of experimental methodology allows psychologists to establish principles of causality in human behaviour*. For example, if in a series of experiments subjects consistently improve their performance on a simple learning task when their correct responses are rewarded, then it could be concluded that rewarding correct responses leads to an improvement in learning.

The work on aggression and violence that I shall be reviewing in this chapter all rests on these three beliefs. In addition, however, such work also seems to be underpinned by a number of other commonly held, though often implicit, assumptions, and I shall describe these in the next section.

## Some Shared Assumptions about Aggression and Violence

On the whole experimental psychologists share a particular assumption about the *origin* of aggressive or violent behaviour. (As will become clear, they are in general less interested in emotions than in behaviour.)[4] This assumption is that *aggressive behaviour is provoked or induced by environmental contingencies*. Although accepting, as Berkowitz puts it, that 'every individual has the neural *capacity* for violence' (1975, p. 217, his italics), they are particularly hostile to the concept of an instinct or innate drive for aggression, as can be seen from the statement by Zillman quoted at the beginning of this chapter.

This, their most central assumption, leads to a second assumption which is that *aggression and violent behaviour are most profitably studied by manipulating environmental contingencies in order to produce such behaviour*. Such manipulation is, as far as they are concerned, best carried out within the confines of the experimental situation.

A third assumption implicit in their acceptance of the second is their belief that the *'aggressive' behaviour that they provoke and measure in the experimental situation is analogous to the behaviour that in everyday life is regarded as 'aggressive'*. I would like to expand on this assumption here by describing the nature of the behaviour which they would describe as aggressive in the experimental situation. In the great majority of such experiments (Baron, 1977), the behaviour is the infliction of an electric shock by the subject on another person. The device used for this is usually the 'Buss aggression machine' or a modification of it. This device consists of a means of administering the shock as well as a dial indicating to the subject the intensity and duration of the shock he or she is administering. In other words, the subject is in control of just how much 'aggression' he or she wishes to display, and the experimenter is able to quantify the 'aggression' by its duration and intensity. (In fact, although the real subject is given an actual shock before the experiment to show that the device works, in the experimental situation, contrary to what he is assumed to believe he is not inflicting actual shocks.)[5]

As this last assumption suggests, experimental psychologists also share a belief that aggression is to be identified with behaviour that results in the infliction of harm or injury. As I mentioned in Chapter 1, this leads them to the assumption that *aggression has no positive aspects*, or to put it more precisely the behaviour that they label as aggressive is behaviour that is specifically directed towards the *intentional infliction of harm or injury*. Berkowitz defends this interpretation as follows: 'If we try to cover such behaviors as assertive salesmanship, striving for mastery, and ethnic prejudice with the same one or two words, we're bound to be somewhat vague and imprecise' (1975, p. 215). So in order to confine their use of the term aggression more precisely, such psychologists have tended to focus on definitions that are concerned with 'the intentional injury of another' (ibid). Similarly Baron defines aggression as 'any form of behavior directed toward the goal of harming or injuring another living human being who is motivated to avoid such treatment' (1977, p. 12). It is this perspective on what may or may not be regarded as aggression that underpins all the work to be discussed in this chapter.

Characteristic of this viewpoint on aggression is an implicit acceptance that violence is simply very forceful aggression. This is seldom explicitly stated, except by Berkowitz who noted that violence is 'the deliberate attempt to do really serious bodily harm' (1976, p. 215). Zillman, for example, in a book of over 400 pages does not even have an entry for violence in his subject index (1979). In general, the assumption of experimental psychologists is that aggression (and violence) are best studied within a tight operational definition which stresses two aspects, first that intentional harm is involved and secondly that the emphasis in such investigation must be on behaviour. Perhaps because of this rather restricted definition of aggression and because of the lack of differentiation between aggression and violence, experimental psychologists display very little interest in what could be called 'pathological' aspects of aggression and violence, for example, sadism. I shall return to this point in the concluding part of this chapter.

Finally, experimental psychologists share an assumption *that it is not important to investigate how subjects view the nature of the experiments they have taken part in*. Thus in the experimental work described below, although subjects are sometimes asked to tick off on a scale how they felt in the experimental situation, they are not asked to explain to the experimenter their own interpretation of the situation they found themselves in.

## Influences on Contemporary Experimental Approaches to Aggression

In an excellent review of what he calls 'aggression in the laboratory', John Sabini (1978) has pinpointed three sets of influences that can be discerned in the evolution of an experimental approach to aggression. These are the study of drive, the study of arousal and the study of social learning. To these three influences could perhaps be added two further and more recent sets of influences – the study of attribution and the study of pro-social behaviour.

## AGGRESSION AND THE NOTION OF DRIVE

The initial model adopted by experimental psychologists to explain aggression was an energy model. That is, they tended to regard aggressive behaviour as resulting from the need to dissipate an aggressive drive. Unlike the ethologists and some psychoanalysts, they did not see this drive as occurring as a result of any innate predispositions, but rather they claimed it arose as a result of a particular set of experiences. Such a view fitted in with the orientation of a group of experimental psychologists in the middle of this century who were working within a motivational viewpoint that tended to place an important emphasis on acquired drives and needs.[6]

To begin with, the particular precipitating circumstances seen as giving rise to a drive associated with aggression were identified *as frustrating experiences*. This association of frustration with aggression was influenced to some extent by Freud's writing on the repression of aggressive and sexual instincts, in that the earliest experimental investigators into frustration, Dollard *et al*. (1939), explicitly attempted to integrate Freudian insights with an experimental methodology. Their earliest formulation of the association of frustration and aggression, quoted at the beginning of this chapter, implied that aggression always occurred as a result of frustration,and frustration always resulted in aggression.

It was soon realized, however, even at the level of general observation, that such an invariance does not hold. For while there is a certain commonsense endorsement that frustrated people can become very angry and indeed antagonistic, there is also an endorsement that continual frustration can sometimes lead individuals to withdraw completely rather than act aggressively. In addition, it soon became obvious that even in laboratory studies frustration did not lead inevitably to aggressive behaviour, so that shortly after Dollard's initial pronouncement, associated psychologists like Miller (1941) amended the link between frustration and aggressive behaviour to the proposition that aggression is the *dominant* response to frustration and that it is really an *instigation to aggressive behaviour* rather than aggression itself that is aroused. Nevertheless, there was a proliferation of experiments designed to show the causal link between frustration and aggression. For example, Barker, Dembo and Lewin (1941) took a number of children to a playroom which contained a large number of very attractive toys. One half of the children were 'frustrated' in that they were only permitted to view these through a window, while the others were allowed to play with them immediately.

Later both groups were allowed to play with the toys and observed. Observers compared the 'constructiveness' of the play between the two groups and it was reported that the first group, who had been frustrated, were more likely to engage in destructive behaviour by, for example, smashing the toys.

The early experimental work on the relationships between frustration and aggression was primarily focused on behaviour designed to vent the hypothesized 'aggressive drive'. No distinction was drawn between the different kinds of motives that might underpin aggressive behaviour. But in the 1960s, experimental psychologists began to distinguish two different kinds of aggression, 'hostile' and 'instrumental', on the basis of a difference between the type of goal the aggressor was trying to achieve (Feshbach, 1964; Buss, 1961).

The first of these terms was used to describe instances of aggression in which the primary or major goal was that of causing the victim to suffer; while the second of the terms was used to describe instances of aggression in which the aggressors sought to assault other persons, not out of a strong desire to see them suffer, but largely as a means of achieving other goals (Baron, 1977). Thus a man who shoots his wife's lover might be assumed to be showing 'hostile' aggression, while a man who in the course of robbing a bank shoots a teller to avoid being apprehended might be assumed to be showing 'instrumental aggression'.

As a result of this rather over-simplified categorization of aggression (and it was the *behaviour* that was characterized rather than the subjective motivation, which was not an area that these psychologists sought to explore), experimental psychologists began to modify their experimental design. The following experiment by Buss (1966) illustrates this twofold categorization of aggression.

In his experiments, subjects were told that they were taking part in a learning task and were to work with another subject (who was in reality a confederate of the investigators). The real subjects were asked to give the dummy subjects an electric shock every time the latter made an error, using the kind of device I have already described, which allowed the subject to vary the intensity and duration of shock and the investigator to measure this as the degree of aggression shown. The real subjects were then divided into two basic conditions, in which some were 'frustrated' and some were not. Those who were frustrated were told either that their own 'know-how' was responsible for their partner's speed of learning, or that their own grade in an introductory psychology course would depend on their partner's speed of learning, while those who were not 'frustrated' were not told of a link between the confederate's performance and their own ability or subsequent psychology grade. In order to investigate the effect of *instrumental* reasons for aggression in this study Buss told some subjects in each of the two 'frustrated' groups and in the 'non-frustrated' group that higher levels of shock would lead to quicker learning, reasoning that this would add an 'instrumental' impetus to the tendency to shock for the groups who were given this information. He found that compared to the 'non-frustrated' groups, only those 'frustrated' subjects who were told that higher levels of shock would be helpful used high levels of shocks. That is, when subjects were not told that higher levels of shock aided learning, there was no difference between 'frustrated' and 'non-frustrated' subjects. Buss concluded from this experiment that frustration does not lead to aggression, *unless* it is accompanied by the knowledge that aggression will be useful in ridding oneself of frustration; that is, frustration does not lead to aggression unless the aggressive behaviour is *instrumental* in achieving other goals.

Returning to the link between frustration and aggression, this experiment, together with a number using the same experimental set-up (electric shocks in a 'learning experiment'), have not yielded any evidence of a strong invariant relationship between frustration and aggression. Some studies like the one just described have shown that frustration in itself is not likely to provoke aggressive responses, but that the knowledge of the efficacy of aggression is likely to enhance aggression; others have shown that whether or not aggression is provoked in an experimental situation will depend on the sex of the subject (Buss, 1963), and yet others have shown that exposure to strong frustration may sometimes serve to reduce rather than enhance aggression. For example, Gentry (1970) showed that male subjects, who were frustrated by an experimenter who repeatedly interfered with their attempts to complete an intelligence test, later delivered lower shocks to the experimenter than subjects who had not been exposed to this treatment. It seems reasonable to conclude with Baron (1977) that in the experimental situation frustration is a relatively weak instigator of aggression and its effect is likely to depend on a number of other variables which may be present in the situation, such as the sex of the participants, the information they may have been given about the efficacy of aggression and the degree of frustration imposed.

But if as a result of these and similar experimental findings few contemporary psychologists continue to believe in a strong and invariant link between frustration and aggressive behaviour, the notion that aggression and frustration are linked continues to exert an influence on some experimental psychologists. Prominent amongst these has been Leonard Berkowitz, who has presented a revised version of the linkage in that he argues that aggression is frequently elicited by 'internal stimulation' which may in many cases derive from frustrating experiences. In essence Berkowitz suggests that the most potent precursors of aggressive behaviour are those emotional reactions which are implicated in what he calls 'impulsive aggression' (a notion rather similar to the concept of hostile aggression). According to Berkowitz (1974), these emotional reactions create a readiness for the performance of aggressive acts, particularly if there are cues (like the presence of weapons) in the environment that may reinforce this predisposition. Such emotional reactions, for example anger, may derive from the experience of frustration, though they may also derive from pain or from the experience of being insulted. I will refer to Berkowitz's views again in the next chapter (and see note 9 below), as he has moved quite substantially away from the views on aggression currently held by experimental psychologists. Before I present these contemporary views, however, I wish to look briefly at other theoretical influences that have shaped these views.

## AGGRESSION AND AROUSAL

As Zillman notes, in the second half of this century a number of theoretical psychologists began to challenge the underlying concepts of drive theory,[7] and consequently experimental psychologists working in the field of aggression began to shun the use of the term because, as he puts it, 'investigators became understandably reluctant to commit themselves to a nomenclature that could make their theoretical positions vulnerable' (1979, p. 158). But even if the term was avoided, or inserted into quotes, the underlying notion of an inner force directing an individual towards aggressive behaviour still remained a very powerful influence on laboratory studies of aggression.

Some aspects of drive theory, as I have noted above, became reflected in Berkowitz's view of anger as a motivator of aggressive behaviour; while another derivation of the energy notion of aggressive behaviour appeared in the work on 'arousal'.

Interest in 'arousal' was stimulated by the work of a number of psychologists (for example, Thompson, 1967) who claimed, as a result of their work in the physiological area, that in vertebrates there was a non-specific energizing force which could be measured through the electroencephalogram, and which was controlled and modified in the brain-stem reticular formation, in particular in what was called the 'reticular activating system'.[8] This force was seen as varying with states of consciousness so that it ranged from its lowest level in the coma state, through deep sleep, light sleep, drowsiness, relaxed wakefulness and alert attentiveness to its strongest level in the state of strong, excited emotions. All these levels of activation were shown to be associated with characteristic wave patterns and rhythms on the electroencephalogram. The term 'arousal' became used to designate the level of activation and to be regarded as a measure, not only of physiological activity in the reticular activating system, but also more loosely to designate an energizing force that potentiates behaviour. It was suggested that in humans arousal could spring not only from physiological processes like the degree to which an individual felt sleepy or alert, but could also be affected by the individual's cognitive and emotional processes. For example, at the cognitive level, if an individual perceived that he or she was in danger he or she could become 'aroused', and at the emotional level, if a person was emotionally upset, he or she could be said to be 'aroused'. The concept of arousal became, in fact, not very different from the concept of a diffuse but energizing drive (see, for example, the discussion in Stonner, 1976).

The concept of arousal was readily incorporated into work on human motivation (Berlyne, 1960), and it was taken up with particular enthusiasm by those experimental psychologists who were working in the field of aggression. It was argued that when an individual became emotionally 'aroused', as for example when frustrated or insulted, he or she became potentiated to take action, and in order to reduce the discomfort that, it was hypothesized, was associated with the emotional arousal, he or she might behave aggressively (if the environment supplied the appropriate cues). But 'arousal' was not only seen as arising from 'internal' conditions, such as feeling emotional, it was also seen as arising from external conditions, and those external conditions that came to be investigated with great vigour were excessive heat, excessive noise, overcrowding and sexual stimulation. It was also suggested that physical exercise which produces higher levels of physiological arousal could intensify aggressive behaviour.

Typically the investigators used the experimental situation that has already been described in that the aggressive behaviour that was measured was giving an electric shock to a confederate of the investigator. For example, Bell and Baron (1976) subjected undergraduates to insults either in a pleasantly cool atmosphere or in uncomfortably hot conditions, and measured the intensity and duration of the electric shocks the subjects subsequently gave to the person who had insulted them. And Geen and O'Neal (1969) investigated the effect of a high noise level by asking subjects to administer shocks to 'victims' at differing noise levels, the subject having being told that the level of shock he was to use was to be related to his assessment of an essay written by the 'victim'.

In general the results of such experiments showed that the relationship between unpleasant environmental conditions and the level of aggressive behaviour displayed was not straightforward. For example, while moderately hot conditions did potentiate aggressive behaviour, excessively hot conditions did not (Baron and Bell, 1975). Further, it became clear that whether or not aggressive behaviour was shown in the experimental situation sometimes depended on the presence or absence of conditions other than a physically uncomfortable environment: for example, whether or not the subjects had been previously angered before being subjected to loud noises (Donnerstein and Wilson, 1976). Yet another variable that appeared to affect the results of such experiments appeared to be the sex of the subject, particularly in the case of overcrowding. In general overcrowding increased the tendency of male but not of female subjects to show aggressive behaviour (Baron, 1977).

The linkage of sexual stimulation to aggressive behaviour in the laboratory situation also showed no straightforward linear relationship between 'arousal' and aggression. Typically these experiments consisted of exposing subjects to erotic stimuli before angering them and then giving them a chance to give an electric shock to the person who had angered them. In general, whether or not erotic stimuli increased the propensity to give shocks appeared to depend on the nature of the erotic stimuli and the sex of the subject (for example, Donnerstein, Donnerstein and Evans, 1975).

Similarly, experiments which investigated the effect of physical exercise on aggression showed that aggression was only intensified by prior exercise under certain experimental conditions, for example, if the aggression could be inflicted on the individual who had directed insults against the subject (Zillmann, Katcher and Milavsky, 1972).

Before I present the theoretical model that Baron has suggested to account for these disparate results on level of arousal and laboratory aggression, I would like to look at the influence of three other important areas of investigation in experimental psychology: social learning, attribution and pro-social behaviour.

SOCIAL LEARNING AND AGGRESSION

While drive theorists and arousal theorists continued to investigate aggressive behaviour from the standpoint of the motive force directing such activity, another group of experimental psychologists, notably Arnold Buss and Albert Bandura, were approaching the experimental study of aggression from quite another direction, influenced by the burgeoning American school of learning theorists.

This school of experimental psychologists concentrated on the study of *learning* because they believed that all behaviour (with the exception of a few reflexes present at birth) is learned. They argued that if behaviour could be broken down into responses, and if psychologists could discover how such responses were acquired or learned, they would be able to build up a science of human and animal behaviour. The three tasks required to understand any form of behaviour were, first, to explain how specific responses *were acquired;* secondly, to explain which features in the environment *elicit specific responses,*[9] and, thirdly, which features in the environment *sustained specific responses.*

Thus Albert Bandura, the most notable exponent of learning approaches to aggression, wrote that 'a complete theory of aggression must explain how aggressive patterns are *developed, what provokes* people to behave aggressively, and *what maintains* their aggressive actions' (1978, p. 31).

In his analysis, Bandura drew on many of the experiments performed by the drive theorists, but he shifted the emphasis away from drives like frustration, which he referred to as 'hypothesized inner determinants', and on to the contingencies that are associated with the appearance and persistence of aggressive patterns of behaviour. In particular, in his experiments he focused on those variables that caused subjects to learn to behave aggressively, and away from the feelings like frustration or humiliation that drive theorists conjectured as underpinning aggressive behaviour. In addition to changing the focus from drive to learning, Bandura also differed from the drive theorists in his insistence that most aggressive behaviour sprang not from the desire to eliminate aversive feelings but from the knowledge that aggression would lead to a desired end. In other words, he argued that drive theorists were too involved with 'hostile' aggression (see above) and did not pay enough attention to the *instrumental* gains that could be accomplished by aggressive behaviour.[10]

In essence, Bandrua was concerned with how people learn to be aggressive, what makes them aggressive in any particular situation and what makes them continue to be aggressive. Indeed, he himself schematized his approach to aggression by dividing the presentation of his theory into the following three categories: the origins of aggression, the instigators of aggression and the reinforcement of aggression. I would like to deal briefly with each of these.

### The origin of aggression
Like other learning theorists, Bandura argued that most complex aspects of behaviour are learned. Aggressive acts could occur spontaneously (as, for example, when a child responds to an attacker by hitting out in a reflex manner) but these would be 'elementary'. For 'most aggressive activities – whether they be duelling with switchblade knives, sparring with opponents, engaging in military combat, or ridiculing an adversary – entail intricate skills that require extensive learning' (1978, p. 31). And learning occurs through observing others – whether this be in the home, in the immediate environment or sub-culture or on the mass media. Such learning occurs because of two 'influences': modelling and reinforcement. (Both these terms have a long and complex history in learning theory, but briefly modelling means imitating and reinforcement means rewarding.)

### The instigators of aggression
Bandura writes that 'a theory must explain not only how aggressive patterns are acquired but also how they are activated and channelled' (1978, p. 39) and he suggests that there are five major instigators of aggressive patterns, once they have been learned. These are modelling influences, incentive inducements, instructional control, delusional control and aversive treatments (these terms will be elaborated below.)

The majority of Bandura's experiments have been concerned with modelling effects. For example, in one particular study (Bandura, Ross and Ross, 1963), young children of nursery-school age were shown a short film in which adults behaved aggressively but in very specific ways to a large inflated toy clown (a Bobo doll, as described on page 42 above), such as sitting on the doll and punching it repeatedly in the nose, hitting it on the head with a toy mallet and saying things like 'Sock him in the nose' and so on. When these children were placed in a room with similar toys they were observed to behave in a very similar manner to the adult models. According to Bandura, such studies indicate that modelling is likely to be enhanced when observers are angered, when the aggression appears to be justified and when the victim has been shown to be associated with aggressive behaviour. While subjects can also refrain from modelling aggressive behaviour when it appears to be unjustified or cruel, according to Bandura, aggression is often facilitated by modelling because the observer loses previously learned inhibitions about aggression and because modelling aggressive behaviour with instruments not previously associated with aggression (for example, the toy mallet in the experiment just referred to) may change the observers' perceptions about the use to which such objects can and should be put.

In modelling, the chief mechanism is, of course, learning. But it is not only in the process of modelling that learning influences aggressive behaviour, for, as we have just seen, Bandura gives three other instigators of aggression that are underpinned by learning. These are incentive inducement (when people are instigated to behave aggressively because they have observed that aggression brings rewards), instructional control (when people learn during their socialization process to obey others and those others instigate or instruct them to behave aggressively) and delusional control (when people believe that others whom they have learned to obey are instigating or instructing them to behave aggressively). In all these cases, aggressive behaviour is both dependent on previous learning and also dictated by 'instrumental' reasons. That is, aggressive behaviour is assumed to be carried out because individuals have learned that it pays off. But does Bandura have no room in his approach for other subjective experiences or reasons that may underpin aggressive behaviour?

The answer to this question is in the affirmative, but with the qualification that Bandura places relatively little emphasis on such issues. For Bandura does accept that occasionally aggression can spring from what he refers to as 'aversive' experiences or treatments. Such aversive treatments include frustration, humiliation, pain and discontent and these experiences Bandura sees as potentiating an emotional state, or in his own terms (and see above) as leading to 'emotional arousal'. This emotional arousal *may*, but only may, lead to aggressive behaviour. For, according to Bandura, emotional arousal may lead as easily to a whole host of other outcomes including dependent behaviour, achievement, withdrawal and resignation, self-anaesthetization with drugs or alcohol, and constructive problem solving. (This conclusion is similar to the approach of the 'arousal' psychologists discussed above.)

## Reinforcers of aggression

If a person behaves aggressively, as a result of aversive experiences or because of modelling influences or because of socialization processes, what is likely to sustain this sort of behaviour? For Bandura the answer is clear cut: 'behaviour is extensively controlled by its consequences' (1978, p. 47). Aggressive behaviour will be repeated when it is rewarding. This may be because it brings direct tangible rewards (for example, when a child seizes a toy belonging to another) or direct intangible ones (for example, when a teenager gains status in the eyes of his peers by acting tough). Yet another form of direct reward is offered when people discover that aggression can lead to the 'alleviation of aversive treatment', as for instance when children who are bullied discover that counter-aggression may bring an end to their own pain and humiliation.

But aggressive behaviour may also, according to Bandura, be indirectly rewarding when it is performed by others. For example, observing that others gain rewards by aggressive behaviour, whether in real life or in the media, offers 'vicarious reinforcement'.

Bandura's earlier social learning approach to aggressive behaviour, focusing as it did on the three traditional prongs of learning theory – acquisition, instigation and reinforcement – placed very little emphasis on internal mental processes as compared to its major emphasis on behaviour, but more recently Bandura (1983) has begun to consider the effect on aggression of what he terms 'self-regulatory mechanisms'.

These mechanisms he traces to the learning of social standards, and he believes they operate in such a way that when an individual transgresses a norm that has been learned, he will disapprove of himself and thus apply a form of 'self-punishment'. So that if children are trained to regard aggression as reprehensible, they are unlikely to engage in aggressive behaviour because of the unpleasant consequences of their self-disapproval. If, however, the situational contingencies do not activate such mechanisms, 'moral people' 'can perform culpable acts' (1983, p. 31). Thus Bandura argues, under the influence of propaganda about one's enemies which dehumanizes them or attributes the blame for conflict to them, even compassionate people can carry out outrageously cruel acts.

In his discussion of these self-regulatory mechanisms, Bandura continues to stress the learning of principles that control behaviour, and he continues to de-emphasize the effect on behaviour of analysis and feelings, arguing that: 'the massive threats to human welfare are generally brought about by deliberate acts of principle rather than by unrestrained acts of impulse' (1983, p. 35). Learning, whether of consequences or principles, remains for Bandura the major mechanisms influencing behaviour. In this view he continues to be somewhat at odds with the later experimental theorists whose work is discussed in the following sections.

## ATTRIBUTION THEORY AND AGGRESSION

In the heyday of behaviourism, when the foundations of much experimental psychology were laid, psychologists were very reluctant to look at the subjective, as distinct from the observable, experience of the subjects they used in their experiments. But, in the 1970s (Billig, 1982), more and more experimental psychologists began asking themselves what kind of 'causal attributions' people make about their own and other people's behaviour? For instance, within the framework of aggression experiments, psychologists began to speculate about how the subjects themselves labelled their own emotional states when, for instance, they were 'insulted' or 'frustrated' (Stonner, 1976). For example, if subjects who are insulted in conditions of extreme heat realize that they are in an extremely hot and uncomfortable situation, do they then show less aggression than subjects who are not feeling hot and uncomfortable, simply because they label their 'aversive condition' as physical discomfort rather than as being upset about being insulted?

Such a reinterpretation of what may have underpinned the inconsistent results referred to above in the experiments on arousal was stimulated by the experiments I described in Chapter 2 by Erdmann and Jancke and by similar ones by Schachter and Singer (1962), in which subjects who had been given a drug which raised their level of physiological arousal reported that they were experiencing particular emotions, such emotions being affected by the cues provided by the experimental situation. These experiments, and the work of attribution theorists such as Kelley (1967), as well as the expanding interest by experimental psychologists in what they called 'cognition' (or more simply 'thinking') led experimental psychologists working in the field of aggression to look rather more intently into their subject's subjective experience. This new focus led them to consider a series of experiments by Stanley Milgram (1974) in which he explored the effect on subjects of social 'obedience'. Using the type of experimental methodology I have already described in which subjects are asked to take part in a 'learning experiment' (see, for example, page 139). Milgram found that the majority of subjects (in his case not only college students but members of the general public) were prepared to administer to their 'pupils' electric shocks at levels that were labelled on the shock-giving device as 'Danger – severe shock', when the experimenter instructed them to do so. In these experiments the subjects had not been 'frustrated' or themselves subjected to unpleasant experiences such as being given electric shocks or insulted; and it was concluded by Milgram and his associates that the only pressure placed upon them was that exerted by the social dynamics of the experimental situation, which forced the subjects, once they had agreed to take part in the experiment, to fall in with the orders issued by the experimenter. In other words, Milgram argued that the major influence contributing to the subjects' infliction of severe electric shocks on their 'pupils' in a learning experiment was their habit of 'obedience to authority' or social conformity.

These experiments led psychologists to speculate whether, in the laboratory as in everyday life, behaviour 'directed towards the injury of others' such as the infliction of electric shocks might spring from causes other than 'frustration', 'arousal' or 'social learning', and they began to consider the effect of the subjects' own 'attributions'. (By this term they referred, as I noted above, to the kind of motives people ascribe to their own behaviour.)

This questioning was given an added impetus by a series of experiments (see Prentice-Dunn and Rogers, 1983) on 'deindividuation'. In such experiments it was shown that subjects who were hooded or who were told that their behaviour would not be evaluated by others were far more likely to behave aggressively in the laboratory situation than controls who were not hooded or who had not been assured that their behaviour would not be subject to scrutiny.

These deindividuation experiments, together with Milgram's and the inconsistent results referred to in the previous sections of this chapter, forced experimental psychologists to question their initial premises concerning the irrelevance of their subjects' subjective experience. But before I describe how their views have been integrated in Baron's more comprehensive interpretation I would like to refer briefly to one final influence on experimental accounts of aggression, the influence of work on 'pro-social behaviour'.

PRO-SOCIAL BEHAVIOUR AND AGGRESSION

It seems rather surprising that approaches to aggression seldom devote any considerable discussion to those factors that might be supposed to inhibit or counteract aggressive behaviour. Indeed, looking back at the three theoretical approaches we have surveyed so far, the physiologically oriented psychobiological, the sociobiological, and the psychoanalytic, the only consideration in any depth that has been given to what could be called 'obverse' factors was in the case of those sociobiologists (Chapter 3) who suggest that there is innate pre-programming for altruism as well as aggression.

The experimental approach to aggression continues this general trend. Although in the last twenty years there has been a slow burgeoning of interest among mainstream psychologists in what is variously referred to as 'moral development', 'moral behaviour' and 'pro-social behaviour' (including the study of altruism and empathy), experimental texts in the area of aggression seldom make any reference to this literature.[11] For example, Bandura's text (1973) of just under 400 pages contains no index references to moral behaviour or development, ethics, pro-social behaviour, altruism or empathy, and Zillmann (1979) covers only one of these aspects, moral judgement, and this in the context of whether or not an act is labelled aggressive by an observer.

In Chapter 7 I shall discuss ways in which the consideration of empathy, altruism, moral development and behaviour and guilt can illuminate our understanding of aggressive and violent behaviour, but at this stage I want to look only at the limited impact the study of these areas has had on experimental work on aggression.

The study of moral behaviour and moral development had until the last two decades received very little attention from mainstream psychologists, but towards the middle of the 1960s and during the 1970s there was a surge of interest amongst psychologists in questions concerned with *moral behaviour*, for example, how moral values are acquired, what factors influence the way people behave in situations requiring moral decisions, and whether or not there are universals in moral development (Lickona, 1976, Kohlberg, 1976). This research has had very little impact on experimental approaches to aggression, except to the extent that it was acknowledged that sometimes, in real life situations, people might censor their own aggressive behaviour in terms of the moral values that they had learned. Thus, typically, Bandura notes that people learn to respond evaluatively to their own behaviour because

> Parents and other socialization agents subscribe to certain norms of what constitute worthy or reprehensible performances. They are inclined to respond approvingly when a child meets moral standards, whereas they are quick to reprimand him whenever he deviates from the way he is expected to behave. As a result of such differential treatment, children eventually come to respond to their own actions with self-approval and self-criticism in accordance with the standards originally set by others. (1973, pp. 208–9)

More recently in mainstream psychology, there has been a proliferation of studies in what has been called 'pro-social' rather than moral behaviour (Eisenberg, 1982). This term is the one used to refer to a person's behaviour when he or she is more concerned with the welfare of others than with their own individual welfare. 'Pro-social behaviour' is often discussed in conjunction with altruism, which is generally taken to mean 'regard for, or devotion to, the interests of others' (Zahn-Waxler and Radke-Yarrow, 1982, p. 110).

Psychological research on altruism (as distinct from the sociobiological approach to altruism discussed in Chapter 3) suggests that it may spring at least in part from empathy (Feshbach and Roe, 1968). By empathy, psychologists refer to what they call a 'vicarious affective response' (Hoffman, 1982), or more simply the emotion that is aroused when an onlooker fully understands and shares the emotions of someone who is in the throes of an emotional state.

A number of developmental studies have been undertaken to show that training in empathy, or the ability to put oneself in the place of others both at the emotional and at the thinking level, is likely to make children more inclined to act in pro-social ways. These developmental studies have also linked empathy training with a reduction in aggressive behaviour because in general it has been found that as children grow older, the ability to empathize with others is likely to be accompanied by a reduction in aggressive behaviour. [12]

Laboratory studies by experimental psychologists working with older subjects have not shown a clear-cut link between empathy and aggression. In such studies it has been assumed that exposing subjects to the fact that their 'victims' experience pain on being shocked is likely to produce feelings of empathy (an assumption that can, of course, be questioned). Studies proceeding on this assumption have sometimes found that exposing subjects to information about the degree of pain felt by their 'victims' after they had given them shocks in a typical 'learning' experiment sometimes caused subjects to give lower levels of shocks and sometimes actually caused subjects to give higher levels of shocks. Not surprisingly the deciding factor appeared to be the relationship between the subject and the 'victim'. For example, in an experiment by Baron (1977), in half the cases subjects had previously been 'angered' by their victim and half the subjects had not. The 'angered' subjects were more likely to intensify shocks and to report that they felt relaxed and cheerful after being given feedback about their victim's pain, while the 'non-angered subjects' after the same feedback lessened the shock level and reported negative shifts in mood. Once again the experiments seem to lead to the conclusion that attributional processes, or learning how subjects interpret their own feelings, must be taken into account in laboratory studies of aggression, and this is an area to which I will return.

## Contemporary Views on Aggression Held by Experimental Psychologists

In the preceeding section, I looked at five threads that have contributed to contemporary views on aggression held by experimental psychologists, reviewing in turn the contributions of the study of drive, arousal, social learning, attribution and pro-social behaviour. In this section I should like to look at the way Robert Baron has united these threads into a comprehensive approach to human aggression.[13]

Baron (1977, 1983), as I have already mentioned, takes the view that aggression should be defined as behaviour that is directed towards harming or injuring others who are motivated to avoid such injury. Like most contemporary experimental psychologists he differentiates between instrumental and hostile aggression, though he prefers Zillman's terms of 'incentive motivated' (for instrumental aggression) and 'annoyance motivated' (for hostile aggression). His general approach is atheoretical in that he directs attention to three 'determinants' of aggressive behaviour, 'social', 'environmental and situational' and 'individual', without explicitly placing either his approach or his general orientation in any particular theoretical context. But he appears implicitly to accept as beyond argument both that psychology is best regarded as a science, and that when an experimental psychologist measures behaviour there are no issues of subjectivity involved. Thus, once he has defined, within any experimental situation, behaviour as aggressive, he never stops to consider the extent to which others might agree that, say, car 'horn honking' (which he has taken as an index of aggression in field experiments) is aggressive behaviour, or whether what he chooses to measure as aggressive behaviour is in fact the only aggressive behaviour displayed by the subject in any particular experiment.

Baron's approach is never explicitly stated as a set of postulates, hypotheses or even assumptions. Rather, as with the work of many experimental psychologists, it is left to the reader to piece together from the empirical findings cited precisely how the psychologist unites the findings within a conceptual framework.

I will now look briefly at Baron's delineation both of the determinants of aggressive behaviour and at measures that can be taken to control such behaviour, attempting as I do this to abstract the conceptual framework that I think underpins Baron's approach to aggression.

## SOCIAL DETERMINANTS

Starting with the premise that 'aggression does not occur in a "social vacuum" ' (1977, p. 122), Baron argues that aggressive behaviour always has 'social antecedents'.[14] In discussing these social antecedents, he draws on experiments relating the effects of frustration, the effect of emotional arousal (for example, experiments when people are insulted), the effects of physical pain (for example, experiments when the subjects themselves receive electrical shocks), the effects of social modelling (Bandura's experiments in which children are exposed to adults beating up a Bobo doll) and the effect of obedience (Milgram's experiments on obedience to authority), concluding that aggressive behaviour often '*stems from aspects of the social environment that instigate its occurrence and influence both its form and direction*' (ibid., p. 122 my italics).

## ENVIRONMENTAL AND SITUATIONAL DETERMINANTS OF AGGRESSION

While acknowledging that such underlying background factors may affect the individual's predisposition to behave aggressively, Baron argues that his or her *actual* behaviour in any given situation will be influenced by additional factors. Prominent amongst these additional factors are those contributed both by the way the subject interprets the situation he or she finds him or herself in, and the actual situation itself.

Looking first at the former aspect, the subject's understanding of the situation, Baron draws on attribution theory to explain some of the seemingly inconsistent results referred to on pages 142–3 above. Take, for example, the inconsistent results on the effects of heating, where mild degrees of heating contributed to higher levels of aggression while extreme degrees did not. In the section on attribution theory, I suggested that this could be explained by arguing that if subjects are hot enough to realize that they are in an uncomfortable physical atmosphere, they may interpret their emotional arousal as due primarily to heat rather than frustration, and consequently be less likely to aggress than subjects who do not make this interpretation. Baron uses this type of explanation, which draws on the experimenter's *interpretation* of the subject's 'attributions', to explain not only the seemingly inconsistent effects of heating, but also the inconsistent results obtained from those experiments which showed that physical exercise only contributed to higher levels of aggression if the target victim had previously frustrated or humiliated the subject. Baron explains this result as follows: physical exercise contributes to higher levels of arousal and such arousal may contribute to different kinds of behaviour. Amongst such potential behaviour is aggressive behaviour. If the victim offers to the subject a justifiable target because he has previously insulted or humiliated the subject, the subject will actually behave aggressively, but if the victim does not appear to be a justifiable target, the subject may refrain from aggression. Thus, as in the case of the heating experiments, the subject's 'attributions' about the experimental set-up are regarded as affecting his behaviour.

But, according to Baron, it is not only the attributions a subject makes that may affect behaviour in a given situation. Baron also argues that behaviour may be affected by other situational variables. Take the inconsistent results on crowding, where crowding contributed to higher levels of aggression for males but not for females. Whether or not crowding contributes to feeling unpleasantly emotionally aroused may depend, according to Baron, on the sex of the subject, because crowding tends to act as an intensifier of already existing emotional moods. If girls quite like the experience of being with others and are thus fundamentally quite well disposed to being in close contact with their peers, then crowding will intensify positive rather than negative feelings. Male subjects, on the other hand, who have been encouraged to view the experimental situation of being herded in with their peers as basically competitive, may find that further overcrowding intensifies their negative feelings against their peers. [15]

Crowding thus has a differential effect depending on situational variables, such as the interaction between subjects. According to Baron, situational variables also play a part in another series of experiments which yielded inconsistent results, the experiments on sexual arousal. I noted earlier that whether or not sexual arousal contributed to higher levels of aggression depended on the nature of the stimuli. In general it has been found, that showing males highly erotic pictures (for example, explicit sexual intercourse) raised levels of aggression when subjects were subsequently insulted, while exposing them to Playboy centrefolds did not. Baron interprets these results to mean that very high sexual arousal spills over into the only active behaviour available, aggression, while mild erotic arousal distracts the subject into thinking about erotica rather than the insults and thus deflects aggression.

This sensitivity to situational factors allows Baron to refine the interpretation of aggression experiments to a limited extent. But the extent remains limited for two reasons: first, Baron makes assumptions about what the subjects' attributions are likely to be, rather than asking them directly (after the experiment) how they viewed the motivations for their behaviour in the experiment, and secondly because Baron never seems to question the extent to which students entering voluntarily into an 'experiment' mirror the reactions and behaviours of people who in everyday life experience frustration, humiliation and other aversive conditions. In particular, psychologists like Baron fail to discuss the effect of the continual frustration and humiliation which occur for some people in their life situations and which are clearly difficult and undesirable to parallel in experimental situations.

## INDIVIDUAL DETERMINANTS OF AGGRESSION

While Baron's approach to aggression is dependent largely on the dynamics of the actual experimental situation, he also turns his attention to certain individual differences which he believes may affect the extent to which people will behave aggressively. These differences he sees as depending on subjects' fear of social disapproval, their feelings of guilt concerning hurting others, their ability to empathize with others and their overall sense of values.

Despite, however, this nod in the direction of normative values, empathy and guilt, Baron, in common with other writers on aggression, as I noted earlier, places very little emphasis on prosocial factors in counteracting aggression, except in as much as these are suggested as a possible alternative to aggressive behaviour when arousal is high. This stance and its emphasis on the control of aggressive behaviour, rather than on the understanding of the motivation for aggressive behaviour, are reflected in Baron's recommendations for the prevention of human aggression.

BARON'S RECOMMENDATIONS FOR THE PREVENTION AND CONTROL OF HUMAN AGGRESSION

For Baron, aggressive behaviour is first and foremost learned:

> it seems to be a learned form of social behaviour, acquired in the same way as other types of activity and influenced by many of the same social, situational and environmental factors. Aggression, in short, is not genetically or instinctively preordained; it arises, instead, from a complex of conditions that encourage – and stimulate – its occurrence. (1977, p. 269)

Because of this emphasis on learning, Baron's first recommendation is that children should be exposed to as little aggression and violence as possible, whether this exposure be in films, television, comic or real life.

Secondly, according to Baron, we should seek to eliminate social conditions that both encourage and reward the performance of overt aggression. Aggression and violence should not be rewarded in any way, as they currently are both in childhood, when 'young children (especially boys) are frequently praised by both peers and their parents for behaving in a tough "macho" manner', or in adulthood, when 'adults are rewarded for acting aggressively in settings ranging from the athletic field to the executive boardroom' (ibid., p. 270).[16]

Thirdly, we should seek to eliminate from the environment those contingencies that either provoke excessive arousal, for example crowding, or provide situational cues, for example the presence of weapons. Fourthly, we should seek to provide non-aggressive models for both adults and children by providing examples of people who when provoked or aroused behave in non-aggressive ways. For Baron, as for Bandura, the concept of modelling is an integral component of an understanding of human psychology in general, and in particular the concept of modelling plays a most important part in their recommendations for the control of aggression. To begin with, according to Baron and Bandura, exposure to non-aggressive models serves to strengthen people's inhibitions and restraints against aggressing. Such exposure also serves to reduce the level of arousal in potentially explosive situations. Further, and most significantly, the model provides opportunities for people to learn to imitate non-aggressive strategies for handling potentially violent situations. Models, of course, must be credible; we are, according to Baron and Bandura, most likely to accept as models those whom we see as attractive, powerful, and similar, at least in some aspects, to ourselves.

A fifth recommendation concerns the provision of alternative outlets for arousal in potentially explosive situations. If, as Baron believes, emotional arousal can be dissipated in a number of alternative ways, we must seek to optimize the chances of people dealing with emotional arousal in a constructive, rather than a destructive, manner. By encouraging empathy, for example, we are likely to open people to understanding why others behave in what may appear to be so provocative and arbitrary a fashion.[17] In addition to encouraging empathic rather than angry emotional responses, Baron believes we should also encourage people to react, when aroused, with humour or lust rather than anger.

In making this recommendation, Baron draws on a field experiment in which male motorists were exposed to three experimental situations, before being frustrated by having a car in front of them stall and thus delay them. In the first experimental condition, the motorists were exposed to 'empathy' (a girl crossed the road in front of them on crutches), in the second they were exposed to humour (a girl crossed the road in front of them wearing 'an outlandish clown mask'), in the third they were exposed to 'mild sexual arousal' (a girl crossed the road in front of them 'wearing a very brief and revealing outfit'). In all three cases the exposed subjects 'honked their horns' less when the car stalled in front of them than subjects who had not been exposed to 'empathy', 'sexual arousal' or 'humour'. (Baron, 1983, p. 186)

I shall return to this experiment when I look at criticisms of experimental approaches to aggression, but here I would like to note that Baron does not explain quite how this methodology for controlling aggression can be used to deflect emotional arousal in circumstances that are rather more serious than minor traffic jams.

The same sort of comment, that it is perhaps inappropriate to generalize from structured experimental or field situations to the complex, multifaceted interactions of real life, can be levelled at Baron's final set of recommendations, which concern the use of punishments and threats of punishment to control aggressive behaviour. Baron claims that the threat of punishment is only effective if the persons who are preparing to aggress are not very angry, the magnitude of the punishment threatened is great, the probability of actually being punished rather than threatened is high and, finally, the potential aggressors have comparatively little to gain from the aggression. Actual punishment, Baron claims, is only effective in stopping aggression when it is administered in a sure, predictable manner, directly after the aggression has been carried out, and it is administered by people whom the aggressor or aggressors regard as legitimate authorities. These recommendations, though Baron does not acknowledge it explicitly, are with the exception of the reference to legitimate authority, derived directly not so much from work on aggression, as from the rather more general 'laws' that experimental psychologists postulated from the series of experiments on learning.

In short, after a comprehensive review of the plethora of experimental studies, Baron produces what amounts to a further development of Bandura's social learning approach. Aggressive behaviour is a way of dealing with social situations. In general an individual is more likely to use it if he or she has been exposed to a great deal of it and has seen it to be an effective manner of dealing with social situations. 'Arousal', whether emotional or physical, energizes behaviour and may energize aggressive behaviour rather than other types of behaviour, depending on the situational cue, the individual's perception of the situation, and the individual's set of values. Further, the predisposition to aggressive behaviour may be weakened in any situation if other alternative modes of behaviour are possible.

Baron's approach, in common with the work of other experimental psychologists discussed in this chapter, rests on a number of implicit assumptions. The most salient of these concern the relevance of findings from controlled studies to everyday life. Before looking critically at these approaches I wish to turn briefly to three areas concerned with aggression and violence which have been continuing foci of concern for experimental psychologists.[18] These are catharsis, sex differences in aggression and violence and the influence of the media on aggression and violence.

## Catharsis

The concept of catharsis can be traced back to the writing of Aristotle, who explained the popularity of Greek tragic theatre by suggesting that the audience, in vicariously experiencing emotions like pity and fear, were able to purge themselves of these emotions. While Aristotle did not himself refer directly to the purging of aggressive emotions in this way, the concept of catharsis was elaborated and extended to aggression by Freud. Freud (see Chapter 4) believed that it was essential for emotional well-being that the aggressive instinct be released, and that one method of doing this was through the expression of aggressive emotions which could provide 'catharsis' for the aggressive instinct. This position has been endorsed by subsequent instinct and drive theorists such as Lorenz, Storr and Dollard, who have argued that letting off steam by giving vent to emotions arising from the aggressive drive is beneficial, not to say therapeutic. 'Catharsis' in this sense has provided a rationale for a number of often diverse recommendations for dealing with aggression. These have ranged from solving international conflict by emphasizing competition in sports, through providing children with aggressive toys so they can sublimate their hostility, to urging people in psychotherapy to vent their repressed feelings of rage and anger by battering large foam cushions.

Contemporary experimental psychologists who, as we have seen, reject the notion of an aggressive drive, have naturally found the concept of catharsis challenging to say the least, and an enormous amount of time and energy has been expended on experiments designed to investigate catharsis. Broadly speaking these have looked at the following issues: is arousal (measured either physiologically or on self report of emotional state) lowered after subjects, who have been frustrated or humiliated, are allowed to behave aggressively to their tormentor by, say, inflicting electric shocks on him, or making negative judgements of him? If so, is this evidence of the 'cathartic' effect of aggression or can similar reductions in arousal be shown, if subjects perform any other activity such as rewarding their tormentor or punishing themselves? Is there any evidence for 'vicarious catharsis': that is, are there reductions in levels of aggressive behaviour after frustrated or humiliated subjects watch aggressive films or listen to videos of 'aggressive humour', or take part in boxing matches or are encouraged to write fantasy stories to express their feelings? Are there sex differences in any of these investigations and, finally, do subjects show any differences that could be ascribed to their usual mode of behaving, for example, are there differences in the effectiveness of catharsis between prisoners who habitually react to threats of violence passively and prisoners who react actively?

Reviewing the often inconsistent results of these studies, contemporary experimental psychologists (for example, Quanty, 1976, Zillman, 1979 and Baron and Byrne, 1981) argue that in general the results support a social learning rather than a drive reduction explanation for 'catharsis'. The social learning interpretation rests on the major premise that arousal, following frustration or humiliation, is reduced *when a subject engages in active behaviour that has previously been effective in reducing arousal*. Thus while some people experience a lessening in arousal following frustration or humiliation after 'aggressive behaviour' (such as inflicting electric shocks on their tormentor), others (predominantly people who are habitually passive rather than active and those who are prone to high levels of guilt) experience a reduction in arousal after self-punishment or even after rewarding their tormentor. In other words, while aggression may be 'cathartic' for some, masochism or appeasement may be cathartic for others.

The results from the experiments on indirect or 'vicarious' catharsis have been particularly inconsistent. These experiments have been concerned with subjects who have been humiliated or frustrated and then exposed to films or videos of aggressive behaviour. For 'vicarious catharsis' to be demonstrated, it has to be shown that viewing such films can serve to lower the tendency to behave aggressively. But as I have noted, the results are so inconsistent that no firm conclusions about the effect of vicarious catharsis can be drawn (see Quanty, 1976).

Currently, despite the large number of experimental investigations of catharsis, few experimental psychologists would be prepared to go much beyond the following rather guarded comments of Baron and Byrne:

> First (as just suggested), catharsis is not nearly as widespread or as general as once believed. Second, while the opportunity to 'even the score' with persons who have provoked us sometimes reduces our tendency to aggress against them on later occasions, this is not always so. Finally, while participation in cathartic activities may sometimes succeed in reducing overt aggression, the potential benefits of such procedures have probably been overstated in the past. (1981, p. 353)

## Experimental Work on Sex Differences in Aggression

That males are more prone to aggression and violence than females is a premise that has been referred to twice before. In Chapter 3 I reviewed empirical studies relating to the physiological sex differences that might underlie such differences and also evidence for sex differences in this area in non-human species. In Chapter 4 I summarized the position held by many psychoanalysts that it is somehow 'healthier' for males to be aggressive and dominant than it is for females. I now want to look at a third approach to sex differences in aggression and violence, that of the experimental psychologists who have documented such differences in experimental or field situations.[19] I also want to look at the interpretation they place on the results of such studies.

As with the majority of studies referred to in this chapter, much of the experimental work on sex differences on aggression has been based on the Buss paradigm, where the subject is told that the experiment is concerned with the effect of punishment (electric shocks) on learning. These studies, and some studies of self-report of aggression, have tended to show, but by no means consistently, that males are more aggressive than females. But other experimental studies, for example of verbal aggression, hostility in dreams, making loud noises to annoy the victim and so on, have not found sex differences on aggression. Certain experimental factors have, however, been shown to effect the results of studies of sex differences in the experimental situation. For example, if the 'aggression' is justifiable, and could possibly be regarded as prosocial, as in the Milgram studies where the aggression was administered in obedience to authority, women are as likely to give electric shocks as men

(Frodi, Macaulay and Thome, 1977). There is also some evidence that although both men and women can be influenced by aggressive cues in the environment, cues such as weapons and aggressive models or other male observers may lead men to be more aggressive than women (for example, Lando *et al.*, 1975). Finally Zillman (1979) suggests that the experimental data supports the conclusion that women are more effective minimizers of annoyance than men; for angered males are more likely to respond aggressively, even when it is clearly counterproductive to do so than females are.

In sum, laboratory studies on sex differences in the propensity to behave aggressively yield no consistent differences and when we turn to the studies psychologists have conducted outside the laboratory the same picture emerges. Such studies centre primarily on the observation of aggressive behaviour in children in their social interactions. In the West, some such studies (for example, Lefkowitz *et al.*, 1977) show boys to be consistently more aggressive and that such sex differences tend to increase with age, but cross-cultural studies do not support this conclusion, indicating rather that where sex differences in aggression exist these are more consistently found in the style and target of aggression rather than in the quantity of aggression displayed (White, 1983).

In interpreting these complex and largely inconsistent results from empirical studies of sex differences in aggression, experimental psychologists tend to minimize the effects of physiological variables (for example, of hormones)[20] and to stress the effect of sex roles and sex stereotypes. For example, Lefkowitz and his colleagues conclude that although the data of their longitudinal study

> cannot refute the possible contribution of biological and hormonal components in the causation of aggressive behaviour, they can and do support the theory that different socialization practices used in rearing male and female children contribute to at least some of the differences in aggressive behaviour attributable to gender. (1977, p. 92)

Thus they argue that women are trained to respond to aggression with more anxiety than men, to suppress aggressiveness and dominance in their behaviour and to avoid situations where they are required to react aggressively, whereas males, because aggression is socially approved for them, are less likely to feel anxious or guilty when they behave aggressively, and indeed are often under social pressure to seek out situations in which they can assert their dominance. While endorsing this view other psychologists point out that as Western societies move towards less clearly differentiated sex roles, and as social forces such as the women's movements reduce the effectiveness of sex stereotyping, we will find decreasing evidence for sex differences in aggression. As Baron puts it, such cultural shifts may

> have served to render women less inhibited about responding aggressively to direct provocation . . . In short the two sexes may gradually become more equal in their propensity for violence as well as in their tendency to more desirable forms of behaviour. (1977, p. 221)

## Experimental Psychologists and the Influence of the Media on Aggression and Violence

In the last decade few aspects of aggression and violence have had more popular impact than the influence of the media on violent behaviour. Recently, for example, the public have been very stirred by the suggestion that not only do a large minority of young children watch 'video nasties', but that such exposure actually desensitizes children to violence.[21] Following the racial disturbances of the early 1980s there were many allegations in the popular press that the televising in news reports of violent incidents induced certain susceptible target groups to mimic these incidents – the so-called copy-cat effect.

Underlying such popular concern has been a belief that a *simple, uni-directional causal relationship exists between watching violence and behaving violently subsequently.* Thus reports on this issue in, for example, daily newspapers, seldom point out that the association of two phenomena does not necessarily mean that one *causes* the other. The fact that a particular country has both higher levels of urban crime than other countries, and also a higher incidence of the televising of urban crime, may be due to factors other than the simple effect of the media on behaviour. It could be that in that country a general belief that violence is permissible under stressful circumstances has led both to less inhibitions about portraying violence on television, and to a more relaxed attitude towards the right of citizens to carry firearms. Similarly, the fact that certain groups of people both watch more violent television than their peers and also behave more violently may be due as much to the fact that they enjoy violence, whether watching or perpetrating it, as to the fact that watching violence makes people behave violently (Eysenck and Nias, 1980).

But it is not only in the popular press that a direct causal link between watching and carrying out violence has been proposed, for much of the experimental work on the media and violence has been done within what Rowland calls the 'restrictive paradigmatic focus' of a causal link between watching violence and behaving violently. This focus has emphasized the connection between the viewing of discrete incidents of violence and subsequent violent behaviour, rather than exploring the association between the media and violence within the 'context of broad, social and cultural questions about, say, meaning, history and community' (Rowland, 1983, p. 229).

The work of experimental psychologists in the area is characterized by two tendencies. First, it is the one area in which they use the term 'violence' in preference to the term 'aggression'. (This may be in response to the manner in which it is referred to at the more popular level.) And secondly, perhaps because of their implicit acceptance of the cause–effect paradigm, their work has been dominated by a tendency to set themselves a series of fairly straightforward questions. These have included the following: does exposing children to films or tapes of models behaving violently make them behave more aggressively or violently (for example, Friedrich and Stein, 1973)? Do people who watch more violent television than their peers behave more violently (for example, Belson, 1978)? Do children who habitually watch more violent television than their peers show less physiological arousal, like a raised heart-rate, when exposed to violent tapes or films in the laboratory than their peers do (for example, Cline, Croft and Courier, 1973)? Does observing violence that subjects are told is 'real' create more physiological arousal than watching violence that subjects are told is just fiction (for example, Geen and Rakosky, 1973)? Are violent television programmes and films more popular than non-violent ones (for example, Diener and deFour, 1978)? And does the extent to which viewers identify with violent protagonists affect the extent to which they subsequently behave aggressively (for example, Eron, 1982)?

The results of the hundreds of studies that have been carried out to answer these and related questions have been summarized both in academic reviews (for example, Geen, 1976, Comstock *et al.*, 1978), and in reports resulting from government sponsored research (for example, the 1972 Surgeon-General's Report in the USA, and Home Office publications such as the one on film censorship and violence, Home Office Research Study, 1977, in the UK).

These reviews seem in general to agree that the experimental and field studies that they summarize reveal the following:

(i) *Observing violence tends to facilitate behaving violently or aggressively*
This generally endorsed finding is explained in different ways by experimental psychologists of different orientations. For example, it is explained in terms of learning theory and modelling and incentive inducement (see pages 143–7 above); in terms of the conditioning of aggressive responses by Berkowitz (see note 9 below), and in terms of the arousal enhancement (see pages 141–3 above).

(ii) *When people observe violence, the meaning that they ascribe to its effects modifies the extent to which it will facilitate violent or aggressive behaviour.*

This finding is interpreted in terms of attribution theory and has been discussed with relation to experiments which demonstrate that in general observing 'real' violence is more facilitative of violent behaviour than observing fictional violence, that observing violence that appears to be justified is more facilitative than observing 'unjustified' violence, and that the extent to which observers identify with violent protagonists affects how violent or aggressively they behave subsequently.

(iii) *The popularity of television programmes does not appear to be affected by the degree of violence they portray.*

These findings and their interpretation have led most experimental psychologists to conclude not only that there is a causal link between media violence and violent behaviour, but that the censorship of violence in the media is both justified and likely to be effective. This conclusion and the findings on which it is based has been challenged on three major grounds.[22] First (for example, Rowland, 1983), experimental psychologists have been criticized for looking at the issue too narrowly, and for not locating the discussion within the complex social climate in which people live and which affects not only their ideology and value systems but also the pressure groups which control and subsidize popular entertainment and news coverage. (I will return to this discussion in the next two chapters.) And secondly (for example, Hall, 1976), experimental psychologists have been criticized for their methodology, which has largely relied on studies in which violent incidents are portrayed in isolation, rather than in the context of the whole film or tape from which they have been abstracted. Thus in the experimental studies the viewing of violence is placed in a context that is not typical of normal everyday viewing, where violence is usually portrayed as part of an extended real or fictional treatment of a particular theme or story. Thirdly (see Howitt and Cumberbatch, 1975 and Howitt, 1982), some social psychologists have claimed that the experimental and field studies on which the conclusions for a causal influence have been based are radically flawed both in design and in the interpretations drawn.

Finally, I would like to look briefly at reported incidents of 'copy-cat' violence. While experimental psychologists such as Bandura, in the defence of the 'copy-cat' hypothesis, often point to explicit incidents where a televised crime is faithfully reproduced by a viewer, Eysenck and Nias (1980) amongst others argue that while the televised incident may affect the precise manner in which a crime of violence is carried out, there is no way of proving that the perpetrator of the crime would not have carried out the same crime using a different technique, even if he or she had not been conveniently provided with a specific example. Turning to the more generalized effect of televising actual events like street disturbances, Tumber (1982) has concluded that there is little evidence that recent street disturbances in Britain were escalated in any way by media coverage.

## Criticisms of the Work of Experimental Psychologists in the Field of Aggression and Violence

> Psychology seems to have wanted to attain respectability by imitating the methods of the natural sciences albeit those of fifty years ago . . . (Fromm, 1977, p. 78)

It should be clear by now that experimental psychologists have striven to investigate aggression and violence as 'objectively' as possible by working within the framework used in the natural sciences. Thus they have based their writing on aggression largely on the results of laboratory or field studies and, unlike the psychoanalysts whose work was covered in the last chapter, they have refrained (on the whole) from drawing on clinical or anecdotal evidence. In conducting their studies they have taken scrupulous care to follow the methodology of the natural sciences by setting up hypotheses, outlining their experimental procedure, quantifying their results, subjecting these results to rigorous statistical tests,[23] and drawing only those conclusions that they consider to be justified by the experimental results.

Before dealing with wider criticisms of their approach, I will touch briefly on some specific criticisms that can be made of their experimental methodology. In the main these criticisms spring from the difficulty of isolating and defining quantifiable instances of behaviour. Unlike the natural sciences, where it is comparatively easy for scientists to agree on fundamental variables and their parameters (for example, measuring temperature in absolute degrees), psychologists have been unable to define or agree about fundamental variables of behaviour.

SPECIFIC CRITICISMS

As I have noted throughout the chapter, some aspects of the experimental methodology used by experimental psychologists are controversial. Take, for example, the behaviour that is labelled as aggressive and remember that, as far as experimental psychologists are concerned, the distinguishing feature of aggressive behaviour is that it is directed towards injuring others. In the Buss paradigm, subjects, nearly always undergraduates, are told that they are to take part in an experiment that

is concerned with the effect of punishment on learning. They are introduced to (or are told about) their 'pupil' who is to be given an electric
shock when he or she makes an error. And they are told to follow this
course of action by a person whom they may suppose to be a responsible
adult – either a member of staff or a graduate student. When they do
actually, in obedience to their instructions, administer an electric shock,
can the experimenter be sure enough of their motives to assume that their
primary aim is to injure?

Perhaps, for example, they trust the experimenter and believe, as
Frodi, Macaulay and Thome (1977) suggest, that their treatment of the
'pupil' is actually in the interest of science and therefore prosocial. Or
perhaps they do not really believe, even if they are first themselves given
a shock on the apparatus, that their victims are actually feeling pain.
They may believe that responsible experimenters would not actually
permit this to happen and they may thus treat the whole experimental
set-up very sceptically.

Perhaps, as Milgram's (1974) experiments suggest, they may be so
trapped in what has sometimes been called the 'demand characteristics'
of the experiment that they inflict the shocks largely because they feel
they have no other choice. Once again the motivation would not
primarily be to injure, but in this case simply to conform to their
instructions. And incidentally, if this does occur, how ethical is it to
expose subjects to the knowledge that they are prepared to actually injure
their fellow students to the extent that they actually 'gasp and groan'
(Frodi, Macaulay and Thome, 1977, p. 639).

In sum, it seems to me that the measure of aggressive behaviour used
in the experiments based on the Buss paradigm does not necessarily fall
within the definition set up by the experimental psychologists themselves: behaviour directed towards the injury of others. I also feel certain
reservations about other measures of aggression used by experimental
psychologists. Take, for example, the Baron field experiment described
above in which the aggressive behaviour measured was 'car honking'.
Can sounding your horn at another driver really be equated with the
desire to injure him or her?

Another controversial area of experimental methodology occurs in the
experiments concerned with 'arousal'. As I noted, arousal is a term that
has been used to refer both to the physiological activity and to the degree
of emotional excitement subjectively experienced. In many experiments
it is assumed that the measurement of changes in physiological activity
(for example elevation of heart rate or blood pressure[24] or increase in
sweat production) can be simply equated with changes in subjectively
experienced emotion. But as Lang (1971) has pointed out, there is no
proof that the one reflects the other in any straightforward manner.

The measurement of physiological arousal itself is by no means a
clear-cut procedure. Sometimes, for example, different measures of

physiological arousal do not agree – that is, there may be an increase in one index but not in another (Malmo and Belanger, 1967). If this is the case, how does an experimenter choose the appropriate measure if he or she only uses one? Thus Stonner (1976) recommends that multiple measures should always be used in order to assess physiological arousal. But it is a precaution seldom taken.

Can the experimenter be sure that the physiological arousal shown may not be due to actually stopping the experiment in order to measure, say, blood pressure rather than to the psychological pressures of being insulted or humiliated? If a subject wishes to retain an impression of outward calm, the prospect of having an involuntary function like blood pressure measured may be as likely to elevate blood pressure as being insulted. Once again, as in the case of 'aggressive behaviour', what is actually measured in the experimental situation may not be quite what the experimenter thinks is being measured.

MORE GENERAL CRITICISMS

For me the approach taken by experimental psychologists to aggression and violence is flawed in three major areas. These are the restricted nature of their discussion, their inability to come to terms with the limitations of positivist methodology, and finally the poverty of their conception of human motivation.

The manner in which they restrict the nature of their discussion has been aptly summed up by Sedgwick when he writes:

Violence, for psychology, becomes translated into a discussion about 'aggression' displayed by individual Ss [an abbreviation commonly used by experimental psychologists to refer to their subjects]; it is never seen as a property of institutions like the police or the Mafia, or of historically contingent situations like a picket-line in a period of intense collision between the State and trade-union militancy. (1974, p. 36)

This quote encapsulates two aspects of the manner in which experimental psychologists narrow down the subject area. To begin with, they seem reluctant to consider either aggression or violence as social phenomena. Perhaps because their conclusions are based on the aggregation of experiments in which the behaviour of subjects is always measured individually, they seem unable to even consider those social or group aspects of aggression and violence which we all know to be relevant. Secondly, they very seldom locate their discussion of aggression and violence in the real world of perceived and actual inequalities, environmental stress and political conflict. Thus, they seem reluctant to come to terms with real-life instances of aggression and violence, like the situation described below where violence is fuelled by the social

dynamics of the actual situation and the political circumstances. This
report, written in the 1960s, is describing what happened after American police officers arrested a black motorist on suspicion of driving with
too high an alcohol level:

> The subject was placed under arrest and the officers attempted to
> escort him to the police vehicle. At this time the subject turned and
> struck the Reporting Officer in the face. He was thrown to the
> ground by the Reporting Officer and an attempt was made to
> handcuff him . . .
> During the struggle with the subject approximately fifteen
> Negroes from the drive-in and occupants of the subject's vehicle
> gathered about the Reporting Officers threatening violence
> towards the police. A statement was yelled at the officers, 'This
> isn't Mississippi, you bastards. We are sick of the police bothering
> the black people.' There were several agitators who consistently
> shouted jeers and abusive statements towards the police. The
> Reporting Officers had been forced to call for assistance over the
> police radio due to the immediate situation which closely
> resembled a near riot. After the subject had been transferred to the
> station for booking the Reporting Officer questioned the subject's
> wife as to the possible reason for his actions. She stated that 'he had
> been drinking and that he was angry because he was unable to find
> a job, etc., and that he was generally angry at all white people,
> because of this.' (Toch, 1972, pp. 86–7)

However, it seems to me that the restrictiveness of the experimental
psychologists is not confined only to their subject matter, for I would
argue that their excessive reliance on a positivist approach blinds them to
even considering whether or not psychology can be legitimately explored
using methods other than those derived from the experimental methodology of the natural sciences. By denying themselves access to introspections, reports of dreams and fantasies and other elements of people's
subjective life, and by considering as legitimate only data gained under
experimental conditions, they lose much. Fromm puts it like this:

> To be sure, the use of 'natural experiments' [by which term
> Fromm refers to interviews, protocols from psychoanalytic
> sessions and observation of incidents in the field] does not permit
> us to arrive at the 'accuracy' of laboratory experiments, because no
> two social constellations are identical; but by observing not
> 'subjects' but people, not artifacts but life, one does not have to pay
> as the price of an alleged (and often doubtful) accuracy the triviality
> of the experiment's results. (Fromm, 1977, p. 79)

Finally, I would argue that the various aspects of restrictiveness that I have just described lead to a conception of human motivation that is excessively mechanistic.

It seems to me that it is just not possible to compare the frustration or humiliation to which psychologists subject students in the laboratory with the smouldering cauldron of resentment and hostility that characterize those individuals for whom life has been a series of disappointments and rejection. Nor do I believe that measuring the behaviour of undergraduates who are placed in an artificial situation gives much insight into the motivations and behaviour of people who exhibit very high levels of violent behaviour, like the sadistic policemen in repressive states who persistently and repetitively torture their victims.

Perhaps the most cogent expression of these criticisms of the experimental psychologists' approach to aggression and violence can be found in Anthony Burgess's novel *A Clockwork Orange*. This book, an odyssey of violence, portrays the anti-social teenage career of Alex and his three friends. It is set in some unspecified future date, when groups of bored teenagers from the lower classes roam the streets of a tightly controlled, arid, consumer-oriented society where the only legitimate activities available are sitting around in cafes, listening to pop music and watching television. School, as Alex puts it in the teenage argot in which the book is written, is 'a great, gloopy seat of useless learning'.

But Alex needs more avenues for self-expression than these restricted and largely passive activities, and so with his friends he sets off on a career of mayhem and violence where excitement is supplied by taking risks, stealing desirable property and destroying the undesirable, beating up the old and raping the young and nubile. Particularly when they are 'feeling like in a hate and murder mood' and out for 'a real kick – and lashings of the ultra-violent', anyone wandering the soulless streets can expect no mercy.

For Alex, however, if not for his less imaginative friends, the violence he perpetrates is inextricably bound up with his feelings about 'Great Music', which 'always sort of sharpened me up, O my brothers, and made me like feel like old Bog himself, ready to make with the old donner and blitzen and have vecks and ptitsas creeching away in my ha ha power' (1972, pp. 35–6). And it is both in great music (as distinguished from the ubiquitous pop) and in violence that Alex experiences what he calls the self, the real essence of his being: like music, 'badness is of the self, the one, the you or me on our oddy knockies, and that self is made by old Bog or God and is his great pride and radotsy' (ibid., p. 34).

Eventually, however, Alex is apprehended and jailed for his excesses. In jail he is subjected to 'Ludovic's technique', a regime that is based on the psychological learning theories referred to in this chapter. According to the criminologists in the jail who advocate the technique, violence is a learned habit which is reinforced when successful, and if violence can be associated with feelings of repulsion, and disgust rather than reward, it will soon be inhibited and will ultimately totally disappear.

So Alex, in a parody of some methods that have been used in what is called behavioural modification, is strapped into a chair, eyelids propped open and forced to watch films of unmitigated violence. Before the films he is given an injection which causes him to experience exquisitely unpleasant nausea at precisely the moment that the violence on the screen reaches its apogee. And it is assumed that as a result, when Alex is faced in the future with opportunities for violence, the very thought of them will conjure up such extreme feelings of revulsion that he will be impelled to behave in a distinctly different manner. As Alex quotes one of the criminologists as saying:

> Our subject is, you see, impelled towards the good by, paradoxi-
> cally, being impelled towards evil. The intention to act violently is
> accompanied by strong feelings of physical distress. To counter
> these the subject has to switch to a diametrically opposed attitude.
> (ibid., p. 99)

When Alex is released, however, the results of his conditioning with Ludovic's technique prove more complex. As Alex is forced to relinquish violence, so he loses his essential self, for all his complex emotions are so interwoven that the revulsion that was conditioned to violence now spreads until when he tries to listen to a Mozart symphony in a record shop:

> what I'd forgotten was something I shouldn't have forgotten and
> now made me want to snuff it. It was that these doctor bratchnies
> had so fixed things that any music that was like for the emotions
> would make me sick just like viddying or wanting to do violence. It
> was because all those violence films had music with them. And I
> remembered especially that horrible Nazi film with the Beethoven
> Fifth, last movement. And now here was lovely Mozart made
> horrible. I dashed out of the shop with these nadsats smecking after
> me and the counter-veck creeching: 'Eh eh eh!' But I took no
> notice and went staggering almost like blind across the road and
> round the corner. (ibid., p. 110)

Burgess, to my mind, thus puts his finger imaginatively and precisely on the chief limitation of experimental approaches to violence and aggression. Such approaches, by concentrating on behaviour, separate it from its complex roots in thought and emotion both at the conscious and unconscious level.

# Overview of the Experimental Approach

EVALUATING THE EXPERIMENTAL APPROACH TO AGGRESSION
AND VIOLENCE

There is no doubt that the experimental psychologists, despite or indeed perhaps because of the narrowness of their approach, bring to the topics of aggression and violence an exactitude that is not found in any of the other approaches so far reviewed. So that using the first evaluative perspective I suggested in the concluding sections of Chapters 2 and 3 it must be granted that if we use criteria like stringent experimental design, replicability of results, adequate sample size and so on, the majority of the studies that have been conducted meet these criteria in the main. The major problem in this area lies, as I indicated in the preceding section, in the validity of the experimental measures. But this aside, I consider that in terms of the first perspective – careful application of generally accepted principles of good scientific design – the work of the experimental psychologists comes off well.

The second perspective I suggested was concerned with the assumptions that are made about human nature, and here I suggested that the criteria used by any evaluator are rather more subjective, and centre around concepts like rigour of thought, consistency and whether or not the approach helps the evaluator extend his or her own understanding of human nature.

Turning first to consistency and rigour, it seems to me that the experimental psychologists again come off well. They seldom make any contradictory statements or draw any contradictory conclusions, and it is unusual for them to make sweeping and unsubstantiated claims. But, as I have indicated both at the beginning of the chapter and in the preceding section, they do make assumptions about human nature which I personally find very limiting, and which centre around their belief that the key to the understanding of the human condition lies in the observation and measurement of human behaviour. As I have indicated throughout this chapter, this leads them to dismiss as irrelevant or too subjective, other – to my mind – most valuable sources of material.

Nevertheless, this emphasis on behaviour has some very positive results which I will return to in the final chapter. In particular, it does suggest some methods for helping individuals, and in particular children, to acquire prosocial rather than anti-social repertoires for dealing with their feelings when they are frustrated or humiliated.

In conclusion it seems to me that the approach of the experimental psychologists has helped to introduce a degree of rigour into the study of aggression and violence. It has also drawn attention to the importance of learning in the acquisition of certain aspects of violent behaviour. For example, as I have just mentioned, it has illuminated how children can learn repertoires of behaviour that serve to escalate conflict, in that learning theory suggests that much of our behaviour is influenced by what we have seen others do and how we have seen others react. It is not, however, an approach which gives us any insight into how people *feel* before and while they are behaving violently. It also, to my mind, gives us very little understanding indeed of the minds of those whose level of aggression and violence are markedly different from the rest of us; into the minds, for example, of those who are labelled as psychopaths. Neither does it give any insight into the nature of sadism.

Finally, while it may illuminate to a limited extent the conditions under which individuals behave aggressively or violently, it offers very little insight into group aggression or violence.

## HOW EXTENSIVE IS THE USE EXPERIMENTAL PSYCHOLOGISTS MAKE OF THE TERMS 'AGGRESSION' AND 'VIOLENCE'?

I will now consider, as I have in the preceding chapters, how adequately the approach of experimental psychology covers the different usages of the terms aggression and violence which I derived in my summational descriptions in Chapter 1.

*Aggression*
(a)  Experimental psychologists, as evidenced in their definitions of aggression, see intention as a major factor; aggressive behaviour is defined as behaviour that is directed towards injuring others. (Note that aggression is almost always discussed with reference to behaviour only; emotion is seldom involved in any discussion.)
(b)  Experimental psychologists do not discuss aggression in the sense of achieving dominance.
(c)  Experimental psychologists would agree that aggression does not necessarily involve physical injury.
(d)  Experimental psychologists (though they may quibble about terms) do distinguish between 'hostile' and 'instrumental' aggression, though they seldom explicitly mention motives.
(e)  Experimental psychologists explictly dissassociate their discussion of aggression from any possible positive aspects of aggression.
(f)  Some (for example, Bandura and Zillman) but not all experimental psychologists discuss the issue of subjectivity in the labelling of aggression. But the discussion is usually in passing and plays a very minor role in their approach to aggression.
(g)  Occasionally some experimental psychologists may mention in passing that values affect whether or not particular behaviour is labelled as aggressive. But, because their definition of aggression tends to be so unambiguous (behaviour directed towards injury),

neither values nor the issues of retaliation and provocation enter centrally into their discussion.

*Violence*

On the whole experimental psychologists write little which is directly about violence (except as I have noted before when they deal with the influence of the media). Their topic is always aggression, and violence is implicitly accepted as that aggressive behaviour which involves physical force and/or is very intense. Such a position with respect to violence as a topic is fully explicable in terms of their focus on aggression as behaviour and aggression as never having any positive aspects.

In general, as should be clear throughout the chapter, experimental psychologists consider the topic of aggression within a range that is considerably more limited than in the other approaches we have so far discussed.

# Notes: Chapter 5

1  Perhaps the most comprehensive recent review of the enormous body of experimental studies on aggression can be found in Dolf Zillmann's *Hostility and Aggression* (1979), although Zillmann's interpretation of the results of these studies would not necessarily be endorsed by all experimental psychologists working in the field. There are also two fairly comprehensive review articles in Kutash, Kutash and Schlesinger (1978). The most straightforward account of contemporary views held by experimental psychologists can be found in Robert Baron's *Human Aggression* (1977) and in Baron and Byrne's *Social Psychology* (1981).

2  Briefly the positivist view may be summed up as follows: 'The view that all true knowledge is scientific, in the sense of describing the coexistence and succession of observable phenomena' (Bullock and Stallybrass, 1977, p. 488). The studies described in Chapter 2 and the ethological studies described in Chapter 3 are also positivist in orientation.

3  The insistence that psychology should be studied within the same paradigm as natural and physical sciences was at its peak between the two world wars and coincided with a general surge of interest in logical positivism, although the roots of psychology as science extend backwards to the end of the last century and its influence is still very strong today (see Harrè and Secord, 1972).

4  This emphasis on behaviour is of course the hallmark of the work of the experimental psychologists in the first half of the twentieth century, and derived from their positivist stance in that they saw the observation of behaviour as the only valid data for social scientists. It is for this reason that their approach became labelled as 'behaviourist'.

5  I shall discuss the ethical implications of allowing subjects to assume that they are going to shock, or have shocked, others at the end of this chapter.

6  Drive theory maintained that increases in drive level increase the motivation to seek out conditions under which activities can be performed that lead to a reduction in drive (Zillman, 1979). Thus, for example, it was contended that when a child investigated his or her environment, this behaviour could be regarded as deriving from the 'exploratory' drive.

7  Theoretical issues in drive theory that became controversial were, for example, the relationship between 'specific' and 'diffuse' drives, whether all 'specific' drives were

acquired in the same way, and finally the relationship between drive and activity in the nervous system (see Cofer and Appley, 1964).

8   The reticular formation is a diffuse system which extends through the brain-stem from the medulla to the thalamus; it has an ascending component which projects to the thalamus and the cerebral cortex and a descending component which influences activity in the extrapyramidal motor system. Physiologists consider that the reticular formation functions to 'alert' the cortex when sensory input is arriving and psychologists have claimed that it then mediates the arousal response which may be detected by electroencephelographic recording (Yeo, 1979).

9   In order to understand the reasoning which places so much emphasis on features in the environment we have to turn to learning experiments on what is called 'classical conditioning', in which a previously neutral stimulus becomes capable of evoking an emotional response. The results of such experiments have been used by learning theorists to explain behaviour like fetishism. For example, consider the development of a sexual fetish when a specific article of clothing (for example, high leather boots), because it has been previously paired with erotic acts, may itself become capable of producing a strong sexual response. It has been suggested (for example, by Berkowitz, 1973) that aggressive behaviour may also be influenced by classical conditioning, in that if, for example, a name is associated with aggressive behaviour at any stage, the mention of the name in a potentially aggressive situation may itself escalate aggressive behaviour. Thus Berkowitz and Geen (1966), in a shock experiment, showed that more intensive shocks were delivered by subjects who had witnessed a boxing film with the actor Kirk Douglas, when the victim was introduced as Kirk Anderson than when he was introduced as Bob Anderson. For a critique of this and similar experiments see Baron (1977).

10  Bandura, however, generally prefers not to classify aggressive behaviour using these terms, noting that 'It would be more accurate to designate aggressive behaviors in terms of their functional value rather than whether or not they are instrumental' (1978, p. 52).

11  Two exceptions being an interesting but rather facile book by H. A. Hornstein, *Cruelty and Kindness* (1976) and a learning-theory oriented text by Kaufman, *Aggression and Altruism* (1970). Neither of these has, however, received much attention in the standard texts either on aggression or prosocial behaviour.

12  This is more likely to apply to boys than girls. A recent review of developmental work in this area can be found in Ellis, 1982 and Zahn-Waxler and Radke-Yarrow, 1982.

13  I have chosen to present Baron's approach rather than Zillman's or Berkowitz's, in Zillman's case because his discussion of the detailed niceties of experimental design has led him to concentrate on technicalities and to limit the discussion of the social implications of his work; and in Berkowitz's case because he places more emphasis on the emotional aspects of aggression than do other experimental psychologists.

14  Although Baron seems to regard his approach to aggression as a social rather than an experimental approach, he falls very much within the tradition of the experimental psychologists whose work he draws on. If his approach is contrasted with those discussed in Chapter 6, it can easily be seen that this is so. For, unlike the theorists to be discussed in Chapter 6, he seldom locates his discussion anywhere other than in the dynamics of specific situations, and he seldom discusses any of the social factors that are normally included within a social rather than an experimental approach. Such factors would include values, attitudes, ideologies, and socio-political movements.

15  The effect of crowding and density on behaviour has been the subject of great interest both to experimental and to social psychologists, who have in general concluded that the effect of crowding is powerfully mediated by subjective factors, such as whether or not people perceive the situation they are in as desirable or undesirable, as well as the objective conditions of actual density of people in any particular physical space. (see, for example, Peay and Peay, 1983 and Freedman, 1975)

16  Although Baron does not draw explicitly on the data, a number of longitudinal studies

of aggression in children have tended to show that children who are aggressive in early childhood are more likely than other children to behave aggressively later in life. For example, Lefkowitz *et al.* (1977), in a study of over 700 American children, claimed that one of their major findings was that aggression at age 8 was the best predictor of aggression at age 19, irrespective of parents' socio-economic class, parents' level of aggressiveness and children's IQ. Lefkowitz *et al.* argue that the major reasons for this consistency in behaviour lie in 'learning factors such as external reinforcement, vicarious reinforcement, and self-reinforcement' (1977, p. 192). I will return to this and other studies in the next two chapters.

17  In discussing this aspect of controlling aggression, Baron draws on a series of experiments by Zillmann and his colleagues, for example, Zillmann and Cantor, 1976, in which they showed that subjects were less likely to show aggression to a fellow subject when they were given reasons for his provocative behaviour, such as that he was 'uptight' about a midterm exam, than when they were not given such explanations.

18  Two of these areas, catharsis and the influence of the media, have stimulated an enormous output of books and articles by experimental psychologists. An excellent review of work on catharsis can be found in Quanty, 1976, and recent books dealing with violence and the mass media from the point of view of experimental psychologists are Eysenck and Nias, 1980 and Comstock *et al.*, 1978.

19  For a review of experimental studies see Frodi, Macaulay and Thome, 1977.

20  An exception to this general rule is Maccoby and Jacklin, 1980.

21  See, for example, the report in *The Guardian*, of 24 November 1983 on 'Video Violence and Children'.

22  However, there are certain dissenting viewpoints which are sometimes, but by no means always, associated with particular vested interests, for instance, in television networks. For a thorough discussion of the ways in which particular vested interests may affect particular positions in the general area of violence and the media, see Rowland, 1983.

23  Rules based on probability theory for deciding from the data whether to retain the initial hypothesis or not.

24  Particular problems arise in the case of assessing arousal by measuring blood pressure. In arousal experiments it is generally systemic blood pressure that is used as an index, and as Stonner (1976), amongst others, points out, there are difficulties in assessing the reliability of this in the experimental situation.

# 6

# Social Accounts of Aggression and Violence

In this chapter, I intend to depart from the pattern of the preceding four chapters where I presented particular theoretical approaches in some detail. In all four cases, the chapters were concerned with coherent and relatively unified perspectives. In the first chapter, the perspective was that aggressive and violent behaviour is controlled by particular physiological substrates; in the second, that human aggression and violence is best understood in terms of evolutionary processes; in the third, that human aggression is inevitable and in essence positive, but that with unfavourable social and emotional influences it can become malign and destructive; and in the fourth, that aggressive behaviour is a learned pattern of behaviour that is largely under the control of environmental contingencies.

In contrast, this chapter will put forward a number of rather different accounts,[1] which I have grouped together because they share one particular assumption; that aggression and violence are best understood in terms of interpersonal relationships within a *social* perspective. They place the emphasis not on individual predisposition (whether innately, physiologically or environmentally determined), but on *social processes*.

In view of this emphasis on social factors, it is not surprising that this chapter deals with the work of social scientists – primarily of psychologists and sociologists, although the work of certain criminologists is also included.

Apart from sharing a general emphasis on social factors, and a training in the social sciences rather than in the natural sciences or the humanities, those workers whose accounts of aggression and violence are covered here also share another commonality, which is that their approaches to the issues of aggression and violence emerge as part of their understanding of social processes, rather than as formal expositions on the nature of human aggression and violence in the sense, say, that

Lorenz wrote on aggression or Storr and Baron their respective versions of *Human Aggression*.

This chapter, then, is concerned with accounts of aggression and violence that share two characteristics; an emphasis on social factors and an assumption that aggression and violence are aspects of social interaction in general, rather than unique categories of social behaviour. Beyond these assumptions, however, the accounts covered share little commonality. This diversity reflects, as it is bound to, the wide divergences in approach within contemporary social psychology and sociology. Nevertheless, I believe it is possible to identify within this heterogeneity three overall perspectives, and in this chapter I present these perspectives in turn, in each case first discussing the rather more psychological accounts and following these with the rather more sociological ones.[2] But before presenting the accounts, I will discuss briefly the rationale that underpins the threefold categorization system I use.

Those accounts that I have grouped in the first category seem to me to be heavily influenced by scientific methodology, and as a result their focus is on observable and measurable behaviour rather than on introspections or individual accounts of subjective experience. In addition, the social scientists discussed in this section *seldom question the subjective issues* involved in labelling behaviour as violent or aggressive. In general the behaviour that they do label thus tends to be behaviour that has been legally proscribed and, as we shall see, their work has centred very often on trying to predict which young people will go on to become violent offenders. Finally they tend to be *deterministic* in their approach, in that they propose that the appropriate model for understanding aggression is a cause and effect one.

These three emphases on scientific measurement, determinist models and the essentially non-controversial nature of applying labels like 'aggressive' and 'violent' can of course be found in the approach of the experimental psychologists (see Chapter 5) and in the work of many of the biologically oriented researchers whose approaches were discussed in Chapters 2 and 3. Indeed, Dallos and Muncie (1982) suggest that it is these very emphases that lie at the heart of the positivist approach. For these reasons it seems appropriate to me to call the approaches discussed in the first category of this chapter 'positivist'.

The second category deals with those workers who have attempted to understand the feelings and behaviour of those who have been labelled as 'violent' and 'aggressive' by seeking to uncover the *meaning* which such behaviour holds for those who practise it. From the psychological stance this orientation has led to attempts to understand, and empathize with, the thoughts and emotions of those who have been labelled violent or aggressive. From the sociological standpoint, attempts have been made to understand violence as a form of social communication. For 'violence is presumed to share with other forms of social behaviour the properties of rationality, motive and meaning' (Downes, 1982, p. 27) and it is the task of the sociologist to uncover these factors because 'violence can be read, appreciated and decoded – in short, understood' (ibid., p. 29). Further, whether approached from a psychological or a sociological standpoint, this orientation is centrally concerned with issues of legitimacy and demands a critical examination of the social variables that are involved when social behaviour is labelled as violent or aggressive. This twofold emphasis on meaning and the relativistic nature of labelling seems to me to bring the work in this section within the tradition in twentieth-century thought that has been called phenomenological. Phenomenology is at root concerned with what Bullock and Stallybrass (1977) refer to as 'a scrutiny of essences and meanings'. Not surprisingly, then, I have called this second section 'phenomenological approaches'.

In the third category I have grouped approaches which move further than the approaches in the second category in their examination of the manner in which particular behaviours become labelled as aggressive and violent. This third approach is concerned with both the *ideological nature* of such labelling, suggesting that the labelling reflects the interests of powerful political groups, and its *political effects*, arguing that the imposition of such labelling allows such powerful groups to 'criminalize, demoralize [and] incapacitate' (Box, 1983, p. 7) those whom the dominant groups perceive to be potentially or actually threatening to the existing distributions of power and privilege. It seems reasonable to me (and see Box, 1983 and Dallos, Hall and Scraton, 1982) to call this third section 'radical'.

## Positivist Social Accounts of Aggression and Violence

PSYCHOLOGICAL ACCOUNTS

> His earlier history was typical of an antisocial recidivist. He was from a poor family, his father had a criminal record and he had an elder brother convicted. He was below average in intelligence and he had performed poorly at school and been a frequent truant. (West and Farrington, 1977, p. 151)

As I noted in the last chapter, many experimental psychologists have chosen to study aggression by attempting to establish a causal relationship between aggressive behaviour in the laboratory and certain selected independent variables. For example, they have investigated whether an increase in heat affects the propensity to give a fellow subject electric shocks. Certain social psychologists have attempted to carry this technique over from the laboratory into social situations and have attempted to measure the effect of specific aspects of the social environment on aggressive behaviour in more natural settings.

Such an approach involves measuring the level of aggressive behaviour shown in a natural setting, and then trying to estimate the effect on such behaviour of particular environmental factors. For example, a researcher may wish to investigate the relationship between aggression in children, as measured by how many fights they are involved in, and how much violent television they watch. She may at the same time want to investigate the effect on the level of fighting of the degree of parental punitiveness.

She would start off with some means of measuring the incidence of fighting in a sample of young children. Simultaneously she would obtain some measure of the amount of violent television they watch and another measure of the level of parental punitiveness. All the measurements would then be subjected to statistical analyses,[3] in order to see whether an association existed between the level of fighting and both, or either, of the environmental factors she measured. Of course, even if an association were established between the two environmental factors and aggressive behaviour such that the more aggressive children watched more violent television and/or the more aggressive children had more punitive parents, she could not be sure that either watching violent television or being punished severely *caused* aggressive behaviour, because it could be that aggressive children prefer violent television and aggressive children provoke their parents to punish them more severely. All she could claim would be that some of *the variation in children's level of aggression*, can be explained by *the variation in the environmental factors she measured*, that is in television viewing habits and/or the levels of parental punitiveness.

She could make her technique rather more powerful by undertaking her collection of data on the same children at two or more points widely separated in time. She could then compare the different sets of data. Such a technique (called a longitudinal study)[4] would enable her to satisfy two further objectives. These are to establish how *consistent* her original findings were and to investigate if she could have used her first measure of environmental variables (in this case television viewing and parental punitiveness) *to predict* which children would be most aggressive the second or subsequent times round. This latter objective, attempting to *predict* from an earlier data sweep which subjects will fall into particular categories on a later data sweep, is used extensively by criminologists in order to see whether particular environmental variables in the home background of young offenders can be used to predict which of them will go on to become hardened criminals.

Perhaps the most comprehensive of such longitudinal investigations has been undertaken by West and Farrington (1973, 1977), who in 1961 began the first of a series of surveys on a group of London schoolboys. This sample of 411 was made up in 1961 of all the boys in the second year of six state primary schools in London who were then 8 years old. They were given a battery of psychometric tests in their schools at ages 8, 10 and 14 and were interviewed at ages 16 and 18. Contact was kept with the majority of the boys and, for example, at age 18 it was possible to reinterview 95 per cent (389) of the boys. In addition to the data gathered from the boys themselves, their parents were interviewed by social workers once a year, from when the boys were 8 until they were 14, and further information was gained from teachers and criminal, social and medical records. This investigation was primarily criminological and was chiefly concerned with the differences in personal history, attitude and behaviour between those of these boys who were subjesequently found guilty of offences in court and those who were not, but Farrington (1978, 1982) has extracted from the data material that has special reference to the longitudinal study of aggressive and violent behaviour.

Aggressive behaviour was measured at ages 8, 10, 12 and 14 from the responses teachers gave to questionnaires filled in at these ages. At ages 8 and 10 the aggressive boys were regarded as those the teachers nominated as being 'difficult to discipline', and at ages 12 and 14 as those who were rated as most 'disobedient, difficult to discipline, unduly rough during playtime, quarrelsome and aggressive, over-competitive with other children, and unduly resentful to criticism or punishment' (Farrington, 1978 p. 76). Measures of aggressiveness at ages 16 and 18 were derived from self-reports at that age, and were related to the degree to which the young men admitted getting into fights, carrying weapons, fighting policemen, and using weapons in fights. A sub-group of 'violent delinquents' was also identified from criminal records, and these were those young men who had been convicted for crimes involving violent assault or violent robbery.

The results of this study showed in Farrington's words that

> violent delinquents, most of whose violent offences occurred when they were aged seventeen to eighteen, tended to be among the more aggressive from age eight onwards. At age eight to ten they tend to have cold, harsh, disharmonious, poorly supervising and criminal parents. They also tended to have low I.Q.s and be rated daring. (1978, p. 90)

Aggressive boys showed much the same characteristics. In terms of the three possible objectives for a longitudinal study that I outlined above, West and Farrington's study indicated that for their sample:

(1)    Certain variables in the environment appeared to be consistently associated with high levels of aggressiveness. These were, notably, parental attitudes, low IQ and parents with criminal records.

(2)    There was a degree of consistency in aggressive behaviour in that, in

general, boys rated as aggressive at earlier ages were also so rated at later ages.

(3) Some factors measured at age 8 appeared to predict both self-reported violence at ages 16 to 18 and violent convictions. These were having cold, harsh disharmonious parents, who were poor supervisors, having low IQs and showing the tendency to be rated daring and aggressive at younger ages.

In Chapter 7 I shall integrate these findings (which are, in general, in agreement with other longitudinal studies) into a theoretical account of the development of aggressive behaviour in children, but it should be noted that West and Farrington themselves make very little attempt to relate their findings to any theoretical perspective on aggression and violence, observing that 'it is not easy to relate these results to theories about the development of aggression' (Farrington, 1978, p. 90) and that

Most longitudinal research on criminal violence has been designed to collect basic information about careers of violence or has been inspired by such policy issues such as incapacitation [preventive detention for the sake, primarily, of prevention of crime, rather than for retribution] or dangerousness' (Farrington, 1982, p. 195)

rather than being designed to develop theories or test hypotheses.[5]

In line with their atheoretical approach, whilst West and Farrington give a very graphic picture of those members of their sample who have been convicted, they show little interest in trying to account for their way of life. Thus they write about their delinquent sample:

They are more immoderate in their smoking, drinking, gambling and sexual habits. They more often become violent after drinking. They drive more recklessly and are more likely to sustain injuries. They are more often spendthrifts. They show little interest in reading or in further education. Their work records are much less stable. They earn more per week, but are in jobs with poor prospects. They mix more with all-male groups of the kind that gets into trouble. They spend more of their leisure time away from home, and indulge more often in seemingly aimless 'hanging about'. They more often take prohibited drugs. They express more pro-aggressive and anti-establishment sentiments in response to an attitude questionnaire. They are more often in conflict with or alienated from their parental home. They are readier to adopt the dress styles and ornaments, notably tattoos, associated with anti-establishment attitudes. (West and Farrington, 1977, p. 78)

Although West and Farrington paint this detailed picture of their delinquent sample, they make little attempt at any stage in their study to understand the behaviour of their sample from the point of view of their subjects. Nor do they explain why they consider that working-class youths are so prone to violence, for while they note that 'violent responses occur *naturally* and readily among working class youths' (1977, p.97, my italics), they offer no coherent account of the origin of what they clearly see as a class difference in aggression. Finally, while they stress the continuity of aggressive behaviour in their sample, they offer no reasons for this continuity, beyond speculating that genetic predispositions may be involved, basing this conclusion on some of the evidence discussed in Chapter 2 above.

This tendency to concentrate on descriptive generalizations rather than on theoretical examinations of aggression is typical of most longitudinal studies on violence and aggression. An exception to this general tendency is offered by some of the work of Lefkowitz et al. (1977)[6]. In an early study, conducted on a sample of middle-class American children which surveyed the subjects at ages 9 and 19, they related the consistency of aggressive behaviour in their sample to Bandura's social learning theory, noting that 'a child learns early on a manner of responding to certain situations which is distinctive to him/her and is perpetuated probably because of the success it brings' (1977, p. 78). But in their later work, they have, like West and Farrington, tended to identify the characteristics of aggressive young people rather than attempt to explain how these characteristics lead to violent behaviour. Thus, Eron, one of the co-authors, noted more recently that

> We know that observation of television violence is a cause[7] of aggressive behaviour in children . . . Also, it seems likely that how closely a youngster identifies with aggressive television characters and how realistic he or she believes aggressive television content to be are related to both aggression and television viewing. We know further that academic achievement is negatively related to aggression and that aggressive youngsters tend not to be popular with their peers. We know that rejection and physical punishment by parents are concomitants of aggression in children and that the attitudes and behaviors of parents, especially mothers, which are known predictors of antisocial behavior, are highly related to the aggressive behaviors of their sons . . . (1982, p. 208)

Despite this detailed portrayal of the characteristics of aggressive young people, Eron, like West and Farrington, does not relate his findings to a theoretical account of how particular characteristics come to be associated with relatively higher rates of aggression.

It is perhaps this reluctance to look more deeply into the viewpoint of their subjects that gives many of the longitudinal studies a certain flavour of dispassion. For while most longitudinal studies have included interviews, the attitude of those who conducted the studies, if not the interviews, sometimes convey the feeling that the subjects were treated rather less than empathetically. Consider, for example, the tone of the remarks made by West and Farrington with respect to the administration of a particular psychometric measure on their sample when they were aged 18.

> The administration of the test created problems: Some youths found the test difficult, and some of them became upset or irritable because they could produce few ideas. Others, who were more perceptive, realised that the test must be a covert method of finding out something about them without their knowing what was being looked for. This often caused resentment and provoked openly facetious remarks. (West and Farrington, 1977, p. 105)

In essence, such studies carry over the flavour of experimental psychology. Motives are attributed to 'subjects' and there is an implicit assumption that measured variables contribute more to the study that is being undertaken than do the subjects' own perceptions and understandings of their own behaviour. Further, as we noted in the previous chapter on experimental approaches to aggression and violence, the emphasis is on empirical data rather than on theoretical explanation.

The same orientation is also to be found in some of the more traditional studies of urban unrest. In order to illustrate this remark I would like to look briefly at one of these. This is an analysis by Leonard Berkowitz of 'riots and other forms of social violence' (1972, p. 77), in which he argues that the American urban disturbances among the black population that occurred in the 1960s should be understood in terms of 'stimulus–response analyses' rather than in terms of disadvantaged people purposefully seeking to redress what they perceive as injustice. Thus, he suggests, the violence that occurs at such times is best regarded as expressive acts that occur in response to aversive conditions. According to Berkowitz, aversive conditions such as heat, frustration, and the actions of unsympathetic policemen create emotional arousal, and this arousal leads to aggressive behaviour.

The urban disturbances amongst American blacks in the 1960s are thus seen as arising primarily from a combination of frustration caused by disadvantaged social conditions, emotional arousal caused, for example, by heat or loud noises, and the cues provided by the presence of stimuli that have previously been associated with angry and hostile responses, such as white policemen carrying weapons. To take a more specific example, here is Berkowitz's account of a disturbance at an athletic event:

In other cases, the arousal can stem from an exciting athletic event. Interracial disorders have erupted in this country following football or basketball games between Negro and white teams, apparently because after the game the excited youngsters were hyper-responsive to the stimulus of someone from another race. Both whites and blacks react in this manner, but, as one illustration, a white university professor recently (March 20, 1969) was pushed, kicked, and shoved off a bus in Milwaukee by a group of black high school students returning from a basketball game. The young people were excited and also upset because their team had lost, and then evidently responded aggressively to the white people in the bus, probably because the whites were symbolic of the frustrations and aggression that had been inflicted on them. (Berkowitz, 1972, p. 89)

As can be seen from this extract, Berkowitz's analysis is not in terms of the rioter's own perception of their intentions, for these are not investigated. Instead, in the tradition of the experimental model we looked at in the last chapter, the emphasis is on the *attribution* of motive. Furthermore, Berkowitz makes little attempt to place the disturbance within a social setting for, as Billig puts it, Berkowitz does not 'seek to relate the riots to the structure of society. Instead he concentrates on the behaviour of the rioters' (1976, p. 169).

A rather similar approach to the study of aggression and violence can also be found in recent cross-cultural studies of aggression and violence by psychologists. For example, Kornadt (1983) has attempted to account for cross-cultural differences in aggressive behaviour in terms primarily of differences in the strength of 'aggression motive'. This energizing force is thought by Kornadt to be dependent on child-rearing variables which differ from culture to culture. Again, as in the case of Berkowitz's analysis of riot behaviour, or in West and Farrington's account of violent delinquency, the emphasis is on the individual motivation in a social setting rather than on the interplay between social forces such as ideology, values and power and the individual experience. The spotlight is on the behaviour of 'subjects' and the variables which are thought to be causally associated with this. The spotlight is not, as it is in the next series of psychological studies which we shall come to, on intention and meaning.

SOCIOLOGICAL ACCOUNTS

It is not far-fetched to suggest that a whole culture may accept a value set dependent upon violence, demand or encourage adherence to violence and penalize deviation. (Wolfgang and Ferracuti, 1967, p. 156)

In 1967, in a book that was designed to provide an interdisciplinary perspective in criminology, two social scientists, one a sociologist and one a psychologist, developed a theoretical framework for investigating violent criminal behaviour which focused on what they referred to as a 'subculture of violence'.[8]

Drawing largely on statistics, Wolfgang and Ferracuti argued that certain societies such as the Colombian society of the 1950s and 1960s, certain sub-groups within societies such as the Mafia in Sardinian society, and certain social classes such as the 'blue-collar, lower social and economic class, especially the laboring, unskilled working group' (ibid., p. 261) were particularly likely to be involved in high levels of criminal violence, particularly homicide.

By focusing on these groups, they argued, it should be possible to 'examine the value system of their subculture,[9] the importance of life in the scale of values, the kind of expected reaction to certain types of stimulus, perceptual differences in the evaluation of stimuli, and the general personality structure of the subcultural actors' (ibid., p. 153). Such an examination would, they believed, allow them to set out a comprehensive way of conceptualizing criminal violence.

The results of their own examination of these issues, set out in *The Subculture of Violence* (1967), led them to propose that violent behaviour results largely from a commitment to a subcultural value and attitude pattern which endorses the use of violence in interpersonal behaviour. People, predominantly young men of lower social status, regard physical combat as a measure of daring or courage, and believe that challenges by others should be met with physical attacks because a failure to strike out could bring disapproval from their peers, and indeed, should it continue, ostracization from the group.

> The juvenile who fails to live up to the conflict gang's requirements is pushed outside the group. The adult male who does not defend his honour or his female companion will be socially emasculated. The 'coward' is forced to move out of the territory, to find new friends and make new alliances. (Wolfgang and Ferracuti, 1967, quoted by Berkowitz, 1982b, p. 92)

Wolfgang and Ferracuti believe that it is an adherence to such values that explains, in a very large part, violent behaviour. Rejecting the notion of aggressive instinct or drive, claiming that there is no indication that any physiological substrates are reliably implicated in violent behaviour,[10] and concluding that there is no firm evidence to link violence with any particular psychological pathology, they argue that overt (and often illicit) expression of violence (of which homicide is only the most extreme) is part of a subcultural normative system, and that this system is reflected in the psychological traits of the subculture participants. (1967, p. 158)

In the book, Wolfgang and Ferracuti acknowledge that it is not always easy to discover how such a subculture emerges: 'We are not prepared to assert how a subculture of violence arises. Perhaps there are several ways in different cultural settings.' They do, however, associate it particularly with the notion of machismo, and in defence of this association point to the fact that

a review of the statistical and clinical literature from many societies indicates that the age–sex category of youthful males exhibits the highest association with violent crime and that physically aggressive behaviour for this group converges with notions about the masculine ideal. (ibid., p. 260)

Wolfgang and Ferracuti's thesis, then, is that where there exists a 'subculture of violence', or shared system of norms, values and beliefs about violence, which sets the group who hold those norms aside from the dominant culture, then it is likely that members of that sub-culture will use violence as a central strategy in their interpersonal relations. Or, as Patrick puts it, 'violence can become a part of the life style, the theme of solving difficult problems' (1973, p. 196). In short, violence is *caused* largely by belonging to a particular sub-culture, because such group identification leads to a violent style of life.

## EVALUATING POSITIVIST SOCIAL ACCOUNTS OF AGGRESSION AND VIOLENCE

As I mentioned at the beginning of the chapter, these accounts are characterized by three orientations, the first of which is a reliance on a 'scientific' methodology. Such a methodology is to be seen more explicitly in the work of West and Farrington and Berkowitz than it is in the work of Wolfgang and Ferracuti. The first three workers place a great deal of emphasis on the statistical testing of particular hypotheses within the framework of elaborate experimental designs (in the case of much of Berkowitz's work, for example, 1973, 1974), or survey designs, as in the case of West and Farrington (1973, 1977). Like the experimental psychologists whose work was discussed in the previous chapter, their work can then be evaluated by criteria such as stringent experimental or survey design, size of sample, reliability of measurement, and replicability of results. In general, it seems to me that their work meets such criteria. For example, the West and Farrington study has shown almost no attrition of sample size in the repeated measures over more than a decade. Further, the psychometric tests they used were consistently and reliably administered, carefully measured and subjected to the appropriate statistical tests of significance before any conclusions were drawn.

Their results were, in addition, consistent with other studies that have looked at the variables associated with 'aggressive behaviour' in children. For example, McCord, McCord and Howard (1961) found that aggression in non-delinquent boys aged 10 to 15 was associated with punitive rejecting parents. And, in the case of their sub-sample of 'violent' young men, West and Farrington's association of such violence with earlier aggressive behaviour has also been reported in other studies such as Mulligan *et al.* (1963).

Applying the same 'scientific' criteria to the work of Wolfgang and Ferracuti produces rather less consistent results. While their demographic data of rates of criminal violence have not been challenged, their interpretation of such differential rates in terms of a 'sub-culture of violence' has been challenged on empirical grounds. When Ball-Rokeach (1973) explicitly tested two hypotheses that derive from Wolfgang and Ferracuti's work – that there will be a strong association, amongst offenders, between a favourable predisposition to violence and their involvement in interpersonal violence, and that men who had been imprisoned for violent offences would show very different values with respect to violence than non-offenders – she found only a very weak association in the first case, and no difference in the second.

The second evaluative perspective I have been using concerns assumptions of a less 'testable' kind; for example, assumptions about human nature. As I noted in previous chapters, these criteria are concerned with issues like rigour of thought, consistency, and whether or not the approach helps the evaluator extend his or her own understanding of the issues in question.

If we look first at the work of West and Farrington, and examine the issues of rigour and consistency, it seems to me that they, like the experimental psychologists whose work was reviewed in the previous chapter, come off rather well. They seldom make loose, overgeneralized statements or extend their findings to make sweeping claims. On the other hand, like the psychologists discussed above, they do appear to adhere to the belief that the social researcher can stand back from his or her research endeavour without any intrusion of values or preconceptions. Thus they appear not to consider that there are substantive problems in defining aggressive or violent behaviour, and they seldom question, for example, the subjectivity involved when teachers label behaviour as aggression, or whether police may provoke violence in young offenders.

While their account is explicitly atheoretical, West and Farrington implicitly appear to accept a social learning model of human interaction.

Like the experimental psychologists their emphasis is always on behaviour. It is true that they extend their consideration of behaviour from
the observable and measurable to include some self-report, but nevertheless the focus is always on the behaviour rather than on the perspectives of those who carry out the behaviour. Thus, like the experimental
psychologists, they lose an important key to understanding aggression
and violence.[11]

Turning to the work of Wolfgang and Ferracuti, I have indicated
above that while their demographic data is not challenged, their hypotheses have not been confirmed by empirical research, so that in judging
their work on the criteria of 'scientific' methodology limitations are
clearly apparent. If we look at the second evaluative strand I have been
using, which is concerned with more subjective aspects of evaluation, it
is fair to say that they are very careful not to make claims about their
formulation of a 'sub-culture of violence' which are not warranted by
existing data. Thus their book is studded with remarks like 'research is
simply not available to permit us to designate where in the world all of
these subcultures [of violence] may be' (1967, p. 272). Nevertheless,
their postulation of such subcultures to account for violent behaviour
seems to me to be an extremely simplistic reading of the complicated and
contradictory attitudes that many offenders hold about the issues of
violence. As I shall indicate in the next two sections of this chapter,
Wolfgang and Ferracuti's conception of clear-cut differences in the value
systems of violent offenders and the rest of the social world is neither
substantiated by the evidence, as already noted, nor tenable in terms of
current strands in sociological theory.

As far as the theoretical underpinnings of their postulation of a sub-
culture of violence are concerned, Wolfgang and Ferracuti do not explicitly acknowledge any orientation which would allow them to explain
why it is that certain Indian tribes, or particular Sicilian families, or
specific Central American countries develop such value systems. As the
remark I quoted above indicates, their concern is with documenting the
existence of such sub-cultures rather than with speculating about their
origins. Nevertheless, although they acknowledge no specific theoretical
underpinnings, their work, like that of West and Farrington and of
Berkowitz, is characterized by certain assumptions: that there is no
ambiguity in defining violence and aggression, that observable and
measurable data is to be preferred to verbal accounts given by subjects,
and that focusing on cause and effect is preferable to focusing on understanding the nature of psychological or sociological processes.

Finally I would like to suggest that, despite its limitations in focus, and
its paucity of theory, the work of positivist social scientists surveyed in
this section has nevertheless yielded some empirical findings that any
comprehensive account of aggression and violence must be able to
explain.

(1)  There appears to be a high level of association between child-rearing practices and aggressive behaviour in children. Those practices which have been so associated are extreme punitiveness and rejection. It is worth noting here that in a cross-cultural survey of research on aggression, Segall (1983) concludes that the association of punitiveness with aggressive behaviour is a finding that extends well beyond Western societies.

(2)  Aggressive behaviour shows a degree of consistency over time, and children who show a relatively high level of aggressive behaviour are more likely than their peers to be indicted for violent crimes later in life.

(3)  There are differences in the rate of indictable violence both across cultures and within them, so that members of the more disadvantaged sections of societies are more likely to be convicted for such crimes.

## HOW EXTENSIVE IS THE USE MADE OF THE TERMS 'AGGRESSION' AND 'VIOLENCE' IN THE ACCOUNTS OF SOCIAL SCIENTISTS?

Before moving onto the next account of aggression and violence, I will look briefly at how adequately those accounts put forth in the present section cover the different usages of the terms 'aggression' and 'violence' that I devised in my summational descriptions in Chapter 1.

*Aggression*
In discussing the use of the term 'aggression', I intend to refer only to the perspective of West and Farrington. This is because Berkowitz's use of the term is subsumed in the discussion at the end of the last chapter, and because Wolfgang and Ferracuti's subject matter is criminal violence and they refer to aggression as a separate concept only when reviewing the work of other social scientists.

West and Farrington's use of the term aggression tends to be very pragmatic and they are not really concerned with issues of definition. Implicitly, then,

(a)  They appear to use the term 'aggressive' to cover behaviour that is inended to hurt or harm others.

(b)  They are not interested in issues of achieving dominance.

(c)  They appear to accept that aggression may not involve physical force, for example, in their description of teachers' reports of aggressive behaviour.

(d)  They do not explicitly distinguish between different classes of motives for aggression.

(e)  They are not concerned with potentially positive aspects of aggression.

(f)   They are not concerned with issues of subjectivity in the labelling of aggression, although (see below) they do accept that there are definitional problems in the labelling of violence.

(g)   They are not centrally concerned with values, and consequently do not see as a major issue how a labellers' value system may intersect with the application of the label 'aggressive' to specific behaviour.

*Violence*

Berkowitz, like the other experimental psychologists whose work was reviewed in the last chapter, seldom deals explicitly with violence, appearing like them to see violence as behaviour which both involves physical force and is very intense. West and Farrington and Wolfgang and Ferracuti are all primarily concerned with criminal or indictable violence. Consequently the issues of defining violence are for them legalistic rather than theoretical:

(a)   Violence is thus seen as necessarily involving physical force.

(b)   Imputing particular intentionalities to violence is seen to be less important than the legal classification of the violent behaviour. In general Wolfgang and Ferracuti appear to believe that most homicides are caused by sudden hostile 'motivational bursts' rather than by rational planning (1967, p. 209).

(c)   No consideration is given to individuals who engage in mutually satisfying violent physical interaction.

(d)   While Farrington does accept that there are problems in the legal definition of criminal violence (1982, p. 171), comparatively little emphasis is placed on issues of the legitimization of violence under certain circumstances, for example, when carried out by agents of law and order.

In general, the work covered in this section, is not concerned with the definitional or conceptual issues that arise in the use of the terms aggression and violence. As I noted above the approach is pragmatic rather than analytical.

## Phenomenological Accounts of Aggression and Violence

PSYCHOLOGICAL ACCOUNTS

*Violent Men*

We must also assume that we cannot make sense of violent acts by viewing them as outsiders. Ultimately, violence arises because some person feels that he must resort to a physical act, that a problem he faces calls for a destructive solution. The problem a violent person perceives is rarely the situation as we see it, but rather some dilemma he finds himself in. In order to understand a violent person's motives for violence, we must step into his shoes, and reconstruct his unique perspective, no matter how strange or odd it may be. We must re-create the world of the violent man, with all its fears and apprehensions, with its hopes and ambitions, with its strains and stresses. (Toch, in *Violent Men*, 1972, p. 38)

Like West and Farrington and Wolfgang and Ferracuti, Hans Toch is concerned with the problems posed for society by violent people. His perspective, however, differs considerably from theirs. Whereas West and Farrington are concerned to identify the characteristics of violent offenders and Wolfgang and Ferracuti are concerned to identify their social milieu, Toch's primary concern, as the quotation above suggests, is with the perspectives and perceptions that violent men hold of their own behaviour and its intentions. Toch sees the individual as immersed in a social context. Within this social context, Toch believes, actions can only properly be understood from the vantage point of those who carry out the actions. Violence must be studied from the perspective of those who commit it. Their points of view must be regarded as primary – their definitions of the social situations, their self concepts and their own perceptions of their emotions and motives. It is this approach with its emphasis on the primacy of individual meanings that I have labelled *phenomenological*.

Toch's own study of violent men centred on a sample of prisoners and paroled men in California and also on a sample of thirty-two policemen who had been habitually involved in violent interactions with detained men. Toch's major source of data was the descriptions these men gave of the violent incidents in which they had been involved.

These descriptions were obtained in lengthy interviews and, in line with his emphasis on the subjective world of his subjects, Toch ensured that such interviews were conducted by the subjects' social peers. For the offenders this meant research assistants who had themselves been convicted for violent offences, and for the police sample this meant academics who had previously served as policemen. By using peers Toch hoped not only to circumvent the barriers to easy communication which occur when a conventional academic interviews a convicted prisoner, but also to create a meaningful dialogue in which interviewer and interviewee could exchange views about mutual experiences of violence. Toch notes that if interviewers are not prepared to exchange views with interviewees on a basis of equality, then the former are 'supplicants and, at worst, invaders demanding booty of captive audiences', who 'expect a person to bare his soul or to make controversial and potentially incriminating statements' in exchange for a modest fee or vague promises (1972, p. 46).

The interviews were tape-recorded and then analysed in group sessions, when both professional and peer researchers tried to extract from the data the common themes and patterns that Toch sought in line with his basic assumption that 'if we want to explain why men are driven to acts of destruction, we must examine these acts, and understand the contexts in which they occur' (ibid., p. 38).

From the analyses that were made of the interviews, Toch concluded that his sample of men were particularly 'prone to violence'. The proneness resulted not from personality traits in the accepted sense of stable attributes, but from an *orientation* which led his subjects to respond with force when in a potentially violent situation. Acknowledging that his sample were often brought up in a world where they could legitimately draw the conclusion that 'power is the only voice that carries', Toch argued nevertheless that it is largely the violent-prone who will interpret the exercise of power as inevitably involving violence.

There were, he suggested, two basic orientations that led to this violence proneness. In the first, the violent-prone individual feels vulnerable to manipulation, and in the second the violent-prone individual sees other people as tools designed to serve his needs. But both perspectives, he argued, shared on closer examination similar roots, for 'both rest on the premise that human relationships are power-centred, one-way affairs; both involve efforts at self-assertion with a desperate, feverish quality that suggests self-doubt' (ibid., p. 226).

Toch extended his consideration of these two orientations to produce a 'typology'[12] of ten categories. Each of these categories, he claimed, represented an approach to interpersonal situations that promotes violence.

The first six categories (and I present these using Toch's own numbering system), derived from the orientation that he saw as being closely tied to vulnerability and inadequacy. These were:

(1) Reputation defending: when violence is used in order to preserve a role which 'has been allocated by public acclaim'.
(2) Norm-enforcing: when violence is used because the individual believes that he is acting to enforce his own values.
(3) Self-image compensation: when violence is used to compensate for low self-esteem. For example, (a) as a form of retribution against people who have cast aspersions against the particular individual; or (b) when violence is used to gain admiration.
(4) Self-defining: when violence is used to preserve the individual from physical harm.
(5) Pressure removing: when the individual tends to deal with social situations by using violence because his social skills are limited.

The other four categories Toch saw as springing from the second orientation in which the violent individual only perceives others as tools designed to serve his needs. These were:

(1)  Bullying: when pleasure is obtained by terrorizing individuals who are particularly susceptible.
(2)  Exploitation: when violence is used to manipulate others into 'being tools of one's own pleasure and convenience'.
(3)  Self-indulging: when violence is used because the individual believes that others exist solely to gratify the individual's own needs.
(4)  Catharting: when violence is used to give vent to emotions or moods.

Violent incidents, according to Toch, were likely to occur when men who fell into any of the categories perceived the social situation as potentially threatening. Further, Toch argues, the members of his sample were very prone to make such an assessment, for they 'scan human contacts assiduously for the possibility of threatening implications' (ibid., p. 229). Once this determination of the situation is made, the violent incident is well on its way, passing through several predictable stages:

> first, the classification of the other person as an object or a threat; second, some action based on this classification; third, the other person may act – if he has the chance – to protect his integrity. The violent incident now reaches its point of no return. The initial stance of the violence-prone person makes violence probable; his first moves increase the probability of violence; the reaction of the victim converts probability into certainty. (ibid., p. 227)

This pattern of reciprocal threat and attack, once established in one or two incidents, is likely to be used by the violent-prone again and again, for as Toch puts it:

> Violence is habit-forming. Aggressors discover that they can satisfy new and unsuspected needs by becoming aggressive. They also learn to view themselves as participants in violent games. Most importantly, they start seeing elements of past violent encounters as they approach fresh situations and begin to respond routinely. They seek and find consistency of self at the expense of their victims. (ibid., p. 229)

A major part of *Violent Men* is devoted to the material I have just covered: the description of the methodology of the study, the case histories that were studied, the derivation of the typology, and the natural history of the violent incident. Rather less space is devoted to three other issues that emerge from Toch's approach. First, why do some men become violent-prone? Secondly, how far does Toch's analysis of violent incidents between two individual contenders extend to group violence? And thirdly, what are the implications for reducing the level of violence in social interaction? I would like to deal briefly with each of these in turn.

Toch has relatively little to say about the origins of 'violence prone orientation'. He suggests, but in bare outline only, that the origins lie in interpersonal relationships in early life. If these lack consistency and stability, according to Toch, the orientation that makes a person feel vulnerable to manipulation arises when there is deficiency in 'stability and emotional support, thus making it difficult for positive self-perceptions to develop' (ibid., p. 231). The second orientation, the predisposition to see other people as tools to satisfy one's own needs, arises when there is a 'failure of socialisation' (ibid., p. 231). When such orientations emerge, and when, in addition, a person grows up in a milieu where violent interactions are commonplace (and here Toch refers to Wolfgang and Ferracuti's concept of a sub-culture of violence), the ground is laid for the emergence of a 'violent man'.

When it comes to extending his analysis from the small group or the two person situation to collective episodes of violence, Toch turns to the American urban unrest of the 1960s, and in particular to what he terms the 'riots' amongst the blacks. In reviewing these disturbances he bases his discussion on the report presented by the President's Commission on Civil Disorder (1968) which listed five ingredients as catalysts of the disturbances. These ingredients were:

(1) Frustration of the hopes which had been generated by the civil rights movement.
(2) A climate which was heavy with the 'approval and encouragement of violence'.
(3) The frustration that was caused by feeling powerless to change the system.
(4) A mood, particularly among younger people, of enhanced racial pride.
(5) A view of the police as a symbol of white racism and repression.

'Riots' occur, then, because in effect an oppressed group suffers the same feelings of inadequacy as the violent-prone individual. Finding in a joint endeavour both support from their peers and sanction of their behaviour, the members of the group seek in violence to redress their grievances and, in Toch's own words, 'every riot is – in extended form – a violent incident of the sort we have described' (ibid., p. 248). Thus, to begin with, according to Toch, 'black citizen A' makes demands of 'white Social Agent B' and, when these are not satisfied, he concludes that white social agents of society 'are his tormentors, and that he must act accordingly. When many individual people arrive at this conclusion, a collective move to act in its spirit can be expected' (ibid., p. 248).

While accepting that the 'rioter is a product of history', that is, that disturbances occur partly as a result of the operation of structural forces within society, Toch nevertheless argues that riots tend to cater for the needs of violence-prone individuals. For Toch claims that in riots, unlike wars, the participant typically wants to commit violence, and 'rioting may thus be an act of revenge for some, and an emotional discharge or an act of rebellion for others. Violence may serve as a vehicle for personal identity, or a means to power or material gain.' War, on the other hand, according to Toch, is typically waged by individuals 'because the individual's military vocation demands it' (ibid., p. 258).

What then are the *implications* of Toch's analyses? He concludes that these fall into two sets of recommendations, those dealing with individual and those dealing with collective violence. *Individual violence,* he believes, can be controlled, in the first instance by an improvement in predicting who will become violence prone and providing emotional succour for such people by the use of group support. When it comes to the man who has a career of violence behind him, Toch believes that the major commitment must be to help him to re-appraise himself and to become redeemed 'through the restorative acts of people bent on rebuilding each other' (ibid., p. 275). Groups of violent men should function as a 'therapeutic milieu' in which they can reinforce each other's strengths, help each other in joint constructive activities and, through the use of techniques such as psychodrama,[13] help each other to handle potentially violent situations in a positive and non-violent manner.

In dealing with *collective violence,* Toch argues that although this 'tends to arise as a reaction against unmet aspirations and consists of retaliation against the symbols of perceived unresponsiveness' (ibid., p. 285), it should not be assumed that such violence can be dealt with by simply meeting the aspirations of those involved. For these aspirations may sometimes be of 'questionable legitimacy'. Where the aspirations, however, are legitimate, Toch argues, potential participants must be taught to seek other means of achieving their objectives. In such cases non-violent resources must be available.

Toch also argues, with respect to collective violence, that the fact must be faced that 'destructive influences are exerted among riot participants by groups and individuals within their ranks. Such centres of violence proneness can be selected for special attention and can be converted or neutralised' (ibid., p. 287). The method of neutralization to be used should be similar to those already suggested for dealing with violent men as individuals – and should centre around therapeutic group support.

Finally, Toch recommends that it is essential that police be retrained if violent encounters between them and offenders are to be reduced. Writing from an American perspective where such violence is relatively common, he notes that

> Our research indicates that the ranks of law enforcement contain their share of violent men. The personalities, outlooks, and actions of these officers are similar to those of the other men in our sample. They reflect the same fears and insecurities, the same fragile, self-centred perspectives. They display the same bluster and bluff, panic and punitiveness, rancour and revenge as do our other respondents. (ibid., p. 288)

The retraining that Toch recommends is once again similar to the rehabilitation that he suggests for violent offenders, and involves the setting up of therapeutic and supportive groups for those officers who are frequently implicated in violent incidents. Such groups, he writes, could utilize the techniques both of psychodrama and of real-life training on the streets in order that the men concerned could acknowledge their own contribution to the escalation of conflict and learn more sensitive and appropriate techniques for dealing with suspects and offenders.

Toch further suggests that police procedures be scrutinized in order to clarify the ambiguities that surround a policeman's role, where he may be told that he may use 'reasonable force' but not be aware how to judge what is, and what is not, reasonable.

In sum, Toch concludes that his view of violent men is neither fatalistic nor over-hopeful, for it suggests that violent men can be assessed, understood and rehabilitated. He warns, however, that such regeneration cannot take place in a society where there are 'men who press explosive buttons or sign bloodthirsty orders'. For such set the stage for the lone operators who he has labelled as 'violent men'.

In looking at Toch's contribution to our understanding of violent men, I believe we must acknowledge how far he moved the debate within social psychology from the positivist tradition of quantifying observable behaviour. By introducing a discussion of what he himself calls 'the phenomenology of violence', he introduced a perspective that allows for an increased sensitivity to the intentions, motives, perceptions and aspirations of people who commit violent acts. I feel, however, that his analysis has some important limitations.

First, it seems to me that he does not relate his discussion of violence to the actions and behaviour of those whom he does not classify as violence-prone. In making this point, I refer both to his very broad use of the term violence and to his rather narrowly focused discussion of it. For Toch, 'violence' embraces not only the use of physical force but also psychological bullying and exploitation. Undoubtedly, it is not only 'violent men' who engage in these non-physical aspects of coercive behaviour. But Toch does not locate his discussion of such aspects of interaction anywhere except in the fulcrum of police–offender or offender–offender confrontations. In the final chapter of this book, I propose how Toch's insights into the understanding of violence can be extended beyond the limited interpersonal situations he describes.

Secondly, and more substantively, Toch does not place his analysis within an overall conceptual framework of interpersonal relationships. If he claims that violence is a strategy that can be used to enhance self-esteem or provide emotional gratification, what does he understand to be the principles that govern the emergence of the sense of self and the satisfaction of emotional needs? This is another aspect that I shall return to in the next chapter.

Finally, his analysis of collective violence does not take into account the fact that behaviour in disturbances can be interpreted, not only as an emotional reaction to perceived frustration, but can also be understood as a rational response to social and economic disadvantages. This additional, if not alternative, perspective on collective violence is taken up by the social scientists whose work is considered in the remainder of this chapter.

Before turning to these, however, I want to present an account of growing up in a black ghetto which provides a subjective and participatory endorsement of Toch's viewpoint:

I remember one time I hit a boy in the face with a bottle of Pepsi-Cola. I did it because I knew the older cats on 146th Street were watching me. The boy had messed with Carole. He had taken her candy from her and thrown it on the ground.

I came up to him and said, 'Man, what you mess with my sister for?'

All the older guys were saying, 'That's that little boy who lives on Eighth Avenue. They call him Sonny Boy. We gon see somethin' good out here now.'

There was a Pepsi-Cola truck there; they were unloading some crates. They were stacking up the crates to roll them inside. The boy who had hit Carole was kind of big and acted kind of mean. He had a stick in his hand, and he said, 'Yeah, I did it, so what you gon do about it?'

I looked at him for a while, and he looked big. He was holding that stick like he meant to use it, so I snatched a Pepsi-Cola bottle and hit him right in the face. He grabbed his face and started crying. He fell down, and I started to hit him again, but the man who was unloading the Pepsi-Cola bottles grabbed me. He took the bottle away from me and shook me. He asked me if I was crazy or something.

All the guys on the corner started saying, 'You better leave that boy alone,' and 'Let go of that kid.' I guess he got kind of scared. He was white, and here were all these mean-looking colored cats talking about 'Let go that kid' and looking at him. They weren't asking him to let me go; they were telling him. He let me go.

Afterward, if I came by, they'd start saying, 'Hey, Sonny Boy, how you doin'?' They'd ask me, 'You kick anybody's ass today?' I knew that they admired me for this, and I knew that I had to keep on doing it. This was the reputation I was making, and I had to keep living up to it every day that I came out of the house. Every day, there was a greater demand on me. I couldn't beat the same little boys every day. They got bigger and bigger. I had to get more vicious as the cats got bigger. When the bigger guys started messing with you, you couldn't hit them or give them a black eye or a bloody nose. You had to get a bottle or a stick or a knife. All the other cats out there on the streets expected this of me, and they gave me encouragement. (Claude Brown in *Manchild in the Promised Land*, 1966, pp. 258–9)

## The Rules of Disorder

Our theory is based on the idea that human social life is a product of interaction between sequences of actions and talk about those actions. Everything we do can be redone by talk . . . A further corollary which has figured largely in our studies is the idea that the best, though not necessarily the ultimate, authorities as to what the action 'actually' is, are the actors themselves. In their accounts are to be found, *prima facie*, the best interpretations of what went on, from the standpoint of the problem of the interpretation of action. This follows almost directly from the fact that the actors were the ones who intended the action in the first place. (Marsh, Rosser and Harré, 1978, p. 21)

The research referred to in *Violent Men* took place in the USA, and was, as I have noted, not explicitly based on any particular theoretical approach to social psychology. In its insistence, however, on paying attention to the world view of its subjects, it comes very close to the perspective of other social psychologists, such as Peter Marsh, working at a slightly later date in Britain. Marsh, however, acknowledges far more theoretical influences on his work than does Toch. These range from de Suassure's work in linguistics, and in particular his discussion of meaning, through recent reformulations of social psychological theory (Harré and Seccord, 1972) to contemporary trends in criminology (for example, the work of Young, 1971). Marsh uses these sources to provide a complex rationale for adopting the same techniques as Toch does –

exhaustive self-reports and attempting to uncover the rules that subjects ascribe to their behaviour.

Unlike Toch, Marsh has not taken as a central area of study either aggression or violence. But in his attempts to interpret the social lives of particular segments of contemporary young people he has looked in some detail at the significance within such lives of gang fights and football 'violence'.

Arguing that all human beings need to achieve personal dignity, 'personal worth and the achievement of identity' (Marsh, 1982, p. 106), Marsh claims that certain sections of young people in contemporary British society are deprived of the means of achieving these within the conventional worlds of school and work. So they are forced to turn for their achievement to the world of their own sub-culture,[14] for such sub-cultures provide a forum for 'a sense of belonging and prestige'. For urban *young men* in particular, it is the football terraces, Marsh believes, that allow for the emergence of sub-cultural rituals. These rituals provide opportunities for the construction of social hierarchies, the establishment of reputations and the waging of contests. The contests are, Marsh argues, mainly waged symbolically and consequently non-violently. Such symbolic battles include the parading of gear – scarves, boots, denim jackets – the yelling of chants and the chorusing of football songs. As is well known, however, confrontation between rival groups at football matches is not only confined to symbolic rituals – it can move, though perhaps less often than the media would suggest,[15] from verbal taunting into physical violence. For Marsh, however, all such confrontations, whether ritualized or violent, are characterized by rules. The rules exist to ensure that aggression, which Marsh sees as an underlying human predisposition, is kept within certain bounds. Such rules applied, for example, to fights between football supporters state that:

> fights should involve equal numbers of protagonists on each side, that some verbal negotiation should precede the introduction of weapons, that certain bodily areas are not legitimate targets for attack, and that attack should be in accord with wrestling and boxing traditions – scratching, spitting, hair pulling and biting are 'out of order'. (Campbell, 1981, p. 147, writing about Marsh's work)

Central to Marsh's position is the belief that aggression is 'inevitable'. And in his conception of aggression, Marsh comes pretty close to the position of Anthony Storr (see Chapter 4), for he defines it as 'a property of human beings in virtue of which they are prone to act upon others in a typically thrusting and imperious way' (Marsh, Rosser and Harré, 1978, p. 27). Its roots, Marsh believes, lie in a biological basis which in a 'global' manner causes individuals to act forcefully upon the world. But

Marsh is less interested in the origin of aggression than he is in the rituals in society which contain it. He sees such rituals as akin, in some respects, to the rituals outlined by ethologists for containing aggression within animal species, but believes that they are not innately laid down; rather they are learned within the cultural environment. It is, for Marsh, the *predisposition to construct rituals that is innate*, rather than the actual ritual.

It is in his investigation and understanding of such rituals that Marsh moves towards Toch's phenomenological perspective. For, like Toch, Marsh believes that the understanding of violence, which he sees simply as 'a consequence of aggression' (ibid., p. 128), lies in entering the world view of the individual who carries it out. In order to enter this, Marsh employs three techniques: first, participant observation, secondly, listening to talk about fighting, and thirdly interpreting such fighting talk, or, as Marsh puts it, uncovering what lies beneath the 'rhetoric of violence'. I would like to deal briefly with these three techniques in turn.

Participant observation is a method of research in which the researcher joins the social group in which he or she is interested and engages, to some extent, in their activities while simultaneously observing and later recording what happens.

The second technique is concerned with collecting the subjects' own accounts of their emotions and intentions both in formal tape-recorded interviews and in casual discussion in the football ground. Here, for example, is a transcript of what a 16-year-old had to say about his own position in his social group and how he rose to a position of leader within it.

> It was about then [three years ago] that I started going with some of my mates like Kevin and Eddie [to football games] . . . and Eddie and me we got into a lot of fights and that . . . and the fucking coppers – they always grab either him or me when there's any bother or that. We been in Cowley nick so many times they keep a special room for us and inside it's got Eddie and Rich written on the walls – and they don't bother to clean it off 'cos they know we'll be back and write it up again . . . A lot of kids – when there's any bother they all start running. That's the trouble with Oxford – they run too much. But Eddie and me and kids like John and Alf we always get left there. These kids was coming at us once and six of them grabbed hold of me and left me to get a kicking . . . I try to keep out of it a lot now but I'm not scared or nothing. If someone wants to have a go I'll give it to him. But I wait for him to start it – and then I just finish it off. (ibid., p. 77)

Marsh, however, is reluctant always to take such accounts at face value. For he argues that boys often report feats of amazing brutality but if pressed will agree that no-one really gets hurt:

Question:     What do you do when you 'put the boot in'?
Fan A:     Well, you kicks 'em in the 'ead don't you – heavy boots with metal toe-caps an' that.
Q:     What happens then?
     (*puzzled look from fans*)
Fan A:     He's dead.
Fan B:     Nah! He's alright – usually anyway.
(Marsh, 1982, p. 105)

The third essential technique is to marry the often apocryphal accounts with observation of actual behaviour. If this is not done, the researcher will be seduced 'by the distortions and transformations that are carried through the rhetorics [which] serve to enhance personal prestige and worth' (ibid., p. 116) into believing that violence occurs far more frequently than it actually does.

Anne Campbell's work with young girls (1981, 1982) is, like Marsh's, primarily concerned with discovering what an individual has to know about the social world in order to take part in the social interaction of the group to which he or she belongs. Consequently, like Marsh, she is not centrally interested in aggression or violence, and investigates them only to the extent to which she sees these issues as playing a part in the social life of the groups she was studying. In Campbell's case the groups concerned were 251 16-year-old working-class schoolgirls in Glasgow, Liverpool, Oxford and London, and another group of sixty girls from a Borstal. Unlike Marsh, however, she did not observe any of the girls' behaviour directly and relied for her understanding of the part that aggression and violence played in their social world on questionnaire responses and group discussions.[16]

Campbell's theoretical stance is less coherent than Marsh's, but she appears to believe, like him, that aggression is a human predisposition arising out of an earlier need to preserve the human species which has been elaborated by both culture and learning so that, looking at her own particular focus of interest in the area, the aggression and violence of adolescent females, she considers that while evolutionary forces have contributed to a higher likelihood of aggression in males than in females, social forces have enhanced this difference. Nevertheless, she argues, it is worth investigating whether aggression in young girls serves a social function in contemporary society.

In the work she describes, however, although she continues to use the term aggression, she focuses exclusively on fighting. Most of her 16-year-old girls (89 per cent) told her that they had been in at least one fight, and all had witnessed one. Like the boys described by Marsh, Campbell's 16-year-old girls appeared to follow implicit rules in these fights so that damage resulting from them was limited. For example, the

most common injuries were bruises (46 per cent), cuts (25 per cent) and
scratches (21 per cent). Like the boys Marsh studied, the fights seemed
to be concerned largely with issues of status, for when the reasons that
girls gave for fights were broken down into categories, the majority of
responses seemed involved with aspects of personal integrity. Girls
fought because they felt the need to retaliate when attacks were made on
their private or public self-concept, or when their friends or relatives
were insulted or when they were jealous. They did not in general fight for
instrumental reasons, for example, to obtain money. Like their male
peers studied by Marsh, Campbell's subjects fought to preserve and
enhance their own status, to reduce or destroy the status of others and to
settle disputes which threatened to disrupt the social order of the group.

AC:   What do girls fight about?
-     Boys.
-     Ripping up one another's clothes and calling each other
      names.
-     Jealousy.
-     Breaking up best friends.
AC:   What sort of names?
-     'Slag', things like that.
AC:   What do boys fight about?
-     Girls.
-     Who's better than who.
-     'I've seen you with her.'
-     Chickening out – they say 'Oh, you chickened out of
      that' and fight about it to show they're tough.
AC:   Does machismo work for girls too?
-     Yeah, yeah.
-     It does.
-     There's always some girl you say 'I wouldn't have a fight with
      her', but when it comes to it you do.
AC:   So do boys and girls fight about the same things or not?
-     Boils down to the same thing really, 'cos girls fight over boys,
      boys fight over girls. Fight for their pride, things like that,
      and boys fight about the same things.
-     A girl that's been called a slag is the same as a boy that's been
      called a chicken.
(Campbell, 1982, p. 142)

Campbell concludes that the picture that emerges of adolescent girls
fighting is 'remarkably similar to that of fights among males' (1981, p.
180). Fights were about keeping 'face' in front of friends and were
provoked as in the case of Marsh's sample by the need to maintain order
within social groups and by issues of personal integrity. In addition, like

boys' fights, rules were acknowledged to exist and were, in the main, followed.

But Campbell's study of fighting amongst Borstal girls yielded rather different results. The girls showed not only more involvement in fighting, but were far more positively disposed to it. Unlike the schoolgirls whom Campbell studied, these Borstal girls believed that fighting was a good way of releasing anger and of settling disputes. Their higher level of fighting and greater intensity of violence when they fought appeared to be related to home backgrounds where violence was imposed on them:

AC:   How did your father hit you?

—    Well, he didn't slap me round the arse. He used to batter my face in. All I had to do to get hit was the littlest thing. If I coughed or sneezed, which you can't help, when one of his operas was on, he used to batter me. He used to really batter me for that. I used to get battered nearly every day. That's no exaggeration. I used to be a right little bastard.

—    My father – he took my arm, right, and he really hammered me. He didn't just smack me, he really laid into me. He got my head and he was sort of punching it.

(Campbell, 1981, p. 182)

In addition to reporting that they were subjected to violence in the home, the Borstal girls also said that they were encouraged by their parents to fight other children in self-defence and that they both fought with their elder brothers and sisters and learned to fight from them.

> When my brother goes, he goes mad. Sometimes he has blackouts and he don't know what he's doing . . . He's done it to me, he stabbed me in the tit once. It bloody hurt. (Campbell, 1981, p. 183)

The reasons these girls gave for fighting, were, like the reasons given by the adolescent schoolgirls, tied up with notions of personal identity, but were slanted in particular in the direction of safeguarding their reputations for *toughness*. Like Toch's sample of violent men, self-worth in the Borstal girls was tied intimately to preserving their own particular sphere of excellence.

> Well, at school I was fighting anybody who wanted to fight – they'd come up to me and say, 'You're meant to be cock of the school,' and I'd say, 'Yeah,' and they'd say, 'Fight me at ten to four when we finish school.' So I'd fight them and I'd beat them, and their mates would come and it was going on like that. I was continually fighting. But when I left school I didn't have half as many fights when I started work, 'cos nobody knew I was a fighter at work. I only fight when it's necessary now. (Campbell, 1981, p. 189)

Finally, unlike the sample of adolescent girls, these girls acknowledge no implicit rules in their fighting nor did they set any limits. Campbell thus concludes that, while the picture of adolescent girls' fighting that emerged from her work was similar to Marsh's picture of boys, both in its rule-bound behaviour and in its aspects of ritualization, the fighting described by her Borstal sample was very different. For these girls, 'fighting seems to have shed its ritual component' (ibid., p. 196) and emerges as a 'vicious expression of hatred and resentment'.

It can be seen that both Campbell and Marsh share certain perspectives with Hans Toch. To begin with, like Toch they believe that the only valid manner in which to investigate aggression and violence is to attempt to understand aggression and violence from the perspective of those who are labelled, or label themselves, as aggressive and violent. Also, like Toch, they conclude that such behaviour is intimately related to the individual's self-concept and the need to preserve self-worth. Unlike Toch, however, they claim that limited involvement in violence can serve a constructive purpose in that, by ritualizing underlying aggression, it can contain such aggression and prevent it escalating in undesirable ways. In developing this aspect of his views on aggression, Marsh comes very close to Lorenz and Storr:

> But there is a sense in which the rituals we have described are in some jeopardy. The fan who, in talking about the wrecked railway carriage, commented that the trouble started because the police were treating them like animals – so they behaved like animals – revealed the fragile nature of the football ritual. Rule frameworks and symbolic systems are not panaceas. They offer solutions to the problem of aggression only to the extent that others in society admit and recognize their value. Eventually, when the fines run into thousands of pounds and longer jail sentences are imposed on football rowdies, the pressure will be sufficient effectively to eradicate the whole phenomenon of the football hooligan. We are right to be concerned with acts of vandalism and assault, but if the official strategies for dealing with law breaking also take away the opportunities for boys and young men to engage in structured aggro, then we might very well be faced with a set of problems that are far more serious and much more difficult to control. (Marsh, Rosser and Harré, 1978, p. 134)

Marsh and Campbell approach their subject matter primarily from a psychological orientation. Their focus tends to be on individuals inter-acting in groups, and on their interpersonal relationships. They are, also like Toch, both concerned with individual self-concepts and how such concepts are risked, defended and enhanced by social interactions. Such emphases are, to my mind, primarily psychological. But in certain other respects, their perspective is very close to that held by a number of sociologists working in the field of deviance. In particular, their emphases on episodes, contexts and rituals, and their claim that behaviour, which may look random and irrational to outsiders, may actually be both planned and rule-governed if viewed from the perspectives of those who are carrying out that behaviour, brings them very close to the accounts of aggression and violence given by a number of contemporary sociologists. It is to these accounts that I will now turn.

SOCIOLOGICAL ACCOUNTS

The sheer proliferation of accounts of delinquency and violence over the past three decades have perhaps sown an undue amount of confusion, which might have been avoided if theorists had specified more carefully what they have been trying to explain. (Downes, 1982, p. 43)

Sociologists have not in general been inclined to write about either aggression or violence as single themes. They have instead tended to regard violence as an aspect of behaviour that is involved in a way of life which is characterized by many kinds of law breaking. Consequently, when most sociologists do write about violence, or less commonly about aggression, they do so within a general treatment of criminal behaviour. In recent years, an underlying assumption that has characterized sociological treatment of criminal behaviour has been one that is endorsed by those psychologists whose work has just been discussed, and that is that such behaviour shares with other forms of social life the properties of motive and meaning. In their search for the understanding of such motives and meanings in violent behaviour, it seems to me that contemporary sociologists have focused on two particular themes: the first is concerned with the value systems of those whose life is characterized by continual encounters with the law, and the second is concerned with the labelling of particular actions as deviant, or in the particular case of our subject matter as 'violent'. I would like to deal with these two themes in turn.[17]

*Anomie, value systems and sub-cultures*
    The Glory Boys
    Sometime heroes
    cold distant
    sharp smart
    walk the two tonic strut
    cheap thrills
    amphetamine smiles
    bitter hate Glory Boys

trying to find themselves in the
faceless crowd
second hand dreams
trying to find our way

It's a teenage dream, a hackneyed theme
A timestained story, a bid for glory . . .
(Page and Cairns, 1979)

At the beginning of this chapter, I quoted Downes's statement that violence can be 'read, appreciated and decoded – in short, understood' (1982, p. 29), and for many contemporary sociologists and their predecessors, the key to such reading, appreciating decoding and understanding has lain in exposing the value systems that are presumed to underpin the commission of violent acts.

In the earlier treatment of these values, the primary emphasis was on *anomie*. Particularly in the USA, it was argued that deviance was likely to be engendered in those societies where, while all citizens are enjoined to strive for worldly success, the possibility of achieving it legitimately is not extended to all. Those who are not able to achieve it legitimately were thought to suffer from *anomie*, and to turn as a result to various kinds of criminal behaviour in order to achieve some measure of financial success. Crime, which might include violent crime, was thus seen as arising from the discrepancy between culturally induced aspirations and realistic expectations (Merton, 1957). In this way both criminal and non-criminal members of society were thought to have no option but to conform to the possibilities facing them: everyone propelled by common values, sought similar aims. In this formulation, criminals did not differ in any substantive manner from non-criminals and violent behaviour was to be understood in terms of the planned pursuit of goals, rather than in terms of psychological pathology (as is suggested by the psychoanalytic perspective of, say, Storr), family background (as is suggested in the social learning perspective) or physiological defects (as is suggested by a biologically oriented approach).

But, when sociologists looked more closely into the actual values endorsed by members of deviant groups, and in particular at adolescent gangs, it soon became clear that while criminal behaviour was planned and intentional as the *anomie* theorists had proposed, the major motive was seldom financial gain. Instead, it seemed (Cohen, 1955) that these gangs were composed of boys from the lower socio-economic classes, who were ill able to compete with their more advantaged peers at school and within conventional career structures. Judged and found wanting by middle-class standards they, formed their own sub-cultures which established new norms and goals which they *could* satisfy. Such gangs legitimized for their own members conduct that was unacceptable to the dominant culture, and boys within such gangs broke the law in order to acquire the status that the gangs endorsed – being tough, daring, hard and combative. In short, gang members not only actively rejected middle-class values but explicitly set up their own in order to satisfy their needs for self-esteem.

Cohen's sub-cultural theory soon produced a series of variations and alternatives. Cloward and Ohlin (1960), for example, argued that there were different delinquent sub-cultures in different neighbourhoods,[18] and that those most involved in *seriously delinquent* sub-cultures were often far more centrally involved with the pursuit of financial gain than Cohen supposed.

More immediately relevant to contemporary sociological thinking about delinquency, however, was the work of Matza (1964), who argued that the causative factors which sub-cultural theory had tried to establish were too far removed from the world that delinquents themselves recognized. Young boys who get into trouble with the law, Matza argued, are not totally opposed to the dominant normative system, nor are they very dissimilar to boys who do not get into trouble. Instead they engage in crime only 'casually, intermittently and transiently', because in general they are committed to conventional morality. When they destroy property because of boredom, or engage in fights to reinforce their status, or steal for gain, they often seek to 'neutralize' their behaviour by justifications like denial of responsibility (I didn't mean it); denial of injury (I didn't really harm him); denial of victim (he deserved it); condemnation of the accusers (they always pick on us), or appeals to higher loyalties (you've got to help your mates). In short, delinquent youths are not an immoral species apart from the rest of us, but ordinary human beings who 'drift' in and out of crimes. Their values are far less deviant than is commonly portrayed and indeed in many ways exaggerate subterranean values of the dominant culture.

According to Matza, the delinquent gang generates meaning for itself within the opportunities offered by the dominant culture; sometimes the paths it takes are legitimate, sometimes not. But even when they are illegitimate, the rationale offered for such behaviour by gang members is in terms that reflect an image, albeit distorted, of the consensual values and underlying themes of the dominant culture. The main thrust, however, of Matza's approach comes very close to that of Marsh: the delinquent youth is not passively acted upon by social forces, but he chooses particular behaviours which, while they may seem irrational and random to others, offer meaning to him himself in that such behaviour satisfies needs for excitement and status. As Downes puts it, the account Marsh and his colleagues give of soccer hooliganism 'chimes extremely well with Matza's notion of delinquency as the "manufacture of excitement", as a contrast to the routine of everyday life' (Downes, 1982, p. 36).

*Labelling*
The earlier perspectives that I have just presented, those of Merton and
Cohen, for example, rested on an assumption that the values of what I
have been referring to as the dominant society can be taken for granted.
Labelling theory looks critically at this assumption and at two aspects of
it in particular. First, it asks what the origins of these norms are, and
secondly it queries the role of the law enforcement agencies and the
media in the amplification of such norms.

This perspective draws heavily on a pluralist vision of society, in that it
asserts that different groups in society hold different values, and that
delinquent acts occur when people find themselves torn between different and competing groups and values (Dallos and Muncie, 1982). It
follows, according to labelling theorists, that the law may be regarded as
enshrining a *particular* rather than an *absolute* set of values, and those
breaking it should be regarded primarily in the light of their deviance
from accepted values, rather than being characterized as having particular personal attributes that cause them to behave immorally.[19] Delinquency should not be regarded as absolute: instead, non-conforming
behaviour should be examined as a social process which involves rule
conformers and rule violators and their social interactions.

Delinquency, or deviance, is thus seen by labelling theorists as depending for its definition on those who are in social control (Downes,
1982). Further, and more importantly from the perspective of this book,
labelling theorists contend that those in social control often amplify
deviance by stressing how different deviants are ('football thugs', 'mindless vandals') from the rest of law-abiding society, and by promoting easy
stereotypes of the deviant which are contrasted with an over-simplified
picture of 'normal' behaviour. Thus the destruction of property by
medical students in charity weeks occurs because of 'youthful high
spirits', but the behaviour of football fans is 'irrational violence'.

Some empirical studies have been made of deviant behaviour in order
to offer support for this perspective. One of the most interesting is that
conducted by Stanley Cohen on the conflict between Mods and Rockers
that occurred in seaside towns in England in the 1960s. In this book
Cohen (1972) suggested that loosely knit associations of young men, who
shared similar styles of dress, social behaviour and choice of music, were
transformed by the agencies of the law and the media into tightly knit,
violent and defiant gangs. 'Ideal-typical "folk-devils" were created: the
youth who offered to pay his fine by cheque was extolled as a symbol of
youthful affluence, defiance and indifference to authority. Even non-
events became news: towns "held their breath for" invasions that did
not materialise' (Downs, 1982, p. 34).

This particular perspective of the symbiotic nature of the relationship
between deviants and those who label them thus is extended by those
sociologists whose work I shall consider in the final section of this

chapter, but before moving on to this section, I would like both to draw out the implications of labelling and sub-cultural theory for the subject matter of this book, and evaluate the work of those whose work I have called phenomenological.

One of the major implications of sub-cultural and labelling theory for the understanding of aggression and violence is very similar, as I have already noted, to the implications of the work of Marsh, Campbell and Toch. This is that violent behaviour, like any other form of social behaviour, is neither random nor senseless. From the point of view of those who perpetrate such behaviour, it is a rational response to a social situation. Gang formation, challenging and daring behaviour, and the violence that may be involved in such behaviour answer needs for status, excitement, identity and occasionally financial gain.

A second implication from labelling and sub-cultural theory which is shared by Marsh and Campbell, if not by Toch, is that the law enforcement agencies and the media, by labelling certain adolescents as 'other' and different from themselves, reinforce in such adolescents a sense of group identity which lead group members to develop and extend their deviant careers. As Dallos and Muncie put it, social reactions to adolescent gangs and their sometimes violent behaviour 'rarely discourage deviant behaviour, but rather reinforce the individual's image of self-as-deviant and thus indirectly promote further and prolonged deviation' (1982, p. 49). Harrington puts this viewpoint at its strongest when he argues,

My own researches support the idea that the mass media focus the attention of the public in a spurious way by giving disproportionate attention to certain forms of group violence. Football hooligans have been hounded by the Press, made infamous by television and given attention far in excess of the seriousness of the crimes they commit. There is little doubt that they have, to an extent, enjoyed the special attention they have been given; it has enhanced their status, given them a social importance they long for. They know they make news and this knowledge increases their vanity and prestige or so they believe. One can easily see how the continuation of their violence is fed by publicity. (Harrington, 1976, pp. 176–7)

Consequently, sub-cultural and labelling theorists recommend, like Marsh, that police should take a less confrontational approach with deviant youths, and as Schur (1973) has suggested the preferred approach should be 'to leave the kids alone whenever possible'. But, in general, methods of controlling or indeed eliminating deviant behaviour, including aggression and violence, is not an issue of central concern to these theorists. In this respect, they differ from all the other theorists whose work has been considered in this book.

It is also worth noting that springing from sub-cultural theory there is sometimes an implicit endorsement of a romanticism that is seen as inevitably attached to those who reject, and are rejected by, respectable society. As Pearson notes,

> The deviant is described as being more colourful than he is, and also less troublesome. He is rarely represented as someone who is unhappy . . . And because he is deviant, he is thought to be spontaneous, free of the hang-ups of the conforming citizen, living 'outside the law'. (Pearson, 1976, p. 195)

Finally, sociologists working within the area of sub-cultural theory have been amongst the most powerful critics of the contention by the experimental social psychologists, discussed in the last chapter, that viewing violent television *causes* violent behaviour. They argue that it is unlikely that television and the values that it transmits, have an effect on the young viewer that is independent of his or her sub-cultural values. In support of this they point to the fact that whereas exposure to television violence is relatively stable across the major social class groups, involvement in violence is heavily skewed towards boys from working-class backgrounds. Sub-cultural theorists thus contend that it is not what they see on television that influences the behaviour of young viewers, rather it is the way in which the content is interpreted, in combination with the viewer's social milieu, that affects the predisposition to become involved in violent behaviour.

## EVALUATING PHENOMENOLOGICAL ACCOUNTS OF AGGRESSION AND VIOLENCE

In evaluating different approaches to, and perspectives on, aggression and violence, I have up to now tended to use two sets of criteria. The first set, which is associated with scientific methodology, asks whether the empirical studies on which the approaches or perspectives are based meet certain conditions such as rigorous experimental or survey design, adequate sampling procedures, the use of appropriate statistical techniques and so on. It is clearly more difficult to apply such criteria to studies like Toch's and Marsh's than it is to the experimental procedures described in the previous chapter. This is largely because those who use the phenomenological approach explicitly criticize a reliance on positivist methodology and explicitly set out to use a methodology which is based on the belief that the understanding of aggression and violence can only emerge through entering the world view of those who are labelled as aggressive or violent.

Nevertheless, it does seem appropriate to consider some aspects of the methodology of the empirical studies on which phenomenological accounts are based (I shall consider here only the work of Marsh, Toch and Campbell, because the sociological perspectives I have presented are not, in general, based directly on particular empirical studies).[20] Looking at Toch's study first, it seems to me that the full description and rationale he gives both for the selection of his sample and the methodology he used in interviews and analysis allows a measure of confidence in the robustness of the findings he reports. Marsh, on the other hand, while acknowledging that there are difficulties in generalizing from an intensive study of a few cases, is less ready to expand on the rationale behind the selections of his sample, or to detail the manner in which he conducted his conversations with his subjects, or the way in which he allocated his subjects to various subgroups. Campbell, too, tends to skirt over issues such as these. While I accept the validity of the phenomenological approach, it does seem to me a pity that some exponents of the phenomenological approach fail to make clear how and why samples are selected and how accounts are collected and subsequently analysed.

I would now like to turn to the second strand that I have been using when evaluating different accounts of aggression and violence. As I have noted before, this strand is concerned with more subjective criteria, such as the extent to which proponents of any particular perspective show a degree of rigour and consistency in their analyses, and whether or not the approach deepens the evaluator's understanding of the issues being considered.

Perhaps because it is the essence of the phenomenological approach to centre on particular perspectives, none of the writers whose work has been discussed in this section resort to the confident over-generalizations that are characteristics of those who, like Lorenz, Freud and Storr, propound macro-theories of aggression and violence. And on the whole their analyses are characterized both by rigour of argument and consistency. Furthermore, unlike the workers in the positivist tradition, they are prepared to tackle the substantive issues of the subjective aspects involved in defining aggressive or violent behaviour and in disentangling, from their theoretical discussions, their subjective preconceptions. Nevertheless, it seems to me that both sets of phenomenological accounts that I have just presented, the psychological and the sociological, are limited in their understanding of aggression and violence.

Turning first to the psychological accounts, in discussing Toch's approach I have already indicated that his account is weakened to some extent, because his discussion of violent behaviour is so firmly located within the confrontations of particular sorts of men, that it throws little direct light on aggression and violence in other settings and amongst other types of people. Extending this criticism, I would argue that because his analysis is so specifically centred, it is difficult to develop it either into a more general approach to aggression or violence, or to absorb it into a comprehensive account of interpersonal behaviour. In short, at the theoretical level it remains limited by its specificity.

Marsh's account, on the other hand, seems to me, at the more theoretical level, to be embarrassed by too much, and too diverse, theoretical underpinning. I have already indicated that Marsh himself acknowledges a number of influences on his work, ranging from de Saussure's epistemological discussion of meaning, through Harré and Secord's reformulation of the theoretical paradigms of social psychology, to Taylor's writing about criminology. But it seems to me that his analysis of aggression and violence owes, in fact, little to any of these sources, and a great deal to the ethological work of Lorenz and of Tiger (1971).[21] This is because ultimately Marsh (like Campbell) appears to believe that violence emerges when rituals break down, and that violence itself derives from an innate predisposition to behave aggressively. Such a reliance on evolutionary determinism would not appear to fit well with the influences he cites in epistemology, contemporary social psychology or radical criminology.

These theoretical considerations aside, further criticisms have been made of the work of both Toch and Marsh and his associates which relate to their inability to come to terms with interaction of social class variables and the behaviour they write about (Pearson, 1976). For example, Pearson criticizes Marsh for not discussing why hooliganism is so much more prevalent among football fans than it is in Rugby League fans. Similarly, Toch spends little time in discussing why it is that violent men are so much more likely to emerge from the most disadvantaged sections of American society. Or, put in other words, it could be argued that psychologists like Toch, Marsh and Campbell locate their search for the meaning behind aggressive and violent behaviour too exclusively within individual perspectives and individual psychological needs, and as a result place too little emphasis on the social, political and economic circumstances of those whose behaviour is under discussion.

On the other hand, it seems to me (and see Berkowitz, 1982b and Patrick, 1973) that the sociologists whose work has been presented in this section are limited in a precisely obverse manner from the way in which the work of the psychologists I have just discussed is limited. The sociologists tend to place too much emphasis on social, political and economic circumstances and too little on individual factors. In particular, I would argue that sociologists working within the tradition of sub-cultural and labelling theories are disinclined to consider whether, within gangs, it is sometimes possible to find particularly violent individuals whose motivations are better accounted for in terms of the individual predisposition to behave violently that Toch writes about, than in terms of the rational meanings that are ascribed to such behaviour by sociologists.

Such a view has been very forcibly expressed by James Patrick (1973). Patrick is a social scientist who was working as a teacher in a Scottish

Approved School (a residential institution catering for boys who had been in trouble with the agencies of law and order) in the late 1960s. During the course of his work he became friendly with one of the pupils, and at this boy's invitation joined him and his friends in their weekend leaves. In order to do this he posed as a member of the gang, and he wrote up this rather unique experiment in participant observation in his book, *A Glasgow Gang Observed* (1973).[22] Here Patrick claimed that although the behaviour of the majority of the gang members could be understood in terms of sub-cultural values and customs, there remained a core of boys whose behaviour was violent enough for both their peers and themselves to explain it in terms of mental illness ('going radio, throwing a maddie, running a psychey', ibid., p. 202). These boys seemed to Patrick to be subject to fits of uncontrollable fury, which were more easily understood as expressions of specific psychological problems and conflicts than as sub-cultural responses to social pressures.

Although I myself would not completely endorse the position of Patrick (and Berkowitz) who see exceptionally violent behaviour as 'pathological' and in essence irrational, I do consider that the sociological perspectives on violent behaviour dealt with here do not take enough account of intentions that are related to individual and psychological needs rather than to sub-cultural meanings. As Tutt puts it, in violent incidents, 'both the violent and the violated suffer, locked in a complex labyrinth of interpersonal relationships from which the only exit is usually violent' (1976, p. 250). I shall return to this discussion in the next chapter.

## HOW EXTENSIVE IS THE USE MADE OF THE TERMS 'AGGRESSION' AND 'VIOLENCE' IN THE ACCOUNTS OF PHENOMENOLOGICAL SOCIAL SCIENTISTS?

I would now like to look, as I have at the end of previous sections of this book, at how adequately those accounts which I have discussed here cover the different usages of the terms 'aggression' and 'violence' that I derived in my summational descriptions in Chapter 1.

### Aggression

In discussing aggression, I intend to refer only to the work of Marsh and Campbell, because Toch does not deal with aggression as a separate topic from violence, and the sociologists whose work has been covered in this section do not regard aggression as a topic at issue in their discussion of law-breaking behaviour.

(a) For Marsh and Campbell, 'aggressive' is a term that covers behaviour that is predominately intended to act on others in a

'thrusting and imperious' manner, rather than in a directly injurious manner.

(b)   Aggression is for them, intimately concerned with issues of achieving dominance.

(c)   Aggression, for them, does not necessarily involve physical force.

(d)   Their work is characterized by specific consideration of the kinds of
motives that underpin aggressive and violent behaviour.

(e)   They are concerned with positive aspects of aggression.

(f)   They are concerned, very explictly, with subjective aspects in the
labelling of aggression. (See particularly the discussion by Marsh,
Rosser and Harré, 1978, of the labelling of 'trouble-makers' in
schools.)

(g)   They are centrally concerned with the manner in which the
labellers' values and perception affect the manner in which the label
'aggressive' is applied.

*Violence*

Toch, Marsh and Campbell deal explicitly with violence; the sociologists
whose work has just been discussed do not explicitly separate violent
behaviour from other law-breaking behaviour.

(a)&(b)   For Marsh and Campbell, violence is seen as an event, while
aggression is seen as a process (Marsh, Rosser and Harré, 1978, p.
128). Violence, for them, is the imposition of physical force on
others that occurs as a consequence (though not an inevitable one)
of aggression.

(c)   The sociologists whose work has been discussed in this section
emphasize that violence is sometimes engaged in for the thrills and
challenge it offers, but Toch places little emphasis on this aspect.

(d)   Phenomenological social scientists all discuss issues concerned with
the legitimization of violence.

In general it can be seen that phenomenological accounts of violence, and
to a lesser extent of aggression, are broadly and comprehensively based.

## Radical Accounts of Aggression and Violence

PSYCHOLOGICAL ACCOUNTS

This line of thinking suggests that the growth of subordinate group
opposition marks a change from an interpersonal mode to an
inter-group mode of thought and action. If a radical ideology is
overtly inter-group, then a conservative ideology, which seeks to
prevent social change, might stress the value of the interpersonal

mode. It may not be altogether fanciful to link this line of thought to the writings of those social psychologists who attempt in their analyses to reduce social frustrations to individual frustrations. Certainly it has been possible to identify a number of normative presuppositions in their formulations – enough to suggest that their 'science' is by no means free from the ideological influences itself or totally neutral with respect to the phenomena it studies. (Billig, 1976, p. 180)

In this section I would like to look briefly at the work on aggression and rebellion by Michael Billig, who in *Social Psychology and Intergroup Relations* (1976) presented a powerful critique of the psychological approaches to aggression that were described in the last chapter. In this critique he suggested that most psychological thinking on aggression has been influenced by the frustration–aggression hypothesis which Dollard and his associates derived from the earlier work of Freud (see Chapter 5 above), and he argues that this reliance on frustration as the most potent progenitor of aggression has led most psychologists to emphasize emotional factors in their account of aggression and to neglect other factors such as cognition and social circumstances. His critique of psychological work on aggression is in two parts. In the first he reviews the experimental work which I presented in the last chapter and comes to a very similar conclusion to the one I reached, which is that this work has, on the whole, neglected to take into account either the subjects' perceptions and understandings of the experimental procedures and their role within it, or the influence of the social dynamics surrounding the experimental situation. He concludes that

The general point is that the subject's hypothesised internal motivational state does not occur in a social vacuum, and that the social context as well as the subject's beliefs and interpretations all combine in determining his course of action. (Billing 1976, pp. 148–9)

Furthermore Billig argues that the terms 'aggressive' and 'violent' are often applied very selectively, particularly by experimental psychologists like Berkowitz who are far more likely to use the terms to describe the behaviour of participants in civil disturbances than they are to the behaviour of the agents of law and order. Moreover, Billig argues, such psychologists are too prone to dismiss the violent behaviour of such dissidents as 'irrational'.[23] Thus far, in the first section of his critique it can be seen that Billig does not extend his arguments much beyond those already presented in the previous section of this chapter.

It is in the second part of his critique of contemporary work on aggression that Billig moves beyond the phenomenological position towards a more radical stance. In this section he asks why it is that most psychologists have confined their inquiries largely to interpersonal aspects of aggression and have refrained from extending their line of inquiry to intergroup aspects of aggression. The answer to this question, he suggests, lies in a deeply rooted bias amongst most psychologists which leads them to avoid looking too deeply into intergroup *conflict*. If psychologists were to look critically at intergroup conflict, he argues, they would be forced to acknowledge the extent to which such conflict is based on inequalities between groups. Not only would they then be led to make prescriptions about reversing, or in some way ameliorating, such inequalities, but they would be forced even further along a line of reasoning which ultimately ascribes rebellion not to frustration or hostility but to a rational intention to remove such inequalities and an associated ideology that provides a reasoned underpinning for such intentions. Acknowledging the existence of such an 'ideology of revolt' would, Billig claims, force psychologists to move beyond looking at the psychological motivations for aggression in group situations and towards ascribing such aggression to a rational cognitive decision on the part of dissident groups to change the nature of social reality.

Thus, for Billig, behaviour by subordinate social groups that is labelled by dominant groups as 'aggressive' or 'violent' is, in essence, behaviour that because it threatens the *status quo* is rejected by most psychologists who are, according to Billig's view, predominantly politically conservative. Because of their implicit political assumptions such psychologists, according to Billig, are unable to accept that lying behind this 'rebellious' behaviour there is, not as traditional psychological approaches would suggest a seething mass of frustrated and hostile feelings, but a political ideology that is a 'revolutionary ideology . . . [which] does not aim at adjusting to the present realities and preserving their social basis – [for] the crucial point about revolutionary ideology is that it aims to change reality' (ibid., p. 171)

In short, according to Billig, most psychologists in their interpretation of which aspects of aggression it is important to study have concentrated on those aspects which do not lead them to ask searching questions either of the society in which they live or of their own underlying ideological assumptions. Furthermore, for Billig, the topic of intergroup aggression cannot be separated from the topic of social inequality, and the (for Billig) inevitable sequel of such inequalities – ideological conflict between groups. It is these dual emphases on the interaction between ideological conflict and aggression, and the political nature of social inquiries, that brings Billig to a more radical and inevitably more political position than other psychologists whose work has been surveyed up to now. But his radical position does find a counterpart in the theoretical position of a group of sociologists to whose work I will now turn.

SOCIOLOGICAL ACCOUNTS

> Most crimes in this country share a single important similarity –
> they represent rational responses to the competitiveness and in-
> equality of life in capitalist societies . . . Many crimes seem very
> different at the same time, but many of their differences – in
> *character and degree of violence* – can usefully be explained by the
> structure of class institutions in this country and the duality of the
> public system of the enforcement and administration of justice.
> (Gordon, 1973, p. 184, my italics)

Billig is chiefly concerned in his writing about intergroup aggression
with a topic to which I shall return in the next chapter, which he calls
'rebellion'. By this term Billig refers to the movements within subordinate groups that challenge the power and interests of dominant groups.
His interest in the issue which has been the central theme of this chapter,
the aggression and violence displayed in law-breaking behaviour, is less
marked. But in his emphasis on the ideological conflict that may spark
off confrontations between groups, Billig comes very close to those
sociologists who propose that the spur for much law-breaking behaviour
lies in a 'culture conflict' between deviant groups, like adolescent gangs,
and the forces of law and order.

Culture conflict theories (for example, those of Miller, 1976) explain
delinquency by reference to the enormous differences which they see
between working-class and middle-class culture. Delinquency is seen as
the product of long-established traditions of working-class life so that,
like Wolfgang and Ferracuti, culture conflict theorists emphasize the
emergence in working-class areas of an ethos which combines an inability
to put off gratification, a stress on *machismo*, and a profound sense of
fatalism about the possibility of influencing external events. But, unlike
the approach of Wolfgang and Ferracuti, culture conflict theorists stress
that the law breaking and violence that emerge from such values are not a
'random outpouring of senseless aggression' (Downes, 1982, p. 38), but
are instead an expression of group cohesion, and an affirmation of group
values. According to Miller, it is the structure of working-class life,
rather than responses to conflicts with middle-class values, which
generate delinquency and the six focal concerns of this life – trouble (the
tension between law-abiding and law-violating behaviour), toughness,
smartness, excitement, fate (being lucky or unlucky), and autonomy
combine to produce patterns of behaviour that produce a continual
challenge to the law. Like Matza (see above), culture conflict theorists
stress the preoccupations of the boys themselves in generating for themselves an environment which meets their needs, but unlike Matza,
culture conflict theorists are not concerned with the complexities of
interpersonal relationships which cause the boys concerned to move in

and out of delinquency; instead they stress the determinism of the social reality in which young delinquents live.

This emphasis on the *determinism* of the socio-economic environment is, of course, taken a step further by those theorists who, working within a Marxist framework, interpret the violence of working-class boys as a by-product of class conflict. For such theorists (for example, Taylor, Walton and Young, 1973), crime and deviance are to be understood as part of the wider aspects of the social control that is imposed on the lower classes by the state. I do not propose to expand on this topic because much of what has been called the new criminology is not of *direct* relevance to the central issues of this book, aggression and violence. However, the clear implication for the topics of aggression and violence of a class conflict[24] analysis is that if class conflict is inevitable in capitalist societies, and if certain areas, like the decayed inner city, concentrate the economic and social contradictions of capitalist political economy, then it is inevitable that conflict will arise between the disadvantaged classes (the unemployed and unskilled working classes) who live there and the agents of the state. Such conflict will inevitably involve violence. But for these theorists violence itself is not a separate issue nor is it problematical. And presumably the amelioration of such violence can only occur as a result of the resolution of the class conflict by another social order.

One radical theorist who does isolate violence as a particular issue in deviance is David Gordon (1973). He proposes (as the quotation at the beginning of this section suggests) that crime, like any social phenomenon, must be related to the structure of the society in which it takes place, for it is the basic structure of social and economic institutions in any society that fundamentally shape the behaviour of its members. In capitalist countries, according to Gordon, 'social relations of production' help define an economic class structure, and one cannot understand the behaviour of individuals unless one understands how such class structures define the economic and social opportunities of the respective economic classes. The state in capitalist societies serves primarily to benefit the members of the capitalist classes, either directly by bestowing further economic privilege, or indirectly by helping them solidify and preserve the inequalities of the class structure. Crime in such societies, argues Gordon, presents a perfectly rational response to the need to guarantee economic security for those who commit such crimes. Clearly it is largely those who are at the lower end of the social spectrum who are more likely to resort to crime in order to guarantee such security for themselves and their dependants. So it is not surprising that there will be a higher incidence of crime amongst the disadvantaged. But class does not only explain the different rates of crimes amongst different social groups; according to Gordon, it also explains the different types of crimes prevalent in different social groups. Thus, while 'relatively affluent citizens have access to jobs in large corporations, to institutions involved in complicated paper transactions involving lots of money, and to avenues of relatively unobtrusive communications' (ibid., p. 177), those raised in poverty are forced to resort to more confrontational and less unobtrusive ways of making money illegally, like robbery. Furthermore, Gordon argues, the police are more likely to counter lower-class crime with violence, and thus they raise the incidence of violence in lower-class life. Thus, according to Gordon, the logic of class conflicts dictates that lower classes will engage in more crime, in more violent crime and that such rational responses to inequalities will be met by a response from the police that escalates the level of violence.

This contention that the lower classes will be more likely to commit violent crimes than the more privileged has been taken up by Steven Box (1983). He argues that many serious crimes involving violence are also committed by people in positions of power and privilege, but that such crimes, including ones in which serious violence is inflicted on victims, are neither publicized in the media nor have they been taken up by criminologists to the extent that crimes committed by the more disadvantaged sections of the community have.

The crimes he refers to are those that take place when, for example, serious injuries occur as a result of negligence, as when working conditions are not maintained at safe levels by employers. Or when deaths occur as a result of drug manufacturers' failures to conduct adequate research on new compounds. Or when car manufacturers refuse to recall and repair known defective vehicles. Even if deaths result from such acts of omission and commission, these deaths are not classified as murder. For Box claims we are encouraged to see murder as 'a particular act involving a very limited range of stereotypical acts, instruments, situations and motives' (ibid., p. 9), an act more likely to involve relatively powerless individuals or groups of individuals rather than an act involving people who are working within powerful and privileged institutions.

Thus, he claims, criminal law categories are ideological constructs because

> Rather than being a fair reflection of those behaviours objectively causing us collectively the most avoidable suffering, criminal law categories are artful, creative constructs designed to criminalize only some victimizing behaviours, usually those more frequently committed by the relatively powerless, and to exclude others, usually those frequently committed by the powerful against subordinates. (ibid., p. 7)

Such biased definitions of serious crimes, Box argues, enable the dominant and privileged group to tighten their *social control* for they:

(1) make the underprivileged more likely than the privileged to be apprehended,

(2) create the illusion that certain disadvantaged groups are more dangerous than others (this point will be taken up again in the next chapter when the nature of 'black muggings' are discussed);

(3) tend to obscure the amount of harm and injury that result from the actions of certain powerful intitutions (for example, the police and certain multi- and transnational corporations);

(4) promote the presentation of criminal justice into a community service which is represented as being above any class or group bias;

(5) make ordinary people more ready to turn to the state for protection against the lawlessness of those groups that (see 2 above) have been presented as dangerous and threatening.

Box's argument about the 'mystification' of issues concerning crime is very similar to Billig's argument concerning the manner in which most psychologists have obscured the real issues about intergroup violence by concentrating on the resistance of particular groups and ignoring the conditions which have caused them to resist. Both theorists stress as well *how important it is to go beyond the given nature of social facts to grasp their significance*. This particular emphasis has shaped the work of the last theorists to be considered in this chapter, whose concern has been with a very specific sort of violent behaviour – violence against wives.

In a study conducted in Scotland in the 1970s, R. Emerson Dobash and Russell Dobash (1980) interviewed 137 women in Scotland who were either living in refuges for battered women or had recently been living in them. In these interviews they were concerned to develop an understanding of marital violence in the context of the wider marital relationship. As the results of these interviews, and in the context of a theoretical position (ibid., pp. 26–7) that suggests that understanding of social processes and interactions emerges from a historical analysis (in their case of 'patriarchy')[25] to an integration of 'the isolated and seemingly unconnected aspects of social life' (ibid., p. 27), the Dobashes concluded that violence against wives occurs as a result of the predisposition of

Many men in Western society [who] learn to expect that their wishes and concerns come first, that because they are males and heads of households they have certain prerogatives and rights that supersede those of women – especially in the family where the rights of males over females are clearly defined from a very early age. The difference between violent men and other males is that the former are prepared to use physical means to enforce or reinforce their own views. When men do use force to chastise and punish their wives for failing to live up to their unilateral standards, they can be very violent indeed. (Dobash and Dobash, 1980, p. 106)

In short, like the other researchers whose work has been considered in this section, the Dobashes conclude that both prevailing ideologies and existing legal, political and economic institutions (which in the case of wife abuse have failed to uphold the needs and rights of women) have reinforced particular kinds of violent behaviour committed by particular (and more privileged) people against others who are relatively powerless.

In this section I have attempted to cover briefly some of the approaches to violence which suggest that violence is inevitable while class, cultural and sexual inequalities exist. A clear implication of this orientation is that the amelioration of social violence can only occur when such inequalities are resolved. An extension of the more radical approach to violence which is put forward by Billig is that it is because of the ideology of those who have investigated aggression that the emphasis within social science in general and particularly within the ranks of psychologists has always been on individual rather than on group aspects of aggression and violence.

## EVALUATING RADICAL APPROACHES TO AGGRESSION AND VIOLENCE

In evaluating radical approaches to aggression and violence, the first set of criteria I have been using, those associated with scientific methodology, would not be regarded as being of particular importance to the theorists under consideration. Nevertheless it is, I believe, important to note that where empirical data is cited by such theorists, it is usually very well documented. For example, Billig's (1976) examination of psychological experiments and studies is rigorously and carefully conducted, and Box's (1983) discussion of corporate crime is well supported by extensive documentation. The Dobashes study of battered wives relied on lengthy and wide-ranging interviews rather than on harder data, and as such might be criticized by behaviourally oriented psychologists for possible bias in interpretation, but as the Dobashes make complete transcriptions of interviews available (see Dobash, Dobash, Cavanagh and Wilson, 1978) such possible biases are open to investigation.

Turning to the second evaluative strand I have been using, it seems to me that the researchers covered in this section, because much of their writing can be construed as overtly political, lay themselves open to criticisms that they go beyond the specific documentation they present to make sweeping generalizations. This kind of criticism is not a point of view that I would endorse, but I am bound to admit it is one that is frequently made of such analyses.[26]

I would, however, like to make two particular points about the radical approach. These are first that theories which, like Billig's, locate violence exclusively as a by-product of structural forces within society signally fail to explain how group violence relates to individual violence.

Secondly, radical theories are subject to the same sort of criticism that I have made of those approaches that I called positivist, in that they are equally deterministic and tend to regard as of comparatively minor importance those meanings, motives and intentions of criminals that are not related to the rectification of economic inequalities. Thus critics of the radical approach to criminolology (for example, Downes and Rock, 1979) argue that it did not really matter that radical sociologists have substituted a Marxist account of the social order for a more conservative one, because neither bridge the theoretical gap between a general analysis of large-scale social processes and an actual explanation of how and why different crimes are committed in any society. Poverty and inequality may explain some forms of crime in all societies – for example, robbery for gain – but they offer little understanding as to why only *some* poor people commit such crimes, and, from the point of view of this book, why some people commit such crimes with so much *more violence* than do others.

Similarly, in their work with battered wives, the Dobashes fail to explore why it is that certain husbands batter their wives violently while others, who may feel equally resentful of their wives' failures to meet what they see as the appropriate wifely role, negotiate changes within the marriage by non-violent means or, as sometimes occurs, withdraw from the marital situation altogether.

HOW EXTENSIVE IS THE USE MADE OF THE TERMS 'AGGRESSION' AND 'VIOLENCE' IN THE ACCOUNTS OF RADICAL SOCIAL SCIENTISTS

Finally I would like to look at how adequately those accounts I have been discussing in this section cover the different usages of the terms 'aggression' and 'violence' which were derived in the summational description in Chapter 1.

*Aggression*
On the whole, the sociologists discussed in this section are not concerned with aggression. Billig is, and for him, although he does not seem to state it explicitly, aggression is an aspect of conflict in which a judgement is made about the behaviour of one party in the conflict who is said to be demonstrating aggression. Thus:

(a)   Aggression is seen as intentional.
(b)   Aggression is concerned with attaining dominance.
(c)   Aggression does not necessarily imply physical force.
(d)   Aggression is regarded as being underpinned largely by cognitive appraisal in that 'aggressors' seek to redress inequalities.

(e)  Aggression can be regarded positively if it is being used to redress inequalities.

(f)&(g)  Ideologies are seen as extremely important in the labelling of behaviour as aggressive and in the extent to which behaviour is seen as reactive or provocative.

## *Violence*

Billig does not separate his discussion of violence from his discussion of aggression. For Box and the Dobashes:

(a)  Violence may or may not involve the use of great physical force. For example, for Box, violence can occur as a result of acts as omission as well as commission, and for the Dobashes violence can be emotional as well as physical.

(b)  Motives for violence are seen to be varied and may include the pursuit of profit (Box) and the extension of social control (Box and the Dobashes).

(c)  Violence as part of a mutually rewarding interaction is not considered.

(d)  Radical theorists are centrally concerned with the manner in which the use of violence is sometimes legitimized and sometimes negatively sanctioned by those in social control.

## Notes: Chapter 6

1   For readers who are interested in following up particular social accounts of aggression and violence, the following references are suggested.

   'Positivist' accounts: for the more psychological orientation, Lefkowitz, *et al.*, *Growing up to be Violent* (1977) and West and Farrington, *The Delinquent Way of Life* (1977); for a more sociological orientation, Wolfgang and Ferracuti *The Subculture of Violence* (1967).

   'Phenomenological' accounts: for a psychological orientation, Marsh, Rosser and Harré, *The Rules of Disorder* (1978); for a sociological one, the Downes and Murdock chapters in Marsh and Campbell *Aggression and Violence* (1982).

   'Radical' accounts: for a psychological orientation, Billig, *Social Psychology and Intergroup Relations* (1976), and for a sociological one, Box, *Power, Crime and Mystification* (1983).

2   In differentiating thus between psychologists and sociologists, I have relied not only on what people tend to call themselves, and the academic departments within which they work, but also on the rather more substantive, if rough and ready, dichotomy that psychologists, even social psychologists, focus on the understanding of social interaction from the point of view of those individuals who take part in such interaction, while sociologists are less concerned with individual perceptions and understanding and are more concerned with group processes and phenomena. (Criminologists, it seems to me, tend, as individuals, to fall into either of the two camps and I will deal with their work within the discipline to which they seem to me to owe their major allegiance.)

3   Such analyses often use multivariate techniques which consist of the simultaneous

analysis of more than one type of measurement or observation. Thus, in the case of the Lefkowitz study described here, simultaneous measures were made of aggressive behaviour and a number of variables that were thought to influence it, for example, intelligence quotient, type of television viewed, parental rates of punitiveness and so on. Then using multiple regression techniques, statistical procedures were performed to produce an equation that best described the relationship of the predictors to the dependent variables, in this case aggressive behaviour. For further reading in the area consult any standard text on statistics for the social sciences.

4   Longitudinal studies can be categorized into three kinds: real-time perspective, catch-up perspective and follow-back studies (Farrington, 1982). The study by West and Farrington described in this section was real-time.

5   In an earlier book, published in 1967, West does provide an overview of current theories about the origin of aggression.

6   This early study by Lefkowitz *et al.* (1977) suffers from a number of serious methodological flaws (Murdock, 1982). For example, retrospective reporting was used to obtain peer assessments of aggressive behaviour, and the definition they made of 'aggressive behaviour' was very broad, so that truanting, drinking alcohol without permission and stealing were all so classified. In addition, there was a very serious attrition in sample size in that by the second stage of the study they were able to obtain information on less than half of their original subjects.

7   Eron here falls into the error of asserting that the studies showing some association between the viewing of violent television and aggressive behaviour have established that such viewing causes aggressive behaviour.

8   In generating this concept of a sub-culture of violence, Wolfgang and Ferracuti (1967) draw to some extent on the sociological writings of Albert Cohen, Matza and Cloward and Ohlin (see Downes, 1982) and to the work of writers such as Yablonsky with gangs.

9   They use the term sub-culture to refer to

> individuals sharing common values and socially interacting in some limited geographic or residential isolation. However, value-sharing does not necessarily require social interaction. Consequently a subculture may exist, widely distributed spatially and without interpersonal contact between individuals. Several delinquent gangs may be spread throughout a city and rarely or never have contacts. Yet they are referred to collectively as the 'delinquent subculture', and properly so, for otherwise each gang would have to be considered a separate subculture. (Wolfgang and Ferracuti, 1967, p. 102)

10   More recently Wolfgang appears to be prepared to give more emphasis to physiological factors in violence (Wolfgang and Weiner, 1982).

11   Much the same criticisms can be applied to Berkowitz's work on group aggression. For a full discussion of this see Billig (1976, Chapter 5).

12   For a comprehensive discussion of the type of taxonomies that have been generated by criminologists about violent offenders see Megargee (1982). Toch's typology differs from the great majority of these in that he does not fall into the easy labelling of 'personality types' that is so typical of earlier classical approaches to criminology (for example, Megargee's own classification of violent offenders into 'chronically overcontrolled assaultive type' and 'undercontrolled assaultive type').

13   Psychodrama is a method of extending social skills and understanding in which group members are asked to simulate particular social situations and in doing this to take particular parts and act in particular roles.

14   Marsh and Campbell (see below) are primarily psychologists and, although they do refer to the work of sociological writers who have dealt with sub-cultural theories, for example Albert Cohen, Cloward and Ohlin, Matza and Jock Young, their discussion of sub-cultures and their norms tends to be psychological rather than sociological in

orientation. That is, they tend to present from their own data the normative values which they believe are held by the groups they are investigating, rather than seek to establish the extent to which those values contradict or endorse those of the dominant groups in society.

15 Like the sociologists whose work will be discussed in the next section, Marsh believes that the violence of young people is sensationalized and amplified by the popular press.

16 Campbell herself admits that relying exclusively on self reports may lead to exaggeration or concealment or indeed both.

17 In extracting these two issues as themes, I have chosen to ignore the boundaries that are often suggested between strain, control, labelling and conflict approaches. For a discussion of these see either Downes, 1982, or Dallos and Muncie, 1982.

18 Cloward and Ohlin (1960) adhered in general to the structurally based model of Cohen (1955) but suggested that there were three different types of sub-culture which arose in different neighbourhoods: criminal (gangs pursuing instrumental kinds of theft), conflict (gangs who spent a great deal of their time fighting) and retreatist gangs (like drug-users).

19 Labelling theory was powerfully influenced by the work of Howard Becker on outsiders. Becker (1963) was among the first sociologists to propound the view that deviance is created and sustained by a community's response to an act as deviant: 'deviance is not a quality that lies in behavior itself, but in the interaction between the person who commits an act and those who respond to it' (1963, p. 14).

20 See Patrick (1973) for a discussion of the link between sub-cultural perspectives and empirical studies.

21 Tiger has proposed that aggression is not so much a general human trait, but a specifically male one which derives from a phenomenon he calls 'male bonding', which stems from a need he sees male social primates as having to work together in exclusively male hunting groups. For a full exposition of his biological approach to aggression, which falls within the sociobiological approach discussed in Chapter 3, see *Men in Groups* (1971).

22 Patrick's perspective on violent gang members has been severely criticized by contemporary sociologists who argue that there is a circularity in accounting for violence by recourse to a psychopathic 'condition' that is manifested largely in the violence it is intended to explain (see Downes, 1982).

23 Billig devotes a fair amount of space in his critique to the work of the political scientist T. R. Gurr (1970). Gurr has attempted to analyse social revolutions in terms of a combination of frustration–aggression theory with the concept of relative deprivation. He argues that it is relative rather than objective deprivation which is the spur to social discontent. According to Gurr, relative deprivation increases when people receive less than they expect to receive; therefore an increase in relative deprivation is likely to lead to an increase in violence. But Billig argues that Gurr's concept of relative deprivation leans too heavily on the motivational aspects of feeling deprived and too little on the cognitive appraisal of inequality and the resultant revolutionary ideology.

24 I have not attempted in this book to look at the earlier versions of conflict theories that are to be found in the writings of, for example, Lewis Coser (1967), as these theories have little immediate bearing on the topics of aggression and violence.

25 Patriachy for the Dobashes relates to both the structural aspects of society and ideological ones which contribute to the maintaining of a hierarchical order in the home which subordinates women to men (1980, pp. 43–4).

26 See, for example (*The Guardian*, 2 July 1984), the criticisms that have been made of the Open University social science foundation course D102.

# 7

# Towards a Synthesis

Violence is here,
In the world of the sane,
And violence is a symptom.
I hear it in the headlong weeping of men who have failed.
I see it in the terrible dreams of boys
Whose adolescence repeats all history
(Jacob Bronowski, quoted by May, 1976, p. 15)

In the Special Forces A Camp at Me Phuc Tay there was a sign that
read, 'If you kill for money you're a mercenary. If you kill for
pleasure you're a sadist. If you kill for both you're a Green Beret.'
(Herr, 1978 p. 205)

In this final chapter I shall present a synthesis of the subject matter I have
been considering. In previous chapters, and sections within chapters, I
have introduced particular approaches by considering the framework
and context within which it seemd to me that the approaches were
located. For example, in the last chapter I examined social approaches to
aggression and violence in the light of three theoretical paradigms:
positivism, phenomenology and structuralism. [1] It therefore seems appropriate in presenting my own synthesis to consider what I perceive to
be its theoretical roots.

My initial training as a psychologist was within a positivist tradition.
That is, I was introduced to psychology as though there were no dis-
puting that its subject matter was observable, and preferably measurable, behaviour and that the mode of studying it should be as closely
modelled on scientific methodology as possible. Psychoanalysis was
regarded with a degree of suspicion because its approach was considered
inherently subjective, and the only fields of study that were accepted as
relevant and germane to psychology were biology and those strands
within psychiatry that were themselves firmly embedded in positivism.

But exposure to the subject matter of psychology, outside academic confines, and the politicization that arose from working in different cultures, soon persuaded me of the validity of the following propositions. First, it is facile and disingenuous to consider human behaviour without looking at the intentions and motivation that lie behind the behaviour. Secondly, it is important to relate behaviour and its intentions to the social situation in which it takes place. Thirdly, there are always a variety of paradigms and approaches that can be used for interpreting or understanding or predicting behaviour. And finally, how a particular individual selects an approach or paradigm for these purposes depends on a host of factors. These range from those that might perhaps be regarded as situational, such as culture, era and discipline, to those that are more idiosyncratic, such as the value systems that the individual endorses and his or her temperamental disposition. Thus, to take an example, it seems to me impossible to extricate a deep belief that aggression is largely innate, and therefore inevitable, from the political implications of that belief. And it seems equally likely that those individuals who present an approach to aggression which argues for one clear and unambiguous root, whether it be innate or environmental, are likely to be people who find ambiguity not only theoretically unsatisfactory but personally threatening.

Endorsing these propositions, however, has not persuaded me that it is necessarily futile to try and obtain empirical data that relate to the understanding of human behaviour. For it seems to me that it is reasonable to assume that when two classes of events are observed to be reliably and repeatedly associated, there is a relationship between them. Just as, say, a medical scientist may deduce that there is a relationship between particular bacteria and a particular set of symptoms, when such symptoms appear whenever an individual has a certain type of bacteria in their bloodstream, so it seems to be reasonable to assume a relationship between certain child rearing practices and aggressive behaviour, if the aggressive behaviour is reliably observed in children brought up in that particular way. Whether the child-rearing patterns *cause* the behaviour is of course quite another matter. For it is in its emphasis on cause and effect, rather than on understanding and interpretation, that I believe positivism is limited.[2] Sometimes, as in the case of the bacteria and the symptoms, it may be possible to be satisfied that the one is a direct cause of the other, but when it comes to the area of psychology rather than physiology, it seems to me that looking for such an unambiguous causal relationship may be an illusionary and ultimately unproductive pursuit.

Nevertheless, in presenting my account of aggression and violence, I will be weaving into it those findings from empirical research that I feel are reasonably robust; for example, that mood may be affected by pathologies in the central nervous system (Chapter 2); that anthropological studies show that there are considerable differences between societies in the level of interpersonal aggression (Chapter 3) that scapegoating is often associated with periods of social turmoil (Chapter 4); that exposing children to aggressive models may often lead to them mimicking such aggressive behaviour (Chapter 5); and that indictable violent offences are more characteristic of disadvantaged social classes (Chapter 6).

Throughout this book I have used a two-pronged evaluative system in assessing approaches to aggression and violence. First, I have scrutinized the empirical findings cited for reliability and validity using the yardstick of scientific methodology; secondly, at a more subjective level I have looked for consistency, rigour and whether or not the approach deepens my understanding of aggression and violence. It is now for the reader to apply these criteria to this chapter.

This chapter is divided into three sections. The first of these suggests a demarcation of the subject area, the second explores the meaning that aggressive behaviour and violence may hold for individuals, and then extends the discussion of individual aggression to group aggression and violence, and the final section looks at ways in which aggressive and violent behaviour can be controlled.

## Demarcating the Subject Area

In this section I suggest that the terms 'aggression' and 'aggressive' should be examined separately. The reasons for this separation will, I hope, become apparent in the discussion and I shall turn first to the term 'aggressive' when it is used to describe behaviour.

### AGGRESSIVE BEHAVIOUR

In considering aggressive behaviour it seems to me appropriate to accept straight away that a specific act of behaviour may be labelled as aggressive by one person, but not by another. (Numerous examples of this have been noted in this book.) But, as has been noted before (for example, Chapter 1), this does not debar us from using the word aggressive very freely in speech or in writing and in such a way that suggests that there is a core of meaning that is shared by those who are in conversation or by a writer and a reader.

It seems to me that it is possible to do this because there is a wide measure of aggreement on the conditions that need to be satisfied for the term 'aggressive' to be used. That is, there is a general acceptance of certain core conditions that underpin the use of the term. *Subjectivity arises, in my opinion, not because there is disagreement about these core conditions, but because for any use of the term, there may be disagreement between observers about whether the conditions are satisfied.* Specifically I suggest that when a labeller applies the term aggressive to describe behaviour, the labeller believes that four conditions apply:

(1) The person[3] carrying out that behaviour, the 'aggressor', does so with intention.
(2) The behaviour is taking place within an interpersonal situation which is characterized by an element of conflict or competition.
(3) The person carrying out the behaviour in question intends by that behaviour to gain a greater advantage than the person being aggressed against.
(4) The person carrying out the behaviour in question has either provoked the conflict or moved it on to a higher degree of intensity.

### The behaviour is intended

This condition is endorsed as far as I can see by all those writing about aggression. As Baron notes (see page 4 above), if a gun goes off accidentally and kills an onlooker while a particular individual is cleaning it, he or she is most unlikely to be labelled aggressive.

### Conflict, competition and advantage

All the uses of the term 'aggressive' that I have come across make the assumption that the aggressive behaviour takes place within a context of conflict or competition; for example, in the *competitive* atmosphere that occurs in sporting contests, or when companies are contesting a market, or in conditions of *conflict*, as for example when verbal sparring occurs against a background of latent hostility in a marriage, or when actual fighting takes place. And, I believe, a labeller is unlikely to apply the label 'aggressive' to behaviour unless the labeller believes the situation to be one of actual competition, or latent or actual conflict. Linked to this I would argue that the labeller is unlikely to apply the label to behaviour unless he or she believes that, by carrying out such behaviour, the 'aggressor' intends to emerge from the conflict or competition in an advantaged position. Thus a child's desire for independence, as evidenced, say, by contradicting a parent, can be called 'aggressive' by Storr, because he believes that parent–child relationships are characterized by conflict, and because he believes that the child wishes by his contradiction to gain mastery of the parent.

### The issue of provocation

Reading accounts of aggression, looking up dictionary definitions of the term 'aggressive', or simply discussing its use with others has convinced me that an important element in using the word 'aggressive' to describe behaviour is the belief on the part of the labeller that the behaviour in question is of a 'first strike' nature. In the case of an obvious conflict like a fight, or an invasion, the 'aggressor' is seen as the initiator of the action, and in the case of competition the person seen as behaving aggressively is perceived as moving the competition on to a more intense plane.

Here, of course, the element of subjectivity in applying the label is clear. While two observers considering the same act may agree that it is intended by the person carrying out the act, that it is taking place in a context of competition or conflict, and that the person carrying it out wishes to gain an advantage, they may well disagree about whether to apply the label 'aggressive' or 'defensive' to the very same act. So that, depending on the viewpoint of the labeller, the parties in a conflict may receive two quite different labels – 'aggressor' or 'defender'. For example, looking at an issue that has figured prominently in news bulletins in the 1980s, President Reagan's policy in Nicaragua is labelled by the Nicaraguans as 'aggressive' and by the US State Department as 'defensive'. In any particular situation of conflict, how the protagonists are perceived, and indeed see themselves, is clearly coloured by a reading of the situation and the circumstances leading up to it which is heavily dependent on values as well as on any description of an objective reality with which all parties could agree.

In sum, it seems that there is commonality of meaning that characterizes the use of the term 'aggressive' to describe a particular act or set of behaviours. The labeller is likely to believe (no matter what his or her theoretical standpoint on aggression is) that the behaviour is taking place in a competitive or conflictual context, that the 'aggressor' not only intends to carry out that behaviour, but intends by so doing to gain an advantage *vis à vis* the person or persons aggressed against, and that the 'aggressor' 'started'. It can be seen, too, that while there is a measure of agreement about what characterizes 'aggressive' behaviour, there is unlikely to be a consensus about whether or not a particular act should be so classified. Much will depend on the labeller's viewpoint.

### AGGRESSION

If there is a measure of agreement in the conditions that an act must satisfy to be classified as 'aggressive', there is little agreement as to the classes of motives or subjective experience that underpin such behaviour. It is here, I believe, that we come to the nub of the issue, for it seems to me that there are three distinct viewpoints about aggression. These are:

(1) 'Aggressive behaviour' is underpinned by a relatively unitary drive which can be called aggression.
(2) Aggressive behviour is underpinned by dispositions that can be

called 'aggression'. These dispositions fall into two classes, 'hostile' aggression and 'instrumental' aggression.

(3) Aggressive behaviour, like any other aspect of human behaviour, is motivated by complex subjective factors. It depends not on forces, drives or dispositions called 'aggression' but on a host of understandings, experiences, feelings and analyses that make up the subjective viewpoint of the person carrying out such behaviour.

## Aggression as a drive

If this viewpoint is accepted, it is not necessary to delve into an aggressor's subjective experience – for aggressors aggress because they experience aggression. Aggression, in this sense, is seen by the biologically oriented theorists as an excitation in the aggressor's physiology, by certain ethologists as an instinct, by sociobiologists as an innately predetermined motivator, by psychoanalysts as an 'instinct' and by certain experimental psychologists as a learned drive. But all would agree that *'aggression' causes aggressive behaviour*.

## Aggression as a dual set of motivations

This is a viewpoint held by a large number of experimental psychologists. Those holding it argue that it is not particularly relevant to look in detail at the aggressor's subjective experience because aggressive behaviour is always perceived as being directed by one or both of two distinct motivating forces. The first of these is a general state of arousal which is accompanied by cues which have in the past been associated with aggressive behaviour; the second is the cumulative effect of past learning experiences in which the aggressor has learned that aggressive behaviour is rewarding. In both cases, however, aggressive behaviour is perceived by experimental psychologists who are associated with this viewpoint as being *caused* by aggression; either an aggressor displays 'hostile' aggression because he or she is driven by a state of arousal, or an aggressor displays 'instrumental' aggression because the aggressor's past history of being rewarded for aggressive behaviour or seeing others rewarded for aggressive behaviour has induced in the aggressor an expectation that aggressive behaviour will bring a desired result.

In this approach to aggressive behaviour, as in (1) above, aggressive behaviour is seen as being caused in a relatively straightforward manner by 'aggression'. The theorists who fall into either (1) or (2) argue that the key to understanding aggressive behaviour lies in understanding their own particular version of 'aggression'. Theorists who fall into the next and third class, however, do not link aggressive behaviour in this causative manner with drives, instincts or dispositions which they call 'aggression'. Instead they argue that aggressive behaviour has the same set of motivations as all other aspects of human behaviour.

*Aggressive behaviour as motivated by complex subjective factors*

This viewpoint, which is held by those theorists whose work was discussed in the last two sections of the previous chapter, rejects the argument that aggressive behaviour is caused by 'aggression' and suggests instead that aggressive behaviour, like all other classes of human behaviour, is underpinned by complex subjective factors which range from diverse and sometimes contradictory sets of emotions to rational and well-thought out plans of action. In short, the argument is that in order to understand why people behave aggressively we should not look for a unitary cause in a particular force called 'aggression', or for dual causes in forces called 'instrumental' or 'hostile' aggression, but we should seek instead to understand the meaning that such behaviour holds for those who carry it out.

The emphasis moves from a cause-and-effect model towards an interpretative one. So that in this approach towards aggressive behaviour there is little room for 'aggression' as a motive force directing aggressive behaviour.

The particular viewpoint that I wish to develop in this chapter is based on this third approach. It seems to me that the earlier parts of this book have illustrated that trying to understand aggressive and violent behaviour by seeking to isolate forces that cause it has not been productive. In Chaper 2 I demonstrated that seeking to identify particular physiological processes as invariably causing aggressive behaviour has not been successful; in Chapters 3 and 4 I demonstrated that there is little evidence either of an instinct or innate drive for aggression, or for arguing that aggression is programmed into our genes in such a sway that it displays itself in an inevitable and identifiable manner; and in Chapter 5 I showed that in confining the discussion of aggressive behaviour only to tightly circumscribed and often very artificial instances, experimental psychologists produced a version of aggression as two motiviating dispositions, which severely limits any understanding of aggressive behaviour in the broader sense in which most people use the term.

The rest of this chapter is not concerned with a theory of 'aggression', but attempts instead to illuminate why it is that human beings are, under certain circumstances of conflict or competition, likely to behave 'aggressively', that is, likely to pursue their own advantage in such a manner that it severely constrains the fortunes of others. It seeks also to identify the factors that act to restrain such behaviour and thus it returns to concepts that have been touched on in earlier sections of this book – the influence on behaviour of empathy, altruism, ideology and fear of punishment. Finally, it looks at methods for controlling the most intense and extreme kind of aggressive behaviour – violence.

VIOLENCE

Throughout this book it has been clear that the term 'violence', though commonly associated with aggression and aggressive behaviour, is not always regarded as an extreme form of aggressive behaviour. For most theorists have, either explicitly or implicitly, taken the view that if violence is retaliatory rather than provocative, or if violence is enjoyed by both the individual inflicting it and the individual on whom it is inflicted, it is not necessarily an aspect of 'aggression'.

The viewpoint that will be taken in this chapter is rather different. It is that, with the single exception of the physical injury that occurs when two or more people voluntarily and with enjoyment engage in behaviour where physical injury is inflicted, violence should always be associated with aggressive behaviour. If it is argued that aggressive behaviour is characterized by the presence of four conditions – intention, a context of conflict or competition, the seeking of a comparative advantage and with the escalation of the conflict – it seems to me that violence, which is the infliction of extreme physical injury, must be regarded as a category of aggressive behaviour. Whether or not it is regarded as justifiable is a subjective question of the same nature as identifying who is the aggressor and who is the defender in a conflict. It is the aspect of subjectivity that leads on to the last issue that I want to discuss in demarcating the subject area.

DOES AGGRESSION HAVE A POSITIVE SIDE?

One of the issues that has continually surfaced throughout this book has been the extent to which aggression and aggressive behaviour can be seen as having a positive as well as a negative aspect. This issue has taken two forms. In the first case, it has been explored in the context of whether or not aggression can, or should, ever be considered in a positive light, and in the second case it has been discussed in the context of particular instances of aggressive behaviour. In the first case it seems to me that the inquiry centres around the nature of the theoretical approach to aggression, and in the second it centres around a series of subjective judgements.

The question as to whether aggression has a positive side presupposes the existence of aggression as a motivating force or drive, and is therefore only of relevance to those theorists who regard aggression in this light. To the social scientists whose work was discussed in the last sections of the previous chapter, the question would appear meaningless, in that they would argue that the judgements made about aggressive behaviour must of necessity be subjective rather than absolute as the question implies.

Where aggression is regarded as a motivating force, it is likely to be regarded as positive as well as negative when it is seen as an innate part of human nature. Thus, Moyer, Lorenz and Wilson claim that certain acts of aggression are healthy and constructive because they derive from innately laid down behaviour patterns that are designed to protect the species, and Freud, Storr and Fromm endorse certain acts of aggression, seeing them as healthy features of human instinctive endowment. Baron, Bandura and Berkowitz on the other hand who, while regarding aggression as a cause of aggressive behaviour, would deny that it is innate, pay little attention to aggression as a positive rather than as a negative force.

In sum, where aggression is seen as a force and particularly where it is seen as an innate drive or instinct, it is likely that aggression will be regarded as having a constructive aspect.

## WHEN IS AGGRESSIVE BEHAVIOUR REGARDED AS POSITIVE RATHER THAN NEGATIVE?

In making judgements about whether or not specific behaviour should be regarded both as aggressive and in a positive light, it is obvious that there is considerable scope for subjectivity.

This is made very clear if we look at the manner in which a particular act may be labelled as aggressive. Take, for example, the case of a 3-year-old child knocking down and shattering one of her mother's favourite ornaments. If the mother applies the label 'aggressive' to the act she is bound to believe that the act is intentional (even if the little girl denies that she meant to break the object); she has to believe that the little girl was in the frame of mind where she wanted to get at or annoy her mother (and the little girl may deny that she is 'in a bad mood'), and she must believe that the little girl was 'starting' because she herself (the mother) had not been behaving irritably.

In short, as noted before, labelling behaviour as aggressive is bound to be subjective to a greater or lesser extent and the subjectivity of applying such labels becomes even more apparent when we consider under which conditions a labeller applies the label: approvingly, neutrally or pejoratively. Turning again to the episode with the mother and child, if the mother is tired and exhausted, she may regard the breaking of the ornament not only as aggressive but as 'extremely naughty and most unwarranted', if she is feeling reasonably cheerful, she may note that it is probably a bit aggressive but 'what can you expect from a 3-year-old', and if she admires spirited children she may, while labelling it as aggressive in intention, feel that it shows that her daughter is capable of 'healthy assertiveness'.

In general, I would argue that the manner in which the epithet 'aggressive' is applied depends on a number of subjective factors. These may include the mood of the labeller, the labeller's value system, how far the labeller believes the person aggressively to have 'overstepped the mark', and the extent to which the labeller identifies or empathizes with either the person he or she regards as behaving aggressively or the person or persons he or she regards as being aggressed against.

## SUMMARY

In this section I suggested that it is fruitful to draw a distinction between the manners in which the terms 'aggression' and 'aggressive' are used.

Turning first to the term 'aggressive' I suggested that running through all usages of the term is an assumption that certain conditions are being met; specifically, that the behaviour labelled as aggressive is intentional, that it takes place in a competitive or conflictual context, that the person carrying out the behaviour is aiming to draw a greater advantage from the behaviour than will accrue to the person or persons against whom he or she is aggressing, and that in carrying out the act the person is moving the competition or conflict on to a more intense plane.[4]

While suggesting that there is a degree of commonality that underpins most, if not all, usages of the term 'aggressive', I noted that the use of the term 'aggression' depends primarily on substantive beliefs about what underpins aggressive behaviour. I suggested that there were three distinctive viewpoints. First, a number of theorists (including those discussed in Chapters 2, 3 and 4) use the term 'aggression' to refer to an energizing drive or force which causes aggressive behaviour. Secondly, and somewhat similarly, another set of theorists (see Chapter 5) use the term aggression to refer to two sets of predispositions (instrumental and hostile aggression) which cause people to behave aggressively. (In both these cases, theorists do not believe it necessary to look too deeply into subjective emotions and thoughts in order to understand aggressive behaviour, for quite simply aggressive behaviour is caused by aggression.) Finally, there is a third set of theorists (discussed in Chapter 6, and amongst whom I would include myself) who do not use the term aggression in a determining manner. In this formulation, in trying to understand aggressive behaviour, we must seek not to identify a force called 'aggression' but strive instead to understand the meaning that the aggressive behaviour holds for those who are carrying it out.

In this latter formulation, 'violence' is regarded as behaviour which involves the intentional use of extreme physical force on another person or persons, and where that force is inflicted without the voluntary consent and enjoyment of the persons on whom it is inflicted, it should be regarded as an instance of aggressive behaviour.

Finally I discussed the *emotional tone* with which the terms 'aggression' and 'aggressive' can be used. I suggested that if aggression is regarded as an energizing force underpinning aggressive behaviour, and further if such force is regarded as innately determined, it is likely that the term will sometimes be used approvingly. Turning to the question of whether the term 'aggressive' can be applied positively or neutrally as well as negatively, I suggested that the emotional tone with which the label 'aggressive' is applied will depend on a number of subjective factors. These include the extent to which the labeller believes the behaviour to be justified, his or her value system, and the extent to which the labeller empathizes or identifies with the person he or she is labelling as behaving aggressively.

## The Meaning of Aggressive Behaviour

> The infant's capacity to cope with necessities becomes, in the growing adult the struggle for self-esteem and for the sense of significance as a person. . . . The cry for recognition becomes the central psychological cry: I must be able to say I *am*, to affirm myself in a world into which, by my capacity to assert myself, I put meaning, I *create* meaning! (May, 1976, p. 21)

If, as the previous section suggests, the concept of a drive that may be called 'aggression' is questioned and aggressive behaviour is seen as similar in its motivation to other aspects of behaviour, can there be any advance in the understanding of aggressive behaviour? I would suggest there can be if we look in depth at two of the conditions that were listed above as holding when aggressive behaviour is seen as taking place. These are firstly that aggressive behaviour is intended behaviour, and secondly that it is intended behaviour carried out by an individual who is not taking into account the welfare of the person or persons against whom he or she is aggressing. The next section then, deals with intentionality in human behaviour, and the following sections consider the aspects of human needs that may be involved when an individual wishes to promote self interest and does not care too much about the consequences for others.[5]

A THEORETICAL BACKGROUND FOR UNDERSTANDING INTENTION IN HUMAN BEHAVIOUR

A central criticism that has been made of many of the approaches to aggressive behaviour which have been discussed is that in proposing a cause and effect relationship between 'aggression' and aggressive behaviour, theorists fail to take into account the motives and intentions of the person carrying out the behaviour. The assumption behind such a criticism is of course that human beings are capable of initiating actions which are anticipated in more or less clear-cut plans, and that such plans depend on the person's understanding of the situation in which they find themselves. Such an assumption seems a truism, but it should be remembered that the second part of it (that the plans depend on the individual's construction of the situation) is one that tends to be glossed over by many theorists who write about aggression and even explicitly denied by the more extreme behaviourists.

In fact, the subject of motives and intentions has created a great deal of difficulty for positivist accounts of human interaction,[6] and it remains problematical even now in such accounts. If, however, the focus is moved, as I intend, from the cause-and-effect paradigm of positivism to a more interpretative approach, the subject of human intentions and motives becomes far easier to integrate into accounts of interpersonal relationships, under which of course the discussion of aggressive behaviour must fall. I would argue that one particular interpretative approach is the most appropriate in seeking to illuminate the kinds of intentions that underpin aggressive behaviour. This approach is located in the very broad theoretical inquiries into what is referred to as 'self'.

Although we all take for granted an awareness, or consciousness, of self, and our ability to monitor the behaviour of that self in the outer world and the thoughts and emotions of that self in the inner one, not all social scientists or philosophers have been content to proceed with this 'taken for granted' conception of self.

Philosophers, in particular, have long wrestled with problems concerning consciousness, while psychologists and sociologists, who have in general been less inclined to delve into the arcane arguments about consciousness, have been more preoccupied with what influences the monitoring process of consciousness. For my purposes, in relating aggressive behaviour to an understanding of self, it does not seem particularly appropriate to examine this wide ranging theoretical debate in any depth at all, and I propose instead to introduce the reader to a particular orientation on self based on eight formal propositions, which together with their appropriate references are listed in the notes at the end of this chapter.[7]

## AN INTRODUCTION TO SELF THEORY

Recently, and noticeably in the late 1970s and the 1980s, a great deal of theoretical and research attention has focused, particularly in the field of social psychology, on what can loosely be called 'self theory'. This interest has roots that are numerous, long standing and extremely diverse, and which range from philosophy (for example, Schutz, 1972) through sociology (for example, Mead, 1934) and psychology (for example, Carl Rogers, 1963) to psychoanalysis (for example, Adler, 1927). This diversity has led not only to substantive differences in the approach to self theory, but also to what Colin Rogers calls a 'confusing mixture of terminology and a frustrating inability to draw together the results of different systems' (1982, p. 140).

In suggesting, at this stage in the book, that a particular orientation to self theory may be useful in understanding aggressive behaviour, I make no more substantial claim than that this approach yields an interpretative paradigm for considering interpersonal behaviour. To some extent, it rests on empirical studies, for example, on those studies that investigate the nature of social and emotional development in infants and young children, and on those studies that have examined the family and social background of people who are regarded by others and by themselves as prone to aggressive behaviour, but to a greater extent it rests on a particular understanding of the nature of human beings. In this, as I hope has been clearly illustrated by now, it is no different from any other account of aggression, except perhaps in its explicit endorsement of the belief that any hypothesis about 'human nature', while it may be empirically testable, cannot be susceptible to scientific *proof* and can be judged only by whether or not it extends understanding of interpersonal relationships.

Studies of child development (see Maccoby, 1980, and Siann and Ugwuegbu, 1980) point to two dominant trends that are apparent from earliest infancy. These are, first, that infants appear to be 'programmed for sociability' and, secondly, that from their earliest weeks infants do not passively receive information from the ouside world, but actively process it in ways that enable them to start building up a symbolic internal representation of the outer world.

For example, the neonate's visual capacities enable him, shortly after birth, to follow with his eyes an object moving at a point about eight inches away from the face, and by three weeks infants' powers of visual processing are accurate enough for them to differentiate their mother's face from that of a stranger. Furthermore, careful studies of the child's first months of life show not only that the child is an active partner in social interactions, but that he or she often initiates such interactions and sets their tone. Indeed, recent detailed studies of infancy are demonstrating that a very large part of early behaviour is directed towards social interaction, aided by what appears to be specific tuning of the sensory organs which make children more likely to pay attention to the human face, voice, and speech patterns than to other classes of incoming information (Kagan, Kearsley and Zelazo, 1980).

Other studies, dealing with the child's developing powers of thought, or cognition, show that even new-born infants are capable of learning to pattern their behaviour, by, for example, turning their head to the right to receive a few drops of sugared water at the sound of a bell but not at the sound of a buzzer. Furthermore when the matters are changed so that the buzzer now signals the water rather than the bell, they can learn to reverse the pattern, indicating considerable flexibility of behaviour (Bower, 1977).

Such studies reveal that by the end of the first year of life the child possesses the perceptual and cognitive abilities and the experience of social interaction that allow him or her to start laying the basis for self-awareness. Indeed, by 20 months of age, it can be shown that young children possess a distinct sense of physical self. This sense of self has been demonstrated by a series of experiments by Lewis and Brooks (1974), in which mothers put spots of rouge on the noses of their infants aged between 16 and 22 months when supposedly wiping their faces. The infants were then shown their reflections in a mirror, and if they touched their own noses rather than the reflection it was inferred that they had some concept of their physical self. By the ages of 20 months most children showed such behaviour and by 22 months all children tested showed this indication of understanding that they had a physical self.

As children grow older, studies show that this awareness of a physical self is accompanied by a maturing sense of self as an object of other people's attention, and a developing understanding of those aspects of self which are private and unique. For example, in a series of studies with children aged 2½ years to 4 years, Flavell showed that well before the age of 5 children think that the 'real me' is somewhere inside 'my head', and they are aware that other people cannot know what they are thinking because, as one child put it,

> (Can I see you thinking?) 'No' (Even if I look in your eyes, do I see you thinking?) 'No' (Why not?) ''Cause I don't have any big holes.' (You mean there would have to be a hole there for me to see you thinking?) Child nods. (Flavell, quoted in Maccoby, 1980, p. 261)

But the child is not, of course, solely preoccupied with a developing sense of self, for the awareness of self takes place against a background of the child's growing understanding of the social and physical world, and with increasing age children begin to relate their understandings of how this world operates, and what other people do, say and mean in this world, to their own place in the world.

As a result of these developmental processes the child begins to appreciate that, as other people have roles to which they, the child, can relate, like 'mommy' or 'brother' or 'teacher' or 'friend', so they themselves have social roles and are other people's son or friend or sister or pupil. Further, the child begins to apply the same sort of categories and labels to themselves as they apply to others, and from the age of 5 onwards children become capable of giving other people quite complex descriptions of who they are, what they are like and what their interests and hobbies are (Maccoby, 1980).

One way of organizing our understanding of these propensities and capacities of children is to see them as pointing to the development of what may be called the individual's sense of self, where by the term self we mean 'the cluster of assumptions, beliefs and hypotheses' (ibid., p. 201) that individuals hold about themselves. Further, it is suggested by self theorists that it is through this system that the individual filters his or her appraisal and understanding of the external world. We react, that is, not to an objective reality that is shared by all observers, but to our own interpretation of that reality and our predictions about how what is happening out there will affect our own particular situation. Of course, the interpretations that we make are shaped not only by our own particular individual experience but also by the values, expectations and attitudes that we have developed as a result of growing up in a particular culture and sub-culture at a particular time.

The influences on the formation of self are obviously manifold. In essence, however, they can be broken down into four sets of factors. First, self is formed in social interaction (Mead, 1934), and to a large extent we learn about the kind of person we are by the way others treat us, what they tell us about ourselves, and the roles they ask us to play.

Secondly, it appears characteristic of human beings (Festinger, 1954) that they evaluate their own abilities and performances against the abilities and performances of those they consider their peers. Such comparisons may be made in a competitive spirit, particularly where the values of the culture encourage competition, but I believe that they are more commonly made because in the same way that humans actively gather information about the external world, so they actively gather and collate information about themselves. Viewed from this perspective, the drawing or making of social comparisons serves to help the individual build up a distinctive personal identity.

Thirdly, people tend to regard themselves as possessing the characteristics of those groups that they regard themselves as belonging to (Babad, Birnbaum and Benne, 1983). Thus some people may accept stereotypes about their ethnic and gender group as applying to themselves (as in someone who says 'we Italians are a very passionate lot'), while others may ascribe to themselves those qualities that they see as permeating ideological or religious groups they have elected to join ('being a socialist means caring about other people').

Finally, an important source of information about ourselves relates to the manner in which we see ourselves as meeting those moral and ethical standards that we personally have adopted as meaningful for, and important to, us. When these are breached we tend to feel shame, or guilt, or both, and our sense of self-worth is assailed.[8]

What has been suggested up to now is that from early childhood human beings consciously observe and monitor their own actions and their own relationships with others. It has also been suggested that in so monitoring they draw on the information given them by others, on social comparison, on the social identity they see as emerging from the groups they belong to and on the comparisons they draw between their performances and behaviours and their individual value system.

It has been further suggested that it is this understanding of self that supplies the major influence on the individual's construction of what might be called 'external reality'. To take an illustrative example: suppose a male teacher in a secondary school offers extra tuition to four girls who have fallen behind in their work. Three of the girls may believe that he does so because, as a concerned teacher, he wants to help them academically; while the fourth girl, who is perhaps more concerned with her burgeoning sense of sexuality, may believe that he does so as a tribute to her personal appeal, and she may even regard his offer of help as presaging a move to make more intimate contact with her.

Two further issues of concern to self theorists need to be briefly touched on. The first of these concerns the dynamic forces that affect the functioning of self, and the second concerns the extent to which the self system is available to conscious examination.

Up to now the self system has been described as a system of feelings and thoughts that individuals hold about themselves; in short, as having both an evaluative and a cognitive aspect. But self theorists argue that this self system is characterized as well by organizational or dynamic tendencies. The most powerful of these is the need to protect and enhance the self system, and self theorists argue that most of our behaviour is concerned with developing and defending our self in the broadest sense. This is not to suggest that self theorists believe that people are motivated simply by self-preservation; rather, they argue, human beings basically behave in such a way as to maintain and defend not simply the physical self but, far more importantly, the sense of personal identity and the values which pertain to it. In this way, self theorists account for the fact that people will go to their deaths for their ideals, or save the lives of others in preference to their own.

It is in this tendency to preserve and enhance self that self theorists believe that unconscious as well as conscious processes may enter into our interpretation of external reality. To illustrate this belief I would like to consider the case of a young woman who regards herself as a very caring and compassionate person, but experiences strong angry and rejecting emotions about her young baby. It may be very difficult for her to consciously admit these negative feelings because in doing so she would need to reconsider her opinion that at heart she is caring, loving and compassionate. One possible manner for dealing with the dilemma would be to dismiss the conscious acknowledgement of the angry emotions and rationalize any impatience she has with the baby by ascribing it to her own tiredness or ill-health, or perhaps the temperament of the child. Such an interpretation of the situation would allow her to defend her self-image, for she could ascribe her impatient behaviour with her child to factors over which she has no control, such as her physical condition or the baby's nature, and not to her feelings of rejection which would, in Ashworth's terms, remain 'undisclosed' to her.

AGGRESSIVE BEHAVIOUR IN THE DEFENCE OF SELF

On pages 226–7 I argued that at the root of aggressive behaviour is the intention on the part of the aggressor to carry through certain actions in such a way as to enhance his or her own advantage at the expense of others. In this section I shall argue that the understanding of aggressive behaviour can be increased if we look in some detail at the kinds of objectives individuals may have in mind when they embark on such behaviour.

In the preceding section it was suggested not only that human beings have a conscious awareness of their own self, but that there is a human need to enhance and defend this sense of self. In an extension of this latter proposition, Rollo May (1976) has argued that the understanding of aggressive and violent behaviour can be increased if we make an assumption that at root all human beings have a need for personal significance. Such a sense of significance does not emerge, as Storr would claim, from dominating over others; rather, according to May, it emerges from a sense of self-affirmation. That is, human beings need to feel valued and effective within the standards that they themselves see as meaningful.

In this view May comes close to two contemporary strands in psychology. First, humanist psychologists argue that the human being has a basic tendency for what they term self-enhancement, and, secondly, certain empirical studies of the social and emotional development of children (for example, Coopersmith, 1967) suggest that such development is optimal when children have a secure sense of their own personal worth. Coopersmith, for example, has suggested that this sense of personal worth emerges from the belief that the individual is successful in terms of:

> *power* – the ability to influence and control others;
> *significance* – the acceptance, attention, and affection of others;
> *virtue* – adherence to moral and ethical standards;
> *competence* – successful performance in meeting demands for achievement.

The assumption that human beings experience the greatest sense of well-being when they feel influential, significant, effective and that they meet their own ethical and moral standards is echoed by Fromm in his postulation of 'existential needs' (see Chapter 4). Fromm argues that inherent in human nature are the needs for close ties with other people, a sense of personal effectiveness and a frame of moral and ethical standards. Further, Fromm claims that when these needs are not met, the groundwork is laid for what he calls 'malignant aggression'.

May takes a similar but rather more carefully argued step to this last argument of Fromm's. For he claims that when self-affirmation is denied, the individual experiences 'a compulsive need which drives an individual all his life' and which leads the individual to actively seek this affirmation, first, according to May (1976, p. 41) by self-assertion; then, if the need is not met, by 'aggression', which May defines as a 'moving into the positions of power or prestige or the territory of another and taking possession of some of it for oneself' (ibid., p. 42); and, if the need for self-affirmation is still denied, ultimately by violence.

My own position is rather similar to May's. I would argue that, irrespective of culture, sub-culture or the era in which an individual lives, all human beings require a sense of personal significance and identity. This sense of significance, or self-affirmation, comes from meeting the standards that the individual has assumed to be important and valid. These standards will vary across time, across culture and across situation. Thus, in the mid-twentieth century, when Storr was writing about aggression, self-affirmation for a man (and Storr writes from a very male oriented position) depended intimately on competing successfully, whereas for a woman living, say, in a Muslim community in the latter part of the century it may rest on satisfying standards of familial and personal honour (Siann and Khalid, 1984). But whatever the standards, if self-affirmation is denied the individual will feel a sense of devaluation that will be deeply distressing.

It is this sense of devaluation that, I believe, may fuel a great deal of aggressive behaviour. For, if aggressive behaviour is defined as behaviour that seeks to advantage self over others, it seems clear to me that the impetus for such behaviour is potently provided when a person wishes to achieve self-recognition. Thus, when self-esteem is attacked, and when affirmation is denied, an individual may experience a number of emotions that may lead him or her to try and exact self-affirmation from others by wresting personal advantage from them. For example, a person who feels humiliated may wish to humiliate others in turn, a person who feels unhappy may wish to make others suffer as well, a person who believes that others have unfairly denied him what is rightfully his may set out to achieve redress. Furthermore, if other methods of recognition are denied, a person craving for recognition may quite systematically seek to achieve it by gaining respect from others for their intransigent and aggressive stance. For example, Jimmy Boyle, describing his early life as a hard man in the slums of Glasgow, writes: 'After the initial shock of entry [to an Approved School] I soon hardened and became very much part of it, trying to gain a position in the only way I knew possible, by violence' (1977, p. 72).

This belief that aggressive behaviour springs from devaluation is one that is of course recognized in a very general way. For example, when people talk about a 'little Napoleon' they refer to a very widely accepted notion that short men feel the need to assert themselves. I am modifying this assumption by suggesting that it is not the need to assert oneself that is fundamental, but that it is in the nature of human beings to wish to be appreciated, valued and affirmed and that when such affirmation is denied, as for example when a society places a value on men being tall, burly and physically dominating, and a man is small, *if he is denied alternative sources of affirmation* he may respond by aggressive behaviour.

Furthermore, I am not arguing that when affirmation is denied aggressive behaviour is the inevitable outcome, for it is quite clear that some people respond to the distress of being devalued and humiliated by retreating into themselves rather than by self-assertion. I am merely arguing that one of the outcomes of such an experience may be the desire to, in a sense, make others pay for the devaluation.

Clearly, the manner in which one deals with the distress is going to depend on a multitude of factors. In particular, if the culture one lives in treats aggressive behaviour as acceptable when it is seen as being justified by antecedent events, then an individual is far more likely to respond with aggressive actions than if a society places a premium on peaceable behaviour. Furthermore, a powerful incentive to respond aggressively rather than in other ways is offered when a person has grown up in a home when aggressive behaviour is the norm and is seen to be effective.

Moving from this rather general statement of my position I would like to look in some detail at the assumptions on which it is based and relate these (where possible) to some of the empirical findings that have been presented in this book. The assumptions are as follows.

(1)  Individuals have a conscious awareness of self that has both cognitive and evaluative components. This understanding of personal identity arises primarily out of social interaction and the monitoring of the behaviour of self against the performance of others and also against the individual's personal value system.

(2)  When an individual experiences this self as affirmed – that is, as being of significance, as valued by others and as effective – he or she finds the experience satisfying and indeed strives to achieve this situation. Conversely, when the individual experiences self as denied affirmation, the experience is arousing and uncomfortable.

(3)  The individual may seek to deal with this latter experience by behaviour which devalues the self of others, and defends his or her own self.

(4)  Aggressive behaviour may be a strategy resorted to consistently, and certain people therefore may be regarded as more 'aggressive' than others.

(5)  Such people are likely to be those who have been denied a sense of their own essential worth. Their backgrounds are likely to have been characterized by a lack of love, by failure and by a continued denial of a sense of affirmation. They are likely therefore to have had parents who are rejecting, to have failed at school, to have been

unpopular as children, and to feel, at the most fundamental level, deeply insecure.

(6) When individuals habitually behave aggressively and violently, they may do so in a conscious attempt to extract from others a degree of respect and affirmation.

(7) It is most likely that individuals will resort to violent behaviour as a means of establishing self-affirmation if other means are denied them and if the culture or sub-culture in which they live places a positive value on such behaviour.

(8) Though particular individuals may resort to aggressive behaviour more consistently than others, most people are likely to behave aggressively at those times when they feel devalued or wish to defend their sense of self.

Assumptions (1), (2) and (3) have been discussed in some detail in the preceding sections of this chapter and have been related both to recent work in developmental psychology and to recent theoretical approaches to interpersonal behaviour. Consequently, I will now look in some detail at the last five assumptions.

## Consistency in Aggressive Behaviour

Although I am not for one moment suggesting that aggression is a measurable personality 'trait', there is no doubt that many studies have shown that certain individuals consistently behave in an aggressive manner both over time and over situations (for example, Lefkowitz *et al.*, 1977, West and Farrington, 1977, Olweus, 1979).

Furthermore, my own subjective experience indicates to me that in general some people are rather more hostile, prickly and suspicious than others and are far more likely to take offence easily and retaliate aggressively. Looking at other people's subjective experience, it seems to me that they too recognize such a constellation of characteristics in particular people. For example, Graham Greene's portrayal of Pinky in *Brighton Rock* presents a frighteningly convincing picture of a very embittered young man whose feelings of hostility and hate not only lead to a terrifying career of violence in the gangland of Brighton in the 1930s, but also move him to vent his hostility even on those who meet him with love and pity. In this extract Pinky and Rose, the girl whom he is forced to marry so that her testimony against him cannot be demanded by the police, are outside a recording booth. Rose has no gramophone but begs him to make a recording:

'I don't want a gramophone,' she said. 'I just want to have it [the recording] there. Perhaps one day you might be away somewhere and I could borrow a gramophone. And you'd speak,' she said with a sudden intensity that scared him.

'What do you want me to say?'

'Just anything,' she said. 'Say something to me. Say Rose and – something.'

He went into the box and closed the door. There was a slot for his sixpence: a mouthpiece: an instruction, 'Speak clearly and close to the instrument.' The scientific paraphernalia made him nervous. He looked over his shoulder and there outside she was watching him, without a smile. He saw her as a stranger: a shabby child from Nelson Place, and he was shaken by an appalling resentment. He put in a sixpence, and, speaking in a low voice for fear it might carry beyond the box, he gave his message up to be graven on vulcanite: 'God damn you, you little bitch, why can't you go back home for ever and let me be?' He heard the needle scratch and the record whirr: then a click and silence.

Carrying the black disc he came out to her. 'Here,' he said, 'take it. I put something on it – loving.' (1975 pp. 176–7).

## Aggressive behaviour springs from devaluation

Both surveys and case studies of consistently aggressive people support the assumption that consistently aggressive individuals have been denied the kind of circumstances that make for a sense of self-affirmation.

Looking first at the manner in which their parents treated them, both West and Farrington and the McCords found that the parents of their aggressive samples were rejecting and punitive (Farrington, 1982). Similarly, Anne Campbell's description of the home background of the Borstal girls she interviewed showed that these were often characterized by extreme rejection and cruelty. In *A Glasgow Gang Observed* writing about the home background of Tim, the boy who introduced him to the gang, Patrick describes the boy's relationship with his father in these words: 'there was no love lost between them' (1973, p. 131). Toch, too, writing about his sample of violent men, suggests that their home background was deficient in emotional support.

Such studies show that people who are habitually aggressive are likely to have been judged as less intelligent (Farrington, 1982) or to have performed badly at school (Lefkowitz *et al.*, 1977, Patrick, 1973), while other studies show that failure extends beyond academic performance (Eron, 1982). For example, in a recent study of bullying, Lagerspetz *et al.* (1982) showed that not surprisingly, bullies were unpopular with their peers.

In general, research on aggressive individuals points to the kind of background which could be assumed to lead to a sense of failure, of lack of personal worth and of insecurity. So it can be conjectured that behind the hard facade lies a deep lack of well being. For example, here is Patrick writing again about Tim:

On a number of occasions, when I was on night duty at the approved school, the night supervisor and I came upon him shouting and screaming in his sleep. Tim later pretended that these outbursts were deliberate practical jokes meant to provoke members of the staff, but such explanations only revealed his concern not to lose face in front of the other boys in the dormitory and convinced nobody. The state of terror in which we found him was all too real for that. (Patrick, 1973, p. 134)

*Aggressive behaviour may be consciously carried out to win affirmation*
That individuals consciously use aggressive and even violent behaviour in order to win affirmation is the central theme of Toch's study of *Violent Men* which was described in some detail in the previous chapter. Although Toch's is the only empirical study I know of that explores this issue in any detail, considerable support for his contentions comes from the writing of people who have themselves had a history of aggressive behaviour, as is revealed for example in the extract from Claude Brown's *Manchild in the Promised Land* quoted in the same chapter. In Jimmy Boyle's description of his life as a gang leader and member in the Glasgow of the 1960s, he makes continual reference to the need he and his friends experienced to gain prestige and respect from violent behaviour. For example:

Our activities on the gang scene became more intense. I was intent on making a name for myself, and the only way it could be achieved was by violence. (1977, p. 67)

and

. . . when I was with my pals, there was the feeling that it was okay and that having attacked a gang single handed the previous night, I had in some way proved myself and gained enough confidence to fight alongside them. I had this hunger to be recognised, to establish a reputation for myself and it acted as an incentive being with the top guys in the district at sixteen. There was this inner compulsion for me to win recognition amongst them. (ibid., p. 79)

and again describing his thoughts in prison:

The fact is that I often thought of the vicious circle of staying places in the Gorbals and how I looked up to the hard men in my street and district. Then the kids looked up to me and saw me as the same guy who would do anything and had done things which they saw as heroic . . . (ibid., p. 239)

*Aggressive behaviour is influenced by cultural factors*
While it seems clear, as Stephen Box (1983) points out, that certain aspects of violent behaviour achieve far more attention in the media and from law enforcement agencies than others do, and that the institutionalized violence of political oppression tends to be ignored in most academic discussions of violence, nevertheless it seems beyond dispute that there is a higher level of violence in certain sub-cultures than others (Wolfgang and Ferracuti, 1967). One way of interpreting this is to locate such differences in the cultural values and norms endorsed by particular sub-cultures, and this interpretation was explored in the previous chapter. Related to this interpretation is the point just discussed, which is that the exercise of violence in such sub-cultures brings with it a degree of public esteem. Consequently it might be expected that people most likely to behave violently will be those whose sense of self-affirmation is low and who belong to sub-cultures which condone or even esteem violence. Thus while aggressive behaviour may be characteristic of particular individuals in all social classes, violent behaviour will be more characteristic of those living within what has been called 'sub-cultures of violence'.

*Hostile feeling may lead to aggressive behaviour*
Few of us, I think, could claim that there are not times when we feel 'aggressive' – that is, we feel hostility towards particular people and feel prepared to act in such a way as to cause them discomfort. In the next section I will explore other reasons for feeling like this, but my own subjective experience of such feelings indicates that they are most likely to arise when I feel I have been personally slighted, or the values that I hold most dear have been attacked, and in such circumstances my hostility tends to be directed not towards the world at large but specifically towards those whom I regard as being responsible for my feelings of humiliation. Some empirical evidence that these are the circumstances that make most people 'feel aggressive' emerges from the experimental studies reviewed in Chapter 5, when it was shown that neither frustration nor arousal consistently produced 'aggressive behaviour', but that aggressive behaviour was most likely to occur if subjects believed that their victims were responsible for their own discomfort. In such cases self was defended.

In this section I have suggested that the major cluster of motivations that underlie aggressive behaviour are those concerned with a desire to defend and enhance self. But it seems to me that there are other sets of subjective experiences that may predispose to aggressive behaviour and I believe that these can be roughly grouped as concerned with the pursuit of excitement, particular aspects of hedonic experience, the defence of ideology and the achievement of instrumental ends. I will now deal with these in turn.

## AGGRESSIVE BEHAVIOUR AND THE PURSUIT OF EXCITEMENT

In Chapter 4 I noted that Erich Fromm suggested that human beings had a number of what he called 'existential needs'. Amongst these was a requirement for what Fromm calls 'stimulation and excitation'. Contemporary psychologists (for example Ball, Farnill and Wangeman, 1984), while not using Fromm's vocabulary, appear to have reached a similar conclusion which is that for optimal well-being the human organism does require a degree of novelty and change in the pattern of stimulation to which it is exposed, and certainly at the subjective level it is clear that, in varying degrees, people become bored by too little change or challenge in their immediate environment.

This pervasive human tendency to seek stimulation bears, I think, on the subject matter of this book in two ways. First, it offers us an understanding of some of the motives and intentions behind the kind of behaviour of young people which is so roundly condemned in the media as 'wanton vandalism', and secondly, it is, I believe, relevant to any discussion of violence in the media.

Turning first to the search for excitement that is characteristic of inner city gangs and some football fans, in the previous chapter I described some of the many studies which attempt to interpret vandalism and hooliganism in terms of the values of groups carrying out such behaviour and in terms of the needs that such behaviours cater for. At this stage I want only to return to the manner in which 'aggressive' behaviour can create a degree of stimulation in an otherwise unchallenging life. Take, for example, this description by Sheila Welsh of the way in which teenage girls in an East End housing estate create diversions for themselves:

> Four of us, Angie, Liz, Nipper and myself were wandering around the estate 'doing nothing'. The sound of an alarm bell took us off the estate and down a nearby side street. The street was narrow with three-storey buildings lining either side and the bell echoed shrilly. Angie started shouting at the top of her voice in an attempt to make herself heard. An unmarked car drew up and the driver began to examine the door with a torch without leaving the car. The content of the shouting changed to:
>
> Angie:   Turn that bloody alarm off.
> Liz:   You silly cunt.
> Angie:   Oy you, y'cunt, turn the light off.
> Liz:   Don't piss about.

The driver wound down the window and shouted back, 'If who-

ever's making the noise doesn't keep their mouth shut you're all
going to end up down the flipping nick.' Liz and Angie were two or
three paces ahead of Nipper and myself. They turned the corner
first and as soon as they disappeared they shouted out something I
could not distinguish. The car shrieked around the corner, having
to go wide because an articulated lorry was parked just around it
. . . we doubled back and ran off the way we had come. For the
next ten minutes we wandered around the streets ready to run
every time we heard a car . . . Plans were made about what to do if
we were caught. It was decided we should deny any knowledge of
the episode. It would be his word against ours and at four to one 'he
wouldn't have a chance'. (Welsh, 1981, p. 262)

Excitement, of course, can be supplied vicariously as well as by
behaviour. It seems to me that while some people undoubtedly watch
violent films because they are turned on by the actual violence, others
watch violent films largely because of the thrills and excitement that
surround the action. Irrespective of whether or not exposure to violence
actually causes violent behaviour, I think it must be accepted that films
or videos concerned with violence offer large numbers of people an
escape from the monotony, cares and routines of day-to-day life. In
seeking this diversion, it seems to me that they are very similar to those
others whose diversions lie in reading romances or going to pop concerts
or attending the opera.

## HEDONIC EXPERIENCE AND AGGRESSIVE AND VIOLENT BEHAVIOUR

As earlier parts of this book have shown, some theorists believe that
behaving violently *is satisfying in itself*. For example, in Chapter 3 I
looked at the work of Fox, who makes this claim most explicitly. Such a
view is also echoed by a number of people I have met and it is certainly
one that is held by some novelists and playwrights. Anthony Burgess, for
example, says: 'But violence needs no pretext. It is good in itself like the
taste of an apple: it is built into the human complex' (1980, p. 689). But
this belief is by no means universally held. Other people, as I noted in
Chapter 3, obviously find violence extremely distressing and some, like
myself, find it very difficult to watch any realistic depiction of violence in
the media.

It seems reasonable to conclude that there are some marked differences in this area, though, as I pointed out in Chapter 3, theorists like
Fox seem reluctant to accept these differences, possibly because the very
existence of substantial numbers of people who find violence repugnant
destroys their thesis that finding violence 'good in itself' is innate.

However, even if it is concluded that enjoying violence is by no means universal, and therefore unlikely to be innate, it must be admitted that there appear to be numbers of people who do find the act of inflicting intense levels of injury satisfying. Were this not the case it would be difficult to account for the fact that in over half of the 164 nations in the world, torture is carried out quite systematically (Gelhorn, 1984). It may well be that those who order their subordinates to get information from prisoners find the idea of torture repugnant, but there seems little doubt from the reports of people who have been tortured that those actually carrying it out do find a certain pleasure in what they do. (See for example, the account of torture in San Salvador in ibid.)

Not surprisingly, the motivation for torture is not a subject that has been studied in any laboratory situation. Thus in attempting to understand why some people enjoy behaving in this way, we have to turn either to psychoanalytic studies like Fromm's or May's, or to accounts of the self-reported feelings of some of Toch's sample of *Violent Men*, or to the self-reports of those who, having carried out torture, now wish to atone for this by helping social scientists to understand how and why they became involved.

Such sources seem to me to focus consistently on one particular theme in their interpretation of why it is that certain people go out of their way to be unfair, unmerciful and inhumane in their violence. This theme is the exercise of power.

This is at the root of the torturer–victim relationship; the torturer exercises almost unlimited power over the victim and in doing so apparently enjoys the experience of seeing the other as completely within his (or less commonly her) power. It is this exercise of power that appears to give the dominant partner or partners a 'pleasure . . . from the exercise of violence and terror against individuals uniquely susceptible to it' (Toch, 1972, p. 176).

In understanding why some people obtain satisfaction in the exercise of power, I believe it is helpful to turn again to self theory. For if part of self-affirmation lies in the ability to influence others, then it might be expected that people whose lives have previously grossly denied them the ability to exercise such influence would be those who derive satisfaction from the exercise of power when the chance is given them. As May (1976) puts it, in such cases it is past impotence that breeds present violence.

But, according to Toch, impotence is not the only past experience that contributes to sadistic or bullying behaviour: linked to the experience of impotence is inevitably a history of fear. Toch claims that dominant amongst the emotions of those men in his sample who appeared to gain a degree of satisfaction from the infliction of violence was a wish to avoid the repetition of previous situations when they themselves had fearfully anticipated the violence of others. Thus, according to Toch, when such men gain the opportunity to exercise violence over others, they do so not only to repay in kind their own past humiliation, but also to exorcise the memory of their own impotence and terror. Such a man, according to Toch, acts unmercifully to others because of the fact that he himself 'as he introspects, feel terribly small and disadvantaged' (Toch, 1972, p. 205).

Toch's interpretation of the emotions of people who bully and torture is substantiated by a recent study of those men who acted as torturers during the regime of the Colonels in Greece.[9] These men were systematically subjected to mortification, degradation, terror, and physical abuse in a training programme. At the end of this period, during which they experienced the extremes both of humiliation and self-abasement, they were gradually given more and more power and eventually, provided that they responded in the appropriate spirit of concentrated violence, they were encouraged to treat their victims in an even more violent manner than they had themselves been subjected to. In this way, like the violent bullies that Toch described, they exorcised their own history of humiliation and terror.

This linkage of the infliction of torture with the desire to avenge past humiliation and the desire to win present self-affirmation, even if it is affirmation of the most malign nature, has been extended recently to the discussion of the motivations underlying rape. A number of studies of rape have pinpointed as the major emotion that is involved, not the simple gratification of sexual urges, but the exercise of power (Groth, 1979). In such formulations, rape is seen as being motivated primarily by the desire on the part of the rapist to be able to exercise control over the victim. Linked to this interpretation is the suggestion that in gang rapes the primary emotional needs catered to are not sexual, but rather they are directly concerned with an enhancement of self. In Groth's terms, the leader in a gang rape may wish to exercise power while the follower 'seeks to find or confirm his masculinity, *achieve recognition*, and/or retain his acceptance with his co-offenders', and Groth continues:

> one of the unique dynamics in gang rape is the experience of rapport, fellowship, and co-operation with the co-defendors . . . It appears [the offender] is using the victim as a vehicle for interacting with other men . . . behaving . . . in accordance with what he feels is expected of him . . . *validating himself* and participating in a group activity. (ibid., pp. 113–15), my italics)

Groth's work, and indeed the work of many others who have researched the motivations of rapists, challenges the direct link between 'aggression' and male sexuality. Instead of the simple equation of high male sex drive with increased levels of aggression in the case of rape, his work suggests that when men rape women (or women rape women, or men rape men), the dominant satisfactions obtained by the rapist centre around the enhancement of self, and the corresponding diminution of other, rather than on concentrated libidinal satisfaction.

At this stage, it seems appropriate to return for the last time to the issue of male sexuality and aggression within 'normal' heterosexual relations (that is, when both partners enter willingly into sexual activity). Returning briefly to the discussion in Chapter 4, I noted there that in contemporary Western society male sexuality has been intimately linked to male aggression, predominantly male aggression towards females, in such a way as to suggest that it is 'natural' for men to wish to dominate and control women within the sexual relationship, and that it is 'natural' for women to wish them to do so. But, even if such a viewpoint is widely held by members of the general public in the West (and it is of course increasingly challenged by feminists, amongst others), the study of sexuality in other societies and at other periods in history points to a different conclusion, which is that this linkage of male sexuality with aggression is culture specific, rather than innately determined. For example, Martin Roth (1982) has recently described how in Japan after a long period in which sexual love was depicted in prints with tenderness and eroticism, towards the middle of the nineteenth century such prints became interfused with blood and violence. Roth suggests that the reason for this change may lie in the increased contact between Japan and the West which occurred at this period. For the substantiation of this latter viewpoint – that male sexuality and aggressive behaviour are not linked because of innate preprogramming – I think we can turn to three lines of inquiry.

The first of these was explored in Chapter 2, when it was demonstrated that there was little evidence to support the hypothesis that there was a causal link between male sexual hormones and aggressive behaviour. The second was explored in the last section of the previous chapter when it was suggested that the belief that men dominate women because it is 'natural' for them to do so rests on the inequality of male–female power relationships and the ideologies that surround such relationships. Finally, a third line of inquiry can be carried out by a visit to any 'porn' shop, where it should be quite clear to even the most ingenuous visitor that a great many men prefer to be dominated and humiliated themselves rather than to dominate and humiliate others.

## AGGRESSIVE BEHAVIOUR AND THE DEFENCE OF IDEOLOGY

In the last three sections, aggressive behaviour has been considered from a psychological perspective which has centred on the emotional needs that it can meet for the individual who is carrying out the 'aggressive behaviour'. In choosing to start off with this focus in my own discussion of aggressive behaviour, I do not in any sense wish to minimize the contribution to aggressive behaviour that can be made by the individual's cognitive assessment of certain social situations. With Billig (see pages 213–14 above), I believe that until very recently most psychologists have tended to underestimate the effect on behaviour of people's *beliefs* about the nature of the social world they live in.

This is very obvious if we look at the way in which psychologists have been inclined to ascribe the radicalization of particular individuals to emotional displacement rather than to political and social beliefs. To take a specific example quoted by Billig, consider the analysis presented by Rainwater of the social attitudes of a black working-class man in the USA in the 1960s, who loses his job for refusing to work extra hours for no extra pay, and suspects that his dismissal has occurred because his employer wishes to employ someone whom he could pay less. Subsequent to losing his job, the man's wife leaves him. Billig (1976, p. 179) notes that Rainwater describes the man's misfortunes as instrumental in changing his viewpoint from moderate to radical, not because the man sensed the inequity of his social and financial position *vis-à-vis* those who held the economic power, but because he projected on to a public race relations issue his own rage and frustration arising from the failure of his marriage.

Such an analysis as Rainwater's (and see the very similar analysis offered by Berkowitz on pages 181–2 above) reflects the reluctance that I have referred to previously of certain social scientists to examine the extent to which their own reading of the social world affects their writing about interpersonal attitudes and behaviour. Two mechanisms seem to be at work in such writing. The first is the implicit belief that such social scientists seem to hold that the attempts to change the distribution of power must of necessity be provocative rather than reactive or defensive, and the second is the belief that such attempts are more likely to be fuelled by emotional sources such as frustration or displacement rather than by rational analysis. My own position is that while motives are always mixed, and the defence of self at an emotional level undoubtedly enters into most aspects of behaviour, it must be accepted that individuals very often act so as to wrest the advantage from others, not because they are motivated by emotional need but because, in their analysis, inequalities should be eliminated. At the individual level, people may behave 'aggressively' in the service of beliefs which they have rationally worked out for themselves as well as in the service of emotions. To take an instance from the early 1980s, while some women from Greenham Common may conceivably have been displacing on to the American personnel their own resentment of men, others behave 'aggressively' by, for example, cutting boundary wires and invading areas from which they were barred because in their own analysis (with which one may or may not agree) nuclear warheads represent a threat to the future of mankind.

In short I believe that ideologies (or systems of interpretative beliefs about the world and our own position in it) must be taken into account when considering the nature of individual aggressive behaviour. For it is ideology which, to a large extent, shapes our definition of behaviour as 'aggressive' or 'defensive', and ideology that frequently impels individuals to behave aggressively in May's sense of moving into the positions of power or prestige or territory of others in order to take possession of some of it for themselves.

Further, I would argue that the consideration of ideology, and its effects, is even more important in considering intergroup aggressive behaviour than it is in considering intra-individual aggressive behaviour, and I shall return to this issue in the discussion on group aggressive behaviour below.

AGGRESSIVE BEHAVIOUR AND ENTRAPMENT ('INSTRUMENTAL' AGGRESSION)

In the previous section I suggested that ideological beliefs should be taken into account when considering the motivations of individuals who take possession of the property, power or prestige of others. But it is also argued (for example, Bandura, 1973) that people may behave aggressively in this sense even though they may regard their own behaviour as neither morally nor socially justifiable, but simply expedient. It seems to me that when this occurs, it represents the only sense in which it would be justified to use the shorthand term 'instrumental aggression' which has been coined by experimental psychologists. In general, I believe that such behaviour is relatively uncommon, because most people tend to justify their own aggressive behaviour in terms of the previous hostility of others or in terms of defending their own rights.

For example, recent work by Dodge and Frame (1982) has shown that boys who were more likely than other boys to initiate aggressive behaviour against peers appeared to believe (and with some justification) that such behaviour on their part was a retaliation for subtle needling from their peers in the past. As was described in the previous chapter on phenomenological approaches to aggression (see pages 203–5 above) studies such as Matza's support the contention that people who behave aggressively in the views of others frequently engage in attempts to 'neutralize' their behaviour by means of justifications which bring such behaviour into line with their moral codes.

Nevertheless, there are times when people inflict violence on others only because they have been placed in such a position where their autonomy to act otherwise, without extremely severe reprisals, is radically limited. For example, soldiers conscripted to fight in wars not of their own making sometimes inflict that ultimate violence – killing others – impelled neither by hostility nor ideology, nor because they wish to achieve medals or decorations, nor even because they believe that they are fighting for the salvation of their country, but because they are caught up in a complex of social pressures from which they are unable to extricate themselves.

Though it is comparatively unusual, similar situations do occur in non-war settings, where group pressures and social dynamics sometimes place individuals in situations where it becomes almost impossible for them to refuse to take part in violent acts. For example, the adolescent on the fringes of a gang, caught up in a heated incident after a football match may find it impossible to withstand the group pressure to take part in a fight, even though he finds the resulting violence distressing and repugnant.

Some experimental parallel to this is offered by the studies of Stanley Milgram (see pages 147–8 above), when members of the public were put into a situation where they administered what they believed to be severe electric shocks to another person because the social pressures exerted by their having agreed to co-operate in the experiment made it very difficult for them to refuse the instructions of the experimenter. Many of these subjects, however, interviewed after they had administered the 'shocks', attempted to rationalize their behaviour in terms of their victim's stupidity, in this way protecting, I believe, their sense of self.

## FACTORS WHICH AFFECT THE PREDISPOSITION TO BEHAVE AGGRESSIVELY

The research quoted on pages 69–70 above showed that the level of overt aggressive behaviour, particularly violent behaviour, varies markedly with culture. For example, it may be recalled that the Canadian Eskimo studied by Jean Briggs condemned open displays of anger and animosity, and that before there was any substantial contact with non-Eskimo societies, observers studying such societies were impressed with the peaceable nature of their social and personal relationships. Even in contemporary times, in societies where aggressive and violent behaviour is strongly discouraged, as amongst the Hutterite communities in the USA, interpersonal aggressive relations amongst children is rarely shown (Eaton and Weil, 1955). Conversely, as the sub-cultural studies of Wolfgang and Ferracuti showed (see Chapter 6), where normative values reward overt aggressive and violent behaviour on the part of young men there is a correspondingly high incidence of violence. For example, in a report about gang violence in San Francisco, Clive Syddall noted that the leaders of the gangs themselves believe that violent behaviour is 'clout. It's like Mastercharge. Young kids look up to you, then the younger kids become eventual gang members. It's natural. It's just like growing up' (Syddall, 1984, p. 7).

But it is not only the more deprived members of Western societies that endorse the use of violent behaviour where it is seen as promoting important values. Here, for example, is an extract from the nineteenth-

century diary of an upper-class American Quaker mother writing about
her 3½ month old baby:

> Logan and I had our first regular battle today, and he came off
> conqueror, though I don't think he knew it. I whipped him until he
> was actually black and blue, and until I really *could not* whip him
> any more, and he never gave up one single inch. However, I hope it
> was a lesson to him. (Mrs Pearsall Smith, quoted in Russell, 1967,
> p. 197)

More recently, John and Elizabeth Newson have noted that when
parents in contemporary Britain chastise their children physically, they
do so in conformity with a cultural norm that endorses violent behaviour
as an agent of socialization (Newson and Newson, 1980).

In Chapter 5, I described the studies of experimental psychologists
which indicated that young children faced with a violent model, who is
seen as powerful and likeable, will tend to model their own behaviour on
such a model. Ample evidence exists which shows that individuals who
behave violently tend to have grown up in violent families and themselves been victims of familial violence as children (Gelles, 1972).

Indeed, interviews conducted by Gelles and his associates with respon-
dents who used high levels of violence on their own families indicates that
not only were techniques of violence passed on from generation to
generation (for example, a mother who used a belt on her children was
likely to have had a belt used on her), but that within such homes there
was a 'subtle teaching' that justified and normalized the use of excessive
violence. Thus one woman, who had herself been a victim of violence
from her husband, observed that:

> My father spanked my mother when I was about 5 years old. I don't
> know what it was for, but I know my mother told me father
> spanked her. That's the only time he ever laid a hand on her – she
> must have done something to deserve a spanking. (ibid., p. 179)

In general, it seems to me that despite the limitations of the social
learning model in accounting for aggressive and violent behaviour over
the whole spectrum of interpersonal behaviour (see page 170 above),
there is little doubt that the extent to which an individual resorts to overt
aggressive or violent behaviour will be powerfully influenced by his or
her own early experiences of the manner in which his or her own parents
or caretakers conducted their interpersonal relationships. It seems from
studies of violent behaviour in the home that 'the more violence is
present in the family, the more a person learns about violence' (ibid., p.
182).

But of course a violent home not only provides models for later behaviour, it also, as I suggested in earlier sections of this chapter, provides direct messages to the victim of violence about his or her lack of personal worth and may, as a consequence, lay the foundations for a style of personal interaction which is intimately concerned with attempting to restore to the individual a sense of personal significance.

Schools, too, may play a significant part in provoking and reinforcing tendencies towards aggressive modes of personal interaction. Recent studies have illuminated the extent to which the ethos of a school can contribute towards lowering or raising the level of interpersonal aggressiveness of its pupils and staff (for example, Power *et al.*, 1967, Finlayson and Loughran, 1976). In general, studies of interpersonal relationships in school support the model for aggressive behaviour that has been suggested in this chapter. Those schools which tend to meet the psychological needs of their pupils by helping them to view themselves as individuals of significance and worth tend to show lower levels of aggressive behaviour amongst pupils both within the school (Johnston and Krovetz, 1976) and outside school (as measured by the tendency to get into trouble with the police (Rutter *et al.*, 1979)).

While schools and homes can influence the predisposition to behave aggressively for particular individuals, I believe it should never be forgotten that the more society as a whole legitimizes violence, the more members are both likely to learn about it and to absorb favourable attitudes towards it. As Toch points out, a society which legitimizes violence on the part of those who exercise law and order must expect moral sanctions against the use of violence to be correspondingly diminished in the minds of the members of that society.

In the same vein I believe that the free availability of weapons like guns and knives makes violent behaviour more likely both by providing the opportunity for their use and, more importantly, by providing implicit messages about the legitimization of violent behaviour. Further, research at the empirical level tends to show that when the possibility of an aggressive interaction exists (as, for example, when a policeman with a record of using force challenges a person with a strong sense of grievance and hostility), the presence of weapons not only influences the occurrence of violence but also the 'severity and lethality' of that behaviour (Monahan and Klassen, 1982, p. 307).

In sum, individuals may wish to promote their own interests in the face of the interests of others in a determined and intentional manner. The extent to which they are prepared to inflict severe disadvantage on the other will depend on their own emotional state as well as on their beliefs about how legitimate their intended behaviour is. These beliefs will be powerfully influenced by the extent to which their own society legitimizes behaving aggressively and violently, the extent to which weapons are available and their own personal experience of aggressive and violent behaviour in the home, in school and in their own social world.

Linked to such a conclusion is of course the question as to whether or not the media can influence people to behave violently. I would now like to turn for the last time to the question of violence and the media.

## AGGRESSIVE BEHAVIOUR, VIOLENCE AND THE MEDIA

In the two previous chapters I explored the topic of violence and the media, and at this stage it might seem appropriate to present those firm conclusions that can be drawn from the plethora of studies that have investigated the topic. I consider, however, that no such firm conclusions can be drawn. To some extent this is due to the sheer volume of research, but it is also because researchers carrying out the research have tended to be so partial that one observer noted that the most that could be said of much of the research was that 'if you torture the data for long enough, in the end you are bound to get a confession' (Tracey, 1984). Nevertheless, it seems to me that there are a few tentative observations that can be made.

The first set of observations concern the issue of a *causal relationship between media violence and violent and aggressive behaviour*. In general, I do not believe that such a causal relationship has been established. This is partly because of the design of the studies which have investigated the relationship, and partly because the researchers who have sought such a causal link have been inclined to draw unwarranted conclusions.

Looking first at the design of the studies, in most of the studies, and particularly the earlier ones, the design has been marred by serious inadequacies, as I indicated in Chapter 5: violent clips were viewed out of context, measures of 'aggressive behaviour' were highly artificial (for example, in a recent study 'aggressive behaviour' was measured by the propensity to push a button labelled 'punish' which was supposed to deliver 'unpleasant blasts of noise' to the victim; Dunand, Berkowitz and Leyens, (1984), and the experimenters seldom considered the issue of pre-existing individual differences in their subjects' attitudes to violence.) A good critical review of these laboratory studies can be found in Rowland (1983).

While later studies sought to remedy some of these deficiencies by moving out of the laboratory, the result of such studies have been inconclusive (Tracey, 1984). To take a specific example, when Belson (1978) conducted a large scale investigation over six years into the viewing habits of 1,500 London schoolboys, he concluded that his evidence pointed to a conclusive support for a causal relationship between television viewing and aggressive behaviour. Other researchers, however (for example, Murdock, 1982), re-analysing his data have pointed out that Belson's study showed the paradoxical finding that the boys who watch most violence are themselves likely to have been least violent (on the measure used by Belson).

Even where there is an agreement between researchers that particular studies show that there is a *correlational* link between watching violence and behaving violently (for example, studies described by Gunter, 1983), there is considerable disagreement as to whether such correlations imply causation, or whether it is simply that people who behave aggressively like watching aggressive and violent programmes. And Hirsch notes of such statistical studies that they

> are not the kind of studies from which I'd be comfortable seeing someone out there basing their policy upon. They're too delimited, they're too partial, [and do not allow researchers to] come up with a strong enough association between watching television and doing anything else that would suggest that television has a causal relationship to people's behaviour. (Quoted by Tracey, 1984, p. 10)

Other more substantive criticisms have also been made of the attempt to obtain a statistical relationship between viewing violence and behaving aggressively or violently, and some of these have been referred to briefly in the last chapter. In general such criticisms centre on the failure of researchers to consider the manner in which people relate to the violence they watch. For example, recent work by Gunter and Furnham (1984) has shown that the effect of violent television programmes on viewers' reports of how upset and disturbed the programmes made them varied in subtle ways depending on a number of variables. These variables included the genre (for example, western *vis-à-vis* crime drama), the type of injury portrayed (for example shooting *vis-à-vis* stabbing), and the extent to which viewers regarded themselves as prone to verbal or physical aggression.

Further, as was indicated in the previous chapter, researchers who attempt to obtain a straightforward causal relationship between media violence and violent and aggressive behaviour have signally failed to take into account the effect of social class. Nor have they been prepared to consider that in a contemporary Western society, there is unlikely to be a normative set of attitudes towards particular media portrayals of interpersonal behaviour that holds over all ages, over both sexes, and for all social classes and sub-cultures.[10]

Finally, as even the most ardent exponents of a causal link between viewing violence and aggressive and violent behaviour concede, viewing television '*by itself* is not going to make any child aggressive' (Husemann, quoted by Tracey, 1984, my italics).

*Should no action be taken to censor violence in the media?*
While the case that watching violence on the media causes aggressive

behaviour is not, as I have indicated above, proven, nor is it likely to be, I personally believe that there is a case for considering the extent to which sanctioning violence by portraying a great deal of it on the media affects the manner in which people regard their fellows. If, for example, a programme or film glorifies the hero who, during its course, repeatedly behaves violently, then viewers may receive the message that it is legitimate, and even admirable, to treat others as objects standing in the way of one's own aspirations. If, on the other hand, a film or programme or video focuses on the effect of violence on its victims, viewers may be forced to consider the implications for others of the violence of those who wield power.

Nowhere, to my mind, are these considerations more important than in the area of the violence towards women that has been characteristic of recent pornography. Research in the area of pornography has revealed that while in many societies both art and pornography have portrayed eroticism (Roth, 1982), it is only very recently that pornography has concentrated on violent sexuality, and particularly on sexual violence perpetrated by men against women (Nelson, 1982). Studies of the effects of viewing such pornography support the contention that the extent to which viewers are sexually aroused following such viewing depends on their prior attitudes towards sex and violence. Where violent sexuality reinforces pre-existing belief systems that men should dominate women sexually, arousal is likely to be raised, in women as well as male viewers (see the work of Malamuth and Check, 1980). It does not seem possible to me, therefore, to separate the subject of violent pornography from the manner in which society as a whole legitimizes male violence against women, and while the viewing of violence may not be the only contributor, and is certainly unlikely to be the direct cause of a man assaulting a woman, it is undoubtedly likely that observing violent sexuality can facilitate sexual violence in an aroused and angered man whose belief system has given credibility to the notion that women enjoy and need to be dominated by men.[11]

### Whose violence?

Before concluding this section on violence and the media, I would like to return to one of the issues that was raised in the last sections of the previous chapter, and consider again how influential the media has been in focusing attention on particular aspects of violence. If we take just two examples, the question of children viewing 'video nasties' and the rate of 'black' violence, it soon becomes apparent that moral panics can become engendered, and subsequently reinforced, by the media.

In the case of 'video nasties', on 25 November 1983, the *Daily Express* reported that four out of ten children watch video nasties, and the *Daily Mail* headlined a similar story 'Sadism for six-year-olds'. These stories were based on a survey carried out by Dr Clifford Hill which gained an immediate hold on the public imagination, even though many social scientists were dubious about the high rate reported. This scepticism was largely based on the difficulty even film critics have of obtaining access to video nasties (Cumberbatch, 1984). Cumberbatch himself suspected that the high rate reported for children even as young as 6 years old was due to the fact that Hill asked children to ring names of videos they had seen; specifically Cumberbatch and his colleagues suspected that young children would ring the names of videos they liked the sound of, as well as those they had actually seen. To test this hypothesis Cumberbatch (1984) and his colleagues asked five classes of 11 year olds to ring videos they had seen and included on the list a number of plausible names of non-existent videos, for example, *Vampire Holocaust*. In line with Cumberbatch's hypothesis, sixty-five per cent of the sample ringed non-existent videos.

But findings such as Cumberbatch's are less newsworthy than Hill's, and have received far less publicity. Like the findings which dispute the causal link between watching media violence and behaving violently, such findings tend to get ignored by the popular press who find the sensational headlines that can be extracted from reports like Hill's far more attractive. Further, I believe that findings like Hill's tend to become more easily absorbed into consensual views because they provide an easy answer for the perennial questions concerning the nature of violence. Also, as Cumberbatch puts it, they do not 'run counter to our entrenched belief'.

Another area which has in recent years received enormous media attention has been the subject of muggings and particularly muggings by black youths; for example, in the huge headlines reported in the *Sun* of 23 March 1983 – 'Black Crime Shock – and in the article the same evening in the London *Standard* headed 'Fury over "blacks and crimes" '. The headlines were based on a figure given for 'robbery and violent theft' in 1982, which the popular press refer to in general as 'muggings'. But technically there is no such crime as 'mugging' and the figures included crimes in the following categories: 'snatches' where the victim is neither threatened nor injured, robberies from open business premises and robberies which specifically exclude street robberies. Only one-third of the total conforms to public images of mugging which is 'robbery in the open following sudden attack'. And, as the press failed to point out, blacks themselves are thirty-six times more likely than whites to *suffer* offences such as violence against the person or robbery (Harris, 1983).

These examples highlight, I think, the real issues concerning the media and violence. These issues are not related to the simple rule – media violence causes violent behaviour, but are instead intimately related to the manner in which the media both reflects and amplifies certain beliefs about violence that lie dormant in the minds of many members of the public. These are, for instance, that there are bound to be easy and straightforward ways of 'stamping out violence', that some people are genetically more predisposed to be violent than others, and that there is a fundamental difference in kind between the violence wielded by the forces of law and order and the violence carried out by ordinary members of society.

## GROUP AGGRESSIVE AND VIOLENT BEHAVIOUR

This book is predominantly concerned with aggression and violence in an interpersonal context. For example, few of the theoretical approaches discussed have extended their analysis of aggression and violence into the fields of war, genocide or even the more bellicose aspects of international bargaining and diplomacy. In this section I propose to similarly limit myself, largely because I believe that such subjects are more germane to a political, historical or economic analysis than they are to the fields of inquiry this book has been concerned with. But partly, too, I would argue with Billig (1976) that such subjects are best understood within a structural model which suggests that where there is an inequitable distribution of resources, and where those who are relatively dis-advantaged perceive the iniquity, conflict is bound to arise, and such conflict may easily lead to aggressive and violent behaviour because, as he puts it, 'vested interests do not readily forgo their social privileges' (ibid., p. 234).

To this extent, then, group aggressive behaviour is likely to be a response to particular social and economic conditions, and to this extent I believe it is best considered within a political framework.

Further, important understandings surround the *political* ideologies that accompany group perceptions of their social, economic and political conditions, and, as Billig has argued, it is such ideologies, which themselves arise out of a subjective interpretation of objective social conditions, that powerfully affect the aggressive interactions between groups.

In this section on group aggression, however, I do not intend to pursue these aspects of social conflict which impinge, as I have indicated, on a far larger canvas than the interpersonal one with which this book is concerned.[12] Instead I intend to concentrate only on those aspects of the understanding of *interpersonal* functioning which affect aggressive behaviour in the group situation.

These understandings relate, I believe, to three aspects of group processes: first, to the processes whereby group membership affects the individual's perception of their social identity; secondly, to the process whereby group members strive to enhance the identity of their social group, because in doing so they enhance and defend their own self image; and thirdly, to the processes whereby group ideologies are seen as justifying aggressive behaviour.

*Group membership and social identity*

I mentioned above that one of the major influences on the self system is the information gained from the process of social labelling in which the individual compares his or her performances with the performances of others, not necessarily in a spirit of competition (although of course in particular cultures and contexts this may be the case), but primarily in order to build up a distinctive social identity.

This process of building up a social identity through comparison seems to be a characteristic of intergroup as well as inter-individual functioning in that, as I mentioned earlier, we are likely to see ourselves as sharing common characteristics with other members of the groups we regard ourselves as belonging to. In doing so, by implication, we classify members of other groups as different. This process of differentiating between members of what is called the 'in-group' and members of 'out-groups' seems characteristic of group processes even within the highly artificial conditions of laboratories. As Tajfel and his associates have shown, even when individuals are assigned to groups on the basis of the most flimsy reason (for example, preferring a particular kind of picture), they tend to generate sets of beliefs about members of their own group compared to members of other groups.

Tajfel (1981) argues that such classifications (or as he tends to refer to them, 'stereotypes') serve three functions. The first is a purely cognitive one, in that classifying and differentiating helps us to organize our understandings of the social world, and the other two are social functions in that such classifying both helps to enhance social and therefore personal identity, and serves to create and maintain group ideologies which enable us to justify and explain our social actions. It is these two social functions which I believe have a powerful effect on interpersonal aspects of aggressive behaviour between groups.

*Group membership and the personal and group worth*

In the earlier sections of this chapter I argued that it appears to be a universal human predisposition to seek to defend and enhance the self system and that where self is seen as being derogated there is a powerful impetus to restore a positive sense of self. It seems to me that where individuals have been denied in any effective manner the possibility of gaining a degree of status and prestige in the social world, they are more likely than those people who have a positive sense of self to seek such positive aspects of personal identity in group membership. Further, I would argue that when people seek group membership for these reasons, it is highly likely that their behaviour in such groups will tend towards aggression in the sense that May uses the term – that is, they will, as a group, tend to move into the position of power, prestige or territory of others and take possession of some of it for themselves.

This is not to say that I believe that the only reason people attach themselves to groups is in order to defend and enhance self. On the contrary, it is clear that people join groups for a great variety of reasons. For example, people identify themselves with others in order to attain shared goals, or because they see themselves as sharing interests, values and ideologies with other members of the group, or simply because they enjoy the close human contact that comes from belonging to a close-knit group. But I believe that for those whose sense of self is insecure, the membership of a group can both provide social identity and a medium for gaining a sense of personal effectiveness.

This line of argument leads to the prediction that there will be a high proportion of socially disadvantaged people in those groups who are renowned not only for their extreme partisanship, but also for their predisposition to behave aggressively (in the sense in which we have defined aggressive behaviour in this chapter). Indeed, if we look at the members of extreme sectarian groups, for example, in Northern Ireland, or at the most fiercely and aggressively loyal members of football supporters' clubs, it would appear that the prediction is supported.[13]

A further corollary to this line of argument is that we can expect the 'senseless violence' of some football fans to continue for as long as social conditions allow a sizeable proportion of young men to lead lives that offer them little sense of personal effectiveness and worth.[14]

*Aggressive behaviour and the ideologizing of collective actions*
If we look at the rhetoric of groups such as football clubs which place a great deal of emphasis on the virtues of their own members, it is immediately obvious that this tendency is accompanied by an equally strong emphasis on the shortcomings of rival groups:

In their (Nottingham) slums,
In their Nottingham slums.
They look in the dustbin for something to eat,
They find a dead cat and they think it's a treat,
In their Nottingham slums.'
(Supporters' chant quoted by Marsh, Rosser and Harré, 1978, p. 88)

Such stereotyping of the negative qualities of the out-group and the positive ones of the in-group not only serves, as we have just noted, to enhance the personal and group identity of in-group members, but serves also to legitimize any aggressive actions that the in-group may decide to take against out-group members. By placing out-group members in a 'different' category, it is possible to subject them to injuries and insults that in-group members would not subject each other to.

This tendency to legitimize aggressive behaviour by creating an ideology of difference is seen at its most explicit and effective in the operation of propaganda machines in times of war when, as Johnson puts it, 'it is easier to kill if one is convinced that the enemy is subhuman or somehow fundamentally evil or disposable' (1972, p. 198). Accordingly, the systematic dehumanization of the enemy has been utilized time and again by those who have directed the course of war. Thus, in the First World War, the Germans were presented to the British people as 'brutal Huns', and in Vietnam American conscripts were encouraged to think of the peasants whose villages they were destroying as 'gooks'.

In considering the exploitation of such social stereotypes, the part played by objective social conditions is very important. It is, for example, relatively easy to get people to accept such blatant propaganda in times of war when they are beset by fear, apprehension and often physical discomforts, but it is, of course, far less easy, for even the most gifted and charismatic demagogue, to get people to accept such stereotypes at times when they do not feel either fearful or under pressure. As Tajfel points out, the prejudicial aspects of such stereotyping 'become especially acute in periods of high stress, social tension and acute intergroup conflict' (1981, p. 58).

It is at such times that 'scapegoating', a phenomenon that was first discussed in Chapter 4, becomes of extreme importance in the understanding of intergroup aggressive behaviour. It is when people feel at risk both psychologically and physically that the displacement of their emotional insecurity on to others becomes particularly rewarding. Scapegoating serves two important psychological functions under such circumstances. First, at the emotional level, it allows people who are feeling particularly emotionally and personally devalued to draw some consolation from the belief that others are even less adequate than they themselves are, and secondly it offers people a means of explaining the parlous nature of their social conditions. For example, anti-Semitism, aside from providing a target for the displacement of emotions, can also

> provide an extensive cognitive interpretation of the world. Above all, crude anti-Semitism is based on a belief that Jews have immense powers of evil in the world. Modern anti-Semitic dogma asserts that Jews control both communism and capitalism and that they aim to dominate the world in a régime which will destroy Western civilization. All facts are explained in terms of this pervasive and perverse belief. (Billig, 1978, p. 132)

In sum, it seems that witch-hunting and scapegoating is a dynamic process in which a particular social group in a period of turmoil creates and maintains not only a positive distinctiveness for itself but a negative distinctiveness for others. In doing this it satisfies not only its own emotional and social needs, but it provides a rationale for itself which helps it to 'understand' the prevailing social conditions.

In this section on interpersonal aspects of group aggression I have suggested that when people come together in groups, they tend to generate shared values about the characteristics of group members and about the characteristics of those who are not group members. This tendency to create such social stereotypes has important implications for aggressive behaviour in that, where self-esteem is low, group members tend to develop highly partisan sets of feelings about members of their own group and highly negative sets of feelings about outsiders. I have further suggested that where self-esteem is devalued, and in addition where social conditions create feelings of apprehension and insecurity, negative feelings about non-group members can lead to an ideology of prejudice which both justifies aggressive actions that are taken against people who are not members of the group, and serves to reinforce and amplify the negative feelings that are already held about them.

In such conditions it becomes, of course, extremely difficult for a member of the in-group to disassociate him- or herself from the negative feelings that the group holds about outsiders. For in doing so the dissenter not only removes himself from the emotional satisfactions that are intimately related to cohesive group functioning, but also exposes himself to being grouped with the hated and rejected outsiders. For example, in South Africa, one of the social sanctions that has been applied to those Afrikaners who throw their lot in with the oppressed non-white majority is for them to be labelled by other Afrikaners as *kaffir boetjies* (literally, brothers of 'kaffirs' – the pejorative word used for blacks). Once a white becomes so labelled, it is relatively easy for the process of dehumanization which is applied by white racists to blacks to be applied to the *kaffir boetjie* him or herself.

## SUMMARY

In this section I have presented a model for understanding aggressive and violent behaviour in human beings, in which I suggested that in attempting to understand the meaning of aggressive behaviour it is helpful to consider such behaviour within the framework of self theory. This approach to interpersonal relationship assumes in the first instance that human behaviour is always underpinned by intentions. It assumes also that human beings possess the capacity to think about themselves and the outside world in a conscious and reflexive manner, and that they also consciously monitor their interactions with the social world. In doing this one of their chief objectives is to enhance and defend their sense of personal significance, for I argued that the experience of feeling oneself to be esteemed, effective and valued is highly positive, while the experience of feeling oneself to be of little significance is extremely unpleasant.

In looking specifically at aggressive behaviour, that is, behaviour which is intended to achieve advantage for oneself relative to others, I suggested that in those people who habitually behave aggressively such behaviour may be related to an attempt to restore to self the effectiveness and significance that has been denied over long periods. Further, I suggested that most people, and not only those who habitually display hostility, may be driven to behave aggressively and with hostility when they feel themselves to be devalued.

I also suggested that in considering interpersonal behaviour other sets of motives, aside from the intention to enhance and defend self, may be considered to underpin aggressive behaviour. The four other sets of motivational states that were considered in the context of aggressive behaviour were the pursuit of excitement, hedonic sensations and experience, the defence of ideology and the achievement of instrumental ends or entrapment. Finally, I extended the discussion of interpersonal aspects of individual aggression to interpersonal aggression in the group situation. In doing this I looked at the function of stereotyping in groups, and suggested that such stereotyping can contribute to aggressive behaviour when people feel devalued both individually and as members of groups, and that under such circumstances, particularly in periods of social strain and stress, an ideology may develop in groups which reinforces such social stereotyping and legitimizes aggressive behaviour.

## Controlling Aggressive and Violent Behaviour

As I have repeatedly stated throughout this chapter, this book is concerned with interpersonal aspects of aggression and does not presume to explore the complexities of intergroup aggression, except at this interpersonal level. Nevertheless, I believe it is important to restate explicitly my belief that where social conditions exist so that one group feels relatively disadvantaged in comparison to others, it is highly likely that the disadvantaged group will resort to aggressive behaviour in order to remedy such perceived disadvantage. Furthermore, as I have noted throughout this book, in so doing it is likely that the disadvantaged group will build up an ideology that legitimizes their behaviour. To this extent, I believe that aggressive behaviour at the intergroup level cannot be substantially reduced until there is a concerted attempt to reduce the glaring inequalities in global resources that exist at the international level, and also in most countries at the domestic level. To my mind, recommendations for reducing group aspects of aggressive and violent behaviour can only be looked at within an explicitly political context. This is not a context with which this book is directly concerned.

Turning to the aspects of aggressive and violent behaviour with which this book has been centrally concerned, I believe that recommendations for reducing aggressive behaviour centre around two sets of concerns:

first, the set concerned with reducing the intention to behave aggressively, and secondly, the set concerned with the consequences for others of the individual's aggression.

## REDUCING THE INTENTION TO BEHAVE AGGRESSIVELY

(1)  If it is accepted, as I have suggested in this chapter, that aggressive behaviour is behaviour that is intentionally concerned to wrest a relative advantage for the aggressor, and that such behaviour often centres around the desire to restore affirmation and significance to self, then it seems clear that considerable attention should be focused on *providing for all individuals in the home, in school and in all social situations, a sense of personal significance and worth.*

In this chapter I have suggested a theoretical rationale for this contention and have also cited some empirical evidence that would appear to support this proposition. At the more personal level, my own experience in working with children and young people has convinced me that where a concerted attempt is made to convince individuals of their significance and worth, aggressive behaviour is considerably reduced (Siann and Ugwuegbu, 1980). And those enlightened experiments in penal reform such as the Special Unit, created in Barlinnie Prison in Scotland in the late 1960s and early 1970s, have suggested that when people with a long history of violent behaviour are encouraged to forge for themselves a modified personal identity which allows them to see themselves as being able to contribute something of worth to others, and to be effective and valued as a result, their reliance on aggressive behaviour as a means of self-assertion is considerably reduced (Boyle, 1977).

(2)  Secondly, I believe that no matter how supportive social conditions are to encouraging the individual's sense of personal significance, there will be times when people will feel personally hostile because they feel themselves to be disparaged or under attack. When such hostility is felt, I believe the individual should be able to utilize strategies other than aggressive behaviour to deal with the hostility. In order to do this I believe that we *have to acknowledge and not deny that we can feel angry with others* (something which it seems to me the experimental psychologists pay little attention to), for only then can we develop alternative strategies to aggressive behaviour in order to cope with this hostility.

(3)  The most successful alternative strategy seems to me to be concerned with *talking as rationally as possible about the feelings we have,* either with a third party or, when the occasion is opportune, with the person we feel angry with. It is my experience that where people are prepared to talk as openly and objectively as possible about their feelings of conflict, they are relatively unlikely to vent them in impetuous aggressive behaviour.

(4)  Other alternative strategies that have proved effective in controlling

aggressive behaviour have been summarized by Kennedy, 1982 (and see also Bornstein, Bellack and Hersen, 1980 and McAuley, 1982). These include training people to think about the long-term consequences for themselves of behaving aggressively, helping them to communicate and negotiate about the issues over which they feel aggressive, and training them to use relaxation techniques and 'thought stopping' about their anger when they feel particularly emotionally aroused.

(5) Aside from developing alternative strategies, I believe that it is important not to present to people, and to young people and children in particular, role models who behave aggressively. As the work of Gelles and others shows, the influence of watching other people deal with their feelings in an aggressive manner, particularly in the home, can have a powerful impact on the disposition to behave aggressively.

(6) While I do not believe (see Chapter 2) that there is any evidence to suggest that there are any specific physiological substrates for aggressive behaviour, I do consider that people are more likely to behave aggressively when they are in a state of physiological discomfort or when they experience mood changes that are consequent on physiological processes. Of course, as I repeatedly stressed in Chapter 2, there are always cognitive circumstances that direct the manner in which the discomfort is perceived subjectively. Nevertheless, in my own experience, when dealing with children and young people with a history of aggressive behaviour, *it is always essential to ensure that they are not placed in situations where they are needlessly exposed to hunger, thirst, excessive heat or other physical discomfort.*

(7) It seems clear to me, as I indicated on pages 247–8 above, that when the social environment in which people, and particularly young people, are required to live offers little scope for excitement and constructive risk-taking, they may turn to provoking and initiating confrontations with others, largely for the thrills such behaviour offers in an otherwise monotonous and featureless existence. Consequently I believe that until *social action is taken in order to provide a stimulating and creative environment for all young people,* those in social control must expect to be faced with what they tend to label as 'mindless vandalism'.

## HELPING PEOPLE TO UNDERSTAND THE CONSEQUENCES FOR OTHERS OF BEHAVING AGGRESSIVELY

Most of us know that we often wish to behave aggressively and violently, and are prevented from doing so, not so much by the fear of punishment or the disapprobation of others, but because we anticipate that the result of such behaviour would bring distress to others to an extent that we either consider morally indefensible or that we find emotionally distressing.

(8) It is for this reason that I believe that one of the most powerful

recommendations that can be made in the area of controlling inter-personal aggressive behaviour is that *we strive to induce both in ourselves and others a degree of empathy with others*. Both at the level of personal experience and as a consequence of reviewing the existing literature in the area (see Ellis, 1982 and Milgram, 1974), it seems to me that en-couraging people to understand and feel sympathetic about the effect of aggressive behaviour on others can act as an important disincentive to aggressive behaviour. To quote an instance that is cited in almost every text on aggressive behaviour, it is far more difficult to kill someone or even hurt them when you are in eye-to-eye contact with them, and thus experience their unique individuality as a human being like yourself, than it is to kill someone at a distance. As the experimental work by Milgram indicates (see Chapter 5), people are far less likely to behave aggressively to others, in conformity with instructions from their superiors, when they actively empathize and identify with their victim.

(9) Linked, of course, to promoting empathy is *the promotion of altruistic or pro-social behaviour*.[15] Whether or not one believes (see Chapter 3) that altruistic behaviour is programmed into the human genotype, it is undoubtedly true that altruistic behaviour is universally seen across all cultures. Indeed, child-rearing would be impossible without it. In the same way as has been suggested that aggressive behaviour can be learned from role models, so too can altruistic and pro-social behaviour (Kaufmann, 1970, Eisenberg, 1982). Surveys of experimental work on pro-social behaviour (Maccoby, 1980) suggests that where children are encouraged to take the perspective of others, and to negotiate rather than confront, their personal relationships are rela-tively free of aggressive interactions.

(10) I personally do not believe that punishment is an effective way of controlling aggressive and violent behaviour to any great extent. As I noted in Chapter 5 even in experimental conditions punishment only succeeds in eradicating particular behaviours if it is always administered in a sure and predictable manner, and it follows aggressive behaviour as closely as possible. In real-life situations neither of these conditions can always hold, and furthermore, in real-life conditions, reacting to aggres-sive and violent behaviour with behaviour that can often be interpreted as violent and aggressive in its turn is more likely to exacerbate hostility than to assuage it. While I do not believe then that punishment which is based on a retributive model can control aggressive and violent be-haviour, it must be acknowledged that some action must be taken to restrain the behaviour of aggressive and violent offenders. The most appropriate model for such restraint seems to me to centre on changing the understanding and perceptions of the violent offender both about him or herself and about the impact of his or her behaviour on others. Briefly, two approaches to this are currently being used. The first, based on the kind of recommendation made by Toch in his discussion of violent

men (see pages 193–4 above), centres on providing a rehabilitative and therapeutic environment in which offenders are encouraged both to gain a positive sense of personal identity that does not involve violence as a central attribute and to learn alternative social skills for dealing with hostility. The second approach is concerned with making violent offenders face up to the implication of their behaviour by encouraging meetings between such people and their victims in an attempt to encourage the development of empathy.

(11)    Finally, it seems to me that the tendency to violent behaviour could be significantly lowered in the general public if there were a serious and concerned debate at the highest level about the contradictions in our own society whereby the 'official' violence of the military, the SAS and, on occasion, the police is treated as fundamentally different in nature from violence committed by others. Until such contradictions are resolved, the full moral, ethical and emotional implications of one human being intentionally injuring another are bound to be obscured.

## Notes: Chapter 7

1    It seems to me that those approaches to aggression and violence that I described in the last section of the previous chapter can reasonably be classified as structuralist in that aggression and violent behaviours are seen as being generated by deep and underlying structures in human society (Bullock and Stallybrass, 1977).

2    This kind of criticism of positivism has often been associated with Habermas (see Giddens, 1984).

3    In this section for the sake of simplicity of presentation I refer to aggressive behaviour as carried out by an individual, but the same criteria apply for the labelling of behaviour as aggressive when it is carried out by more than one person.

4    In this formulation, aggressive behaviour comes very close to Tedeschi's concept of coercion (see Chapter 1).

5    I will also take for granted at this stage that aggressive behaviour takes place in a context of implicit or explicit conflict – for there is always a shortage of resources, emotional, social and financial, and therefore always a source of potential competition if not conflict.

6    In approaching the subject of the intentions that lie behind behaviour, I do not propose to refer to the debates about motives that have taken place in either psychology (for example, Heider, 1958, Kelley, 1971), or in sociology (for example, Mills, 1940, Taylor, 1972). Instead the discussion of intention is located in contemporary approaches to the theory of self.

7    There are eight formal propositions underpinning the introduction to self theory that is presented in this chapter.

(1) Human beings are born with a capacity for consciousness. By consciousness I mean an awareness both of themselves and an outer world which is not themselves. Further, they are capable of monitoring not only their consciousness of self, but also their relationship with the world. In short, people can reflect about themselves, about their relationship with others and about their actions in the social and physical world. (See Ashworth, 1979, for a further discussion of consciousness.)

(2)    As human beings are born with a capacity for consciousness, so they seem born with a predisposition to seek for meaning both in their subjective world and in their encounters and relationships with the social and physical world (Schutz, 1972).

(3)  These joint capacities for consciousness and for extracting meaning result in the formation of organized systems of understandings (Kelly, 1955, Kelvin, 1970).

(4)  Perhaps the most powerful of these systems of understandings are the individual's conceptions of self. Loosely speaking we can perhaps call these conceptions of self-as-a-systematized-object-of-awareness – the person's self system (Ashworth, 1979).

(5)  In considering the self system, it is convenient to make a distinction between the individual's set of beliefs about himself, which are commonly referred to as the individual's self-concept, and the individual's evaluation of himself, commonly referred to as 'self-esteem' (Burns, 1979, Rogers, 1982).

(6)  The self system has a dynamic as well as an evaluative and organizational aspect and it is suggested that the two tendencies that characterize the dynamic aspect of the self systems are, first, that in general individuals strive to *protect and enhance self-esteem*, and, secondly, that interacting with the tendency to protect self-esteem is the tendency to retain a degree of *consistency of the self system*. In general those components of the self-concept that are most central are most likely to be defended and those components that are less central are more likely to be modified in order to retain a degree of consistency (Carl Rogers, 1963, Burns, 1979, Colin Rogers, 1982).

(7)  In defending the self, the individual will not only draw on those aspects of feeling and thinking that he or she is consciously aware of, but he or she may also be influenced by emotions and thoughts that are not currently at the centre of consciousness, that is, certain aspects of the self systems may remain in Ashworth's phrase 'undisclosed to their "owner" ' (1979, p. 196). In psychoanalytic terms, 'unconscious' or 'pre-conscious' thoughts and feelings may influence those thoughts and emotions which are consciously experienced as the self system.

(8)  When people behave in particular ways, it is more meaningful to interpret such behaviour as intended actions that arise from the individual's construction of the situation they are in and its implications for his or her self system than it is to seek for antecedent causes in the environment (Mead, 1934, Schutz, 1972 and Ashworth, 1979).

8   It has been suggested (see Ashworth, 1979) that in different cultures different emotions are involved when individuals breach the standards they have adopted for themselves. For instance, when a Japanese person breaks such standards he is likely to feel 'shame', whereas a Westerner might feel guilt. In both cases, however, experiencing emotion is likely to prove uncomfortable because self-esteem is diminished.

9   See *The Listener*, 23rd February, 1984 p. 38 for a description of the Danish study on which the *Everyman* television investigation, *Your Neighbour's Son –The Making of a Torturer*, was based.

10  In particular, considerable controversy has surrounded the work of Professor Gerbner and his associates at the Annenberg School of Communications in Philadelphia (for example, Gerbner, 1975). Gerbner contends that, in general, heavy television viewers come to see the world as a fearful, mean place – the 'mean world syndrome'. But other researchers who have reanalysed Gerbner's data draw very different conclusions (see Rowland, 1983, for a discussion of Gerbner's work).

11  For a comprehensive review of the experimental literature on pornography and violence see Nelson (1982) and for a perspective on feminist approaches to the subject area see Brownmiller (1975).

12  As I have indicated in the last chapter, this book has dealt only at the most cursory level with conflict theory. For an introduction to earlier approaches to conflict theory see Coser (1967), and for an introduction to contemporary approaches see Billig (1976).

13  See, for example, the discussion of the social class background of British football 'hooligans' abroad in Williams, Dunning and Murphy, 1984.

14  This is of course not to suggest that the aggressive behaviour displayed by such groups should be interpreted only in the sense of enhancing a sense of self effectiveness, for, as

has been argued both in this and the previous chapter, other aspects of personal functioning are clearly involved, for example, the attainment of economic goals, the enhancement of group cohesiveness and the generation of excitement.

15  I have not discussed the role of 'moral development' in reducing aggressive behaviour because in general, *teaching* morality does not seem to have any consequent effect on aggressive behaviour (see Krebs, 1982).

# References

Adler, A. (1927) *Understanding Human Nature*, trans. W. Wolfe (New York: Greenberg, 1946).

Adler, A. (1931a), 'Compulsion neurosis' in *Superiority and Social Interest*, ed. H. Ansbacher and R. Ansbacher (London: Routledge & Kegan Paul, 1965).

Adler, A. (1931b), 'Individual psychology and psychoanalysis' in *Superiority and Social Interest*, ed. H. Ansbacher and R. Ansbacher (London: Routledge & Kegan Paul, 1965).

Anderson, A. (1982), 'Environmental factors and aggressive behavior', *Journal of Clinical Psychiatry*, vol. 43, no. 7, pp. 280–3.

Ardrey, R. (1982), 'The violent way', in *Readings in Social Psychology: Contemporary Perspectives*, 2nd edn, ed. D. Krebs (Cambridge, Mass.: Harper and Row).

Ardrey, R. (1976), *The Hunting Hypothesis* (London: Collins).

Ardrey, R. (1966) *The Territorial Imperative* (New York: Atheneum).

Ardrey, R. (1961), *African Genesis* (New York: Atheneum).

Armistead, N., ed. (1974), *Reconstructing Social Psychology* (Harmondsworth: Penguin).

Ashworth, P. D. (1979), *Social Interaction and Consciousness* (Chichester: Wiley).

Babad, E. Y., Birnbaum, M. and Benne, K. D. (1983), *The Social Self: Group Influences on Personal Identity* (Beverly Hills: Sage).

Balasubramaniam, V., Ramanujam, P. B., Kanaka, T. S. and Ramamurthi, B. (1972), 'Stereotaxic surgery for behavior disorders' in *Psychosurgery*, ed. E. Hitchcock, L. Laitinen and K. Vaernet (Springfield, Ill.: Thomas).

Ball, I. L., Farnill, D. and Wangeman, J. F. (1984), 'Sex and age differences in sensation seeking: Some national comparisons', *British Journal of Psychology*, vol. 75, pp. 257–66.

Ball-Rokeach, S. J. (1973), 'Values and violence: A test of the subculture of violence thesis', *American Sociological Review*, vol. 38, pp. 736–49.

Bandler, R. (1982), 'Neural control of aggressive behavior', *Trends in Neuroscience*, vol. 5, part ii, pp. 390–4.

Bandura, A. (1983), 'Psychological mechanisms in aggression', in *Aggression: Theoretical and Empirical Reviews*, vol, 1, *Theoretical and Methodological issues*, ed. R. G. Geen and E. I. Donnerstein (New York: Academic Press).

Bandura, A. (1978), 'Learning and behavioral theories of aggression', in *Violence: Perspective on Murder and Aggression*, ed. I. L. Kutash, S. B. Kutash, L. B. Schlesinger and associates (San Francisco: Jossey-Bass).

Bandura, A. (1973), *Aggression: A Social Learning Analysis* (New Jersey: Prentice-Hall).

Bandura, A., Ross, D. and Ross, S. A. (1963), 'Imitation of film-mediated aggressive models', *Journal of Abnormal and Social Psychology*, vol. 66, pp. 3–11.

Barker, R. G., Dembo, T. and Lewin, K. (1941), 'Frustration and regression: an experiment with young children', *University of Iowa Studies in Child Welfare*, vol. 18, no. 1.

Barnett, S. A. (1973), 'On the hazards of analogies', in *Man and Aggression*, 2nd edn, ed. A. Montagu (New York: OUP).

Baron, R. A. (1983), 'The control of human aggression: a strategy based on incompatible responses', in *Aggression: Theoretical and Empirical Reviews*, vol. 2, *Issues in Research*, ed. R. G. Geen and E. I. Donnerstein (New York: Academic Press).

Baron, R. A., (1977), *Human Aggression* (New York: Plenum).

Baron, R. A. and Bell, P. A. (1975), 'Aggression and heat: Mediating effects of prior provocation and exposure to an aggressive model', *Journal of Personality and Social Psychology*, vol. 31, pp. 825–32.

Baron, R. A. and Byrne, D. (1981), *Social Psychology: Understanding Human Interaction*, 3rd edn. (Boston: Allyn & Bacon).

Becker, H. (1963), *Outsiders* (New York: Free Press of Glencoe).

Bell, P. A. and Baron, R. A. (1976), 'Aggression and heat: the mediating role of negative affect', *Journal of Applied Psychology*, vol. 6, pp. 18–30.

Belson, W. A. (1978), *Television Violence and the Adolescent Boy* (Farnborough: Saxon House).

Benedict, R. (1934), *Patterns of Culture* (Boston: Houghton Mifflin).

Berkowitz, L. (1982a), 'Simple views of aggression', in *Readings in Social Psychology: Contemporary Perspectives*, 2nd edn, ed. D. Krebs (Cambridge. Mass.: Harper & Row).

Berkowitz, L. (1982b), 'Violence and rule-following behaviour', in *Aggression and Violence*, ed. P. Marsh and A. Campbell (Oxford: Blackwell).

Berkowitz, L. (1975), *A Survey of Social Psychology* (Hinsdale, Ill.: Dryden).

Berkowitz, L. (1974), 'Some determinants of impulsive aggression: Role of mediated associations with reinforcement for aggression', *Psychological Review*, vol. 81, no. 2, pp. 165–76.

Berkowitz, L. (1973), 'Words and symbols as stimuli to aggressive responses', in *The Control of Aggression*, ed. J. F. Knutson (Chicago: Aldine).

Berkowitz, L. (1972), 'Frustrations, comparisons and other sources of emotional arousal as contributors to social unrest', *Journal of Social Issues*, vol. 28, no. 1, pp. 77–91.

Berkowitz, L. (1962), *Aggression: A Social Psychological Analysis* (New York: McGraw Hill).

Berkowitz, L. and Geen, R. G. (1966), 'Film violence and the cue properties of available targets', *Journal of Personality and Social Psychology*, vol. 3, pp. 525–30.

Berlyne, D. E. (1960), *Conflict, Arousal and Curiosity* (New York: McGraw Hill).

Bexton, W. H., Heron, W. and Scott, T. H. (1954), 'Affects of decreased variation in the sensory environment', *Canadian Journal of Psychology*, vol. 8, pp. 70–96.

Bibring, E. (1941), 'The development and problems of the theory of the instincts' *International Journal of Psychoanalysis*, vol. 22, pp. 102–31.

Billig, M. (1982), *Ideology and Social Psychology* (Oxford: Blackwell).

Billig, M.G. (1978), *Fascists: A Social Psychological View of the National Front*, European Monographs in Social Psychology No. 15 (London: Academic Press).

Billig, M. (1976), *Social Psychology and Intergroup Relations* (London: Academic Press).

Bioulac, B., Benezech, M., Renaud, B., Noel, B. and Roche, D. (1980), 'Seretoninergic dysfunction in the 47, XYY syndrome', *Biological Psychiatry*, vol. 15, no. 6, pp. 917–23.

Birch, H. G. and Clark, G. (1950), 'Hormonal modification of social behavior. iv. The mechanisms of estrogen-induced dominance in chimpanzees', *Journal of Comparative and Physiological Psychology*, vol. 43, pp. 181–93.

Birket-Smith, K. (1959), *The Eskimos* (New York: Dutton).

Blumenthal, M. D., Kahn, R. K., and Andrews, F. M. (1971), 'Attitudes towards violence', *Proceedings of the 79th Annual Convention of the American Psychological Association*, vol. 6 (summary).

Boice, R. (1976), 'In the shadow of Darwin', in *Perspectives on Aggression*, ed. R. A. Geen and E. C. O'Neal (New York: Academic Press).

Bornstein, M., Bellack, A. S. and Hersen, M. (1980), 'Social skills training for highly aggressive children', *Behavior Modification*, vol. 4, no. 2, pp. 173–86.

Bower, T. G. R. (1977), *The Perceptual World of the Child* (London: Open Books).

Box, S. (1983), *Power, Crime and Mystification* (London: Tavistock).

Box, S. and Hale, C. (1983), 'Liberation and female criminality in England and Wales', *British Journal of Criminology*, vol. 23, no. 1, pp. 35–49.

Boyle, J. (1977), *A Sense of Freedom* (London: Pan).

Breger, L. (1981), *Freud's Unfinished Journey* (London: Routledge & Kegan Paul).

Bremer, J. (1959), *Asexualisation* (New York: Macmillan).

Brenner, C. (1973), *An Elementary Textbook of Psychoanalysis* (New York: International Universities Press).

Briggs, J. L. (1970), *Never in Anger* (Cambridge, Mass.: Harvard University Press).

Brown, C. (1966), *Manchild in the Promised Land* (London: Cape).

Brownmiller, S. (1975), *Against Our Will: Men, Women and Rape* (New York: Simon & Schuster).

Bullock, A. and Stallybrass, D. (1977), *The Fontana Dictionary of Modern Thought* (London: Fontana).

Burgess, A. (1980), *Earthly Powers* (New York: Avon Books).

Burgess, A. (1972), *A Clockwork Orange* (Harmondsworth: Penguin).

Burns, R. B. (1979), *The Self Concept: Theory, Measurement, Development and Behaviour* (London: Longman).

Buss, A. H. (1966), 'Instrumentality of aggression, feedback and frustration and determinants of physical aggression', *Journal of Personality and Social Psychology*, vol, 3, pp. 153–62.

Buss, A. H. (1963), 'Physical aggression in relation to different frustrations', *Journal of Abnormal and Social Psychology*, vol. 67, pp. 1–7.

Buss, A. H. (1961), *The Psychology of Aggression* (New York: Wiley).

Bylinsky, G. (1982), 'New clues to the causes of violence', in *Readings in Social Psychology: Contemporary Perspectives*, 2nd edn, ed. D. Krebs (Cambridge, Mass.: Harper & Row).

Campbell, A. (1982), 'Female Aggression', in *Aggression and Violence*, ed. P. Marsh and A. Campbell (Oxford: Blackwell).

Campbell, A. (1981), *Girl Delinquents* (Oxford: Blackwell).

Campbell, C. (1976), 'Perspectives of violence', in *Violence*, ed. N. Tutt (London: HMSO).

Clare, A. (1980), *Psychiatry in Dissent*, 2nd edn (London: Tavistock).

Cline, V.B., Croft, R.G. and Courrier, S. (1973), 'Desensitization of children to television violence', *Journal of Personality and Social Psychology*, vol. 27, pp. 360–5.

Cloward, R. A. and Ohlin, L. E. (1960), *Delinquency and Opportunity* (Glencoe, Ill.: The Free Press).

Cofer, C. N. and Appley, M. H. (1964), *Motivation: Theory and Research* (New York: Wiley).

Cohen, A. K. (1955), *Delinquent Boys: The Culture of the Gang* (Glencoe, Ill.: The Free Press).

Cohen, Stanley, (1972), *Folk Devils and Moral Panics* (London: McGibbon & Kee).

Comstock, G., Chaffee, S., Katzman, N., McCombs, M. and Roberts, D. (1978), *Television and Human Behavior* (New York: Columbia University Press).

Coopersmith, S. (1967), *The Antecedents of Self-Esteem* (San Francisco: Freeman).

Coser, L.A. (1967), *Continuities in the Study of Social Conflict* (New York: The Free Press).

Cowden, J. (1969), 'Adventures with South Africa's Black Eagles', *National Geographic*, vol. 136, pp. 533–43.

Crook, J. H. (1980), *The Evolution of Human Consciousness* (Oxford: Clarendon).

Cumberbatch, G. (1984), 'Sorting out little white lies from nasty pieces of work', *The Guardian*, 25 April 1984.

Curran, D. and Partridge, M. (1969), *Psychological Medicine* (London: Churchill Livingstone).

Daleski, H. M. (1965), *The Forked Flame* (London: Faber & Faber).

Dallos, R., Hall, S. M. and Scraton, P. (1982), 'The person and group reality: Law, class and control', in *Thinking about Crime: Theories of Crime and Justice*, D335 3 (1–4) (Milton Keynes: Open University Press).

Dallos, R. and Muncie, J. (1982), 'Moral development and the family: Humanizing the deviant', in *Thinking about Crime: Theories of Crime and Justice*, D335 3 (1–4) (Milton Keynes: Open University Press).

Dart, R. (1953), 'The predatory transition from ape to man', *International Anthropological and Linguistic Review*, vol. 1, pp. 201–19.

De Saussure, F. (1974), *A Course of General Linguistics*, trans. Wade Baskin (London: Collins).

DeSisto, M. J. (1970), 'Hypothalamic mechanisms of killing behavior in the rat', Doctoral Thesis, Tufts University.

De Vore, I. (1982), 'The new science of genetic self interest: An interview with Irwin de Vore by Scot Morris', in *Readings in Social Psychology: Contemporary Perspectives*, 2nd edn. ed. D. Krebs (Cambridge Mass.: Harper & Row).

Dienner, E. and DeFour, D. (1978), 'Does television violence enhance program popularity?', *Journal of Personality and Social Psychology*, vol. 36, pp. 331–4.

Dobash, R. E. and Dobash, R. (1980), *Violence Against Wives* (London: Open Books).

Dobash, R. E., Dobash, R., Cavanagh, C. and Wilson, M. (1978), 'Wifebeating:

The victims speak', *Victimology*, vol. 2 (3–4), pp. 608–22.

Dodge, K. A. and Frame, C. L. (1982), 'Social cognitive biases and deficits in aggressive boys', *Child Development*, vol. 53, pp. 620–35.

Dollard, J., Doob, L. W., Miller, N. E., Mowrer, O. H. and Sears, R. R. (1939), *Frustration and Aggression* (New Haven: Yale University Press).

Donnerstein, E., Donnerstein, M. and Evans, R. (1975), 'Erotic stimuli and aggression: Facilitation or inhibition', *Journal of Personality and Social Psychology*, vol. 32, pp. 237–44.

Donnerstein, E. and Wilson, D. W. (1976), 'The effect of noise and perceived control upon ongoing and subsequent aggressive behavior', *Journal of Personality and Social Psychology*, vol. 34, pp. 774–81.

Downes, D. (1982), 'The language of violence: Sociological perspectives on adolescent aggression', in *Aggression and Violence*, ed. P. Marsh and A. Campbell (Oxford: Blackwell).

Downes, D. and Rock, P. (1979), *Deviant Interpretations* (Oxford: Martin Robertson).

Dunand, M., Berkowitz, L. and Leyens, J. P. (1984), 'Audience effects when viewing aggressive movies', *British Journal of Social Psychology*, vol. 23, pp. 69–76.

Durham, W. H. (1976), 'Resource competition and human aggression: Part 1: A review of primitive war', *Quarterly Review of Biology*, vol. 51, pp. 385–424.

Dyson-Hudson, R. and Smith, E. A. (1978), 'Human territorality: An ecological reassessment', *American Anthropologist*, vol. 80, pp. 21–42.

Eaton, J. W. and Weil, R. J. (1955), *Culture and Mental Disorders* (New York: Free Press).

Egger, M. D. and Flynn, J. P. (1963), 'Effect of electrical stimulation of the amygdala on hypothalmically elicited behavior in cats', *Journal of Neurophysiology*, vol. 26, pp. 705–20.

Eisenberg, L. (1973), 'The *human* nature of human nature', in *Man and Aggression*, 2nd edn, ed. A Montagu (New York: OUP).

Eisenberg, N., ed., (1982), *The Development of Prosocial Behavior* (New York: Academic Press).

Ellis, P. L. (1982), 'Empathy: A factor in antisocial behavior', *Journal of Abnormal Child Psychology*, vol. 10, no. 1, pp. 123–34.

Erdmann, G., and Janke, W. (1978), 'Interaction between physiological and cognitive determinants of emotions: Experimental studies on Schachter's theory of emotions', *Biological Psychology*, vol. 6, pp. 61–74.

Erhardt, A. and Baker, S. (1974), 'Fetal androgens, human central nervous system differentiaton and behavior sex differences', in *Sex Differences in Behavior*, ed. R. Friedman, R. Richart and R. Vande Wiele (New York: Wiley).

Eron, L. D. (1982), 'Parent–child interaction, television violence, and aggression of children', *American Psychologist*, vol. 37, no. 2, pp. 197–211.

Eysenck, H. J. (1952), 'The effects of psychotherapy: An evaluation', *Journal of Consulting Psychology*, vol. 16, no. 5, pp. 319–24.

Eysenck, H. J. and Nias, D. K. (1980), *Sex, Violence and the Media* (Frogmore, St Albans, Herts.: Paladin).

Farrell, B.A. (1981), *The Standing of Psychoanalysis* (Oxford: OUP).

Farrington, D.P. (1982), 'Longitudinal analyses of criminal violence', in

*Criminal Violence*, ed. M. E. Wolfgang and N. A. Weiner (Beverly Hills: Sage).

Farrington, D. P. (1978), 'The family backgrounds of aggressive youths', in *Aggression and Anti-Social Behaviour in Childhood and Adolescence*, ed. L. A. Hersov and M. Berger (London: Pergamon).

Feshbach, S. (1964), 'The function of aggression and the regulation of aggressive drive', *Psychological Review*, vol. 71, pp. 257–72.

Feshbach, N. D. and Roe, K. (1968), 'Empathy in six and seven year olds', *Child Development*, vol. 34, pp. 133–45.

Festinger, L. (1954), 'A theory of social comparison processes', *Human Relations*, vol. 7, pp. 117–40.

Finlayson, D. S. and Loughran, J. L. (1976), 'Pupils' perceptions in high and low delinquency schools', *Educational Research*, vol. 18, no. 2, pp. 138–43.

Fox, R. (1982), 'The violent imagination', in *Aggression and Violence*, ed. P. Marsh and A. Campbell (Oxford: Blackwell).

Freedman, J. L. (1975), *Crowding and Behavior* (San Francisco: Freeman).

Freud, S. (1905), 'Three essays on the theory of sexuality', in *The Complete Works of Sigmund Freud*, ed. J. Strachey, vol. 7 (London: Hogarth Press, 1953).

Freud, S. (1909), 'Analysis of a phobia in a five year-old boy: "Little Hans" ', in *The Pelican Freud Library*, ed. J. Strachey, vol. 8 (Harmondsworth: Penguin, 1977).

Freud, S. (1915), 'Instincts and their vicissitudes', in *Standard Edition of the Complete Psychological Works of Sigmund Freud*, vol. 14 (London: Hogarth Press, 1957).

Freud, S. (1920), 'Beyond the pleasure principle', in *Standard Edition of the Complete Psychological Works of Sigmund Freud*, vol. 18 (London: Hogarth Press, 1961).

Freud, S. (1923a), 'The Ego and the Id', in *The Complete Works of Sigmund Freud*, ed. J. Strachey, vol. 19 (London: Hogarth Press, 1953).

Freud, S. (1923b), 'The infantile genital organisation', in *The Pelican Freud Library*, ed. J. Strachey, vol. 7 (Harmondsworth: Penguin, 1977).

Freud, S. (1930), 'Civilization and its discontents', in *Standard Edition of the Complete Psychological Works of Sigmund Freud*, vol. 21 (London: Hogarth Press, 1961).

Freud, S. (1932), 'Why War?' in *The Complete Works of Sigmund Freud*, ed. J. Strachey, vol. 22 (London: Hogarth Press, 1953).

Freud, S. (1933), *New Introductory Lectures on Psycho-Analysis* (New York: Norton).

Freud, S. (1940), *An Outline of Psycho-Analysis* (New York: Norton).

Friedrich, L. K. and Stein, A. H. (1973), 'Aggressive and prosocial television programs and the natural behavior of preschool children', *Monograph of the Society for Research in Child Development*, vol. 38, no. 4.

Frodi, A., Macaulay, J. and Thome, P. R. (1977), 'Are women always less aggressive than men? A review of the experimental literature', *Psychological Bulletin*, vol. 84, no. 4, pp. 634–60.

Fromm, E. (1977), *The Anatomy of Human Destructiveness* (Harmondsworth: Penguin).

Geen, R. G. (1976), 'Observing violence in the mass media. Implications of basic research', in *Perspectives on Aggression*, ed. R. G. Geen and E. C. O'Neal (New York: Academic Press).

Geen, R. G. and O'Neal, E. C. (1969), 'Activation of cue-elicited aggression by general arousal', *Journal of Personality and Social Psychology*, vol. 11, pp. 289–92.

Geen, R. G. and Rakosky, J. J. (1973), 'Interpretations of observed violence and their effect on GSR', *Journal of Experimental Research in Personality*, vol. 6, pp. 289–92.

Gelhorn, M. (1984), 'Testimony', *Granta* no. 11, pp. 141–54.

Gelles, R.J. (1972), *The Violent Home* (Beverly Hills: Sage).

Gentry, W.D. (1970), 'Effects of frustration, attack and prior aggressive training on overt aggression and vascular processes', *Journal of Personality and Social Psychology*, vol. 16, pp. 718–25.

Gerbner, G. (1975), 'Scenario for Violence', *Human Behaviour*, pp. 64–9.

Giddens, A. (1984), 'The return of grand theory V: Politics has become a kind of technology', *The Listener*, 3 May 1984, pp. 12–13.

Golding, W., (1958), *Lord of the Flies* (London: Faber).

Goldstein, J. H. (1975), *Aggression and Crimes of Violence* (New York: OUP).

Gordon, D. M. (1973), 'Capitalism, class and crime in America', *Crime and Delinquency*, April 1973, pp. 163–86.

Gorer, G. (1973), 'Ardrey on human nature: Animals, nations, imperatives', in *Man and Aggression*, 2nd edn, ed. A. Montagu (New York: OUP).

Gould, S. J. (1984), *The Mismeasure of Man* (Harmondsworth: Penguin).

Graham, H. D. and Gurr, T. R. (1969), *The History of Violence in America* – A Report to the National Commission on Causes and Prevention of Violence (New York: Bantam).

Gray, K. G. and Hutchinson, J. C. (1964), 'The psychopathic personality. A survey of Canadian psychiatrists' opinions', *Canadian Psychiatric Association Journal*, vol. 9, pp. 452–61.

Greene, G. (1975), *Brighton Rock* (Harmondsworth: Penguin).

Groth, A. N. (1979), *Men Who Rape: The Psychology of the Offender* (New York: Plenum Press).

Gunn, J. and Fenton, G. (1971), 'Epilepsy, automatism and crime', *Lancet*, Vol 1 pp. 1173–6.

Gunter, B. (1983), 'Do aggressive people prefer violent television?' *Bulletin of the British Psychological Society*, vol. 36, pp. 166–8.

Gunter, B. and Furnham, A. (1984), 'Perceptions of television violence: Effects of programme genre and type of violence on viewers' judgement of violent portrayals', *British Journal of Social Psychology*, vol. 23, pp. 155–61.

Gurr, T. R. (1970), *Why Men Rebel* (Princeton: Princeton University Press).

Hall, S. (1976), 'Violence and the media', in *Violence* ed. N. Tutt (London: HMSO).

Harré, R. and Secord, P. F. (1972), *The Explanation of Social Behaviour* (Oxford: Blackwell).

Harrington, J. (1976), 'Violence in groups', in *Violence*, ed. N. Tutt (London: HMSO).

Harris, M. (1983), 'The media muggings', *New Society*, 31 March 1983, p. 509.

Hartmann, H., Kris, E. and Lowenstein, R.M. (1964), 'Papers on psychoanalytic psychology', vol. 4, New York: International Universities Press).

Hawke, C. C. (1950), 'Castration and sex crimes', *American Journal of Mental Deficiency*, vol. 55, pp. 220–6.

Heath, R. G. (1962), 'Brain centers and control of behavior – man', in *Psychosomatic Medicine: First Hahnemann Symposium*, ed. J. H. Nodine and J. H. Moyer (Philadelphia: Lea & Fabiger).

Heider, F. (1958), *The Psychology of Interpersonal Relations* (New York: Wiley).

Heilbrun, A. B. Jr. (1979), 'Psychopathy and violent crime', *Journal of Consulting and Clinical Psychology*, vol. 47, no. 3. pp. 509-16.

Helmuth, H. (1973), 'Human behavior: Aggression', in *Man and Aggression*, 2nd edn, ed. A. Montagu (New York: OUP).

Henderson, D. and Gillespie, R. (1969), *Textbook of Psychiatry*, 10th edn (London: OUP).

Herr, M. (1978) *Dispatches* (London: Pan Books).

Hinde, R. A. (1982), *Ethology: Its Nature and Relation with Other Sciences* (Glasgow: Fontana).

Hinde, R. A. (1974), *Biological Bases of Human Social Behavior* (New York: McGraw-Hill).

Hoffman, M. (1982), 'Development of prosocial motivation: empathy and guilt', in *The Development of Prosocial Behavior*, ed. N. Eisenberg (New York: Academic Press).

Home Office Research Study (1977), No. 40, *Screen Violence and Film Censorship* (London: HMSO).

Hornstein, H. A,. (1976), *Cruelty and Kindness: A New Look at Aggression and Altruism* (Englewood Cliffs, N.J.: Prentice-Hall).

Howitt, D. (1982), *Mass Media and Social Problems* (Oxford, Pergamon).

Howitt, D. and Cumberbatch, G. (1975), *Mass Media, Violence and Society* (London: Elek Science).

Hutchings, B. and Mednick, S. A. (1974), 'Registered criminality in the adoptive and biological parents of registered male adoptees', in *Genetics, Environment and Psychotherapy*, ed. S. A. Mednick, F. Schulsinger, J. Higgins and B. Bell (Amsterdam: North Holland).

Hynes, S. (1968), *William Golding* (New York: Columbia University Press).

Jasper, H. H. and Rasmussen, T. (1958), 'Studies of clinical and electrical responses to deep temporal stimulation in man with some consideration of functional anatomy', *Association for Research in Nervous and Mental Diseases Proceedings*, vol. 36, pp. 316–34.

Johnson, R. N. (1972), *Aggression in Man and Animals* (Philadelphia: Saunders).

Johnston, K. D. and Krovetz, M. L. (1976), 'Levels of aggression in a traditional and a pluralistic school', *Educational Research*, vol. 18, no. 2, pp. 146–51.

Jones, A. D. (1965), *Ictal and Subictal Neurosis: Diagnosis and Treatment* (Springfield, Ill.: Thomas).

Kagan, J., Kearsley, R. B. and Zelazo, P. R. (1980), *Infancy: Its Place in Human Development* (Cambridge. Mass.: Harvard University Press).

Kahan, V. (1976), 'Violence – nature or nurture?', in *Violence*, ed. N. Tutt (London: HMSO).

Kaufman, H. (1970), *Aggression and Altruism* (New York: Holt Rhinehart and Winston).

Kedenberg, D. (1979), 'Testosterone and human aggressiveness: An analysis', *Journal of Human Evolution*, vol. 8, pp. 407–10.

Kelley, H. H. (1971), *Attribution in Social Interaction* (New Jersey: General Learning Press).

Kelley, H. H. (1967), 'Attribution theory in social psychology', in *Nebraska Symposium on Motivation*, ed. D. Levine (Lincoln: University of Nebraska Press).

Kelly, G. A. (1955), *The Psychology of Personal Constructs*, 2 vols. (New York: Norton).

Kelvin, P. (1970), *The Bases of Social Behavior* (London: Holt, Rhinehart and Winston).

Kennedy, R. (1982), 'Cognitive-behavioral approaches to the modification of aggressive behavior in children', *School Psychology Review*, vol. 11, pp. 47–55.

Kohlberg, L. (1976), 'Moral stages and moralization: The cognitive-developmental approach', in *Moral Development and Behavior: Theory, Research and Social Issues*, ed. T. Lickona (New York: Holt, Rhinehart and Winston).

Kornadt, H. J. A. (1983), 'A cross-cultural analysis of the development of aggression', in *Expiscations in Cross-cultural Psychology*, ed. J. B. Deregowski, S. Dziurawiec and R. C. Annis (Alblasserdam, Netherlands: Swets & Zeitlinger).

Krebs, D. (1982), 'Altruism – a rational approach', in *The Development of Prosocial Behavior*, ed. N. Eisenberg (New York: Academic Press).

Krebs, D. and Holder, M. (1982), 'Evolution, Altruism and reinforcement', in *Readings in Social Psychology: Contemporary Perspectives*, 2nd edn, ed. D. Krebs (Cambridge Mass.: Harper & Row).

Kreuz, L. E. and Rose, R. M. (1972), 'Assessment of aggressive behavior and plasma testosterone in a young criminal population', *Psychosomatic Medicine*, vol. 34, pp. 321–2.

Kristal, L. (1982), *The ABC of Psychology* (Harmondsworth: Penguin).

Kushler, M. G. and Davidson, W. S., II (1981), 'Community and organizational level change', in *In Response to Aggression*, ed. A. P. Goldstein, E. G. Carr, W. S. Davidson II and P. Wehr (New York: Pergamon).

Kutash, S. B. (1978), 'Psychoanalytic theories of aggression', in *Violence: Perspectives on Murder and Aggression*, ed. I. L. Kutash, S. B. Kutash, L. B. Schlesinger and associates (San Francisco: Jossey-Bass).

Kutash, I. L., Kutash, S. B., Schlesinger, L. B. and associates, eds. (1978), *Violence: Perspectives on Murder and Aggression* (San Francisco: Jossey-Bass).

Lagerspetz, K. M., Bjorkqvist, K., Berts, M. and King, E. (1982), 'Group aggression among school children in three schools', *Scandinavian Journal of Psychology*, vol. 23, no. 1, pp. 45–52.

Lando, H. A., Johnson-Payne, E., Gilbert, L. A. and Deutsch, C. J. (1975), Sex differences in response to physical and nonphysical instigators, Paper presented at the 83rd Annual Convention of the American Psychological Association, Chicago, August, 1975.

Lang, P. J. (1971), 'The application of psychophysiological methods to the study of psychotherapy and behavior modification', in *Handbook of Psychotherapy and Behavior Change: An Empirical Analysis*, ed. A. E. Bergin and S. L. Garfield (New York: Wiley).

Lange, J. (1931), *Crime as Destiny*, translated by C. Haldane (London: Allen & Unwin).

Lawrence, D. H. (1971a), *Psychoanalysis and the Unconscious* (Harmondsworth: Penguin).

Lawrence, D. H. (1971b), *Fantasia of the Unconscious* (Harmondsworth: Penguin).

Lawrence, D. H. (1960), *Women in Love* (Harmondsworth: Penguin).

Lefkowitz, M. M., Eron, L. D., Walder, L. O., and Huesman, L. R. (1977), *Growing up to be Violent* (New York: Pergamon).

Lewis, M. and Brooks, J. (1974), 'Self, other and fear: Infants' reactions to people', in *The Origins of Fear*, ed. M. Lewis and L. A. Rosenbloom (New York: Wiley).

Lickona, T., ed. (1976), *Moral Development and Behavior* (New York: Holt, Rhinehart and Winston).

Loehlin, J. C. and Nicols, R. C. (1976), *Hereditary Environment and Personality* (Austin: University of Texas Press).

Lombroso, C. (1876), *L'Uomo delinquente* (Turin: Bocca).

Lorenz, K. (1966), *On Aggression* (London: Methuen).

Lorimer, F. M. (1972), 'Violent behavior and the electroencephalogram', *Clinical Electroencephalography*, vol. 3, p. 193.

McAuley, R. (1982), 'Training parents to modify conduct problems in their children', *Journal of Child Psychology and Psychiatry*, vol. 23, no. 3, pp. 235–42.

Maccoby, E. (1980), *Social Development: Psychological Growth and the Parent-Child Relationships* (New York: Harcourt, Brace, Jovanovich).

Maccoby, E. E. and Jacklin, C. M. (1980), 'Sex differences in aggression: A rejoinder and reprise', *Child Development*, vol. 51, pp. 961–80.

McCord, W. and McCord, J. (1956), *Psychopathy and Delinquency* (New York: Grune & Stratton).

McCord, W., McCord, J. and Howard, A. (1961), 'Familial correlates of aggression in non-delinquent male children', *Journal of Abnormal Social Psychology*, vol. 62, pp. 79–93.

McEwan, I. (1982), *The Comfort of Strangers* (London: Picador).

Malamuth, N. M. and Check, J. V. P. (1980), 'The effects of mass media exposure to an acceptance of violence against women: A field experiment', *Journal of Applied Social Psychology*, vol. 10, pp. 528–47.

Malmo, R. B. and Belanger, D. (1967), 'Related physiological and behavioral changes. What are their determinants?, in *Sleep and Altered States of Consciousness*, ed. S. S. Kety, E. V. Evarts and H. L. Williams (Baltimore: Williams & Wilkins).

Maple, T. and Matheson, D. W., eds, (1973), *Aggression, Hostility and Violence: Nature or Nurture?* (New York: Holt, Rhinehart and Winston).

Mark, V. H. (1978), 'Sociobiological theories of abnormal aggression', in *Violence: Perspectives on Murder and Aggression*, ed. I. L. Kutash, S. B. Kutash, L. B. Schlesinger and associates (San Francisco: Jossey-Bass).

Mark, V. H. and Ervine, F. R. (1970). *Violence and the Brain* (New York: Harper & Row).

Mark, V. H., Sweet, W. H. and Ervine, F. R. (1967), 'Role of brain disease in riots and urban violence' (letter to journal), *Journal of the American Medical Association*, vol. 201, p. 895.

Marsh, P. (1982), 'Rhetorics of violence', in *Aggression and Violence* ed. P. Marsh and A. Campbell (Oxford: Blackwell).

Marsh, P. and Campbell, A., eds. (1982) *Aggression and Violence* (Oxford: Blackwell).

Marsh, P., Rosser, E. and Harré, R. (1978) *The Rules of Disorder* (London: Routledge & Kegan Paul).

Marsh, W. (1973), *The Bad Seed* (Bath: Cedric Chivers).

Mattsson, A., Schalling, D., Olweus, D., Low, H. and Svensson, J. (1980), 'Plasma testosterone, aggressive behavior and personality dimensions in young male delinquents', *Journal of the American Academy of Child Psychiatry*, vol. 19, pp. 476–90.

Matza, D. (1964), *Delinquency and Drift* (New York: Wiley).

May, R. (1976), *Power and Innocence: A search for the Sources of Violence* (London: Fontana).

Mayfield, D. (1976), 'Alcoholism, alcohol intoxications, and assaultive behaviour', *Diseases of the Nervous System*, vol. 37, no. 5, pp. 288–91.

Mazur, A. (1983), 'Hormones, aggression and dominance in humans', in *Hormones and Aggressive Behaviour*, ed. B.B. Svare (New York: Plenum).

Mead, G. H. (1934), *Mind, Self and Society* (Chicago: Chicago University Press).

Mednick, S. A. Pollock, V., Volavka, J. and Gabrielli, W. F. Jr. (1982) 'Biology and violence', in *Criminal Violence*, ed. M. E. Wolfgang and N. A. Weiner (Beverly Hills: Sage).

Megargee, E. I. (1982), 'Psychological determinants and correlates of criminal violence', in *Criminal Violence*, ed. M. E. Wolfgang and N. A. Weiner (Beverly Hills: Sage).

Meller, R. (1982), 'Aggression in primate social groups: Hormonal correlates', in *Aggression and Violence*, ed. P. Marsh and A. Campbell (Oxford: Blackwell).

Merton, R. K. (1957), *Social Theory and Social Structure* (New York: Free Press of Glencoe).

Meyer-Bahlburg, H. F. and Erhardt, A. A. (1982), 'Prenatal sex hormones and human aggression: A review, and new data on progestogen effects', *Aggressive Behavior*, vol. 8, no. 1, pp. 39–62.

Milgram, S. (1974), *Obedience to Authority* (New York: Harper & Row).

Miller, J. B. (1973), *Psychoanalysis and Women* (Harmondsworth: Penguin).

Miller, N. E. (1941), 'The frustration–aggression hypothesis', *Psychological Review*, vol. 48, pp. 337–42.

Miller, W. (1976), 'Youth gangs in the urban crisis era', in *Delinquency, Crime and Society*, ed. J. F. Short, Jr (Chicago: University of Chicago Press).

Mills, C. W. (1940), 'Situated actions and vocabularies of motive', *American Sociological Review*, vol. 5, pp. 904–13.

Mitchell, G. D. (1969), 'Paternalistic behavior in primates', *Psychological Bulletin*, vol. 71, no. 6, pp. 398–416.

Mitchell, J. (1974), *Psychoanalysis and Feminism* (New York: Pantheon Books).

Monahan, J. and Klassen, D. (1982), 'Situational approaches to understanding and predicting individual violent behaviour', in *Criminal Violence*, ed. M.E. Wolfgang and N. A. Weiner (Beverly Hills: Sage).

Money, J. and Erhardt, A. (1972), *Man and Woman, Boy and Girl* (Baltimore: John Hopkins University Press).

Money, J. and Schwartz, M. (1976), 'Fetal androgens in the early treated androgenital syndrome of 46XX hermaphroditism: Influences on assertive and aggressive types of behavior', *Aggressive Behavior*, vol. 2, no. 1, pp. 19–30.

Montagu, A. (1978), *The Nature of Human Aggression* (Oxford: OUP).

Montagu, A. (1973), *Man and Aggression*, 2nd edn. (New York: OUP).

Moody, P. (1966), *Golding: Lord of the Flies* (London: Macmillan).

Moos, R. H. (1977), *Menstrual Distress Questionnaire Manual* (Stanford, Cal.: Social Ecology Laboratory, Department of Psychiatry and Behavioural Sciences, Stanford University).

Morris, D. (1968), *The Naked Ape* (New York: McGraw-Hill).

Morris, S. (1982), 'The new science of genetic self-interest: An interview with Irven DeVore', in *Readings in Social Psychology: Contemporary Perspectives*, 2nd edn, ed. D. Krebs (Cambridge, Mass. Harper & Row).

Moyer, K. E. (1976), *The Psychobiology of Aggression* (New York: Harper & 2nd edn, ed. D. Krebs (Cambridge, Mass.: Harper & Row).

Mulligan, G. Douglas, J. W. B., Hammond, W. A. and Tizard, J. (1963), 'Delinquency and symptoms of maladjustment', *Proc. Roy. Soc. Med.*, Vol. 56, pp. 1083–6.

Murdock, G. (1982), 'Mass communication and social violence: A critical review of recent research trends', in *Aggression and Violence*, ed. P. Marsh and A. Campbell (Oxford: Blackwell).

Narabayashi, H. and Uno, M. (1966), 'Long range results of stereotoxic amygdalotomy for behavior disorders', *Confinia Neurologica*, vol. 27, pp. 168–71.

Nelson, E. C. (1982), 'Pornography and sexual aggression', in *The Influence of Pornography on Behaviour*, ed. M. Yaffé and E. C. Nelson (London: Academic Press).

Newson, J. and Newson, E. (1980), 'Parental punishment strategies with eleven-year old children', in *Psychological Approaches to Child Abuse*, ed. N. Frude (London: Batsford Academic & Educational).

Olweus, D. (1979), 'The stability of aggressive reactions in males: A review', *Psychological Bulletin*, vol. 86, pp. 852–75.

Olweus, D., Mattsson, A., Schalling, D. and Low, H. (1980), 'Testosterone, aggression, physical and personality dimensions in normal adolescent males', *Psychosomatic Medicine*, vol. 42, no. 2, pp. 253–68.

Ounsted, C. (1969), 'Aggression and epilepsy rage in children with temporal lobe epilepsy', *Journal of Psychosomatic Research*, vol. 13, pp. 237–42.

Page, I. and Cairns, D. (1979), 'Glory boys', from the record *Secret Affair* (London, Arista Records).

Parlee, M. B. (1976), 'The premenstrual syndrome', in *Female Psychology*, ed. S. Cox (Chicago: Science Research Associates).

Patrick, J. A. (1973), *A Glasgow Gang Observed* (London: Eyre Methuen).

Pearson, G. (1976), 'In defence of hooliganism', in *Violence*, ed. N. Tutt (London: HMSO).

Peay, M. Y. and Peay, E. R. (1983), 'The effects of density, group size, and crowding on behaviour in an unstructured situation', *British Journal of Social Psychology*, vol. 22, pp. 13–18.

Pihl, R. O., Zeichner, A., Niaura, R., Nagy, K. and Zacchia, C. (1981), 'Attribution and alcohol-mediated aggression', *Journal of abnormal psychology*, vol. 90, no. 5, pp. 468–75.

Pilbeam, D. (1973), 'An idea we could live without: The naked ape', in *Man and*

*Aggression*, 2nd edn, ed. A. Montagu (New York: OUP).

Pinion, F. B. (1978), *A D. H. Lawrence Companion* (London: Macmillan).

Pizzey, E. and Shapiro, J. (1982), *Prone to Violence* (Feltham, Middlesex: Hamlyn).

Plomin, R., Foch, T. T. and Rowe, D. C. (1981), 'Bobo Clown aggression in childhood: Environment not genes', *Journal of Research in Personality*, vol. 15, no. 3, pp. 331–42.

Poirer, F. E. (1974), 'Colobine aggression: A review', in *Primate Aggression, Territoriality and Xenophobia*, ed. R. L. Holloway (New York: Academic Press).

Power, M. J., Alderson, M. R., Phillipson, C. M., Schoenberg, E. and Morris, J. M. (1967), 'Delinquent schools?' *New Society*, 19 October 1967.

Powers, R. J. and Kutash, I. L. (1978), 'Substance-induced aggression', in *Violence: Perspectives on Murder and Aggression*, ed. I. L. Kutash, S. B. Kutash, L. B. Schlesinger and associates (San Francisco: Jossey-Bass).

Prentice-Dunn, S. and Rogers, R. W. (1983), 'Deindividuation in aggression, in *Aggression: Theoretical and Empirical Reviews*, vol. 2, *Issues in Research*, ed. R. G. Geen and E. I. Donnerstein (New York: Academic Press).

President's Commission on Civil Disorder (1968), *Report of the National Advisory Commission on Civil Disorders* (New York: Bantam Books/E. P. Dutton).

Quanty, M. B., (1976), 'Aggression catharsis: Experimetnal investigations and implications', in *Perspectives on Aggression*, ed. R. G. Geen and E. O. O'Neal (New York: Academic Press).

Reid, W. H. (1981), 'The anti-social personality and related syndromes', in *Personality Disorders: Diagnosis and Management*, 2nd edn for DSMIII, ed. J. R. Lion (Baltimore: Williams & Wilkins).

Reinisch, J. M. (1981), 'Prenatal exposure to synthetic progestins increases potential for aggression in humans', *Science*, vol. 211 (13 March), pp. 1171–3.

Rodin, E. A. (1973), 'Psychomotor epilepsy and aggressive behavior', *Archives of General Psychiatry*, vol. 28, pp. 210–13.

Rogers, C. (1982), *A Social Psychology of Schooling* (London: Routledge & Kegan Paul).

Rogers, C. R. (1963), 'Towards the science of the person', *Journal of Humanistic Psychology*, vol. 3, pp. 79–92.

Rohrbaugh, J. B. (1980), *Women: Psychology's Puzzle* (London: Abacus Sphere).

Rose, R. M., Bernstein, I. S. and Gordon, T. P. (1975), 'Consequences of social conflict on plasma testosterone levels in rhesus monkeys', *Psychosomatic Medicine*, vol. 37, pp. 50–61.

Rosvold, H. E., Mirsky, A. F. and Priabam, K. H. (1954), 'Influence of amygdalectomy on social behavior in monkeys', *Journal of Comparative Physiology and Psychology*, vol. 47, pp. 173–8.

Roth, M. (1982), 'Pornography and society: a psychiatric view', in *The Influence of Pornography on Behaviour*, ed. M. Yaffé and E. C. Nelson (London: Academic Press).

Rowland, W. D. (1983), *The Politics of TV Violence* (Beverly Hills: Sage).

Russell, B. (1967), *The Autobiography of Bertrand Russell, 1872–1914* (New York: Bantam).

Rutter, M., Maughan, B., Mortimore, P. and Ouston, J. (1979), *Fifteen Thousand Hours: Secondary Schools and their Effects on Children* (London:

Open Books).

Rycroft, C. (1972), *A Critical Dictionary of Psychoanalysis* (Harmondsworth: Penguin).

Sabini, J. (1978), 'Aggression in the laboratory', in *Violence: Perspectives on Murder and Aggression*, ed. J. L. Kutash, S. B. Kutash, L. B. Schlesinger and associates (San Francisco: Jossey-Bass).

Sano, K., Mayanagi, Y., Sekino, H., Ogashiwa, M. and Ishijima, B. (1970), 'Results of stimulation and destruction of the posterior hypothalamus in man', *Journal of Neurosurgery*, vol. 33, pp. 689–707.

Schachter, S. and Singer, J. (1962), 'Cognitive, social and physiological determinants of emotional state', *Physiological Review*, vol. 69, no. 5, pp. 379–99.

Schneirla, T. C. (1973), 'Instinct and aggression', in *Man and Aggression*, 2nd edn, ed. A. Montagu (New York: OUP).

Schulsinger, F. (1974), 'Psychopathy: Hereditary and environment', in *Genetics, Environment and Psychopathology*, ed. S. A. Mednick, F. Schulsinger, J. Higgins and B. Bell (Amsterdam: North Holland, American Elsevier).

Schultz, A. H. (1969), 'Comments on Mrs Roper's "Infrahuman Killing" ', *Current Anthropology*, vol. 10, p. 454.

Schur, E. M. (1973), *Radical Non-Intervention* (Engelwood Cliffs, N. J.: Prentice-Hall).

Schuster, R. H. (1978), 'Ethological theories of aggression', in *Violence: Perspectives on Murder and Aggression*, ed. I. L. Kutash, S. B. Kutash, L. B. Schlesinger and associates (San Francisco: Jossey-Bass).

Schutz, A. (1972), *The Phenomenology of the Social World* (London: Heinemann).

Sebastian, R. J. (1978), 'Immediate and delayed effects of victim suffering on the attacker's aggression', *Journal of Research in Personality*, vol. 12, pp. 312–28.

Sedgwick, p. (1974), 'Ideology in modern psychology', in *Reconstructing Social Psychology*, ed. N. Armistead (Harmondsworth: Penguin).

Segall, M. H. (1983), 'Toward a global strategy for research on aggresion', in *Expiscations in Cross-Cultural Psychology*, J. B. Deregowski, S. Dziurawiec and R. C. Annis (Alblasserdam, Netherlands: Swets & Zeitlinger).

Serafetinides, E. A. (1970), 'Psychiatric aspects of temporal lobe epilepsy', in *Epilepsy, Modern Problems in Pharmacopsychiatry*, ed. E. Niedmeyer (New York: Karger).

Serafetinides, E.A. (1965), 'Aggressiveness in temporal lobe epileptics and its relation to cerebral dysfunction and environmental factors', *Epilepsia*, vol. 6, pp. 33–42.

Shah, S. A. and Roth, L. H. (1974), 'Biological and psychophysiological factors in criminality', in *Handbook of Criminology*, ed. D. Glaser (Chicago: Rand McNally).

Shaw, D. M., Kellam, A. M. P. and Mottram, R. F. (1982), *Brain Sciences in Psychiatry* (London: Butterworth).

Siann, G. and Khalid, R. (1984), 'Muslim traditions and female education', *Journal of Adolescence*, vol. 7. pp. 191–200.

Siann, G. and Ugwuegbu, D. (1980), *Educational Psychology in a Changing World* (London: Allen & Unwin).

Simon, M. A. (1982), 'Sociobiology: The Aesop's Fable of science', in *Readings in Social Psychology: Contemporary Perspectives*, 2nd edn, ed. D. Krebs (Cambridge, Mass.: Harper & Row).

Slater, P. J. B. (1980), 'The Ethological approach to aggression', *Psychological Medicine*, vol. 10, pp. 607–9.

Smith, D. D. (1976), 'The social content of pornography', *Journal of Communication*, vol. 26, no. 1 pp. 16–21.

Smith, P. K. (1983), 'Human sociobiology', in *Psychology Survey No. 4*, ed. J. Nicolson and B. Foss (Leicester: The British Psychological Society).

Spilka, M. (1978), 'On Lawrence's hostility to wilful women: The Chatterley solution', in *Lawrence and Women*, ed. A. Smith (London: Vision Press).

Steffensmeir, D. J., Steffensmeir, R. H. and Rosenthal, A. S. (1979), 'Trends in female violence 1960–1977', *Sociological Focus*, vol. 12, no. 3, pp. 217–27.

Stepansky, P. E. (1977), 'A history of aggression in Freud', *Psychological Issues*. vol. 10, no. 3, monograph 39.

Stewart, O. C. (1973), 'Lorenz/Margolin on the Ute', in *Man and Aggression*, 2nd edn, ed. A. Montagu (New York: OUP).

Stonner, D. M. (1976), 'The study of aggression: Conclusions and prospects for the future', in *Perspectives on Aggression*, ed. R. G. Geen and E. C. O'Neal (London: Academic Press).

Storr, A. (1970), *Human Aggression* (Harmondsworth: Penguin).

Surgeon-General's Scientific Advisory Committee on Television and Social Behavior (1972), *Television and Growing Up: The Impact of Televised Violence* (Washington, DC: US Government Printing Office).

Surwillo, W. W. (1980), 'The Electroencephalogram and childhood aggression', *Aggressive Behavior*, vol. 6, no. 1, pp. 9–18.

Swanson, H. (1976), 'The biological value of aggression', in *Violence*, ed. N. Tutt (London: HMSO).

Syddall, C. (1984), 'The gangs in Olympic City', *The Listener*, 7 June 1984, pp. 5–7.

Tajfel, H. (1981), 'Social stereotypes and social groups', in *Intergroup Behaviour*, ed. J. C. Turner and H. Giles (Oxford: Blackwell).

Taylor, I., Walton, P. and Young, J. (1973), *The New Criminology* (London: Routledge & Kegan Paul).

Taylor, L. (1972), 'The significance and interpretation of replies to motivational questions: The case of sex offenders', *Sociology*, vol. 6, pp. 23–39.

Taylor, S. P. and Leonard, K. E. (1983), 'Alcohol and human physical aggression', in *Aggression: Theoretical and Empirical Reviews*, vol. 2, *Issues in Research*, ed. R. G. Geen and E. I. Donnerstein (New York: Academic Press).

Tedeschi, J. T. (1983), 'Social influence theory and aggression', in *Aggression: Theoretical and Empirical Reviews*, vol. 1, *Theoretical and Methodological issues*, ed. R. G. Geen and E. I. Donnerstein (New York: Academic Press).

Tedeschi, J. T., Smith, R. B., III and Brown, R. C. Jr. (1974), 'A reinterpretation of research on aggression', *Psychological Bulletin*, vol. 81, no. 9, pp. 540–62.

Thompson, R. F. (1967), *Foundation of Physiological Psychology* (New York: Harper & Row).

Tiger, L. (1971), *Men in Groups* (London: Granada/Panther).

Tiger, T. (1980), 'On the biological basis of sex differences in aggression', *Child Development*, vol. 51, pp. 943–63.

Tiger, V. (1974), *William Golding: The Dark Fields of Discovery* (London: Calder & Boyars).

Toch, H. (1972), *Violent Men: An Inquiry into the Psychology of Violence* (Harmondsworth: Penguin).

Tracey, M. (1984), 'Television affects everything we do, everything we think', *The Listener*, 9 January, 1984, pp. 2–4, 19.

Treves–Brown, C. (1977), 'Who is the psychopath?', *Medical Science and the Law*, vol. 17, no. 1, pp. 56–63.

Trivers, R. L. (1971), 'The evolution of reciprocal altruism', *Quarterly Review of Biology*, vol. 46, pp. 35–57.

Tumber, H. (1982), *Television and the Riots* (London: British Film Institute Publications).

Tutt, N. ed. (1976), *Violence* (London: HMSO).

Twito, T. J. and Stewart, M. A. (1982), 'A half-sibling study of aggressive conduct disorder', *Neuropsychobiology*, vol. 8, no. 3, pp. 144–50.

Vine, I. (1983), 'Sociobiology and social psychology – rivalry or symbiosis? The explanation of altruism', *British Journal of Social Psychology*, vol. 22, pp. 1–11.

Virkkunen, M. (1983), 'Insulin secretion during the glucose tolerance test in antisocial personality', *British Journal of Psychiatry*, vol. 142, pp. 598–604.

Vowles, D. M. (1970), *The Psychobiology of Aggression*, lecture delivered at the University of Edinburgh on 15 April 1970 (Edinburgh: University of Edinburgh Press).

Welsh, S. (1981), 'The manufacture of excitement in police–juvenile encounters', *British Journal of Criminology*, vol. 21, no. 3, pp. 257–67.

West, D. J. (1967) *The Young Offender* (Harmondsworth: Penguin).

West, D. J. and Farrington, D. P. (1977), *The Delinquent Way of Life* (London: Heinemann).

West, D. J. and Farrington, D. P. (1973), *Who Becomes Delinquent?* London: Heinemann).

White, J. W. (1983), 'Sex and gender issues in aggression research' in *Aggression: Theoretical and Empirical Review*, vol. 2, *Issues in Research*, ed. R. G. Geen and E. I. Donnerstein (New York: Academic Press).

Whitman, S. Hermann, B. P., Black, R. B. and Chabria, S. (1982), 'Psychopathology and seizure type in children with epilepsy', *Psychological Medicine*, vol. 12, pp. 843–53.

Williams, J., Dunning, E. and Murphy, P. (1984), *Hooligans Abroad* (London: Routledge & Kegan Paul).

Wilson, E. O. (1978), *On Human Nature* (London: Harvard University Press).

Wilson, E. O. (1975), *Sociobiology: The New Synthesis* (Cambridge, Mass.: Belknap Press of Harvard University Press).

Witkin, H., Mednick, S., Schulsinger, F., Bakkestrom, E., Christiansen, K., Goodenough, D., Hirschhorn, K., Lundsteen, C., Owen, D., Philip, J., Rubin, D. and Stocking, M. (1976), 'Criminality in XYY and XXY men', *Science*, vol. 193, pp. 547–55.

Wolfgang, M. E. (1958), *Patterns in Criminal Homicide* (Philadelphia: University of Pennsylvania Press).

Wolfgang, M. E. and Ferracuti, F. (1967), *The Subculture of Violence Towards an Integrated Theory in Criminology* (London: Tavistock).

Wolfgang, M. E. and Weiner, N. A. (1982), 'Introduction', in *Criminal Violence*, ed. M. E. Wolfgang and N. A. Weiner (Beverly Hills: Sage).

Yablonsky, L. (1967), *The Violent Gang* (Harmondsworth: Pelican).

Yeo, C. H. (1979), 'The anatomy of the vertebrate nervous system: an evolutionary and developmental perspective', in *Brain, Behaviour and Evolution*, ed. D. A. Oakley and H. C. Plotkin (London: Methuen).

Yoshii, N., Shimolochi, M. and Tani, K. (1961), 'The electroencephalogram in juvenile delinquents', *Folia Psychiatrica et Neurologica Japonica*, vol. 15. pp. 85–91.

Young, J. (1971), 'The role of the police as amplifiers of deviancy', in *Images of Deviance*, ed. S. Cohen (Harmondsworth: Penguin).

Zahn-Waxler, C. and Radke-Yarrow, M. (1982), 'The development of altruism: Alternative research strategies', in N. Eisenberg (ed.) *The Development of Prosocial Behavior* (New York: Academic Press).

Zillman, D. (1979), *Hostility and Aggression* (Hillsdale, NJ: Lawrence Erlbaum Associates).

Zillman, D. and Cantor, J. R. (1976), 'Effect of timing of information about mitigating circumstances on emotional responses to provocation and retaliatory behavior', *Journal of Experimental and Social Psychology*, vol. 12, pp. 38–55.

Zillman, D., Katcher, A. H. and Milavsky, B. (1972), 'Excitation transfer from physical exercise to subsequent aggressive behavior', *Journal of Experimental Social Psychology*, vol. 8, pp. 247–59.

# Index